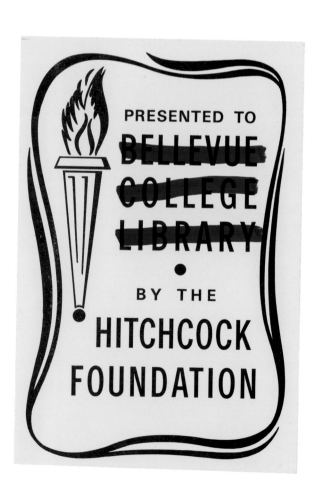

Russian Research Center Studies, 66

The Kurbskii-Groznyi Apocrypha

The Kurbskii-Groznyi Apocrypha

The Seventeenth-Century Genesis of the
"Correspondence" Attributed to Prince A. M. Kurbskii
and Tsar Ivan IV

Edward L. Keenan

With an appendix by Daniel C. Waugh

Harvard University Press   Cambridge, Massachusetts   1971

19 526

© Copyright 1971 by the President and Fellows of Harvard College

The Russian Research Center of Harvard University is supported by grants
from the Ford Foundation. The Center carries out interdisciplinary
study of Russian institutions and behavior and related subjects.

Library of Congress Catalog Card Number 70–154501

SBN 674–50580–8

Printed in the United States of America

For Joan

...Она же, вздохня, отвещала:
«добро, Петрович, ино еще
побредем.»

Аввакум, *Житие*

Preface

Let us commence with a violation of scholarly convention and the revision of a cliché: the error, if such it be, is mine alone. Those whom I mention in gratitude have given much but bear no responsibility for my use of their contributions.

This is a heretical book, but not a passionate one. Heretical it is, in the word's primary sense, since I have taken or chosen for myself a conclusion which is unorthodox. But as I search (*myslenne obrashchaiasia*, Semen Shakhovskoi would say) for the passions which move the heretic beyond the defense of his own conclusion and into the attack upon the belief of others, I am able to discern only a mild indignation that so much has been so piously taken for granted for so long. I cannot accept the fundamental assumptions of my colleagues, past and present, yet I admire and am grateful for their scholarship. I have had no intention to debunk, or to deprive Ivan IV, Andrei Kurbskii, or sixteenth-century Muscovy of achievements rightfully theirs. But I could not be silent about information which I consider vital, simply because my observations will be controversial.

Thus the personal predispositions reflected in this book; it is for others to judge whether I have deceived myself. In order to aid them, and perhaps to make the following exposition clearer, I think it worthwhile to sketch the genesis of its major aspects.

I cannot recall when I began to have doubts about the history of the *Correspondence*, doubts originally based upon the considerations discussed in Chapter 3 and, to a lesser extent, upon the linguistic peculiarities of the texts. In retrospect it is clear that Professor John Fennell's remarks at a Russian Research Center seminar held on February 4, 1964, had a deep influence upon my thinking, although I do not remember that the question of the authenticity of the *Correspondence* was raised at that time.

Nor indeed was the problem of authenticity foremost in my mind as I began to prepare a graduate seminar on the *Correspondence* in the fall of 1968. But the simple procedures of planning the necessary exercises—of gathering information on the extant manuscripts, on the textual relationships among them, and on their literary "convoys"—produced results very much like those set forth in Chapter 1, and revived old doubts. The search for texts of the works associated with the *Correspondence* led, with the help of a timely bibliographical reference from my colleague, Professor Omeljan Pritsak, to Isaiah of Kam'ianets' in Podillia and the first concrete textual evidence that something was awry in the traditional attribution. I attempted to repeat the procedure, turning via the convoy to Peresvetov, to the Muscovite Chronographs, and to Ivan Khvorostinin, whom I considered for a time the probable author of Kurbskii's first letter. But this identification was, as we shall see, forced, and as I rejected it I quite suddenly realized that the man whom I had been pushing aside in almost every source I consulted about Khvorostinin—Semen Shakhovskoi—was more like the man portrayed in Kurbskii's first letter than was Khvorostinin or, for that matter, any person of whom I knew. It was at this point that I could no longer work with any other hypothesis. Here—in Shakhovskoi's relationship to Kurbskii's first letter—lies the crux of the matter. The outline of the later development of the *Correspondence*, which follows directly from the history of the extant manuscripts, depends heavily upon this identification. The relationship of Kurbskii's *History* to Lyzlov's *Skifskaia istoriia* is an independent matter, which I have chosen to discuss only in passing, since it will require extensive further study.

Many of the ideas and lines of argument to follow have emerged as the natural result of conversations and collaborative work with students and colleagues. In the seminar mentioned above, a number of students produced original work which helped to shape my thinking. Most important was the stimulus which my students provided in forcing me to set forth and test my hypotheses as they developed. For this I thank Messrs. Wayne Dowler, Lubomyr Hajda, Thomas Owen, Orest Subtelny, and Donald Suda. For many helpful suggestions and patient counsel I thank Professors John L. I. Fennell, Oleksander Ohloblyn, and Richard Pipes. And for moral support, countless wise hints, and that crucial reference to Isaiah, Omeljan Pritsak.

I must acknowledge my special debt to my friend and colleague, Daniel C. Waugh, who generously took time from his own work in Soviet archives to copy texts and to answer a number of specific queries about manuscripts, and who has since his return been a constant source of accurate information, sound skepticism, and moral support. This book could not have appeared as it is without his tireless assistance and the many fruitful suggestions which find reflection not only in his excellent appendices, but throughout.

Finally, I should like to pay my grateful tribute to Mary Towle and Vicki King, who typed and retyped this difficult manuscript professionally, attentively, and gladly.

Wheatley, Oxon., England
October 12, 1970

Contents

Note on Transliteration

The Harvard College Library modification of the Library of Congress system is used throughout. In the case of pre-1918 and Slavonic orthography, spellings are modernized first, according to the system adopted by *TODRL*. In the citation of texts, the spellings of the originals are retained, and no attempt is made to standardize orthographical variants.

Geographical names have been rendered in forms appropriate to the official language of the locality involved, thus Valmiera, Vilnius, Ostroh, in preference to Vol'mer, Vil'no, Ostrog.

Introduction

In June 1564, Prince Andrei Mikhailovich Kurbskii, a member of one of Muscovy's great princely families and an experienced military leader, abandoned his post as commandant (*voevoda*) of the city of Tartu in Estonia (Derpt, Iur'ev) and took previously arranged asylum in the lands of Sigismund, King of Poland and Grand Prince of Lithuania. Historians agree that his defection had a profound impact upon Tsar Ivan Vasil'evich (Ivan IV, "Groznyi" or "The Terrible," 1530–1584), and that the exchange of letters between them, shortly instigated by Kurbskii, contains the most significant documents of Muscovite political thought in the sixteenth century. There can be little question that their *Correspondence* has become the most influential source of factual information and interpretative nuance available to historians of Muscovy's later sixteenth century. The paucity of contemporary narrative accounts has assured these texts the attention of scholars; their literary qualities have made them popular classics.[1] More even than More's and Shakespeare's Richard, the Ivan portrayed in the *Correspondence* has dominated posterity's perception of the historical ruler and his time, to the exclusion of other, often contradictory, evidence. These are the texts which inspired Karamzin, Repin, and Eisenstein: their Ivan is the Ivan perceived by Peter I and Stalin. Latter-day historians have, thanks to the great progress of recent decades in the discovery and elucidation of documentary sources, relied less heavily upon the *Correspondence* and the closely related *History of Ivan IV*, also attributed to Kurbskii; but the conceptual and chronological frame derived by older scholarship from our texts remains an important part of even the most original interpretations.[2]

How paradoxical it is, then, in view of the importance of these letters, that their provenance has never been properly established. There is no complete variorum edition of the *Correspondence*. No adequate study of its extant copies, of their paleographic and diplomatic features, dates, or origins has even been attempted.[3] No modern scholar has tested this keystone, above whose arch so much has been built since Karamzin set it; we have no current estimate of its ability to support the accumulated weight of two centuries of hypothesis and generalization.

This neglect of the essentials of source study can be attributed in part to the success of an incompetent trailblazer: the first edition of the *Correspondence* was published at an early stage of the development of Russian historical science by Nikolai Gerasimovich Ustrialov (1805–1870), a much-honored but little-respected historian of the Nicolaevan period.[4] Ustrialov was apparently fascinated by what he took to be the personality of Kurbskii; he seems truly to have spared no exertions in seeking out information about the self-exiled prince. "And could I have done otherwise," he says in the preface to his second edition of Kurbskii's works, "when Fate had given me the opportunity of being Kurbskii's publisher?"[5]

Ustrialov paid his debt to Fate in bad coin, for his enthusiasm far outran his historical training and judgment. In the examination and attribution of texts presumed to be Kurbskii's, he had the discretion of a billy-goat. He never revealed in print any of his reasons for attributing any single work to Kurbskii, nor did he discuss adequately the pertinent features of the manuscripts containing these works, either those which he used for his editions or those which he chose not to use. His choices, not surprisingly, were in many cases highly unsatisfactory.[6]

The popularity of Ustrialov's editions, and perhaps his personal prominence, seem to have discouraged other scholars of the nineteenth century from preparing a proper edition, although a number of critical comments had accumulated by the time of the third edition in 1868.[7] Some effort was made to correct the idealized picture of Kurbskii created by Ustrialov and by Gorskii's abysmal biography;[8]

the documents concerning Kurbskii's later life published from former Lithuanian archives were particularly important in this regard.[9] At the same time, an increasingly skeptical evaluation of Ivan IV's character began to emerge; stimulated by dilettantish applications of early psychopathological techniques, some writers began to challenge the grand picture of Ivan projected by the erudite and witty polemics of Ivan's great first letter, which by now was familiar to every schoolboy.

But still no one even attempted a critical edition or a serious study of the manuscripts. It was apparently to fill this lacuna that the energetic and erudite G. Z. Kuntsevich undertook early in this century a new edition of Kurbskii's works (together with Ivan's portion of the *Correspondence*). The first volume of Kuntsevich's work was indeed an improvement upon Ustrialov's editions, and in many respects it remains unsurpassed.[10] But the second volume, in which he had planned to provide full descriptions of all manuscripts— and, presumably, some attempt at a history of the text—never appeared.[11] Moreover, although he quite scrupulously provided numerous variant readings, he, too, seems to have excluded from consideration a number of the earliest and most important copies.[12]

A leading Soviet medievalist, Iakov Solomonovich Lur'e, corrected many of Kuntsevich's oversights in a new edition of the letters of Ivan IV, but, in accordance with the limitations of his task, he published critical editions of Ivan's letters only, providing for purposes of reference the text of Kurbskii's first letter, taken from a single manuscript.[13] Lur'e's great contribution should nonetheless be acknowledged: he provided for the first time the integral text of the second version of Ivan's first letter, on the basis of the earliest extant copies. Moreover, Lur'e examined and briefly described many of the most important manuscripts and attempted to construct a textual history of Ivan's first letter.[14]

Lur'e's highly competent work shows clearly how encumbering is the burden of the traditional views. He seems never to have questioned the most basic of them, but rather to have accepted failure in his remarkable efforts to explain the incongruities of the *Correspondence* within its traditional context. It may indeed be said that Lur'e has done all that can be done without challenging the very bases of our acceptance of these texts. No one has attempted to do so, and as a result, the available evidence has never been systematically analyzed.

Thus we are still without a thorough study of the provenance of the *Correspondence*, based upon systematic review of the manuscript evidence and analysis of textual features. The purpose of this small monograph is to initiate such a study. There can be no grander claim: this is a preliminary report. It is based upon the limited evidence provided by published sources, augmented by such information as has been provided by thoughtful colleagues.[15]

What I intend, quite simply, is to examine *de novo* the texts known as the *Correspondence* between Ivan IV and Prince Andrei Kurbskii, posing such questions as are always obligatory for the establishment of provenance. Having considered the available paleographic and circumstantial evidence, which under normal circumstances should provide some indication as to the period and milieu in which the texts were produced, I shall turn to a close reading of the texts, with the hope of finding justification for the identification of an author or authors.

Since it is clear that Kurbskii's first letter is not only the earliest letter in the *Correspondence* but the source of many of the major themes—and indeed of much of the actual text—of the following letters, I have studied it most intently, dealing with later letters in proportion to their decreasing relevance to the problem of the genesis of the *Correspondence*. I have assumed from the beginning that if one can establish the date and authorship of Kurbskii's first letter, the major questions concerning the origins of the *Correspondence* will have been brought much nearer solution.[16]

Clearly, then, there is little that may be considered innovative in my methods, which amount in essence to little more than close reading and the application of the rules of simple probability. In order to provide the argument with the necessary evidential basis at each stage of its exposition, however, it has been necessary to include in the text a considerable amount of rather detailed evidence and textual analysis. Repeated attempts to exile this information to the footnotes for the sake of readability led to an unevenness of argumentation, as did efforts to organize the argument along the lines indicated by the logic of the conclusions. As a result, the chapters are organized to reveal the progress of research, rather than the harmony of the conclusions. Not all readers will find these central chapters as interesting as the conclusions to which they so cumbrously lead; I shall therefore summarize, without extensive argument or qualification, my conclusions concerning the genesis and growth of the *Correspondence*.

Semen Ivanovich Shakhovskoi wrote, sometime between 1623 and 1625, a letter to Tsar Mikhail Fedorovich in which he complained of the persecution visited upon himself and his clan by the tsar and the tsar's father, Patriarch Filaret. Among his sources were a "Complaint" written in 1566 by a little-known Ukrainian monk named Isaiah and a foreword, "To the Reader", written around 1620 by Prince Ivan Andreevich Khvorostinin. Shakhovskoi apparently did not send his letter and, after he returned unexpectedly to favor, found it expedient to add a postscript and heading in which the letter was indirectly attributed to his distant relative Kurbskii.

Some time in the later 1620's or early 1630's (probably before the death of Filaret in 1633), Shakhovskoi, or someone close to him, composed a first version of Ivan's first letter, that is, a response to Shakhovskoi's own letter, now attributed to Kurbskii. This text appears to be both a part of the new history writing of the post-*smuta* period and a disguised commentary upon the political situation during Mikhail Fedorovich's reign, in particular upon the role of Filaret. Shortly afterward, a second version of this same letter, expanded through the interpolation of extended historical and theoretical digressions, was produced by someone with views very much like Shakhovskoi's, perhaps by Shakhovskoi himself.

At this point the growth of the *Correspondence* halted for some decades, but in the latter years of Tsar Aleksei Mikhailovich's reign some representative of the upper bureaucratic elite, a supporter of Aleksei Mikhailovich and of his vision of autocracy, wrote a précis of Ivan's first letter in a style somewhat plainer than the ornate Slavonic of that letter. Still later, and in the same milieu, an author with a different view of the Romanovs and of their absolutist rule composed the texts which are known as Kurbskii's second and third letters, and the *History of Ivan IV*, which has been attributed to Kurbskii. These works, too, were political allegories, which commented, under the guise of a discussion of Ivan's military record and domestic tyranny, upon the contemporary issues of Russia's relations with Poland and the role of the old Muscovite aristocracy in the increasingly bureaucratic monarchy.

These conclusions are developed and supported in the chapters that follow. First, the earliest extant manuscripts are "sorted" by age and contents; the individual letters are arranged in order of "literary time," according to their interrelations, and grouped according to linguistic style.

These procedures lead to the conclusion that the extant copies fall into three rather distinct chronological groups, each of which is characterized by certain features of language, "convoy," and combination of letters. These groups display, moreover, perfect correlation with the evidence of the literary interdependence of the individual letters.

Since it is clear that Kurbskii's first letter was the keystone of the *Correspondence*, Chapter 2 deals exclusively with the origin of that text. A detailed textual analysis of the letter reveals numerous features that provide appropriate evidence for attribution. This evidence is considered in the context of the biographies of the writers whose names are put forward by the examination of manuscripts in Chapter 1. This juxtaposition leads to the conclusion that, in all probability, the kernel of the Kurbskii letter was written to Tsar Mikhail Fedorovich by Semen Ivanovich Shakhovskoi.

Chapter 3 is a digression into the evidence which has commonly been adduced in support of the traditional attribution of the *Correspondence*. This evidence is seen to be insubstantial, and further argument leads to the conclusion that, on the basis of existing documentary evidence, neither Ivan nor Kurbskii can be considered the author of any part of the *Correspondence*.

Chapter 4 returns to the examination of texts and manuscript evidence, finding that the remainder of the *Correspondence* may be assigned with some confidence to the period and milieu in which the earliest manuscripts of these texts apparently appeared, and argues briefly that the content of the later texts reflects the political concerns of the individuals most closely associated with the manuscript tradition.

A final word about the nature of the conclusions: this is not another "interpretation" of the *Correspondence*; I have consciously kept interpretative comments to a minimum, reserving them for a later stage of the study of the problems raised here. What is presented in this book is a study of the textual evidence provided by the extant manuscripts, with the aim of determining the origin and history of the texts which they contain. In this context, it should be said that these manuscripts provide our *only* evidence, and that all further discussion of the main conclusions must be based upon them. These are "either-or" conclusions, more like a group of geometrical theorems than a body of historical hypotheses. If any of them is accepted, one must then accept the main conclusion—that the traditional attribution of the *Correspondence* to Ivan and Kurbskii must be rejected.

Chapter 1

The Manuscript Evidence

Chronology of Manuscripts

Some two dozen seventeenth-century manuscripts contain copies of one or another part of the *Correspondence*.[1] Although the precise dating of Muscovite manuscripts of the seventeenth century by either paleographic or watermark evidence is particularly difficult, it appears that these copies may be arranged in approximate chronological order as follows (Table 1).

The earliest *dated* copy of any letter is found in MS 1615 of the Pogodin collection, which contains only Kurbskii's first letter to Ivan.[2] Four other copies written on paper used in the late 1620's or 1630's (MSS 197, 4469, 603, and 1584) belong in the same chronological cluster. In addition to their presumed time of origin, these copies have in common the fact that they—and they alone of the manuscripts described in available literature—contain *only* Kurbskii's first letter.

A second chronological cluster of manuscripts, closely related in many ways to the first, seems to date from the 1630's and 1640's (MSS 1573, 2524, 1551, 32.8.5, V.2.11, 1567, 1581, 230). As in the case of the first cluster, these manuscripts are linked as well by a common feature: they all contain either the "full" or the "abbreviated" version of Ivan's first letter, and two of them contain only that letter. Six contain Kurbskii's first letter, but *none* contains other parts of the *Correspondence*.

TABLE I. Manuscripts Grouped Chronologically and according to Contents

MS	DATE[a]					CONTENTS					
		KI[a]	KI[b]	GI[a]	GI[b]	KII	GII	KIII	KIV	KV	HIST
197	Early 1630's	X									
1615	Early 1630's	X									
603	Early 1630's	X									
4469	1630's	X									
1584	1633–36	X									
[43]	?[c]	X									
1551	Early 1630's	X	X								
1567	ca. 1630	X			X						
1581	ca. 1640	X			X[g]						
230	ca. 1640	X			X						
2524	ca. 1650	X		X							
1573	ca. 1650	X		X							
32.8.5	ca. 1650 ?			X							
V.2.11	?[b]										
79.1	1670's						X				
1311	ca. 1675			X							
41	?[i]			X							
623[h]	1677		X		X	X		X	X	X	X
1582	1679		X		X			X	X	X	X
639	1684		X		X			X	X	X	X
181/60	After 1682		X	X	X			X	X	X	X
1494	After 1682		X	X	X			X	X	X	X
136	After 1675[e]		X	X	X			X	X	X	X
1/91[d]	1680's	X[f]			X[g]						
F.IV.165	1680's	X[f]			X[g]						
F.IV.198	1680's[b]	X[f]			X[g]						

Note: It appears that other seventeenth-century manuscripts, Titov 2350 and F.XVII.15, might be added to this table, but since their contents are not clearly established, they have been omitted. See App. I, pt. a, Titov 2350 and F.XVII.15.

KI[a] = First version of Kurbskii's first letter
KI[b] = Second version of Kurbskii's first letter
GI[a] = First version of Ivan's first letter
GI[b] = Second ("full") version of Ivan's first letter
KII = Ivan's second letter.
GII = Ivan's second letter.
KIII–V = Kurbskii's later letters
HIST = Kurbskii's *History of Ivan IV*

  [a] Bases for all dates are given in App. I and Chap. I, n. I. See also Chap. 4, Table 3.
  [b] A copy of the preceding.
  [c] This very corrupt copy forms part of a chronologically mixed manuscript, parts of which are of the late seventeenth century. The brackets here indicate that

The remaining seventeenth-century copies seem to have been produced in the seventies and eighties of that century. Some of these copies are found in collections of the type known as "Kurbskii Collections" (*Sborniki Kurbskogo*); others are found together with rather late versions of the so-called "Chronograph of 1617." An exception is MS 79.1, to which Lur'e ascribes an origin in the seventies.[3] This collection contains the only known seventeenth-century copy of Ivan's second letter to Kurbskii, and no other directly related texts.

In summarizing the chronological data, one should note the remarkable correlation between the dates of the clusters described and the presumed sequence of the letters (the earliest copies contain the earlier letters, etc.). At the same time, a striking time lag (70–100 years) exists between the presumed dates of the letters (as given in the texts or established by scholarly deduction) and the dates of the earliest extant copies.[4]

Incidence of Individual Letters

We may observe another significant correlation in comparing these time-clusters with the patterns of incidence of various combinations of letters. Thus, Kurbskii's first letter, which occurs in almost all manuscripts containing any part of the *Correspondence*, is found *alone* in only six of our collections, five of which seem to belong in the earliest cluster. Similarly, the "abbreviated" version of Ivan's first letter is found in only five copies, *all* of which seem to have been made around the same time. Moreover, within each of the first two clusters, copies which represent incomplete, and apparently earlier, versions of the text (MSS 197 and 1551) are among the earliest copies according to dating procedures.

Ivan's first letter in the "full" version, by contrast, is found in many copies made over a long period. Here, too, certain correlations

what is meant is the protograph of 43, which apparently was used in the production of 1567, 1581, and 230, and therefore belongs in the first group. See App. II, notes to stemma of GI[a].

[d] This and the following two manuscripts contain, together with 1581, the so-called "Chronograph" version of Ivan's first letter.

[e] Information unclear; see *Poslaniia*, p. 548.

[f] On the relationship between the first and second versions of KI, see Chap. 4. I have been unable to determine which of the versions is represented in this group of manuscripts, but the more logical assumption is that they contain GI[a].

[g] This is the "Chronograph" version of GI, in later discussion, "GI[c]."

[h] Protograph of 623; see Chap. I, n. I.

[i] Information unclear; see *Poslaniia*, pp. 540–541.

with the chronological data are to be noted: it appears together with Kurbskii's first letter, and with no other works of either author, only in the earlier cluster (MSS 1567, 230, 1581) *or* in the so-called "Chronograph" collections (which apparently stem from a copy much like MS 1581), while the manuscripts in which it is accompanied by other works of Kurbskii are of nearly identical, also very late, provenance.

Some further comments are apposite concerning the combinations of incidence. The *Correspondence* is *nowhere* found complete in a single manuscript: Ivan's second letter appears only alone. The earliest manuscript containing all other letters is dated 1677. The later letters of Kurbskii (i.e., other than his first) appear *always* in the company of his *History of Ivan IV*.[5] It is, finally, in these manuscripts, and *only* here, that the second version of Kurbskii's first letter appears.

Summing up, one notes that although these seven letters are found in two dozen pre-1700 copies made over a long time span and a broad geographical area, they occur *only* in the following combinations (chronological clusters indicated at left):

(I)   a. First of Kurbskii (first version)
(II) b. First of Ivan ("abbreviated")
      c. First of Ivan ("full")
      d. a and b
      e. a and c
(III) f. Second of Ivan
      g. a (second version) and c and later Kurbskii letters (and *History*)

Linguistic Styles

A number of detailed observations concerning the language and style of the various letters will be made in Chapters 2 and 4, but it is appropriate here to point out certain general features that seem to provide additional justification for the groupings established above.

One may distinguish three rather sharply differing styles in these letters: Kurbskii's first letter and both versions of Ivan's first are written in a rather ornate and erudite late Muscovite Slavonic; Ivan's second letter is for the most part distinctly in the "plain style" most often associated with the Muscovite chancelleries;[6] the later Kurbskii letters—and these alone—bear heavy traces of the "Polish" (more properly Ukrainian) lexicon and grammar so often cited as characteristic of Kurbskii's style. These Western features are also to be found in the *History*.[7]

The introduction of the linguistic criterion permits us to make two additional comments. First, by reducing this information to the simple opposition—Muscovite Slavonic/other—we may establish two groups which conform entirely to the chronological and incidence groups, and may indeed be indicated by the dotted line drawn through Table 1. Second, the linguistic distinctions do *not* coincide with the traditional attributions—the first letters of *both* Ivan and Kurbskii fall above our line, while the other letters of *both* writers are below it.

Combining these three criteria (i.e., date, coincidence, and language) it is possible to form three quite distinct and strikingly homogeneous groups of the manuscripts that contain the *Correspondence*.

Group I embraces copies of the first version of Kurbskii's first letter and both versions of Ivan's first, found alone or in combination, but accompanied by no other parts of the *Correspondence*. This group contains the earliest available copies of all of the works mentioned, and all of them are written in the same Slavonic.

Group II is represented by a single letter, Ivan's second, which is found alone and stands alone with respect to language.

Group III contains all of Kurbskii's letters, together with Ivan's first, only in the "full" version (in corrupt form: see below) and Kurbskii's *History*. The second version of Kurbskii's first letter is found only in manuscripts of this group. Kurbskii's later letters are never found separate from the *History*. These texts are similar in style and are found only in very late copies.

Textual Relationships

The various letters are interrelated in terms of "literary time," that is, in terms of what textual evidence (cross-references, etc.) reveals about the order in which the letters were written.

The "abbreviated" version of Ivan's first letter was clearly written after, and as a response to, the first version of Kurbskii's first letter.[8] As we shall see (Chap. 4, below), the "full" version of Ivan's first letter was written on the basis of the "abbreviated" version and the earlier version of Kurbskii's first. It is to this, the "full" version, that Kurbskii's second letter responds, as indicated by the well-known derisive mentions of "bodywarmers," and so forth, which are not mentioned in the "abbreviated" version.[9] Ivan's second letter, oddly, gives no indication of being a response to Kurbskii's second letter, but was clearly written on the basis of Ivan's first, of which it is a kind of paraphrase in "plain style."[10] Finally, the remaining letters of Kurbskii make reference to the second ("full") version of Ivan's first letter and to the second version of Kurbskii's first, together with both of which they are normally found.[11]

It is thus possible to construct a diagram combining chronological and literary "time," in accord with all of the above information (Fig. 1).

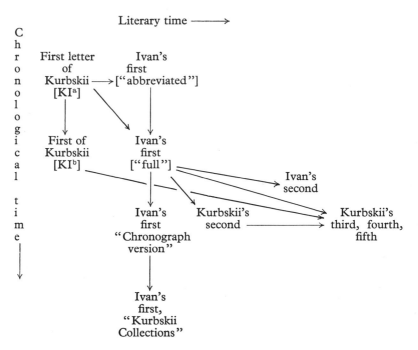

Fig. 1. Time relationships of the letters in the *Correspondence*.

"*Convoy*"

The "convoy," or literary milieu, represented by other works with which the copies of any manuscript text are bound together is of particular importance in considering its possible provenance.[12] The *Correspondence* travels in rather interesting company in the manuscripts known to me, and certain observations must be made concerning this fact. As will be seen from Table 2, where all texts that appear twice or more with any seventeenth-century manuscript of the *Correspondence* are represented, one must note a rather close relationship between the *Correspondence* and such seventeenth-century "documentary belles-lettres" as the so-called "Correspondence with the Sultan," the "Tale of the Two Embassies," the "Extracts from the Kizilbash Books," and so forth. This is true of the earliest copies, in particular, while the later groups (the Chronograph and "Kurbskii Collection" groups) are linked largely with the cosmographic and historical literature which was popular at the time of their production. It thus emerges from Table 2 that the same general groups which have been indicated above are here again adumbrated: groups established by date or combinations of parts of the *Correspondence* tend to contain the same accompanying works. These works are for the most part anonymous; some of them may possibly be associated with Prince Semen Ivanovich Shakhovskoi (fl. 1606–1653).[13] Other seventeenth-century figures whose names are mentioned, either in works found in our manuscripts or in marginal notes, are Isaiah, a monk from the Ukrainian city of Kam'ianets' in Podillia, Ivan Fedorovich Khvorostinin, Nikita Ivanovich Romanov, Bogdan Matveevich Khitrovo, Vasilii Vasil'evich Golitsyn, Andrei Lyzlov, F. I. Divov, a certain Semen Ivanov (Shakhovskoi?), and one Ivan Mikhailovich (Katyrev-Rostovskii?).[14]

A final indicator of the relationships among these manuscripts may be found in a minute textual comparison of the text which they most often have in common: Kurbskii's first letter. Although the variant readings are neither numerous nor divergent enough to provide conclusive evidence of the relationships among all manuscripts, a plausible and tentative chart of filiation may be constructed (Stemma A).[15] From this graphic representation of the variant readings it should be clear that even minute differences tend to separate our texts into groups very similar to those established by other procedures: the most common opposition is 197 + 43 + 4469 + 1584 + 603 + 1581 vs. 2524 + 1615 + 1573 + 1567, that is, the manuscripts containing only Kurbskii's first letter against those containing it together with Ivan's first (1615 and 1581 are exceptions, but their convoys in some respects link them with the expected groups). That the protograph of the second version has most in common with the earlier group does not contradict this observation: the second version apparently represents a late version of the letter, made from a copy like those of the group 4469/1584/603, if not in fact from 603 itself (see Stemma I, Appendix II).

Conclusions

Let us now consider some matters of greater and lesser probability with regard to the history of these manuscripts and their texts. The

TABLE 2. Selected Parts of Manuscript Convoy

	197	1615	603	4469	1584	43	2524	1573	1551	32.8.5
VYM				X	X		X	X		
PRE				X	X		X	X	X	
T				X	X	a			X	
P				X	X					
COR						X	X	X		
EMB	X	X	X				X	X	X	
KOR				X			X	X		
KIZ				X			X	a		
MEG							X	X		
SYN			X	X						
PERE				X	X					
CHRON/ STEP										X
GUAG and STRY										

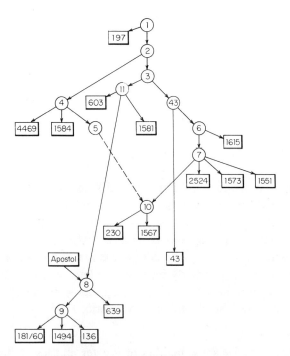

STEMMA A. Kurbskii's First Letter

TABLE 2 (*continued*).

1567	1581	230	41	1/91	F.IV.165	1494	136
X							
X		X	X	X	X	X	X
X		X					
	X		X	X	X		
						X	

Note: For abbreviations, see App. II.
a = Fragment; see App. I.

compactness of the chronological groups, and the consistency of content within these groups, should under normal circumstances indicate that we are dealing with a number of clusters, each produced around a single time. That the chronological limits of the groups are so narrow should indicate that, in all probability, the prototype of each group was produced in the same time period. One should assume, then, that the first five manuscripts in Table 1 (and the protograph of MS 43) represent the first stage of growth of the *Correspondence*, the period ca. 1625–1635, with the probable date of the protograph of Kurbskii's first letter falling at the beginning of that period. The seventh (MS 1551) may represent a second stage, probably around 1630, which may tentatively be considered the date of the protograph of the first version of Ivan's first letter. The two other copies of the same text probably appeared at a somewhat later time.

The next three texts (1567, 1581, 230) belong to a slightly later period, as does, presumably, the protograph of the text which they have in common—the second version of Ivan's first letter. The remaining groups are also quite discrete: MS 79.1 stands alone by all criteria, around 1675, the most likely date of origin of the second letter of Ivan; the last three groups are to be bracketed in the late seventies or early eighties, the most probable date of creation of the

texts which appear first in them—the remainder of the Kurbskii
letters.

It must be stressed that these are hypotheses based upon the
incomplete manuscript information alone and represent but the *most
probable* conclusions on the basis of this evidence, considered
independently of existing traditions. It should be stressed, however,
that all of the groups as established by whatever criterion—date,
contents, language, filiation—display a striking internal consistency
and have a perfectly logical relationship with one another. Intuition
and the general laws of probability indicate that if one has a significant
number of manuscripts of the same general date and of similar
composition, it is most logical to consider, as a first assumption, that
a text which they contain is roughly contemporaneous with the oldest
of them.

These conclusions become more striking when one considers the
logical consequences of the juxtaposition of these probabilities with
the extremely low probabilities which must be associated with the
traditional dating of these letters. Letter collections, as a rule, appear
in scriptoria associated with the authors and are most commonly
found in sets, complete or one-sided. One would expect these letters
to be found either among the copious files of the Muscovite diplomatic chancelleries or in some collection associated with Kurbskii's
Lithuanian activities. There seems to be no trace of the *Correspondence* in either place. There is no manuscript of the whole
Correspondence, or of Ivan's part of it, and none of Kurbskii's letters
made before 1677. Most striking of all is the fact that, if we accept
the existence of sixteenth-century originals in two separate archives,
we must assume not only that all copies of both halves of the exchange
made before ca. 1625 were lost, but that the losses were extra-
ordinarily systematic; the losses included all copies of Kurbskii's first
letter before ca. 1625, all of Ivan's first (first version) before ca. 1635,
of the second version before the same date, and so forth (see below,
Chap. 3). Such an assumption violates normal probability, strains
credulity, and is, as we shall see, unnecessary.

Chapter 2

The Textual History of Kurbskii's First Letter

It is thus . . . apparent, that only the full history of the text of a work can provide a final attribution. However convincing certain considerations and individual facts might be, if the texts of all versions are not elucidated, if variant readings of passages which serve as the basis of attribution are not taken into account, if the question of the textual boundaries of the work is not cleared up, if its date is not established etc., no attribution can be considered convincing.—D. S. Likhachev

Ivan's great and grandiloquent first letter has been for most readers the crucial portion of the *Correspondence*, by virtue of its sheer bulk and the political ideas which it seems to contain. From it come most of the loci classici; it is to this text that most scholars have turned for corroboration of one or another view of the etiology of Russian political thought. In the study of the history of the texts themselves, however, Ivan's letter is of secondary importance: the textual and thematic keystone of the *Correspondence* is Kurbskii's first letter. Here most of the themes elaborated in the later letters are established; verbatim citations or indirect references to this letter are found in all of the later ones.[1]

We shall, therefore, devote considerable attention to this short letter, for in elucidating the details of its origin, we may hope to explain, in large measure, the genesis of the *Correspondence* as a whole. Appendix III contains a tentative critical text of the assumed first version of Kurbskii's first letter, based upon the earliest texts. This version is reproduced below without notes or variants for convenience in following the necessarily detailed analysis.

1	Царю, от Бога препрославленному, паче же во православии пресветлу явльшемуся. Ныне же грех ради наших, супротивным
2	
3	обретшемуся. Разумеваяй, да разумеет, совесть
4	прокаженну имуще, якова же ни в безбожных языцех обретается.
5	И болши сего глаголати о всем поряду не попустих
6	моему языку, но гонения ради прегорчайшаго от
7	державы твоея, и от многие горести сердца потщуся мало
8	изрещи ти.
9	Про что, царю, сильных во Израили побил еси,
10	И воевод, от Бога данных ти на враги твоя
11	различными смертьми разторгал еси
12	И победоносную святую кровь их
13	во церквах божиих пролиял еси,
14	И мученическими кровьми
15	праги церковныя обагрил еси
16	И на доброхотных твоих и душу за тя полагающих
17	неслыханные от века муки и смерти и гонения
18	умыслил еси,
19	Изменами и чародействы и иными неподобными
20	Облыгая православных
21	И тщася со усердием свет во тьму прелагати
22	И сладкое горькое прозывати?
23	Что провинили пред тобою
24	И чем прогневали тя
25	Християнские предстатели?
26	Не прегордые ли царства разорили,
27	И подручные тобе их во всем сотворили,
28	У них же преже в работе были
29	Праотцы наши?
30	Не претвердые ли грады германские тщанием разума их
31	От Бога тебе данны быша?
32	Сия ли нам бедным воздал еси, всеродно погубляя нас?
33	Али бессмертен, царю, мнишися, и в небытную ересь прельщен,
34	аки не хотя уже предстати неумытному судье,
35	надежде християнской, богоначальному Иисусу,
36	хотящему судити вселенней в правду, паче же не обинуясь
37	пред гордым гонителем, и хотяще истязати их до влас прегрешения
38	их, яко же словеса глаголют. Он есть, Христос
39	мой, седяй на престоле херувимском одесную силы величествия
40	во превысоких, судитель межу тобою и мною.
41	Коего зла и гонения от тебе не претерпех!
42	И коих бед и напастей на мя не воздвигл еси!
43	И коих лжей и измен на мя не возвел еси!

44 А вся приключившая ми ся от тобе различныя беды
45   поряду за множество их не могу изрещи
46 И понеже горестью еще душа объята бысть.
47 Но вкупе вся реку: конечне всего лишен бых
48 И от земли божия тобою туне отогнан бых.
49 И за благая моя воздал ми еси злая, и за возлюбление
50 мое — непримирительную ненависть. И кровь моя, яко вода
51 пролитая за тя, вопиет на тя к Богу моему. Бог сердцам зри-
52 тель: во уме моем прилежно смышлях и совесть мою сви-
53 детеля поставлях, и исках, и зрех, мысленне обращаяся,
54 и не вем себе и не найдох, в чем пред тобою
55 согреших.
56   Пред войском твоим хожах и исхожах,
57   И никоего тебе безчестия приведох,
58   Но разве победы пресветлые помощью
59   ангела господня во славу твою поставлях,
60   И никогда же полков твоих хребтом к чужим обратих,
61   Но паче одоления преславна на похвалу тобе сотворих.
62 И сие не во едином лете, ни в двою, но в доволь-
63 ных летех потрудихся, многими поты и терпением;
64 яко мало и рождешии мене зрех и жены моея не поз-
65 навах, и отечества своего отстоях, но всегда в
66 дальних и окольных градех твоих, против врагов
67 твоих, ополчахся и претерпевах естественныя бо-
68 лезни, имже господь мой, Иисус Христос, сви-
69 детель; паче же учащен бых ранами от варварских
70 рух в различных битвах и сокрушенно уже ранами
71 все тело имею. Но тебе, царю, вся сия ни во что
72 же бысть.
73 Но хотех рещи вся поряду ратные мои дела, ихже
74 сотворих на похвалу твою, но сего ради не изре-
75 кох, зане лутчи Бог весть: он бо есть всим сим
76 мздовоздаятель, и не токмо сим, но и за чяшу
77 студеные воды.
78 И еще, царю, сказую ти и х тому: уже не узриши, мню,
79 лица моего до дня Страшного суда. И не мни мене
80 молчаща ти о сем: до дни скончания живота моего
81 буду непрестанно со слезами вопияти на тя пре-
82 безначальной тройцы, в нея же верую, и призывая
83 в помощь жерувимского Владыки матерь, надежду
84 мою и заступницу, владычицу богородицу, и всех
85 святых, избранных божиих, и государя моего, князя
86 Федора Ростиславичя.
87 Не мни, царю, ни помышляй нас суемудренными мыслми
88 аки уже погибших и избьенных от тебе, неповинно заточенных
89 и прогнанных бес правды. Не радуйся о сем, аки
90 одолением тщим хваляся: избиенные тобою у пре-

91 стола господня стояще отомщения на тя просят, за-
92 точенные же и прогнанные от тебе без правды от
93 земля ко Богу вопием день и нощь на тя. Аще и
94 тьмами хвалишися в гордости своей, в привременном
95 сем и скоротекущем веке, умышляючи на христьянский
96 род мучительные сосуды, паче же наругающе и попи-
97 рающе ангельский образ, согласующем ти ласкателем
98 и товарищем трапезы, бесовския, согласным твоим бояром, гу-
99 бителем души твоей и телу, иже и детьми своими,
100 паче Кроновых жерцов, действуют. И о сем, даже и
101 до сих. А писаньце сие, слезами измоченное, во
102 гроб со собою повелю вложити, грядущи с тобою
103 на суд Бога моего, Иисуса. Аминь.
104   Писано во граде в Волмере, государя моего Ав-
105 густа Жигимонта короля, от него же надеюся много
106 пожалован быти и утешен ото всех скорбей моих,
107 милостию его господарскою, паче же Богу ми помо-
108 гающу.
109   Слышах от священных писаний хотящая от дьявола
110 пущенну быти на род христианский губителя, от
111 блуда зачатого, богоборного антихриста, и видех
112 ныне сигклита, всем ведома, яко от преблуждения
113 рожден есть, иже днесь шепчет во уши ложная царю
114 и льет кровь христианскую, яко воду, и выгубил уже
115 сильных во Израили, аки согласник делом антихристу. Не при-
116 гоже у тебя быти таковым потаковником, о царю! В
117 законе господни во первом писано: «моавивтин и
118 аммонитин и выблядок до десяти родов во церковь
119 божию не входят» и прочая.

A close reading of the first letter, in the context established by the discussion in Chapter 1, permits us to establish a plausible hypothesis concerning its origin.

The first feature to strike the careful reader of this text is its inconsistent prosody: passages of rhymed prose (of the type known as *tserkovnyi stikh* or liturgical verse) are interspersed with passages which reveal no such organization.[2] Consider, for example, lines 9–18:

Про что, царю, сильных во Израили побил еси,
И воевод, от Бога данных ти на врага твои
    различными смертьми расторгнул еси,
И победоносную святую кровь их
    во церквах божиих пролиял еси,
И мученическими кровьми
    праги церковные обагрил еси,

И на доброхотных твоих и душу за тя полагающих
   неслыханные от века муки и смерти и гонения
                    умыслил еси,

or lines 56–61:

Пред войском твоим хожах и исхожах
И никоего тебе безчестия приведох
Но развее победы пресветлые
   помощью ангела господня во славу твою поставлях,
И никогда же полков твоих хребтом к чужим не обратих,
Но паче одоления преславна на похвалу тобе сотворих.

Not all passages adhere to this principle, of course: there are some individual lines which break the rhyme, a feature not uncommon in other essentially rhymed texts of the same period.[3] There are also three passages which display little if any attempt at poetical organization. They are:

     1. Али бессмертен... мною (lines 33–40)
     2. И за благая... согреших (lines 49–55)
     3. Писано... to end (lines 104–119).

These unrhymed passages constitute a rather significant portion of the letter and contain some of the more important themes which are to be developed in the *Correspondence*. Why are they so distinct, in terms of prosodic texture, from the remainder of the letter?

The answer to this stylistic query lies in a reexamination of the manuscript evidence. It will be remembered that early copies both of Kurbskii's first letter and of the first version of Ivan's first letter are found in a manuscript (MS 1573) which also contains a biographical text, "Spisok s pravoslavnogo spiska Isaina."[4] The Isaiah whose life is there briefly recounted merits a brief digression, which will explain the special prosaic nature of passages 1 and 2.

Isaiah and Kurbskii

In the "glorious and beautiful" capital of Vilnius, in early summer, 1561, Isaiah joined the party of the Greek Metropolitan of Cyzicus, Ioasaf, for the last leg of its journey from Constantinople to Moscow. Ioasaf's mission is well known; it was he who brought to Ivan IV the Patriarch's formal sanction of the use of the title "Tsar."[5] Isaiah's mission, now little remembered, was cultural: he was to obtain, if possible, fair manuscript copies of the Bible edited by Gennadius (Archbishop of Novgorod, 1484–1504) and other religious texts to be used in the printing of books for the Orthodox population of the Grand Principality of Lithuania.[6] Encouraged by the reports of previous emissaries, and bearing a letter from Sigismund August in behalf of his undertaking, Isaiah had good reason to believe that his mission would achieve its purpose and give the lie to the well-meaning skeptic who had foretold failure.

In the event, the warning against joining a party of Greeks bearing gifts to Moscow was a prophetic one: denounced by Metropolitan Ioasaf as a (Roman) heretic, Isaiah was arrested, abused, and sent into monastic confinement, first in Vologda and later in Rostov. Here, far from his native Kam'ianets', this *rusin ot oblasti kievskiia* was to spend the remaining three decades of his life.

It is difficult to establish the details of Isaiah's life and activities in the Muscovite North. The terms of his confinement apparently permitted him access to books and the freedom to write: he continued, in his writings, to insist stoutly upon his innocence and the purity of his Orthodoxy. These protestations, it appears, gained him a personal audience with Ivan IV in 1582, after which the tsar granted him permission to return to Vilnius. The renewal of hostilities against Stefan Batory and the death of Ivan in 1584 prevented the realization of Isaiah's dream, however, and he returned to Rostov, where he died sometime after 1591.

We possess a number of texts which are attributed to Isaiah: a translation or copy of a translation of Feofilakt the Bulgarian's *Tolkovanie na Evangeliia Matfeia i Marka*;[7] a short biographical notice of Maksim Grek (in whom Isaiah had a special and quite understandable interest);[8] a "Letter" (*list*) to Ivan IV; a "Conversation with His Soul," or "Lament," in which Isaiah attempts to answer his soul's lament about the bitterness of imprisonment with traditional arguments about the transitory nature of this life; a "Complaint" against his denouncer, Ioasaf; a "Deposition" concerning his original mission, and the "Prophecy" of his tragedy.[9]

All of Isaiah's original writings, with the exception of the biographical notice about Maksim Grek, are found together in two manuscripts.[10] A close reading of these texts permits a number of preliminary conclusions.

(1) The five texts (the "Letter," the "Lament," the "Complaint," the "Deposition," and the "Prophecy") are separate entities, written at different times, in varying styles, and for different purposes.[11]

(2) The known copies seem not to have been Isaiah's work; from the headings provided, it would appear that this collection was compiled by someone else, also a Ukrainian or Belorussian, some time after the composition of the original texts.[12]

(3) Isaiah was an educated man and a talented writer. His Slavonic is correct and graceful, and his "plain style" (Lithuanian version) is authentic. In his "Letter," which is devoted to proofs of the purity of his Orthodox faith, he displays a proper knowledge of theological texts and tradition, and in the "Lament" he reveals a modest literary talent.[13]

It must be admitted, however, that Isaiah's place among sixteenth-century authors would remain insignificant, were it not for the fact that one of his texts, the "Complaint," coincides, word for word, over slightly more than half of its total length, with Kurbskii's first letter to Ivan.

One need hardly stress the importance of this coincidence: if it can be shown that Isaiah used Kurbskii's text, the "Complaint" is by far the earliest proof of the existence of that version of Kurbskii's letter which Ivan himself presumably read; if, on the other hand, it can be demonstrated that Kurbskii's letter depends upon Isaiah's "Complaint," we must examine the possibilities either that Kurbskii obtained a copy of the "Complaint" before his departure for Lithuania in 1564 or that Kurbskii did not in fact write the letter.

There remains the possibility of a common source. Although unlikely, this solution cannot be eliminated at the present stage of our knowledge, and it sets an important task for future research.[14]

Let us then examine the similar passages, in an attempt to come to some tentative conclusion concerning their relationship.[15] The four marked passages occur close together in both texts, and in neither do they seem to break the line of reasoning. Our analysis, therefore, should consist in a reconstruction of the two possible presumed editorial processes: how did the author of the dependent text adapt the original, and for what reasons?

The author of the dependent text made three decisions in adapting his original: (a) a choice of which passages to borrow; (b) a change of referent (expressed by grammatical alterations); and (c) a change of context (achieved by a change in the order in which the passages occur).

(a) The two hypothetical decisions concerning choice of borrowing are as follows: either (1) Isaiah chose to remove scattered unrhymed

Isaiah

Мнитмися же, недобрый пастырь словесных овец и неистинный учитель… митрололит Кизитский Иоасаф… помыслил злая мне и слово законопреступно возложил на мя, яко несмысленный старец и блекотливая баба не с очей на очи, якож есть обычай правде,

1/2 бездоводно *неподобными* своими мене *оболгал.* | *За благая моя воздал ми злая, и за возлюбление* мое *непримирительну ненависть, и*

3 *кровь моя яко вода пролитая* туне *вопиет к Богу моему.* | *Али бессмертен мнит себе, аки не хотя уже предстати* доброму пастырю и истинному учителю и *неумытному судии,* надежи христианской, *богоначальному Исусу, хотящему судити вселенней в правду, и истязати* всяко колено *до влас прегрешения их.* Днесь аз в темницы,

4 и слова ради истинного христова во юзах яко злодей зле стражу. | *Бог сердцам зритель —* в разуме *моем прилежно смышлях, и совесть мою свидетеля поставлях, и зрех, мысленне обращаяся, и не найдох в чем* бых *пред* ким *съгрешил,* или кому чим повинен в чужей и незнаемеи земли.

prose passages from the middle of Kurbskii's letter, eschewing adjoining rhymed material, or (2) Kurbskii chose to use a compact text forming most of Isaiah's letter, breaking and changing the order of the text to suit his purposes. Clearly the second is the more probable procedure.

(b) The grammatical changes occur in passages 2, 3, and 4; namely, the second person singular of the Kurbskii text (*mnishisia, esi, na tia, za tia*) corresponds to the third person singular of the "Complaint." In one case (Kurbskii's *vopiet na tia*), the "Complaint" has no personal referent; in another, Kurbskii's *pred toboiu* is found instead of Isaiah's interrogative *pred kim?* If we assume the dependency of the Kurbskii text, these changes appear consistent and logical, while the opposite assumption requires us to explain why Isaiah did not adapt Kurbskii's *vopiet na tia* as *vopiet nan'* and his *pred toboiu* as *pred nim.*

Finally, the comparison of the passages *iako voda prolitaia tune* (Isaiah) and *iako voda prolitaia za tia* (Kurbskii) reveals a subtle grammatical change ("like water spilt in vain"/"spilt like water for thee") which is of some interest: if we assume that Isaiah was borrowing from Kurbskii, we are left once again with the puzzle of why Isaiah did not simply replace the "thee" with "him," leaving the sense (i.e., "spilt like water for him"). Assuming, however, that the borrower was Kurbskii, we may explain the introduction of *za tia* as consistent with all of the cases already reviewed—but we should note that Isaiah's "and my blood cries out to my God, like water

Kurbskii

1   ...изменами и чародействы и иными *неподобными облыгая* православных, и тщася со усердием свет во тьму прелагати и сладкое
горьким прозывати ?..

3 | *Али бессмертен*, царю, *мнишися* быти, и в небытную ересь прель-
щен, *аки не хотя уже предстати неумытному судье, надеже христианской, богоначальному Иисусу, хотящему судити вселенней в
правду, паче же не обинуясь пред гордым гонителем и хотяще
изтязати их до влас прегрешений их, яко же словеса глаголют.* Он
есть, Христос мой, седяй на престоле херувимстем, одесную Силы
величества во превысоких — судитель межу тобою и мною.

2   Коего зла... | *И за благая моя воздая ми еси злая, и за возлю-
бление мое — непримирительную ненависть. И кровь моя, яко вода
пролитая за тя, вопиет на тя к Богу моему.* | *Бог сердцам зритель —
во уме моем прилежно смышлях и совесть мою свидетелем поставлях,
и исках, и зрех, мысленне обращаяся, и не вем себе, и не найдох в
чем пред тобою согреших...*

4

spilt in vain" has a distinctly Old Testament ring (the wasting of
precious water being a crime among Semites) while Kurbskii's
reconstruing, "and my blood, spilt like water for you, cries out to
my God," is decidedly trite by comparison.

(c) A study of the differences in the use of the parallel passages in
context leads to similar conclusions. If one assumes that the Kurbskii
letter depends upon the "Complaint," the editorial process presents
itself quite readily: the author borrowed the whole of Isaiah's text
after *nepodobnymi* . . . , consistently omitting passages which pertained
only to Isaiah or Ioasaf and were inappropriate to Kurbskii (i.e., the
beginning passage; *Dnes' az v temnitsy . . .; . . . v chuzhei i neznaemei
zemli*) and adding some redundant passages of his own (*i v nebytnuiu
eres' . . . ; pache zhe ne obinuiasia . . .*). The text was then divided and
incorporated, in changed order, into the Kurbskii letter. All of this
is quite logical, in terms of the texts themselves and the personae of
Kurbskii and Isaiah which they present.

If, however, we proceed on the assumption that Isaiah used the
Kurbskii letter as a source, we encounter, once again, some puzzling
inconsistencies. For whereas the "omissions" of the Kurbskii letter
can be explained, the cases of "omission" in the "Complaint"
cannot. What reason would Isaiah have to omit the passages just
cited, or the text which divided, in his supposed original, passages 3
and 2 (*On est' . . .*)? These general appeals for justice are as appropriate for Isaiah as for Kurbskii.

Conversely, there seems no reason for the Kurbskii letter to omit *dobromu pastyriu i istinnomu uchiteliu*, except for the fact that it appears at the beginning of the "Complaint" in a passage not found in the Kurbskii letter, but *specifically associated with Ioasaf*.

In sum, it must be concluded that the available evidence indicates that the Isaiah's "Complaint" served as a source for Kurbskii's first letter. It appears, moreover, that Kurbskii's letter was written sometime after 1566, since the undated "Complaint," itself probably written in 1566, is accompanied in the known copies by another text which apparently influenced Kurbskii's letter and bears the date 1566.[16]

One question remains, however: why did Kurbskii choose to separate and reverse the passages marked 2 and 3? The change in order was clearly dictated by compositional considerations which need not occupy us here; as to the interposed paragraph (*Koego zla . . .*), a surprising explanation presents itself, as in the case of the passages from Isaiah, after a reexamination of the manuscript evidence.

Ivan Khvorostinin and Kurbskii

One of the earliest and best copies of the "full" version of Ivan's first letter to Kurbskii was once a part of a manuscript which belonged to Ivan Fedorovich Khvorostinin, cousin of the well-known writer and heretic, Ivan Andreevich Khvorostinin.[17] A perusal of the latter's works indicates that the passage of Kurbskii's first letter which is interposed between the two citations from Isaiah's "Complaint" shows remarkable similarities with Khvorostinin's foreword "To the Reader," presumably written about 1620.[18] This text is reproduced in full in Appendix IV; the pertinent passages follow:

Khvorostinin	Kurbskii
И что еще безумне глаголю? Остаток понуждает беды моея сетования и плача глаголати. *Бог* убо *сердца* моего *зритель* и всякому благодеянию податель. *Он* бо *есть Христос* Господь *мой* всем Владыка и Бог, Иже *седяй на престоле величествия* своего *в превысоких,* всем богатный дарователь, *и всем сим, не токмо сим, но и за чашу сту-*	Али бессмертен, царю, мнишися быти, и в небытную ересь прельщен,... яко же словеса глаголют. *Он есть, Христос мой, седяй на престоле* херувимстем одесную силы *величествия во превысоких,* судитель межу тобою и мною. *Коего зла и гонения* от тебе *не претерпех!* И *коих бед и напастей* на мя не воздвигл еси! И *коих лжей и измен на мя*

деныя воды. Той бо весть, *коего злаго гонения не претерпех, коих напастей не претерпех, коего зла не возведоша на мя, коего лжееретичества* и *лжеизменных* малодушеств не приложиша ми. Но *вся сия* безвинно претерпевая, хотех мало написати...

не возвел еси! А *вся* приключившая ми ся от тебе различныя беды по ряду за множество их, не могу изрещи... И за благая моя воздал ми еси злая...

As is clear from the above, all of the similarities to the Khvorostinin text are found, in the Kurbskii letter, *between the two separated and transposed portions of the text borrowed from Isaiah*. At first glance, it appears that we are here dealing not with a verbatim borrowing, but with a kind of paraphrase, rhymed in the Kurbskii letter, unrhymed in Khvorostinin's. Closer examination, however, permits some rather interesting comments with regard to the closeness of the two texts and the possible directions of borrowing. Once again we may consider the two possible editorial processes. (a) Khvorostinin had Kurbskii's text before him and adopted for his own use precisely the words which lie between the long passages from Isaiah's "Complaint," *which he must have consulted.* That he might have had Isaiah's text before him for this purpose is quite unlikely, in view of its rarity. And even assuming that this is possible, the editorial process we must assume to accommodate this hypothesis is illogical: what reason would he have to suppress Isaiah's text systematically, particularly since the passages in question would suit his purposes? Finally, even if we were to posit some reason for such suppression, why would he, having made such a decision, go out of his way to insert two phrases (*Bog serdtsam zritel', i vsim sim*) from portions of the text he was suppressing and to eliminate the obvious poetical organization of his original? All of this is illogical, and improbable in an author of the caliber of Khvorostinin. (b) Assuming the opposite direction of borrowing, we can reconstruct the following editorial process: the author of the Kurbskii letter, having decided to incorporate the portion of Khvorostinin's letter beginning *Bog ubo ...*, could not use the first sentence, since an almost identical phrase was to follow, in the passage from Isaiah's "Complaint," which he had already read, divided, and prepared for inclusion in his text. He thus began with *On bo ...*,—but with a changed syntax and meaning, since his *On* refers to Jesus, who is mentioned in the preceding passage from Isaiah's text, while Khvorostinin's *On* had referred to

God the Father. This conscious change explains the editorial changes in the following sentences as well: God, but not Jesus, is *vsiakomu blagodeianiiu podatel'*; God sits on the throne of his own majesty, while Jesus sits at the right hand of God's majesty; God is Khvorostinin's "Lord, master, and God," but in the Kurbskii text "He [i.e., Jesus], my Christ, . . . is judge," and so on.

Next, the *studenaia voda* passage is suppressed, like the *Bog ubo* . . . , because it is to be used below (lines 76–77), while the *Toi bo* . . . , which in Khvorostinin's text refers again to God, is eliminated, to suit the change of grammar in the following enumeration of Kurbskii's sufferings.

Throughout, moreover, we observe that the author of the Kurbskii letter carries out the same grammatical transformation as in the adaptation of Isaiah's text: forms of the second person singular are systematically introduced (*goneniia* OT *TEBE, vozdvigl ESI, vozvel ESI*).

From these observations it follows that the editorial process which links our two texts corresponds to our second hypothesis: the Kurbskii letter is dependent upon the Khvorostinin text. Our separate proofs may not be considered conclusive, but taken together, the "textual triangle" (i.e., the relation of both Isaiah's and Khvorostinin's texts to, and within, Kurbskii's), certain general editorial traits (Khvorostinin's consistent references to God the Father, Kurbskii's inconsistency), and the chronological data at hand (Khvorostinin d. 1625; earliest copy of Kurbskii letter ca. 1630)— all suggest that this is the more logical and probable relationship.[19]

The third long passage of the Kurbskii letter which shows no tendency to rhyme is the long postscript after the word *Amin'*. The reason for the change in style at this point is not, in all probability, to be found in comparison of these paragraphs with other texts, but rather in the fact that the letter, in its original form, ended with the *Amin'* after the concluding formula, *o sikh, i do sikh,* and a final invocation of Christ as ultimate judge. Khvorostinin, indeed, ends the letter which we have been considering in just this way.[20]

Very strong support for this hypothesis is provided by MS 197, which, in addition to being one of the oldest (if not the very oldest) of the first (Kurbskii letter only) group of manuscripts, is textually closest both to Isaiah's text (it alone has the passage *I za blagaia moia* . . . as it appears in the "Complaint") and Khvorostinin's (only it and MS 43 have *sediai,* as against *sediachshe* in other copies).

MS 197 alone among the copies known to me ends with the word *amin'*, followed by one and one-third pages of blank paper.[21]

The possibility that Kurbskii's letter in its original form ended at this point is of considerable importance: it is only after the *Amin'* that there appears anything in the text which specifically links the letter to Kurbskii.[22]

Our analysis of the structure of the Kurbskii letter may be summarized as follows:

(a) the letter displays a tendency, over much of its length, toward "liturgical verse";
(b) three portions of the text are sharply set apart by the absence of such a tendency;
(c) comparison of these passages with other texts permits the stylistic divergences to be explained: the first two passages are verbatim borrowings from the "Complaint" of Isaiah of Kam'ianets', in reverse order, and interrupted by a paraphrase of a portion of Khvorostinin's "To the Reader"; the third, which follows the word *Amin'*, was probably not a part of the original text.

Kurbskii's Letters to Vas'ian

At least one other text stands in a close relationship to Kurbskii's first letter: this is a very similar letter, attributed to Kurbskii, and addressed to a certain Vas'ian, Elder of the Pskov Monastery of the Caves.[23] It is apparently found in at least six copies (MSS 1567, 4469, 1584, 2524, 1551, 1573) all of which contain Kurbskii's first letter. In addition, all of these manuscripts are linked by numerous other common texts and similar readings. The earliest of these copies date from the late 1620's; MS 4469 seems to be closest to the assumed protograph.[24] It seems, indeed, that this "Epistle" was written by the author of the Kurbskii letter: the language is identical, the subject matter and order of exposition very similar, and the biographical information entirely compatible.[25] Moreover, in addition to a number of similar wordings, there are passages which are nearly identical:

Letter to Vas'ian	Kurbskii Letter
Колико трудихся, вхождах и исхождах пред полки господскими и с воинством Бога живого, и никогда же бегуном быв, но паче одоления пресветла Христовою силою поставлях; и	Пред воиском твоим хождах и исхождах... и никогда же полков твоих хребтом к чужим не обратих, но паче одоления преславныя на похвалу тобе сотворих... [Кунц., стб. 4]

колико бед претерпевах, и нужд телесных, и учащение ран! Иного же мню, яко и вы не весте, яже приях в варварских различных ополчениях. Но сия ли ми бедному воздасте и всего лишенному? Бог судитель праведный и крепкий межу вами и мною: и аще ко вратом смертным приближуся, и сие писанеице велю себе в руку вложити, идущу с ним к неумытному судии, к надежи християнской и к Богуначальному моему Исусу... [Кунцевич, стб. 408–9]

...и претерпевах нужды многие и естественные болезни... паче же учащен бых ранами от варварских рук... [там же] Сия ли нам бедным воздал еси ... [стб. 2] Он есть... судитель межу тобою и мною [стб. 3] ...писание сие... во гроб со собою повелю вложити, грядуще с тобою на суд Бога [стб. 6] ...аки не хотя уже предстати неумытному судии, надежи христианской, богоначальному Иисусу [стб. 3]

While juxtaposition of these texts yields no decisive evidence of borrowing in one direction rather than the other, one fact is indicative of their relationship: the most extensive common passage begins in the middle of a sentence in the letter to Vas'ian, but constitutes the beginning of a sentence in the Kurbskii letter, immediately after the end of the borrowing from Isaiah. That this is not mere happenstance is indicated by the fact that, with the exception of the passages *neumytnomu sudii* ... and *bed i napastei*, which may have been favorite formulae of the writer, none of the common passages or words occurs in the portions of the Kurbskii letter which are borrowed from Isaiah or Khvorostinin.[26] We may thus tentatively assume that the letter to Vas'ian, like Isaiah's "Complaint" and Khvorostinin's "To the Reader," served as a source of Kurbskii's first letter.

We have now established a tentative critical text of Kurbskii's first letter, traced a number of internal boundaries and probable sources, and adopted, as a working hypothesis, the most likely date indicated by the manuscript evidence (ca. 1625) as the time of its appearance.

In view of the chronological problems raised by the above conclusions (i.e., the possibility that Kurbskii's letter was written as late as ca. 1625) and the tenuous relationship of the postscript (the only explicit link with Kurbskii) to the rest of the text, we must now analyze the content of the letter with a view to determining its probable author.

The Author of the First Kurbskii Letter

This author is rather well educated and not poorly informed in theological matters, especially for his time, but he is excessively prolix.[27]

Among the features of the letter that seem to reveal biographical information about its author are the following:

(1) The letter's liturgical verse form, its simple *Amin'* ending, and numerous religious allusions and analogies indicate that the author was not a layman, or, at the very least, that he was a man who had had a thorough literary education in the religious tradition. This conclusion is supported by the observation that the author was master of a facile and correct Slavonic.

(2) The tendency toward rhymed prose betrays an author with specific literary tastes and pretensions, typical of the period in which the earliest extant manuscripts were produced.

(3) The author seems to have suffered repeated injustices and prolonged oppression at the hands of the addressee, to have been exiled and deprived of his property (*vsego lishen bykh . . . otognan bykh*).

(4) The author accuses the addressee of oppression of others as well, specifically of the family or clan of the writer (*vserodno pogubliaia nas*).

(5) The author seems preoccupied with death: he speaks of the coming Judgment, taunts the addressee with thinking him already dead, and indicates that his letter will be placed in his grave.

(6) The author is a military man, repeatedly wounded, but never defeated, during a long and arduous service.

(7) The author rarely saw his wife during his service in distant and nearby cities.

Having established features that may possibly identify the author of the letter, let us examine the available biographical and literary evidence concerning the individuals who have been associated with the text and its manuscript tradition in our previous discussion: Kurbskii, Isaiah, Khvorostinin, and Shakhovskoi. Kurbskii's biography is relatively well known;[28] Isaiah's has been discussed above. The careers of Khvorostinin and Shakhovskoi, however, merit brief biographical digressions.

Ivan Andreevich Khvorostinin (Starkov) was, like Kurbskii, a descendant of the Rurikid princes of Iaroslavl'.[29] His father, who bore the nickname Starko (hence Ivan's second surname), had been a courtier under Godunov; Ivan began his public career, it seems, at the court of the first Pretender. Ivan was quite young at the time; Platonov implies that his position at the court of the Pretender was based upon an "exceedingly shameful intimacy," which Massa quite openly assumes to have been of a homosexual nature.[30] It was apparently this relationship, rather than "heresy," which led to Khvorostinin's exile, during the rule of Vasilii Shuiskii, to the Volokolamsk Monastery, from which he returned in 1610 or 1611.

Under the new Romanov regime, Khvorostinin did not regain his previous status. Even before the coronation of Mikhail Fedorovich, he was sent out on the first of the numerous and arduous military assignments which were henceforth to occupy such periods of his life as were not spent in monastic incarceration. He was sent first to the South, where he engaged the Poles and became involved in a controversy with Prince Andrei Khovanskii concerning the responsibility for a bungled campaign and an apparent flight before the forces of the enemy. Until 1619, he seems to have served in various campaigns against Zarucki, Władysław, and Sahaidachnyi. In March of that year he returned to the court.

The army had not, apparently, "straightened out" the imperious and licentious youth whom Massa had known fifteen years before. If anything, the army had further corrupted him, for in addition to his other unusual tastes, he had acquired a liking for Polish books and manners. Very shortly after his demobilization, official attention was drawn to Khvorostinin's new passions: searches of his quarters produced "Latin" books and icons. A warning was issued, but went unheeded—indeed, the dissident nobleman seems to have progressed from heresy to outright apostasy and treason. In the official document remanding him to another term of monastic confinement in 1622, he is accused not only of heresy, drunkenness, and general moral turpitude, but of a "lack of firmness towards treasonable activity," a weighty charge in those security-conscious times. In addition, he found himself accused, as have many since his time, of disrespectful attitudes toward Muscovite culture. He had said, it seems, that "the whole populace (in Moscow) is stupid, and there is no one (sufficiently intelligent) to live with" and many other things, some of them in *virshi*, of a highly unflattering and unpatriotic nature. Most heinous of all, it appears, was the fact that in a letter which had been uncovered by the investigation, Khvorostinin had called Mikhail Fedorovich a "despot" (*vladyka*) rather than "Tsar and Autocrat"; this should have been severely punished, but in his boundless mercy, the tsar chose not to have Khvorostinin executed, but rather to send him, "for the correction of his beliefs," to the Kirillo-Belozerskii Monastery.

This second exile lasted from the end of 1622 until the beginning of 1624, when Khvorostinin was pardoned after having expressed contrition and a sincere intent to sin no more. He returned to Moscow and the court, but was not to enjoy his liberty for long. Apparently in ill health (there is some indication that he was an alcoholic),[31] he took the cowl in the Troitse-Sergiev Monastery and died, under the monastic name Joseph, in 1625.

Prince Semen Ivanovich Shakhovskoi, known as "Kharia," was a prolific and remarkable writer, in spite of numerous personal tragedies and professional catastrophes during his long life of military and diplomatic service.[32] Although he is primarily known as a religious writer, he was not a monk—he was, like Khvorostinin, one of the first lay persons in Muscovite literary history to become known as a facile master of Slavonic and the religious literary culture.[33] He wrote hagiographic works, religious services, and prayers, as well as historical narratives, many of which contain passages in verse.[34] In the latter works, as well as in his numerous epistles, he displayed a strong tendency to revert to religious themes and examples from Biblical and patristic literature.

Shakhovskoi was a friend, correspondent, and distant relative of Khvorostinin, and their biographies are in many ways similar, although, if we are to judge from the well-known letter to Khvorostinin, Shakhovskoi not only did not share, but deplored the hauteur and heretical views of his contemporary.[35] Christian humility, rather than pride, seems to have been Shakhovskoi's defense against the misfortunes and injustices of which his life was so full.

Like Khvorostinin, Shakhovskoi began his career in the Time of Troubles.[36] First he served Vasilii Shuiskii, but after having been exiled by Shuiskii and then pardoned, he betrayed the Boyar Tsar and joined the group of renegades at Tushino, whence he soon defected to the Lithuanian side and was granted (1610) lands by Sigismund. He returned to Muscovy very shortly thereafter and spent the following years in service against the Swedes and the Poles, during which time he was twice wounded. In 1615 he complained of having been "dragged about from one post to another" to which the official response was a period of exile in the Unzha region.

He was shortly thereafter returned to active service, but in 1620 and 1621 two misfortunes occurred. In the summer of 1620, most of his male relatives became involved in a bizarre incident which led to their being convicted of treason. It seems that a number of

Shakhovskoi brothers and cousins had a gay reunion in Moscow after the long and trying campaigns in which they had engaged, and toward the end of a relaxing evening they staged an inebriated parody of the election of Mikhail Romanov in 1613, choosing one of their number as "tsar." After appropriate additional libation, he anointed all of them as his "Boyar Duma," and further toasts were drunk. Some member of the company, presumably more sober than the rest, reported this innocent skit to the proper authorities the next day, and the government began an investigation and trial. Semen was thrown into the dock along with his relatives, in spite of the fact that he was in Tula at the time, and all were sentenced to death.[37]

The sentences were commuted to exile, but at this point a second misfortune came upon Semen. In 1621 he was forcibly divorced from his wife, his lands were confiscated, and he was imprisoned. Including the two happy years spent with this fourth wife, Shakhovskoi spent, as we learn from his writings, a total of only six and one-half years with his wives.

It seems from his own account that Shakhovskoi spent but a short time in prison, but he remained out of favor for two or three years during which time he wrote a number of letters, which have been preserved, claiming that he had been unjustly treated and begging his friends to intercede with the tsar and Patriarch, that he might be restored to his former position. It was apparently through the intercession of two of his correspondents, Kiprian, Metropolitan of Krutitsy, and Semen Gavriilovich Korob'in, whose brother Vasilii was involved in Persian affairs, that Semen was chosen by Patriarch Filaret to compose an important formal letter to Shah Abbas in May of 1625. Filaret hoped to convince the Shah to embrace Orthodoxy, and he apparently turned to Shakhovskoi as a facile letter-writer, well versed in politics and the theological culture. But the performance of this Christian duty seems not to have moved the Patriarch to restore Shakhovskoi to favor: there is no evidence of him at court or in official position until 1628/1629, when he was sent to Eniseisk as voevoda, an assignment which for the cosmopolitan prince must have been an ill-disguised exile.

But happier times were ahead. He was permitted to return to Moscow in August 1632, and a year later Filaret, whose treatment of the Shakhovskois had been harsh, to say the least, passed from the scene. (Semen's cousins, culprits of the "Game of Tsar," were rehabilitated four days after the Patriarch's death.) Semen's political fortunes apparently changed immediately, and the following years were a time of administrative and diplomatic service in Moscow and provincial posts, including a major embassy to Warsaw in 1637. By 1643 he was apparently an important figure at court, for he formed, it seems, a close relationship with the Danish Prince Waldemar, who had come to Muscovy in the vain hope of gaining the hand of Mikhail's daughter Irina. Indeed, Shakhovskoi's relations with the Prince were deemed excessively close: after Mikhail's death and the decision not to conclude the marriage, Shakhovskoi was tried in the *Posol'skii prikaz* for treason and heresy (he had given the opinion that Waldemar might marry without embracing Orthodoxy) and sentenced to death at the stake.[38] This second capital sentence was also commuted: Shakhovskoi was sent to the Far North, where he apparently spent most of the rest of his life. The last evidence of his activities is a letter written to Simon Azar'in in 1653.[39]

We may now turn again to our text, examining its main features, as noted above, in the context of the biographical information now at hand. Kurbskii, Isaiah, Khvorostinin, and Shakhovskoi are the only known writers whom we have been able to associate with this text; it is appropriate to suspect that one of them may have been its author. Considering then, point by point, the features listed above, we find the following correlations.

(1) The religious tone and polished Slavonic of the letter are entirely compatible with the known works of all the possible authors, save Kurbskii: many of the works attributed to him are, as has been noted, written in a "western" Slavonic, no traces of which are present here.[40] Isaiah and Khvorostinin were monks and known writers of religious texts in Slavonic, and although Shakhovskoi was never a monk (he was excommunicated as he was exiled, and therefore could not be shorn), he was a monk in all but name, as he himself says:

> And lo, Sire, a great and special grief and
>   woe has assailed me for my sins
> And has utterly shorn me [*postrigla*] without
>   black habit or willing vow.[41]

(2) The tendency toward rhymed prose which has been noted is not a characteristic of the known works of Isaiah or Kurbskii; both Khvorostinin and Shakhovskoi are known as authors of such texts. It may be noted, in addition, that most authorities consider them

among the earliest Muscovite practitioners of the rhymed prose style; it is utterly out of place in the 1560's.[42] Shakhovskoi, in particular, is known to have written a considerable amount of "liturgical verse," some of which is strikingly similar to the verses contained in the Kurbskii letter. Compare, for example, the first verse passage pointed out above with the *irmos* of the first canticle of Shakhovskoi's Mass for Sophia the Divine Wisdom:

Неизреченным велением пеша ходяща приял еси,
И непроходимое море изсушил еси,
Израильтеские люди обращенныя от Египта спасл еси,
Исходную песнь пою тебе господи.[43]

(3) The wrongs committed against the author require special comment. Isaiah, Shakhovskoi, and Khvorostinin, as we have seen, had experienced such insults and injuries in full measure. Shakhovskoi in particular, complains in numerous extant letters of the injustices committed against him.[44] Kurbskii, by contrast, was apparently not oppressed by Ivan before his defection. Although the contrary view, based largely upon the *Correspondence* and the *History*, has often been expressed, the contemporary documentary sources do not support it.[45] Bielski's comment that Kurbskii fled out of fear of the tsar's wrath after an unsuccessful campaign is but a supposition; extant documents indicate that Kurbskii betrayed his master and homeland after protracted negotiations with Sigismund, for very prosaic motives of personal gain.[46] Until the very night of his defection, the future renegade was held in honor befitting his services and given responsibilities (including the governorship of an important frontier town) and rewards appropriate to his talents and station.[47]

Of particular significance are the words "of everything have I been deprived" (Fennell, *Corresp.*, p. 5). Kurbskii could not legitimately complain of this—at the presumed time of writing he could hardly have known of the confiscation of his estates in retribution for his flight, and in any case he had himself to blame (not to mention the fact that his rewards in Lithuania were more than adequate compensation). Shakhovskoi, on the other hand, apparently *did* have his property, and that of his relatives, confiscated by Mikhail Fedorovich after the "Shakhovskoi affair" of 1620, as is clear from an official document which mentions an inventory of their confiscated possessions (*opal'nye zhivoty*).[48]

(4) As to the oppression of the writer's family, our candidates

arrange themselves as follows: we have no information about Khvorostinin's family which indicates that they suffered as a group; about Kurbskii, it is known that his only brother, Ivan, died in 1553 of wounds suffered in battle.[49] Shakhovskoi, however, suffered in precisely the way indicated by the words of the Kurbskii letter (*vserodno*) from a vindictive political repression directed against his whole clan.

(5) The preoccupation with death that is apparent in the Kurbskii letter might be characteristic of any of our possible authors; it is least probable, however, that Kurbskii, safely established at the age of 35 in his new homeland, and vigorous enough to have two marriages and two decades of military service ahead of him, would be drawn to this theme. The other three candidates might well succumb to such morbid thoughts. Shakhovskoi, especially, was known to be subject to similar moods, as his other letters show. For example, the writer's prediction that the addressee will not again see his face (lines 78–79), while in theory applicable to all candidates, is less likely to have been written by Kurbskii, who surely expected to engage in warfare against Ivan, than by Isaiah, Khvorostinin, or Shakhovskoi, all prisoners in exile. The last, under a commuted death sentence, wrote to a friend in much this same tone: "And I know not the end of my woes, . . . Christ having condemned me for my sins to end my days in exile and detention and poverty."[50] Elsewhere, in a letter to Prince D. M. Pozharskii, Shakhovskoi is even more dramatic:

> Thou knowest, Sire, that I suffer and perish
>   wrongfully,
> Neither helper, nor protector find I in my
>   utter misfortune,
> I would joyfully go alive into the earth,
>   our common mother,
> For I suffer each day the mortal beatings of
>   the executioners,
> But I cannot put myself to death,
> And send my immortal soul and body to Hell.[51]

(6) The military exploits of the author are central to his plea; this aspect of his biography excludes Isaiah, a monk since adolescence, from further consideration. The remaining three were military men, but the specific discussion of the author's career seems to suggest that neither Kurbskii nor Khvorostinin is here indicated. There is no record of Khvorostinin's having been wounded, and unless we

are to assume prevarication by the author, neither he nor Kurbskii (because of the defeat at Nevel') could claim never to have retreated from the enemy (*polkov tvoikh khrebtom k chuzhim ne obratikh*). Shakhovskoi, on the other hand, was, according to contemporary evidence, twice wounded and apparently never defeated in battle.[52]

Another complaint of the author, that he had "marched to and fro at the head of [the tsar's] armies" (*pred voiskom tvoim khozhakh i skhozhakh*) is reminiscent of Shakhovskoi's petition, mentioned above, in which he objected to being "dragged about from one post to another."

(7) It is of course natural that a busy military commander should see his wife only rarely; it is odd that one should mention this fact of garrison life in a letter such as the present one. There is no record of Khvorostinin's having been married; Kurbskii quite light-heartedly abandoned his wife in 1564 when he defected, and was anything but a loving husband to the two brides he took in Lithuania.[53] Here again, however, Shakhovskoi fits our information perfectly. We know that he had very little time with any of his wives, all but the last of whom died after but a few years of marriage, and that this was the cause of considerable personal sorrow. We have his own testimony, from a letter to Filaret probably written during his first exile (ca. 1622):

Forgive me as the Prodigal, O our good teacher and pastor, and remit a single fault amongst my manifold transgressions; three wives of mine having died in a very short passage of time (nor did I live with even one of them for long enough—I only cast my eyes upon them—with one I lived three years, with the second eighteen months, with the third nineteen weeks), I was greatly saddened and fell into melancholy, and my mind became feverish, because I am young and cannot overcome the sweet passions of the flesh, and eschewing sundry and frequent fornication, I united myself in wedlock with a true maiden, and lived with her two years, and, Sire, God gave us the gift of children. But now I am deprived of my conjugal state and of my children for my heinous lawlessness, but thou, O wisest doctor, cure me, do not permit me in my melancholy to fall into the hand of the Devil![54]

Noting that the Kurbskii letter associates the complaint "and I did not know my wife" with the long years of military exertions by the writer, we may well associate the phrase with Shakhovskoi's military career, specifically with the period between the end of 1619, when he married his fourth wife, and the time of his trial and exile (1621), most of which he apparently spent in Viaz'ma. That Shakhovskoi reverted to the misfortunes of his family life in a prayer which he composed for the souls of his wives further supports this correlation.[55]

In concluding this analysis of the biographical hints contained in the letter, it is necessary to clear up the seeming contradiction between points 1 and 7, that is, that the author was both a man with considerable religious training and a military man. This is an unusual combination in Muscovy before the middle of the seventeenth century; one would require some specific information resolving this paradox before the candidacy of any author could be accepted. There is nothing, aside from the works uncautiously attributed to him, which would serve to identify Kurbskii as a religious, or even an educated, man,[56] and no reason for him to be indignant about the debasement of the monk's cowl, considering his own disregard of canon law.[57] Khvorostinin might fit our specifications, but he apparently took the cowl *in extremis*, and his religiosity is known to have been idiosyncratic.[58] Here again, however, we possess information which permits us to link the words of the letter with Shakhovskoi. For although he was never shorn, Shakhovskoi, as we have seen, apparently thought of himself as a monk in all but name, "shorn by fate." In addition, of course, there is ample independent evidence that Shakhovskoi was both an erudite and prolific writer of religious literature and an experienced military commander.

We may summarize in tabular form our attempts to associate the biographical information of the Kurbskii letter with the candidates considered (+ = firm positive correlation; − = firm negative correlation; ? = unclear):

	1	2	3	4	5	6	7
Isaiah	+	?	+	?	?	−	−
Kurbskii	?	?	−	−	?	−	?
Khvorostinin	+	+	+	−	+	?	?
Shakhovskoi	+	+	+	+	+	+	+

On the basis of biographical information alone then, it would appear that Isaiah and Kurbskii could not have been the author of this letter, that Khvorostinin might have been, and that the most likely of the candidates who suggest themselves on the basis of the manuscript tradition is Shakhovskoi.[59] Certainly no other individual can at present be so securely linked, by so many criteria, with this text. The analysis of biographical data coincides entirely with the chronological parameters established by the study of the manuscript tradition, confirms the formal and stylistic observations made in the preceding sections, and is supported by information linking Shakhovskoi with the "convoys" of the earliest copies of this letter.

Unfortunately, it has been impossible to compare the style of Kurbskii's first letter with appropriate exemplars of Shakhovskoi's style, which remain in manuscripts.[60] Even among the few texts available in print, however, there are a number of intriguing similarities with Kurbskii's first letter, both in style and content.

The most striking of these are found in a letter which Shakhovskoi wrote to his protector Kiprian, Metropolitan of Krutitsy (later of Novgorod, d. 1634) probably in the latter part of 1625:

…предстани государь со дерзновением и теплым заступлением, разреши держимые на мне многовременные узы и терпение. Свидетельствуют о мне самом дела мои, яко ниже по умышлению ниже по лукавству некоему сицевое дело приключися ми, о нихже по неведению умолчах и за то разхищен… Ни в помысл мой вниде нелепотное что. О богохранимой государской державе не буди мне окоянному таковое безумие что благодатью же божиею и соблюден есмь доселе даже и до последнего издыхания моего соблюденну ми быти тако доброхот есмь по всему и раб верен еще и богомолец о богохранимой государской их державе… И работах им государем на ратях вседушно, не щадя головы своей, даже и до крови подвизахся. Аще бы и смерть приях за них государей, то рад бых тому, и аще ли бы ныне и прегреших что яко человек, и неугодно сотворих пред очима их по неведению или по небрежению некоему, а никакоже реку по лукавству или по умышлению (да исчезнет от мене таковое вредоумие), то уже и суд приях доволен, четыре времени летних минуло в терпении моем, гоним и прегоним, и всячески озлоблен и расхищен… не ослабей помогающе ми и не отвергися слова уст твоих, еже ми обещало преподобство твое яще ли государь мой и неполезный отказ слышал еси о нас убогих оного дня, и времени. Не отступлю от твоей святительской помощи по вся дни, дондеже получу отраду своему терпению. Вемы упование твое Владыко, аще подвигнешися на прошение, умолишь благоутробие государя нашего светлейшего патриарха, понеже он, человеколюбец и врач духовный, носяще великий образ горнего архиерея Господа нашего кротчайшего Исуса Христа… и сия возглаголеши. О честный отче яко просте: И без подобы пришедши ми в таковую вину им государем вся ведома суть, о сих, что моей худости и на Москве не было в те дни, в нихже случися братьям нашим в таковое беззаконие впасти, и не разумехом о том, но не вем отколе постигоша мя таковая пагуба, грех моих ради.[61]

Another significant, if minor, link with Shakhovskoi's prose is the somewhat unusual *neumytnyi sud'ia* found in the Kurbskii letter, in the "Epistle" to Vas'ian, and in a more intimate letter to Shakhovskoi's friend Tret'iak Vasil'ev.[62] Elaborations on the common formula *Bog sertsam zritel*, found in the Kurbskii letter and in the Epistle to Vas'ian, appear twice in Shakhovskoi's letter to Pozharskii.[63] A more significant and particularly striking parallel may be noticed in a letter which Shakhovskoi wrote to Mikhail Fedorovich, just before the unfortunate dénouement of the Waldemar affair. Two passages of this letter correspond almost verbatim to parts of the Kurbskii letter and they are, perhaps by coincidence, the very first and very last sentences of that letter (see below, Chap. 4).

There is another seventeenth-century text that exhibits an interesting resemblance to Kurbskii's first letter—the "Tale" or narrative account of the events of the Time of Troubles usually attributed to Prince Ivan Katyrev-Rostovskii. The similarities are not extensive, and the relationship between the texts cannot be determined by their juxtaposition—but their stylistic similarity is worth noting, in view of the fact that the "Tale" may well have been written by Semen Shakhovskoi.[64] The passages in question are:

"Tale"	"Letter"
«О преславный царю Борисе, паче же неблагодарный! По что душегубного такового дела поискал еси и властолюбию восхотел еси? Почто беззлобного младенца, сына царева суща, смерти горькие предал еси и царский род на Российском государстве пресекл еси?[65]	«Царю от Бога препрославленному, паче же во православии пресветлу... Про что, царю, сильных во Израили побил еси, и воевод данных ти от Бога на враги твоя различными смертьми разторгал еси, и победоносную их ...кровь... пролиял еси... и т.д.

In the course of the previous discussion we confirmed the traditional assumption that the "Epistle to the Elder Vas'ian," copies of which are always found together with Kurbskii's first letter, was probably written by the author of that letter. The "Epistle" is linked textually to two other letters to Vas'ian, also attributed to Kurbskii, and it becomes appropriate here to support our previous remarks about the textual origins of Kurbskii's first letter with a brief consideration of these letters to Vas'ian, in the light of the hypothesis of Shakhovskoi's authorship.

The "Epistle," as has been mentioned, is always found together with Kurbskii's first letter (in MSS 4469, 1551, 1584, 1573, 1567, and 2524), and all of the previous remarks about these collections apply equally to it. The other two letters (known as the "first" and "second" letters to Vas'ian), by contrast, are found in a rather different "convoy," which, however, has a number of features in common with certain of the earliest manuscripts of the *Correspondence*.[66] These three letters are written in standard late Muscovite Slavonic, a feature which they share only with the first letter to Ivan (and one other text) among texts attributed to Kurbskii.[67]

Most important of these letters, for our purposes, is the "Epistle" whose relationship to Kurbskii's first letter we have examined above. Close examination of the text indicates that, while no definitive attribution is possible, much of the information provided by the letter may much more appropriately be associated with Semen Shakhovskoi than with Andrei Kurbskii. All copies of this letter bear an inscription containing the name of Andrei Kurbskii; this seems to be a later addition, because its attribution is contradicted by the contents of the letter, as the following observations indicate.

Kuntsevich, column 405, lines 5–10: Whether one assumes that Kurbskii wrote this letter before his flight or after he was established in Lithuania,[68] it is difficult to imagine a time during which he would have sent to a monastery for "supplies" (*potrebnaia zhivotu*): before his flight, Kurbskii was in no position to need anything from a monastery; after, he would hardly have turned to the Pskov monastery for such. Shakhovskoi, however, was apparently often hard put to provide himself with a few items to soften the hardship of his exile—witness his request, written in exile, to Tret'iak Vasil'ev for money, caviar, and sturgeon.[69]

Lines 10–13: There is no record of any financial transactions of Kurbskii before 1564, but this is negative evidence of little weight. More important is the fact that Kurbskii could have little reason, before or after his flight, to say "but at present I didn't want to be in debt to your Reverence." Shakhovskoi, on the other hand, having in the early period of his exile been deprived of his possessions, might well have hesitated to borrow after 1620, although in earlier times he did so with the confidence of one who could repay.

Lines 13–20: The words "when I first was on my way for the first time to do battle against the Germanic foreigners [*nemtsy*]" might just as well apply to Shakhovskoi's participation in 1611 in the unsuccessful struggle against the Swedes in Novgorod[70] as to

Kurbskii's participation in the early stages of the Livonian War.

Lines 20–21: The mention of "seven years of warring without respite" might just as well refer to the years 1611–1618, during which Shakhovskoi was continually, when not in banishment, engaged in military campaigns, as to the six and a half years which Kurbskii spent in the saddle between the beginning of the Livonian War and the presumed time of this letter (1564).

Lines 22–25: It is highly unlikely that Kurbskii would speak of the "quietude and profound peace" in which the Pskov Monastery of the Caves found itself in 1564, in the very midst of the Livonian War; Shakhovskoi, by contrast, might well speak of such conditions, in 1620 or 1621, after the peace treaties concluded with Sweden (1617, Stolbovo) and Poland (1618, Deulino).

Column 406, lines 7–25: This is not Kurbskii speaking; he had not, as we have seen, suffered before his exile, and after it he would hardly choose to complain in this tone to Vas'ian. Shakhovskoi, however, *had* suffered (assuming that this was written after 1621) and indeed had appealed to *arkhierei i sviatiteli*, specifically to Filaret and Kiprian, in letters which have already been cited. Kurbskii had not, if our documentation is to be trusted, been called a "heretic" by 1564; Shakhovskoi had, by 1621, as a result of his uncanonical fourth marriage.

Column 407, line 1: The long complaint which begins here is not entirely rhetorical—the references and biblical citations are all intended as allegorical criticism of the times in which the letter was written, as is the last sentence (col. 408, line 13) "and in these times he [who?] has betrayed our whole ruined land." The culprit is not named, but it is clear that he is a clerical figure, who has failed and continues to fail in his responsibility to speak out against the excesses of the tsar and curb his tyranny. In particular, a parallel is drawn between the object of the author's criticism and Theophilus, Patriarch of Alexandria (385–412 A.D.; col. 407, line 4). It seems unlikely that Kurbskii would complain in this way either against Makarii, who was anything but a toady in his relations with Ivan IV, and who had in any case died some six months before Kurbskii's flight, or against Afanasii, who had been appointed mere weeks before the presumed time of this letter.[71] There is no evidence of the participation of either of these hierarchs in any persecution of Kurbskii before 1564, if in fact such occurred.

The Patriarch Filaret Romanov, however, took, a direct part in the punishment of Semen Shakhovskoi, as we have seen, and it is most logical to assume that it is he who is meant in this passage. This view is supported by the appropriateness of the allegorical reference to Theophilus, who was

Energetic, intelligent, cunning, and proud. . . . He subjected those subordinate to him to chains, imprisonment, and banishment for their resistance [to his imperious rule]. He had a superlative understanding of the significance of the imperial power in the religious matters of the Eastern Church, and he attempted to rely on that basis. . . . His omnipotence in the two spheres—the religious and the political—gained Theophilus the epithet of the Christian Pharaoh.[72]

From line 15, col. 408, the author turns to personal matters, and at this point the letter reveals its closeness to Kurbskii's first letter. Here, among other matters discussed above, are contained the passages indicating that the writer was "deprived of everything" and that he will place his letter in his grave, both of which, as we have seen, have greater correlation with Shakhovskoi's biography than with Kurbskii's.

The final paragraph of this letter (col. 410, lines 5–10) contains a reference to another letter, also attributed to Kurbskii (Kuntsevich, cols. 383–404). This other letter to Vas'ian, known in the scholarly literature as the "second" letter of Kurbskii to that still imperfectly identified personage, raises a number of questions. In view of the clear link between this letter and the "Epistle to Vas'ian" which we have associated with the author of Kurbskii's first letter, it must here suffice for us to establish whether this "second" letter contains any information which would conclusively link it with Kurbskii or with Shakhovskoi. It does not. One piece of information contained in the "second" letter, which has been used as the basis of an argument that it was written around 1564, is a reference to Skorina's edition of the *Psalter* "translated not many years ago, something like fifty years or a bit more" (col. 402). Skorina's *Psalter* first appeared in Vilnius in 1525, significantly less than fifty years before the presumed time of this letter (before 1564). A second edition of the very same text appeared, however, also in Vilnius, in 1575, almost precisely fifty years before the time when we have been assuming Shakhovskoi wrote the letter to which this "second" letter of Vas'ian is indirectly linked.[73]

Numerous other details support the assumption that Shakhovskoi might have written this letter, in particular the description of the ills of the writer's time and another indirect reference to the Patriarch (col. 396, lines 17–18). Finally, it should be noted that this letter was clearly written in Muscovy and in standard Slavonic—which Kurbskii, in his own words (in so far as any are his), claims to have learned only after his emigration.[74]

This digression into matters associated with the "letters to Vas'ian" has not attempted to establish the provenance of these letters or to study their contents closely. Occasioned by the previous association of these texts with Kurbskii's first letter, it has been intended solely to establish whether anything about these letters contradicts or confirms the hypothesis of Shakhovskoi's authorship of the Kurbskii letter. We have found no contradictions; neither have we found any definitive support, although some of our observations have provided some evidence that these letters, too, may have been written by Shakhovskoi.

The sum of our evidence, then, whether provided by manuscript tradition (the coincidence in manuscripts of the *Correspondence* and works by Shakhovskoi), by textual history (the passage from the "To the Reader" of Shakhovskoi's friend and relative Khvorostinin), by stylistic (the tendency toward rhyme) or biographical content analysis, indicates that under any normal conditions of evidential argument, and on the basis of present information, one should conclude that the most probable author of the first letter of Kurbskii is Semen Ivanovich Shakhovskoi.

Conclusions

Our study of the significant features of Kurbskii's first letter has led us, then, to three conclusions:

(a) It was written before 1632 (the date of the first dated manuscript) and probably after 1620 (the date of Khvorostinin's "To the Reader"). These dates coincide very well with those indicated by the study of the manuscript groups in Chapter 1 (i.e., first group ca. 1625–1635).
(b) The text following the word *Amin'* was very probably not a part of the original letter.
(c) The text of the letter up to the word *Amin'* is in fact a letter written to Mikhail Fedorovich by Semen Shakhovskoi, most probably during his exile after 1621.[75]

These are the most logical and probable conclusions from the available evidence. When one considers the evidence at hand concerning "Kurbskii's first letter" without any a priori dispositions, without any attempt to "explain" this evidence in the light of what we know or think we know about Kurbskii, but simply as evidence which reveals and obeys the same rules of statistical, linguistic, and logical regularity as any other evidence, it becomes rather obvious that, unless we are willing to suspend such rules on faith, we cannot attribute this letter to Kurbskii.

It remains for us to provide, by way of hypothesis, some narrative explication of the genesis of Kurbskii's first letter, as we now possess it. The kernel of the letter (as far as the word *Amin'*) was apparently written by Shakhovskoi in exile, after the affair of the Shakhovskoi princes in 1620, probably in 1621. Shakhovskoi borrowed passages from Isaiah's "Complaint," which was strikingly apropos, from Khvorostinin's "To the Reader," and perhaps from his own letter of the same period to Vas'ian. The letter may never have been dispatched; later, perhaps after he was pardoned and returned to Moscow to serve Filaret, Shakhovskoi took the precaution of adding the postscript, in which the letter became associated with his distant relative Kurbskii. This metamorphosis completes the genesis of the first letter and begins the later development of the *Correspondence*, which we shall discuss in Chapter 4.

The implications of these conclusions are, of course, far-reaching; they will be developed in the Afterword.

Because of the importance of our main conclusion, however, and because the unanimous and unchallenged historiographic traditions identify Kurbskii as the author, we shall turn now to a consideration of the possibility that Kurbskii might, in spite of the positive evidence to the contrary, have written this letter.

Chapter 3

The Pseudo-Ivan and the Pseudo-Kurbskii?

Your desire to include facsimiles of the handwriting of Tsar Ivan and Prince Kurbskii (be magnanimous toward my frankness!) demonstrates your still meagre experience in our ancient literature. These things are possible only for a Sulakadzev or a Svin'in.—P. M. Stroev to N. G. Ustrialov, 1832

Our purpose in this chapter is to establish whether Andrei Kurbskii, as he is portrayed in available documentary evidence, might indeed have written the first letter—or, for that matter, any of the works attributed to him—whether his milieu, as we understand it, could have been that in which these works appeared, and whether any independent evidence is to be found of the existence of these works before ca. 1620.

The broadening of our scope to any of the work attributed to Kurbskii is logical and necessary: while the method used in Chapter 2 allowed the study of the first letter in isolation, the nature of the argument to follow requires that we first consider the possibility that Kurbskii wrote anything at all, returning to the narrower question later, if necessary. Similarly, we shall broaden our inquiry to include Ivan, for if the conclusion of Chapter 2 is to be accepted, the tsar could not have written the parts of the *Correspondence* attributed to him.

The essence of the accepted views concerning the origin and authorship of the *Correspondence* has been stated in the Introduction: these letters were exchanged by Ivan and Kurbskii over the years

1564 to 1579. Certain corollaries to these views have arisen, presumably as the result of scholars' attempts to compensate for the
absence of concrete evidence in support of the main hypothesis.
Most important among these supporting hypotheses are:

(a) that the *Correspondence* was by no means a personal exchange of
letters, but a series of "open letters." This suggestion has usually been
brought forward as an explanation of the highly unusual epistolary
forms found in the texts.[1]
(b) that Ivan possessed not only an enormous erudition, but unprecedented
stylistic virtuosity, which permitted him to move easily from the most
elevated and convoluted Slavonic to seemingly colloquial and even
vulgar Russian. The assumption that Ivan possessed this talent has its
basis in the observation that, indeed, the letters and other writings
attributed to Ivan display an enormous range of knowledge and
stylistic virtuosity.[2]
(c) that "much has been lost." It has been assumed that much evidence
relating to Ivan's education and literary interests including his
Kremlin library has been lost. This assumption, too, has arisen as a
partial explanation of the fact that the *Correspondence* contains
evidence corroborated nowhere else, and that the author of the letters
was indeed a very well-educated man, by sixteenth-century standards.

It will be noted that these three corollaries are but logical extensions
of the main theorem they are intended to support: that Ivan and
Kurbskii wrote these texts. If this point d'appui is removed, even
tentatively, it becomes clear that there is inadequate independent
evidence to support any of the corollaries, and the serious paradoxes
which they are intended to resolve are restored.

Indeed, to say the least of it, the whole structure of those arguments
which attribute the *Correspondence* to Ivan and Kurbskii is so ridden
with logical, conceptual, and methodological faults that it cannot by
rigorous standards be accepted as proof of anything.

Yet, as we have noted in the Introduction, neither Ustrialov nor
anyone has ever asked, in print, "How do we know that these extraordinary texts are genuine?"[3] To my knowledge, no one has ever
analyzed the manuscript tradition, no one has properly studied the
texts as linguistic evidence, no one has permitted himself, in discussing the manifold contradictions and anachronisms of the texts, to go
beyond the pious perplexity with which a believer confronts a
mystery.[4]

But the scholar, however painful his ignorance, may not accept
the solace of mysteries. And the objective scholar must conclude that

an enormous burden of proof still rests with those who assert the authenticity of the *Correspondence*.

The Meaning of Silence

We examined in Chapter 1 some of the reasons why this is so: there is simply no manuscript evidence for the existence of even Kurbskii's first letter before the late 1620's, and the likely dates for other portions of the *Correspondence* are scattered over decades until the seventies or eighties of the same century.

One may not, of course, disregard entirely the possibility that originals of this *Correspondence*, written by Ivan and Kurbskii and presumably kept by them or their disciples in concealed personal or official archives, have simply been lost. This possibility, however, can be shown to be quite remote, in ways which add authority to the argument *ex silentio*.

We possess a large and representative array of the manuscript and printed material produced in Muscovy and in the territory where Kurbskii found refuge.[5] More specifically, we possess an enormous part of the Grand Princely archive as it was in 1575 and an even larger portion of what was recorded in an inventory of 1614, including Ivan's Lithuanian correspondence for the 1560's and 1570's.[6] And yet, as our previous discussion has revealed, there exists not only no official copy of the *Correspondence*, but no copy of any part of it of any period, which can in any way be associated with Ivan's archive or his chancelleries. Similarly, no early manuscript of any part of this *Correspondence* can be linked to any of the seats of Kurbskii's presumed activities in the Polish-Lithuanian territories.[7]

Let us pause briefly to consider all of the logical consequences of these observations. If one accepts the traditional dates, he must assume that manuscripts of the *Correspondence* were produced as follows: Kurbskii wrote his first letter in Valmiera in 1564 in two copies, of which he kept one and sent the other to Moscow. In the same year, Ivan responded, basing his letter on Kurbskii's. At some later date, a second version of Ivan's letter was made in two copies, based upon a slightly different copy of Kurbskii's letter, like that found in MS 43. In writing his later letters Kurbskii apparently referred to still another version of his own first letter, like that found in the "Kurbskii Collections," and to a copy of the second version of Ivan's first letter. In 1566, Isaiah used a copy of the first, and Fedorov, in 1574, a copy of the second version of Kurbskii's letter.

Thus, by the death of Ivan and Kurbskii in 1584 and 1583, respectively, there must have existed at least six different copies of three
different versions of Kurbskii's first letter, two copies of the second
version of Ivan's first, and one copy of each of the others. Sometime
around 1625 or 1630, a copy of Kurbskii's first letter was made from
a copy of the earliest version, and somewhat later copies from copies
of both the versions of Ivan's first letter. Much later, around 1675,
a copy of Ivan's second letter was made, and, at about the same time,
copies of the second version of Kurbskii's first, together with the
remaining Kurbskii letters.

But only the seventeenth-century copies of all of these letters are
preserved, which means that we must assume the following losses:

three sixteenth-century copies of the first version of Kurbskii's first letter,
one in Lithuania and two in Moscow;
one sixteenth-century copy of the second version of the same, in a different
part of Lithuania;
one sixteenth-century copy of Ivan's letter in the first version, in Moscow;
two copies of the second version of same, in two places;
two sixteenth-century copies of each of the remaining letters.

To these lost copies, whose existence must be assumed if the
traditional attribution is to be retained, may be added:

one copy of the first version of Kurbskii's first letter, which Isaiah obtained
in exile by 1566;
one copy of the second version, used by Ivan Fedorov in L'viv in 1574.

Thus, assuming that these letters were exchanged as is alleged,
we may posit the existence, around 1575, of at least nineteen separate
manuscripts containing at least one letter (not to speak of *sborniki*)
scattered throughout East Slavic territory from Kovel' to Rostov and
from Valmiera to L'viv. And we must assume, on present evidence,
that every one has been lost.

Now, the disappearance of all of these letters, particularly from
the generally well-preserved Lithuanian correspondence of the
Grand Princely archive, and from Kurbskii's personal archive,
requires no little explanation; but nearly 400 years have elapsed,
many of them stormy, and such losses are not beyond imagining. Yet
we still have to account for the loss of a number of copies which
disappeared *after* they were used in the seventeenth century:

a copy of the first version of Kurbskii's first letter, which was available in
Muscovy in the early 1630's (i.e., common protograph of MS 4469,
etc., and of Khvorostinin's "To the Reader");

a copy of the version of the same as reflected in MS 43, which was available in Muscovy late in the seventeenth century;

a copy of the first version of Ivan's first letter, used by a Muscovite copyist around 1630;

a copy of Ivan's first letter in the second version, extant at about the same time;

a copy of Ivan's second letter, used in 1675;

copies of the remaining Kurbskii letters, together with a copy of the *second* version of Kurbskii's first letter (which must have been transported from Lithuania) from which the extant copies of the 1670's and 1680's were made.

All of these later copies, of course, must have been, if not the originals, copies from the originals which somehow bridged the chronological gap between the assumed date of the letter and the dates of copying. Thus, we must assume that at *each* of the stages of seventeenth-century copying, the copyist had at his disposal a copy, now lost, of a text which represented not only a stage of the textual and literary history of the *Correspondence*, but also the very same stage in the sequence in which the extant texts were copied from now lost original or earliest copies in the seventeenth century. This colossal coincidence may be represented as follows:

	Presumed date of original	Date of earliest known copy
Kurbskii 1 (first version)	1564	ca. 1630
Ivan 1 (first version)	1564	ca. 1630 (later)
Kurbskii 1 (variant)	?	? (i.e., protograph of MS 43)
Ivan 1 (second version)	1564 (shortly after)	ca. 1630 (after GI[a])
Kurbskii 2	1565	1677
Ivan 2	1577	1675
Kurbskii 1 (second version)	1578 (before)	1677
Kurbskii 3 et seq.	1578	1677

Thus, the study of the textual evidence indicates a sequence which is, quite logically, the sequence of the letters, with a few modifications (the second versions of the first letters of Ivan and Kurbskii). The extant copies reproduce this sequence. That the pattern of loss of all originals and sixteenth-century copies, in two distant places of collection, should perfectly duplicate this sequence is, to say the least of it, miraculous. The possibility of a vast international conspiracy being excluded, we should conclude, as a first approximation,

that, although we may not possess all of the protographs, we do have the texts which reflect, and are essentially contemporary with, the protographs of the Kurbskii–Ivan IV *Correspondence*.

This conclusion is supported by what may seem a more startling and categorical statement: there is, quite simply, no evidence of any kind of the existence of *any* part of the *Correspondence* before ca. 1630. Of course, such an argument *ex silentio* bears only the force of the anticipated probability that the reverse should be true; in this case there are at least three considerations which justify our stressing this fact:

(a) None of the well-known itinerant foreigners, most of whom were particularly interested in Ivan's relations with his nobles, makes any mention of the *Correspondence*.[8]

(b) Kurbskii is nowhere mentioned in the extensive printed Ukrainian polemical literature of the late sixteenth and early seventeenth centuries, notwithstanding the fact that the energetic editors of such works, desperate for authoritative defenses of Orthodoxy, should have welcomed such an articulate and well-educated spokesman, especially a noble layman (conversions to Catholicism among the Ukrainian Orthodox nobility having been a particularly dangerous trend). It is doubly curious that Kurbskii should be unknown in these circles, since many religious and semireligious works attributed to him are written in the style and language of the polemical literature of the western areas and deal with the vexed questions of that time.[9]

(c) The later Muscovite chronicles, some of which were edited, presumably, by Ivan himself, make no mention of any correspondence, in spite of the fact that, as Al'shits has shown, Ivan's first letter is somehow linked to them.[10]

It should be clear from this brief sketch that the above arguments undermine very seriously two of the corollaries of the authenticity hypothesis mentioned above: one can hardly explain away the stylistic and formal peculiarities of this extraordinary *Correspondence* by declaring it an exchange of "open letters" when there is no evidence that anyone had ever heard of it before ca. 1625; the "much has been lost" dodge is highly questionable. However much has been lost, enough has survived to create a source pattern in which such losses could be identified and even reconstructed. Shelves of official documents, the originals of the testaments of the Grand Princes from Dmitrii Donskoi, printed volumes of diplomatic correspondence, including the exchanges with Sigismund August for the period in question, which make no mention of any correspondence, two published volumes of documentary evidence reflecting Kurbskii's

activities in exile, hundreds of pages of foreigners' accounts, several hefty volumes of Ukrainian polemical works, thousands of manuscripts—we possess a quantity and variety of source material that makes it unconvincing indeed for us to throw up our hands and complain about "losses," however regrettable they may have been.

Thus the logic of our source pattern and the absolute absence of any evidence of the *Correspondence* before the 1620's make our first two corollaries doubtful. Before consideration of the third (the nature of Ivan's style and erudition), other matters must be reviewed, which have to do with certain patterns of culture in Muscovy and, in particular, with Ivan's education.

Paradoxes of Culture, Style, and Ambience

Discussions of the "level of culture" in Muscovy have traditionally dealt in value judgments: Muscovy was "higher" than one culture, "lower" than another, "ahead" of one, "behind" the other. Were we to attempt to place Ivan and Kurbskii within the culture of their time and place on the basis of such judgments, we would fall into circular reasoning: their works contain much of the evidence usually cited in establishing the "level" of Muscovite culture.

In considering the possible attribution of the *Correspondence* to Ivan's time, it is desirable to attempt to establish not whether Muscovy was "capable" of producing such texts, but whether the texts are consistent with that pattern which we know to have been characteristic of Muscovite culture. Regardless of "level," artifacts, material or spiritual, must "fit": assuming, let us say, that Muscovite culture of the time was "superior" to that of the Australian aborigines, one should still be suspicious of a boomerang attributed to Ivan.

Thus in considering Ivan's education, we must attempt to establish not whether he was "educated enough" to produce such letters, but rather whether the kind of education he presumably received would normally prepare him to produce letters like these.

One of the distinctive features of Muscovite cultural life in the mid-sixteenth century is a rather sharp contrast between secular and religious cultures. Russian monastic culture, having inherited traditions and techniques familiar to students of medieval Western literature and philosophy, remained relatively free, during the sixteenth century, of outside influence, while the traditions and techniques of the court and counting-house continued, by and large,

the practices evolved by the great states which had preceded Muscovy
as lords of the East European plain. There are very limited inter-
change and interaction between these cultures: no strong traditions
of formal education in the essentially religious formal culture were
developed by the ruling dynasty or the warrior class; few if any
princes of the Church succumbed to the lure of secular culture
which so compromised Western clerics.[11]

The distinctiveness of these cultures was clearly reflected in the
forms used by each. The medium of the formal monastic culture was
the Muscovite recension of Slavonic; its genres were the saint's *vita*,
the homily, the pastoral letter, and, originally, the chronicle. In the
secular culture, the medium was the so-called "*prikaz* language," a
kind of "plain style,"[12] which, while linked to very ancient conventions, was more flexible and open to the influence of colloquial
speech than the "classical" Slavonic; and the forms were the
charter, the petition, the ambassador's report, and so on. Later, the
distinctions between these forms and cultures became less rigid, and
in the seventeenth century, documentary forms played, briefly, the
role of tentative premodern belletristic genres, but for the mid-
sixteenth century, the old distinctions remain characteristic, and the
"etiquette" of the traditional literary forms was observed.[13]

The formal and stylistic features of the letters in the *Correspondence*
appear extraordinary in the mid-sixteenth-century context, to say
the least of it. As we have observed above, three distinct literary
languages are used—and the differences in style do not reveal any
correlation with presumed authorship. Kurbskii's first letter is
linguistically identical with Ivan's first (both are written in rather
ornate Slavonic), while the other letters are different from these and
from each other (Ivan's second in a kind of mixed "plain style,"
Kurbskii's remaining letters in a "Western" Slavonic).

This evidence conflicts in a number of ways with almost any
justifiable assumption about the nature of the education presumably
received by either correspondent. Since there is no documentary
evidence about this education, we must assume that both were
trained in the secular tradition, and that if they were literate at all,
it was in the language used in their own, the secular, culture. Further,
we must assume that Ivan, all of whose "genuine" letters (i.e.,
unquestionably authentic letters signed with his name)[14] to lay
persons are written in "plain style," would have chosen to write
Kurbskii in that language, especially since after his flight Kurbskii

was, strictly speaking, a foreigner, and Ivan's diplomatic correspondence was conducted exclusively in "plain style."[15] All of the
same assumptions should apply to Kurbskii. And yet in the early
letters both men use Slavonic, the medium of the religious culture.

Much has been made, by way of explaining the oddities of these
letters, of Ivan's "vulgarity" and of Kurbskii's use of "polonisms."
Let us consider these features, too, in the context of contemporary
epistolary culture. True, some of Ivan's more colloquial phrases in
these letters are remarkably like those found in some "genuine" letters
of a diplomatic and official nature: the famous letter to Vasilii
Griaznoi is the usual exemplar.[16] But such colloquial devices reflect
the circumstances of production (transcription of speech) and the
linguistic medium (the plain style) of the documentary genre; in
the higher epistolary style with which Slavonic is associated in the
sixteenth century, they are irregular, to say the least.[17]

Thus, Ivan's letters are highly unusual in form and style: he
would be expected to write to Kurbskii in "plain style," adhering to
the epistolary formulae of the chancellery. Instead, he chose, for his
first letter, Slavonic—and by sixteenth-century standards, a stylistically impure Slavonic—into which some inappropriate plain-style
elements were imperfectly incorporated. And for his second letter
he chose an even more unprecedented medium—mixed Slavonic and
plain style, which, although increasingly common in the seventeenth
century, is very rare in the sixteenth.[18]

Concerning Kurbskii's letters, many of the same comments are in
order. One must presume that his education, if any, was much like
Ivan's; in letter-writing he, too, should be expected to use "plain
style." In fact, however, all of the letters here attributed to him are
written in Slavonic—but in two different recensions of Slavonic, the
Muscovite and the "Western."[19] The traditional explanation of this
stylistic inconsistency (i.e., the influence of a Polish linguistic
environment) is illogical for a number of reasons. First, it should be
pointed out again that the non-Muscovite elements of Kurbskii's
later letters are not Polish, but Belorussian or Ukrainian. A second
observation concerns the fact that Kurbskii's second letter, presumably written but a few months after the first, is already entirely
identical in its Westernisms with all of the later letters, written,
according to most authorities, as much as fifteen years later.[20]

That the "Polish" environment could have changed the formal
literary language of a mature individual in such a short time is

manifestly doubtful. It must be remembered that Slavonic was not a spoken but a conventional literary language, and the degree to which it could be "influenced" by colloquial speech is questionable. This was an idiom which one learned, with some difficulty, at an early age, in one or another of the established local recensions, and it remained, like the literary Italian of a Roman who has moved, say, to Brescia, essentially immune to nonliterary influences.

Thirdly, Kurbskii was writing to Ivan, who, having had the same Slavonic education as Kurbskii, would find the "Western" version of Slavonic somewhat confusing. What conceivable purpose, in 1565, could Kurbskii have had in choosing this idiom?[21]

Similar doubts must be expressed about the kind of erudition which is clearly possessed by the authors of these texts. Without, once again, making any comparative evaluations of culture, we may note the patterns which are characteristic of Muscovy and the letters' lack of conformity with these patterns.

The chasm between the clerical, primarily monastic, culture and that of the court is particularly important here. These texts, if they appeared in the sixteenth century, must clearly have originated within the religious realm of the Muscovite culture. Although the second version of Ivan's first letter contains a great deal of political history and personal reminiscence, the enormous body of information concerning Byzantine, Old Testament, and classical history, the citations from the Church Fathers, and so forth, create a dissonance with everything we know from other sources about the culture of the Muscovite court.[22]

Considering the patterns of Muscovite culture in the mid-sixteenth century as a whole, we note a similar discordance. While much of what Ivan cites is well known in sixteenth-century works, there are many authors and allusions that are highly unusual for his period, although they became popular in the seventeenth century. The same can be said of Kurbskii, whose translation of Cicero, for example, is without parallel in his time.[23]

It is useful here to recall for a moment a larger pattern of Slavic culture, of which Muscovy's culture was but a part. It is a general characteristic of the cultural history of the Slavs, in the medieval and early modern periods, that such cultural movements and influences as are received from the West can be seen to move gradually eastward across the various Slavic cultural communities, and to be passed by each to its neighbors, as well as directly from the western sources.

Particularly in the case of the humanistic writings, popular after the Renaissance, which so unexpectedly appear in the writings of Ivan and Kurbskii, it has long been noted, and fully elucidated, that the culture of the Renaissance traced a procession from the areas in most direct contact with the Italian and Central European centers (Dalmatia, Moravia) via Poland and the Ukraine to Muscovy.[24] The importance of Polish transmission in the evolution of Muscovite culture, particularly in the seventeenth century, is quite obvious, although its full scope and significance has not, in recent decades, found sufficiently explicit treatment in Soviet and even Polish works.[25] An even more neglected element of the general pattern of Slavic cultural development is the role of the Ukrainian cultural awakening of the later sixteenth and seventeenth centuries, when, in the environment created by the struggle of the Orthodox population against the Catholic and Polish culture of its masters, many of the most important links of the chain joining Muscovy with the West were forged.

There are some particularly important features of this Ukrainian experience which must be considered in any discussion of the patterns of Muscovite culture in the sixteenth and seventeenth centuries.[26] First, it must be stressed that in the case of the Ukraine, we are dealing not with the simple transmission of early modern Western ideas, but with a bitter, life-and-death struggle for religious freedom and cultural integrity between the Ukrainian and Belorussian Orthodox establishment and the powerful forces of official counterreformation, in a context created by reformation ideas. It was here that the East Slavs threw up their first lines of defense against the encroachment of the Catholic West, here that Orthdoxy was reinfused with the cultural vigor required for the struggle, here that the first significant printing establishments appeared, and that the first attempt at an East Slavic vulgate Bible was made. And in this territory first appeared those traditions of polemical literature, based both upon interpretation of Orthodox tradition and scholarly analysis of Catholic and Protestant works, which were to prove so important for Muscovite cultural life in the seventeenth century.[27]

In the late sixties and seventies of the sixteenth century, this ferment was well begun in the Ukrainian and Belorussian territories, but nothing comparable can be observed in Muscovy, which seems to have been untouched by all but the faintest echoes of the *Kulturkampf* which was convulsing Europe. Here doctrine was unchallenged (save for a few internal heresies) and polemics traditional. Here the genres, language, and content of the (predominantly religious) literature were quietly canonical, and the manuscript book was unchallenged by Ivan Fedorov's unsuccessful attempt to introduce printing.[28]

The general features of this late sixteenth-century pattern are well known and indisputable; it may indeed be one of the sources of Muscovy's later strength that she was spared, at this stage of her development, the convulsions that generated the cultural efflorescence in the western parts of East Slavic territory. But can Ivan and Kurbskii and their *Correspondence* be placed within the context so defined? For these texts, and previous scholarly literature, ask us to believe that our correspondents were Renaissance men, keenly interested in the questions which were stirring all of Europe *except* Muscovy, well-versed in precisely the texts which were the marching chants of peoples *outside of* Muscovite territory, eager to refute heresies which had not yet challenged Moscow's Orthodoxy.

Can it be? Can we accept the notion, crucial to the traditional attribution, that Kurbskii composed or translated after his flight a number of polemical works, extremely topical for the time in his new home—some even credited as the first of their kind—and that no one in Lithuanian territory even knew about them, or at least mentioned them? Can it be that a layman of Muscovy's warrior class became in effect the teacher of the learned clerical defenders of Orthodoxy in the Polish-Lithuanian state? Can it be that Ivan, who in the *Correspondence* appears more ponderously erudite, if less versatile, than Kurbskii, was a Renaissance prince of a realm with no Renaissance—that he was decades ahead of his subjects in cultural development? No, if what we think we know of the cultural history and cultural patterns of East Slavic territory is to be credited, it cannot be.

Kurbskii and Ivan: Biographical Considerations

It cannot be, that is, unless there exists some firm evidence that Kurbskii and Ivan were, indeed, exceptional within the general context of Muscovite culture and had somehow become particularly well-educated men. A considerable amount of biographical source material about Kurbskii, and rather less concerning Ivan, does exist, and we may turn to it now, with the hope of establishing some record of their literacy and literary education.

About Kurbskii's childhood there is no evidence. He first appears in our sources in 1550 as a warrior, and all of his activities before his flight to Lithuania were essentially military.[29] After his defection, Kurbskii continued to distinguish himself primarily as a military man, and the documents make clear that he was a litigious adulterer, an accessory to murder, a thief, and a general blackguard. There is no evidence that he owned a single book. His will, which details his possessions with great care (he was apparently extremely avaricious), bequeaths to the well-known patron of early Ukrainian book publishing, his friend and executor, Konstantin Ostroz'kyi, not some prized incunabula, but a suit of armor![30]

There is, of course, nothing in the general run of human experience to indicate that a base adventurer cannot ipso facto be a man of some erudition. But given the traditions and techniques of education of Kurbskii's time, and the rigid differentiation of the roles of scholar and warrior characteristic of Muscovy, his imputed erudition must be considered highly improbable, to say the least.

One need hardly go into the contradictions of this nature in the case of Ivan, before whose exploits Kurbskii's adventures seem the peccadillos of *un homme moyen sensuel*. Concerning his education we possess, as in Kurbskii's case, no reliable information.[31] Note should perhaps be taken, however, of the recurrent myth of the existence of a library of Latin and Greek books which presumably were Ivan's, and are thought by some to be buried to this day under the Kremlin wall. Proving that they are not buried there, or anywhere else is, of course, similar to proving that one is not a camel. The possibility that some trusting individual will someday uncover such a collection cannot be entirely excluded, but, within the limits of present knowledge and the parameters of normal logic, Belokurov long ago showed that this library is the figment of a number of overheated imaginations.[32]

Thus, to put the contradiction in its starkest form: if these letters are to be accepted as genuine, one must then also accept the compound paradox that the two most erudite authors of their age, who anticipated by two generations later formal and philosophical developments in Muscovite literary culture, whose careers are otherwise rather well illuminated in documentary sources, left no evidence of their literary activities, nor indeed of their functional literacy, aside from texts questionably attributed to them, and that their innovative and heroic intellectual achievements remained entirely unknown to their contemporaries.[33]

A final comment about the content of the *Correspondence*: the main attention of scholars in the past has been attracted by the presumed political polemic conducted in these letters, in which Ivan has been assumed to be defending the absolute autocracy with which he is traditionally identified, while Kurbskii has been variously described as the representative either of the "old feudal order" or of a more modern oligarchic point of view. As Nørretranders has shown in his minute and thoughtful analysis of these letters, there is strikingly little basis for either of these views.[34] Kurbskii, in particular, never really does make clear what he believes in, aside from his complaints against Ivan's personal tyranny, while Ivan, for the most part, is at pains to justify his own actions on personal and historical grounds, rather than by any consistent theoretical program.

As we shall see below, many of the numerous oddities, inconsistencies, and anachronisms of the *Correspondence* may be explained and removed by a single step—the rejection of the traditional dating and attribution.

The Traditional Attribution: Logical Flaws

The traditional attribution of the *Correspondence*—to the extent that it has been justified at all—has relied heavily upon the obvious similarities between certain of its letters and other texts ascribed to Ivan or Kurbskii. Attribution through juxtaposition with similar texts is of course an entirely legitimate method; its importance in establishing authorship increases as the number and conclusiveness of other sources of attribution decreases. But attributions based upon comparison are rarely conclusive in themselves, and can in no case be more reliable than the attributions of the texts chosen for comparison.

In the present instance, comparison of the *Correspondence* with other texts attributed to Ivan or Kurbskii yields results which are so inconclusive as to be meaningless. There are no works which may be considered as unquestionably composed by Kurbskii; among those attributed to Ivan, only a few that he may have dictated to other writers may, with the attendant qualifications, be called his.

A review of the literature in which various texts are attributed to Ivan or Kurbskii would detain us inordinately and without profit; to establish proper attributions would require several small monographs. We shall, however, consider in the briefest outline the features of the texts most commonly associated with the names of our authors.

As one examines the "passports" of the works published in Kuntsevich's "Works of Prince Kurbskii" things become "curiouser and curiouser." The Hatter, it develops, is Ustrialov, who rarely mentions any reasons for his belief that Kurbskii wrote any of these works, but in his unspoken judgments reveals an utter lack of methodological rigor and a rare gullibility. In most cases, he apparently relies upon the judgment (and honesty!) of the late seventeenth-century copyists who provided the manuscript headings in which Kurbskii is credited as author; occasionally he accepts the chance remark or speculation of a contemporary.

If there exists any single copy of any original work attributed to Kurbskii which was manufactured within a generation of his death, or any text of his which has been preserved in a Lithuanian environment, such manuscripts are not mentioned in the literature on the subject. Assuming that Kuntsevich displayed his customary assiduity in searching for manuscripts, we may conclude that, with the exception of the first letter of the *Correspondence*, the major original works attributed to Kurbskii exist in copies made no earlier than 1675, a century after their presumed appearance.

Like the *Correspondence*, the works of Kurbskii are written in at least three styles, so different as to be termed three distinct literary languages. Some of his letters—precisely those found in the earliest manuscripts—are, like his first letter to Ivan, written in a normal late Muscovite Slavonic; others, like the later letters to Ivan with which they are always found, are full of "westrussianisms." The third group, also usually found together with the later stages of the *Correspondence*, are entirely "westrussian," being exemplars of the epistolary Slavonic in use among Orthodox literati in Ukrainian and Belorussian territory at the end of the sixteenth century.

Now it is possible that Kurbskii dictated these letters at different times to scribes of widely different training. If there were any explicit evidence to support this argument, it could be an important one. There being none, it remains a speculative device for the reconciliation of contrary evidence with the accepted view.

Although such a hypothesis might explain stylistic incongruities in letters of lesser significance and more ordinary contents, it collapses the moment one begins to consider the logical limits set by the nature of our letters. Can we assume that Kurbskii, who translated Cicero and in general displayed erudition unheard-of in his time, cared so little about his prose style that he entrusted his text to a scribe unable to write Muscovite Slavonic, and then didn't even bother to edit the final version? Can we accept the notion that Ivan, author (by dictation?!) of perhaps the longest epistle ever composed in Muscovite Slavonic, one fairly bristling with syntactic virtuosity and erudition, would permit a stylistic pastiche like the second letter attributed to him to go out over his name? Both answers must be negative, as must the response to the "scribe" objection. If, finally, one assumes that the scribes themselves composed the letters from general instructions, it follows that we are then dealing not with the works of Ivan and Kurbskii, but with those of two unjustly forgotten literary geniuses of the sixteenth century.

The Traditional Attribution: Kurbskii's Other Writings

Let us now turn to a cursory review of the major original works attributed to Kurbskii.

Although he is nowhere explicitly identified, Kurbskii appears from internal evidence to be the real or imputed author of the remarkable work, the *History of Ivan IV*. Its convoy, language, and contents link it very closely with the latest portions of the *Correspondence*, those parts found only in copies of the last third of the seventeenth century.[35] It was probably composed at the same time, and by the same person, who wrote the last letters of Kurbskii. It is particularly noteworthy that the *History* is often found together with excerpts from Guagnini's "Description of Muscovy," with which it shares certain information.[36] Guagnini's work was apparently brought to Moscow in 1653, and translated somewhat later.[37]

Many scholars have noted, but found explanations for, the oddities, anachronisms, and paradoxes in which this text abounds.[38] The very title—*History*—is questionable in two respects. The term *istoriia* was uncommon in Muscovite usage in the 1570's, if it was used at all; certainly the "history" form, the thematic narrative in which events are organized by an author in order to illustrate historical development, cause and effect—or, as here, psychological evolution of a protagonist and its influence upon events—is highly unusual for that time and place. In Muscovy the annalistic form remained the norm until the Time of Troubles, when the first rather primitive efforts in the "history" genre began to appear.[39] One might turn once again to Kurbskii's Lithuanian acculturation in order to find an explanation for his precocity. But this too is speculation, unacceptable in view of the fact that everything about this work suggests that it was written in Muscovy, for Muscovite readers, and on the basis of Muscovite sources which could hardly have been available in Kovel' in 1577.[40]

A considerable literature and a number of serious historiographic disputes have been generated by the incompatibility of information contained in the *History* with other, in some cases massive, documentary evidence. The prime example of such problems is the question of the Chosen Council (*Izbrannaia rada*), a term and indeed a concept which seems to have been invented by the author of the *History*. Historians have long been aware that the term appears nowhere else, and that much of the *History*'s information about the Chosen Council and its members (notably Adashev) is erroneous or misleading, but only recently has a systematic monographic discussion of the paradoxes here involved shown the unreliability of the *History* and the chaos which has been created by historians' overly trusting use of it. But even the author of this meticulous study apparently did not ask himself the essential question: can the *History* be accepted as the genuine sixteenth-century testimony of a participant in the events described, and what evidence is there of its authenticity ?[41]

There is very little such evidence, and prior to further attempts to reconcile the *History*'s testimony with genuine sources, historians must examine its origins most carefully. No amount of ratiocination about Kurbskii's possible motives for prevarication, or about sources he might possibly have used in his distant exile, or about copyists' errors and emendations, can replace a serious examination of the *History*'s passport, and it may develop that such a study will at a stroke resolve the contradictions which have for so long taxed historians' imaginations.

Thus, for example, a comparison of the *History* with the "History of the Scythians" (*Skifskaia istoriia*), written by Andrei Lyzlov in the late seventeenth century, indicates that the *History* can hardly be older than Lyzlov's work, or, if such be found, than their common source. More than forty pages of the *History* coincide nearly verbatim with sections of Lyzlov's work, and there are strong indications that the *History* borrowed from it.[42] This observation is in accord with the chronological information about the manuscript copies of the *History*, many of which contain Lyzlov's translation of Stryjkowski's "Chronicle."

The second major narrative work attributed to Kurbskii is the

"History of the Outlaw Eighth Council," a polemical, Eastern Orthodox interpretation of the Council of Florence-Ferrara.[43] Like the *History of Ivan IV*, this work apparently is found only in copies made in the last decades of the seventeenth century, and in Muscovite rather than Polish-Lithuanian environments.[44] Its close relationship to a work with the same title attributed to an otherwise unidentified "Cleric from Ostroh" has been noted by a number of scholars, most of whom have assumed, after Hrushevs'kyi, that this resemblance is the result of Kurbskii's use of an earlier version of the published text.[45] There is, however, no evidence of the existence of such a common source, and it can be shown that the text attributed to Kurbskii is in fact a translation and condensation of a Ukrainian text written after the Union of Brest.[46] In all probability, the "History" is a Muscovite translation of the printed version of 1598, similar to numerous other seventeenth-century manuscript translations of Ukrainian and Belorussian printed books (*knigi litovskoi pechati*), and has nothing to do with Andrei Kurbskii.

There are two groups of texts which stand apart from the works heretofore discussed, in that they seem to contain no evidence contradictory to documentary information or to the general patterns of Muscovite and non-Muscovite East Slavic cultural history. The first group is composed of a number of letters attributed to Kurbskii. Cursory examination indicates that these are genuine letters, written in Polish-Lithuanian territory, by an Orthodox writer, in the late sixteenth century. Although they may well have been written by Kurbskii, this attribution has not been satisfactorily established, and the question of how they came to be included in the late Muscovite collections of Kurbskii's works remains unanswered.[47]

The second group is composed of translations, mostly of a religious nature, which have been attributed to Kurbskii on the flimsiest of grounds.

In summing up the evidence provided by other texts attributed to Kurbskii, the following points may be made with reference to the question of his authorship of the *Correspondence*:

(1) There is no single text which can without serious qualifications be ascribed to Kurbskii.
(2) As in the case of the *Correspondence*, no part of the remainder of the oeuvre attributed to Kurbskii is to be found in sixteenth-century manuscripts or in a "western" manuscript environment.
(3) Like the several letters of the *Correspondence*, the other works may be

divided, by the linguistic/stylistic criterion, into groups so different as to raise doubts about a common authorship.

(4) Some of these works (the "History of the Eighth Council," the letters to Vas'ian) are almost surely not Kurbskii's; others (the *History*, the letter to Ioann the Learned) are doubtful; a third group (the "western" letters) seem to have been written in Kurbskii's time and in Polish-Lithuanian territory, but not necessarily by Kurbskii. Oddly, the letters of this third group, which might have been written by Kurbskii, are, of all the works here considered, the least similar in language and content to Kurbskii's part of the *Correspondence* and are found in the latest (ca. 1680) manuscripts.

Thus, while our cursory review has not permitted us to declare definitively either for or against the traditional attribution of these works to Andrei Kurbskii, it has shown that that attribution is questionable and insufficient, and that it can provide no basis for the attribution, on grounds of similarity, of the Kurbskii portion of the *Correspondence* to Kurbskii or to the author of these texts.

The Traditional Attribution: Ivan's Other Writings

What then of Ivan's half of the *Correspondence*, and of the traditional attribution, which is based in large measure upon similarities with other works attributed to him? Here we face problems even more complex than those that encumber the discussion of Kurbskii's authorship. It is difficult, indeed, to decide which of the texts attributed to Ivan should even be considered here. Numerous works attributed to him have been shown to be seventeenth-century fabrications;[48] others are apparently questionable.[49] The problem of determining whether one or another letter sent over Ivan's name is "genuine" is a complex one: surely the hundreds of official letters sent in his name to Muscovite and foreign dignitaries and preserved in the diplomatic and domestic archives of the Muscovite chancelleries are "genuine" in the sense that they are authentic contemporary documents, written in the name of the tsar.[50] But which, if any, of them did the tsar compose or dictate, and which were composed by clerks of his chancelleries? No attempt has been made, it appears, to answer this question, and it is difficult to conceive of such a study, since there exist no texts indisputably written by Ivan himself and therefore no criterion for judgment.

After thoughtful consideration of this problem, Iakov Solomonovich Lur'e selected, on the basis of "individual peculiarities," a number of texts as representative of Ivan's epistolary style, and we may accept these letters as most characteristic of the style identified as Ivan's.

Muscovite chancellery practice, in matters of diplomatic form and stylistic norms, was quite elaborate and firmly established by the second half of the sixteenth century. The "plain style" of the *prikaz* represents, indeed, such a consistent linguistic material as to permit its description as *the* language of Muscovy in the sixteenth century, although it was clearly neither the spoken nor the literary language of the time.[51] Similarly, the chancelleries had elaborated a consistent and obligatory set of forms for each of a number of types of document. Extensive chronological and typical series of these documents have been preserved, and the patterns of this preservation are entirely regular: all but an insignificant number of extant genuine diplomatic documents remain to this day in the archive of the *Posol'skii prikaz*, to which they were sent, apparently, shortly after they lost currency;[52] while charters, land-grant documents, and the like have been preserved among the records of the beneficiaries, especially monasteries.[53] The normative patterns of style, form, and preservation are quite clear, then, for the overwhelming majority of indisputably genuine documents of the period, and they provide us with certain bench marks against which we may measure the evidence provided by the letters which Lur'e considers the most probable examples of Ivan's own prose.

Ivan's famous letter to Elizabeth I is unquestionably an authentic communication produced in a Muscovite chancellery in 1570. Its language is that of the *prikaz*; its form raises no questions; its content is in full accord with other documents with which it forms a series; its contents seem appropriate. Whether it was *composed* by Ivan himself must remain an open question.[54]

Ivan's two letters to Johann III of Sweden seem, like the letter to Elizabeth, quite probably "genuine." They, too, are found where they belong, among the series of documents from the Grand Princely archive.[55] Two features of style arouse some interest, however; these are particularly insulting and humiliating letters, and they clash somewhat in tone with those which follow immediately in the same "book" of which they occupy the first pages. Secondly, one notes an almost pathological repetition of certain phrases which are somewhat unusual for Muscovite chancellery practice in general and for the immediately adjoining letters.[56] These unusual features might, with the support of additional evidence, either provide arguments in favor of the traditional attribution to Ivan, and of the "unorthodox" style with which he is credited, or (if no compatible evidence be found) encourage a skeptical view of the origin of these two letters.

The well-known letter to Vasilii Griaznoi is, from all appearances, "genuine." Nothing about its form or style is exceptional; it is found in the expected archival environment. Whether the animus it reveals belongs to Ivan or one of Griaznoi's superiors in the Muscovite diplomatic service cannot now be established.

Thus, with some qualifications, we may accept the letters to Elizabeth, Johann, and Griaznoi as "genuine" on the basis of normal patterns of diplomatic practice and the preservation of Muscovite archives, although Ivan's composition of them remains to be proven. The same criteria, however, which permit us to accept these letters cause certain doubts about the "genuineness" of *all* of the other letters included in the standard edition of Ivan's works.

A particularly interesting problem is raised by the four letters presumably written by Ivan for some of his boyars in 1567, in response to an apparent proposal by Sigismund II August that they betray Ivan. In form and style, at first glance, these letters seem normal: they are written not in Muscovite, but in Lithuanian *prikaz* style, but such a style was not uncommon in Muscovite letters to Lithuanian addressees. They are, as well, preserved among the records of the *Posol'skii prikaz*, a fact to which we have given considerable importance in discussing the previous letters. Closer examination, however, reveals something rather unusual about this group of letters—they are found not among the correspondence of the period to which they pertain, but in a separate book, which contains nothing else and violates that series' chronology.[57] It appears, moreover, that they were not a part of the archive when it was inventoried in 1614.[58] While the unusual and presumably secret nature of the letters might be considered sufficient reason for their being out of place (although if Ivan wrote them it is hard to imagine where, other than in his archive, they would be preserved), this circumstance requires that we examine the documents somewhat skeptically.

Indeed, the form and style of these letters, if closely examined, do reveal some questionable features. To begin, the writer uses a number of formulae which are simply not appropriate to non–Grand Princely writers, particularly the address of Sigismund, a crowned head (whatever his origin) as "our brother" and the

exclusively sovereign formula *slovo nashe to*.[59] Lur'e notes some of
these features, and explains them with the observation that the
boyars are manipulating this traditional formulaic system in order
to show the non-princely origins of Sigismund and their own princely
antecedents, which make them his equal or "elder."[60] This is an
intelligent guess, but not an entirely convincing one, for Lur'e seems
occasionally to forget that it is presumably Ivan who is the writer,
and he would not be expected either to use style appropriate to him
and him alone (or did he slip ?) in speaking for his boyars, or to stress
their descent from rulers whom his ancestors recognized as
"brothers."[61] Moreover, at least one of the nominal writers (Bel'skii),
however proud he may have been of his antecedents, was apparently
reconciled to the fact that the *pany* of the Lithuanian state were his
peers—he calls them "brothers" in a genuine document of the same
period.[62] It is similarly questionable that Ivan, who was at the
presumed time of writing engaged in breaking the power of the old
boyars and princely families, would go out of his way to magnify the
ancestry and nobility of the likes of Bel'skii, whose usual title is here
embellished to ludicrous proportions.[63]

In sum, while these letters, if they were indeed written by the tsar
after his discovery of Sigismund's attempt to lure the boyars to his
side, may be considered so exceptional as to be beyond the realm of
normal criteria of authenticity, their authenticity remains unproven.

Much the same must be said of the strange document known as
"The Petition of Ivanets Vasil'ev to the Tsar and Grand Prince
Simeon Bekbulatovich." The peculiar story of Ivan's "political
masquerade" in which he abdicated his throne to the Tatar prince
Sain Bulat is well known; this document is usually associated with
that incident.[64] The "passport" and stylistic features of this letter
are as strange as its contents: it is found among the historical pot-
pourri apparently assembled for Aleksei Mikhailovich in his Privy
Chancellery (*Tainyi prikaz*), and its origin is not clearly established.[65]
The extant document is clearly a later copy: the heading was probably
written in the seventeenth century.[66]

Stylistically, the letter takes the form of a *chelobitnaia* in which
the petitioner, Ivan, in apparently satirical, self-abasing language,
asks permission to "pick over" his "mannies," that is, to exile,
reassign, and generally shake up his boyars and *dvoriane*. In its
excessive use of diminutives, and particularly in the concluding
formula (*Gosudar' smiluisia, pozhalui!*) the text is reminiscent of

seventeenth-century petitions, and its content is clearly satirical, since Ivan was politically in charge through his little charade. Perhaps normal judgments should be suspended in this case—we are obviously dealing with a little joke. But it is not at all clear whose little joke.

A number of letters which Ivan presumably wrote during the devastatingly successful campaign through Livonian territory in 1577 seem to form a separate group and may be treated together. They are found among the "Polish Dossiers" of the Central State Archive of Ancient Acts and among the papers of A. N. Popov.[67] The Popov copy is apparently a copy of the archival one, or of one very much like it.[68] If we may judge from the convoy (these manuscripts contain a copy of the "Titulary" [Tituliarnik], written for Aleksei Mikhailovich in 1673), the common protograph of these collections was composed in the latter part of the seventeenth century. This fact, and the observation that the documents are not found among the official records of that expedition,[69] may be considered irregular, although perhaps easily explained by the disruption in normal practices caused by field conditions.

There are, however, some other odd features of this group of letters which deserve mention. The letter to Aleksandr Polubenskii is dated "Preskov [sic—Pskov]" July 9, 1577, which is odd, since Ivan apparently was in Novgorod on that day.[70] It is similarly unusual that Ivan should say in the text that he is sending the letter with Timofei Romanovich Trubetskoi, who was not a messenger, but the commander of a large army dispatched from Novgorod on that day in the direction of Valmiera to execute reconnaissance and "pacification" measures in the area surrounding, but which did not apparently have as its object the siege and capture of the city.[71]

This letter contains other noteworthy features: it is full of affect (threats, insults) but has no real message, and can hardly be compared with functional diplomatic documents; Trubetskoi, the bearer, is provided with a genealogy going back to Ol'gerd; the introduction, containing the tsar's title, is fantastically long and complex. Particularly interesting is the fact that, as Lur'e notes,[72] the text seems to contain citations from Ivan's earlier works, notably his first letter to Kurbskii, and echoes of a number of other literary works. The imagination staggers at the thought that Ivan remembered all of these sources so well, particularly a letter sent thirteen years before, which he quoted almost verbatim, and it is almost equally unlikely that on this extensive and arduous campaign he took along parts of his library and his old correspondence.

The other published letters found in the manuscripts mentioned above are somewhat similar, in their irregularities, to that addressed to Polubenskii. The letter to Jan Chodkiewicz, dated Valmiera, September 12, shares with the Polubenskii letter a lack of any effective or operative portion—it is largely a boastful and somewhat insulting declaration. It does contain some uncharacteristic praise of Chodkiewicz's bravery, which is couched in Slavonic, although the rest of the letter adheres by and large to the norms of plain style. The praise of Chodkiewicz causes Lur'e to comment, on the basis of other, indisputably genuine letters, on Ivan's radical change of attitude toward his addressee; it is altogether possible that not the attitude, but the author, was different in the two cases.[73]

The final letter of the group associated with the 1577 campaign is the short letter to Timofei Teterin. It exists only in the copy of the "Titulary" made for Popov, but the existence of a seventeenth-century original for Popov's copy may be assumed. If Polubenskii's confused *Sprawa* is to be trusted,[74] Ivan did send some letter to Teterin, but is this it? If it is, it was a waste of time for all concerned, for it contains no message, being little more than a resumé, in scornful and imprecatory tone, of things which we know Teterin did (wrote to Morozov, took Izborsk, etc.). Why in heaven's name write such a letter, in response, as it indicates, to a letter written more than a decade before, to Mikhail Morozov in Tartu? Why mention that Teterin once (*twenty* years earlier) delivered a letter to Ivan from Andrei Shein? Why, finally, does Ivan call Kurbskii Teterin's "master," when he was not? These latter two questions apparently bothered Lur'e—he provides clever but not entirely satisfactory answers for them,[75] but does not seem to question the raison d'être of the letter as a whole.

There is one letter among those which are included in *Poslaniia* which stands apart from the rest, by virtue of its personal and religious nature. The letter, presumably written to the abbot of the Kirillo-Belozerskii Monastery in 1573, has long been known to scholars and has served as the basis of a good deal of what has been written about Ivan's epistolary style. There is, however, no compelling evidence that it was written by Ivan—or even for him—and some considerable justification for concluding that it could not have appeared before the late seventeenth century.[76]

The final letter attributed to Ivan in *Poslaniia* is one addressed to Stefan Batory in 1581. It seems to be preserved in quite early copies, in the expected archival environment, and does not contain, apparently, any striking incongruities of style or contents. It seems analogous to other letters of the time in which Ivan (or his chancellery) set forth long historical justifications for Muscovite claims to disputed territory.[77]

Our brief review of the most important features of the letters other than those of the *Correspondence* which are most authoritatively attributed to Ivan has indicated that their probable authenticity fluctuates over a wide spectrum: some (those addressed to Elizabeth and Griaznoi) are almost certainly "genuine," in the sense that they are authentic letters written in Ivan's chancelleries, while others (the "boyar" group and those to Teterin, Polubenskii, and the Kirillo-Belozerskii Monastery) are very questionable for a number of reasons, and cannot confidently be considered "genuine" even in the limited sense which we have indicated.

For our present purpose of determining the origins of the *Correspondence*, two observations about this spectrum of relative probabilities are of significance:

(1) even the "genuine" letters cannot definitively be considered the compositions of the tsar himself;
(2) the letters which are "genuine" are least, and the questionable letters most, like the *Correspondence* in date, place of preservation, and style. Specifically, the second letter to Kurbskii clearly forms a part of one of the more questionable groups, the so-called "Collection" of 1577.

Conclusions

In concluding our review of the negative and circumstantial evidence, we may sum up as follows: the acceptance of the traditional attribution of these letters, an attribution which has never been properly questioned or justified, forces one to accept on faith a number of extraordinary corollaries which, in combination, are nothing short of miraculous, namely:

—that Ivan and Kurbskii, known from ample documentary evidence as men of action, to say the least, had at some time received what amounts to a complete monastic education, which made them utterly unique among lay figures of their time;
—that their erudition and tastes, particularly with regard to Western culture, were generations ahead of their time;

—that they were stylistic virtuosi and innovators, who anticipated by
decades the evolution of literary genre and language which was to
characterize the early seventeenth century;

—that these extraordinary documents were unknown in their own time,
both to curious foreigners and to the Ukrainian publishers and polemists
who would have been desperate for the kind of defenses of Orthodoxy
which are attributed to Kurbskii;

—that neither of these extraordinary figures left so much as a scrap of
text which can be identified as an autograph, and indeed no conclusive
evidence of his literacy;[78]

—that most of the other works attributed to Ivan, and all of those ascribed
to Kurbskii, are of questionable provenance and display the very same
doubtful features of chronology, style, and content as the parts of the
Correspondence with which they are most closely linked.

There being no sufficient evidential proof of the traditional
attribution of these letters, one is forced to employ logical deductive
proofs, which depend upon combinations of greater and lesser
probabilities. All of the positive probabilities established by analogy
with the known facts of biography, text history, and cultural context
are infinitesimal: in combination they approach zero. On the basis
of available evidence, there is no substantial reason to believe that
Ivan or Kurbskii wrote any of the letters of the *Correspondence*.

Chapter 4

The Growth of the *Correspondence*

It will be remembered that the life of the *Correspondence* does not, strictly speaking, begin with the composition of the original form of Kurbskii's first letter, because, if our previous conclusion is to be accepted, the kernel of the letter was composed not as a spurious letter from Kurbskii to Ivan, but as a personal letter from Shakhovskoi to Tsar Mikhail Fedorovich. Under these circumstances, the question *cui bono ?*, vital in the consideration of fabrications, does not arise.

Very shortly after its composition, however, the letter seemingly underwent a radical metamorphosis: the portions now found after the word *Amin'* were apparently added, along with a caption, in which the letter was reattributed to Kurbskii.[1] It is in this form that it found its way into all but one of the extant manuscripts.

Thus the point at which the last two paragraphs were added to the original letter may be considered the moment of conception of the Kurbskii-Ivan *Correspondence* as such. It is quite important, therefore, to establish the date and possible author of this transformation.

Since no copies of the first letter without some form of caption seem to exist (and only one without the postscript), and because the letter was used in the composition of the first version of Ivan's first letter, it seems plausible that the same individual, whom we consider to have been Shakhovskoi, composed both letter and postscript. A comparison of the added text with another work by Shakhovskoi provides interesting support for this view, and indeed for the larger hypothesis concerning Shakhovskoi's authorship of the letter itself.

In 1644, during the discussion of the proposed marriage of Prince Waldemar to the tsarevna Irina Mikhailovna (see above, Chap. 2), Semen Shakhovskoi composed for Mikhail Fedorovich a brief on certain problems of canon law raised by the prospective groom's Protestant faith. This document, about whose authenticity and authorship there seems to be little question, contains two passages which reproduce verbatim parts of the first letter of Kurbskii:

Shakhovskoi 1644	First Letter
Царю, от Бога препрославленный, паче же благочестивый!...	Царю от Бога препрославленному, паче же во православии пресветлу явльшемуся...
Писано бо есть в законе божии: моавитин и аммовит и всяк иноплеменник да не внидет в церковь Божию.[2]	В законе господни во первом писано: «моавитин и аммонитин и выблядок по десяти родов во церковь божию не входят» и прочая.[3]

These passages are, of course, precisely the first words of the original text and last words of the postscript of Kurbskii's first letter—an extraordinary coincidence, which seems to indicate that Shakhovskoi wrote the postscript as well as the body of the letter.

This information permits us tentatively to reconstruct the moment of metamorphosis of Shakhovskoi's original letter to Mikhail Fedorovich into Kurbskii's first letter as follows. Having retained the original of his letter to the tsar, Shakhovskoi must have felt that it was a rather embarrassing document to have in one's possession. There is nothing overly conspiratorial about this assumption: in order to understand what Shakhovskoi may have thought about the matter, one need only recall the arbitrary political repression of the Shakhovskoi clan in 1620, or the repeated searches of his cousin Khvorostinin's books and personal effects.[4] Loath to destroy his letter (he apparently kept collections of his own writings),[5] he hit upon a simple device—the attribution to Kurbskii—which made of what could be termed a treasonous letter a relatively harmless historical document.

This kind of dissimulation is entirely in character for Shakhovskoi, who displays in his known writings an almost pathological love of anonymity and secrecy. He is known for the concealment of his name in number codes, acrostics, and the like. In a number of his works he even elaborates his reasons for preferring to remain anonymous.[6] Certainly his bitter letter to Mikhail Fedorovich was not the kind of thing the newly pardoned "traitor" and "heretic" would want discovered in an unexpected house search by his enemies within the government. Thus our hypothetical time span for the attribution to Kurbskii and the addition of the postscript is ca. 1623–1632 (from Shakhovskoi's return to favor to the date of MS 1615).[7]

Why did Shakhovskoi choose Kurbskii? This question is vital, for, having assumed that Shakhovskoi was the agent of the attribution, we must find a satisfactory reason for him to choose Andrei Kurbskii as his "cover," at a time when Kurbskii was by no means a well-known figure, and probably was in no way associated with the ideas which modern scholars attribute to him.

An explanation of the choice presents itself when one considers some details of Shakhovskoi's early life. As we have seen, Shakhovskoi was a distant relative of Kurbskii and, like him, a prince of the Iaroslavl' line. In 1610, he betrayed Tsar Vasilii Shuiskii for Sigismund, King of Poland, and was granted some *pomestie* land in the Toropets region.[8] It was the practice in the *Rzeczpospolita*, where possible, to justify land grants to exiles on the basis of ancient historical and genealogical claims. Kurbskii, it will be remembered, styled himself *Kniaz' Iaroslavskii i Smolenskii* while in Lithuania; it is perfectly possible that Shakhovskoi hoped to do the same, and that while he was under Sigismund's rule, he inquired into the Lithuanian period of Kurbskii's biography.

That Shakhovskoi had some special interest in Kurbskii is indicated by an event which occurred shortly after Shakhovskoi's death, during the prolonged Muscovite-Polish war which began in 1654. In July 1656, the new Muscovite military commander of Vilnius wrote the following in a report to Aleksei Mikhailovich:

It became known to me . . . that Prince Andrei Kurbskii [Kurbskii's grandson] was living with his brother Jan in his estates in the province of Volkomir, and I . . . wrote and sent Mikhail Vlasov to him, Prince Andrei, [telling him] to recall his Orthodox faith and his native kind [*prirodu svoiu*] . . . [and] to come over to you with his brother.[9]

Kurbskii did so, as it appears from Muscovite documents, although he remained in Polish territory and even, some years later, maintained in a court of law that he had never had any treasonous dealings with the Muscovite occupation authorities.[10] It is not Kurbskii's activities that are of interest here, however, but the fact that a Muscovite *voevoda*, on his own initiative, sought out the entirely undistinguished landowner, had him come to Vilnius, and persuaded him of his duties to Orthodoxy and to Muscovy. Now if, as we have concluded above, the original Andrei Kurbskii was little remembered in Muscovy at this time, and if only his first letter to Ivan was in existence—and at that in perhaps a dozen manuscript copies—we must conclude that the Muscovite *voevoda* was someone who had special reason to know of the original Kurbskii, someone, perhaps, who had even read the letter. Such, apparently, was the case, for the *voevoda* in question was Mikhail Semenovich Shakhovskoi, son of Semen Ivanovich.[11]

Coincidence ? Perhaps, as indeed the similarities between Kurbskii's first letter and Shakhovskoi's letter concerning Waldemar, and even Shakhovskoi's defection to Sigismund may be. But they *are* facts, and at some stage enough facts coincide to permit us to speak not of mere coincidence but of mutually supporting, if diverse, bits of evidence which suggest, without fully explaining why, that Shakhovskoi had some reason to choose Kurbskii as his "cover."

These suggestions are no more than that; fuller evidence may lead to their revision. But they are the best explanations we can offer at this point concerning the date of the postscript, its raison d'être, and the choice of Kurbskii as the author ex post facto. Having put them forward, we may move to the next stage of the development of the *Correspondence*.

The First Version of Ivan's First Letter

In all publications of the *Correspondence* the so-called "abbreviated" version of Ivan's first letter has been relegated to an inferior position vis-à-vis the "full" versions.[12] Most recently, Lur'e, while preferring the "full" version, of which he is the first to provide an acceptable text, noted that one must take into consideration the fact that the "abbreviated" version contains the best readings of certain passages and must have originated very early, perhaps even with the author.[13]

This observation is supported by all the evidence to be gleaned from the manuscript tradition and from textual analysis. The group of manuscripts which contain the "abbreviated" version is of generally earlier manufacture than the group containing the "full" text, and it is connected by its "convoy" with the earlier manuscripts which contain only the first letter of Kurbskii, while other collections containing the "full" version show no such correlation.[14] Detailed examination and comparison of the texts, moreover, show not only that the "abbreviated" version is superior in many regards, but that some of the oddities of the "full" version seem to have appeared as a result of misunderstandings by the author of the "full" version of the "abbreviated" text.[15] Finally, it appears that the changes in the order of exposition are best explained by the assumption that the "abbreviated" preceded the "full," and there is even a suggestion that we possess the very texts from which the "full" was composed.[16]

Turning to the extant manuscripts of the first version (thus henceforth the "abbreviated" version), we note that they form two groups of radically different content and apparent provenance. The three earlier collections (MSS 1573, 1551, and 2524) are those most closely linked with the earlier manuscript history of the *Correspondence*.[17] The other pair (MSS 32.8.5 and V.2.11; one is apparently a copy of the other) seem not to be associated with the earlier manuscript tradition, and are somewhat later in origin, although the earlier of them apparently belonged to the great boyar Nikita Ivanovich Romanov, cousin of Mikhail Fedorovich.[18]

The earlier three manuscripts, although they are similar in contents and, apparently, textual variants, may also be divided into two groups: MS 1551 stands alone as the earliest copy of Ivan's first letter in the first version, while MSS 1573 and 2524, perhaps as much as two decades younger, clearly form a closely related pair.

In spite of the earlier date of MS 1551, it is the northern pair which is probably of greater significance in the history of the *Correspondence*. These manuscripts were probably written in the same place (the Dvina-Arkhangel'sk region) and at approximately the same time (1645–1650).[19] By their convoy, they are most closely linked to MS 4469, which contains only Kurbskii's first letter.[20] In addition to the first letters of Kurbskii and Ivan, they have in common the tale *Vypisano iz Kizilbashskikh otpisok*, and MS 1573 contains copies of documents concerning Muscovite negotiations with Władysław in 1635.[21]

All of these features link these two collections with the known facts of Semen Shakhovskoi's biography. They were composed in the region to which he was sent after the Waldemar affair, and they appeared at the time of his exile. The text *Vypisano . . .* is a literary reworking of the embassies exchanged with Shah Abbas, in which Shakhovskoi played an important part.[22] It was immediately after the departure of the Polish envoys Piesoczyński et al., whose reception in Moscow in 1635 is described in MS 1573, that Semen Shakhovskoi was sent after them to continue negotiations.[23] Thus these manuscripts seem to represent a kind of personal archive, in which were collected texts reflecting a number of episodes of Shakhovskoi's private and public life. It may be noted, finally, that MS 4469, the manuscript of the first group with which these two collections are most closely linked, bears on its last page the inscription, described by the cataloger as a *proba pera*, "Semen Ivanov," that is, Shakhovskoi's name and patronymic.[24]

But although MSS 2524 and 1573 permit us to link the text of the first version of Ivan's letter with Shakhovskoi, they are not the earliest copies, and they clearly were written some time after the text first appeared. The watermarks of MS 1551, together with those of MS 1567, which must have appeared after the first version, upon which its text of the second version is based, indicate that the first version must have appeared before the mid- to early 1630's. Thus we may establish a probable period for the creation of the first version: between ca. 1621 (i.e., the *terminus post quem* of KI[a]) and ca. 1633.

The text of the first version of Ivan's first letter is, in style, nearly identical with the first letter of Kurbskii. The one significant divergence from the standard literary Slavonic is seen in the occasional use of cliches from the language of the chancellery (*pochen ot ... Vladimera*; *vedomo da est'*; *pisanie tvoe priiato byst'*, etc.)[25] which are altered to fit the general Slavonic linguistic structure and not altogether properly used.[26] This kind of denatured diplomatic formula is common in the "documentary belles lettres" of the first half of the seventeenth century, and some of the phrases found here are entirely inappropriate calques from Turkic diplomatic jargon (not used in the Lithuanian correspondence) like those used in Ivan's spurious correspondence with the Sultan, which often forms part of the convoy of the *Correspondence*.[27] Shakhovskoi, whose major known works were written in the formal religious and Slavonic mode, but who took part in the affairs of the *Posol'skii prikaz* (and was officially under its jurisdiction), is one who might well have attempted the integration of documentary cliches into the literary language.

The contents of the letter deserve extended commentary, but for our present purposes only those items which relate to questions of dating and attribution will be discussed. The letter begins with an utterly uncharacteristic *intitulatio*, which is unlike those of genuine documents of this period, but nearly identical with one found in the spurious correspondence noted above.[28] It is of very questionable authenticity.

A second feature of Ivan's letter in this version is the predominant role of religious themes, as opposed to the political, biographical, and historical arguments introduced in the second and better-known version of the letter.[29] While the letter is composed as a point-by-point refutation of Kurbskii's first letter, the commentary on the passages cited and refuted tends to be couched almost exclusively in religious terms. This is not Ivan's way, if one is to judge from indisputably genuine letters sent in his name; the reversion to religious themes, even in discussion of historical questions, is characteristic of the known works of Shakhovskoi.[30]

There are many important themes of the letter which seem entirely anachronistic and are puzzling for the fact that Ivan seems to be refuting arguments which Kurbskii never made in his first letter. Ivan goes on at some length about Kurbskii's presumed apostasy— yet as we know, Kurbskii remained faithful to Orthodoxy (as he understood it!) until his death, and indeed is portrayed in other texts attributed to him as a militant defender of the Eastern Church.[31] It was not until after the union of Brest that political allegiance to the Polish-Lithuanian Crown became, in Muscovite eyes, ipso facto evidence of apostasy, and not until well after the Time of Troubles (1620) that mere presence in Lithuanian territory raised official suspicion of heretical taint. It is unlikely that Ivan should have raised this issue in 1564, but perfectly natural that Shakhovskoi, writing in the 1620's (after his own brush with the heresy-conscious authorities), should project the concerns of his own time into the past.

Even the central theme of the letter—the nature of the tsar's power—is presented in a puzzling context. Ivan waxes prolix in justifying the untrammeled rule of divinely appointed rulers and denounces the usurpation of power by both clerics and clerks of state (*d'iaki*). But no opposite view is even hinted at by Kurbskii, who in fact criticizes the sycophancy of Ivan's boyars in his letter (*tovarishchi trapezy, boiare, gubiteli dushi tvoei i telu*).[32] The essence of his complaint is that Ivan had mistreated his military leaders (*voevody*), but Kurbskii makes no suggestion of the necessity of sharing power with them.

It is particularly strange that Ivan should make such a pointed reference to the interference of religious counsellors in the exercise of the tsar's power and enunciate the principle that "it is not befitting for priests to assume the authority of tsars" (*ne podobaet sviashchennikom tsarskaia tvoriti*).[33] Kurbskii never raises this subject—why should Ivan? And to whom might this allude? Certainly not to Makarii (d. December 31, 1563), one of the few persons who apparently had a good relationship with Ivan. The answer, it seems, lies in an examination not of Ivan's, but of Shakhovskoi's time. There was but one "priest" in Muscovite history who succeeded in assuming the plenitude of "the authority of tsars"—Filaret, alternately the tormentor and protector of Semen Shakhovskoi. It was Filaret, probably, who, shortly after his return from Poland, ordered, or at the least condoned, the senseless punishments of the Shakhovskoi family for "playing at tsars." It was Filaret, without any doubt, who forced Semen's separation from his fourth wife and ordered his punishment in 1622. Filaret probably had some role in the assignment of Shakhovskoi to Eniseisk in 1629, a kind of semiexile after five years at the court. Finally, it was only with Filaret's death that Semen—and the rest of his family—were returned to their rightful positions, in Semen's case to the important diplomatic and military service which his talents doubtless warranted.

Thus, as in the case of the "Epistle to Vas'ian," there is good reason to assume that the reference to the worldly and powerful cleric is an allusion to Filaret. That such is the case is further indicated by another passage in the letter (Fennell, *Corresp.*, pp. 30–32) where Ivan speaks of those who have been forcibly tonsured (Filaret was tonsured by Boris Godunov in 1599): "Did not Climacus say 'I have seen people receive monasticism against their will and then mend their ways even more than those who received it voluntarily.' Why have you [plural] not imitated these words, if you are so pious?"

This passage, and its possible allusion to Filaret, is particularly interesting for the fact that in the second version of this letter, to be discussed below, Ivan adds what seems to be a much more direct comment: "Many who even in recent years have received the tonsure at the command of the great council when they returned to their former dignity [*chest'*], sinned still more than their predecessors, who did not dare to do such things."[34]

The context—and indeed the very meaning—of these comments is unclear, but it is clear that Kurbskii was never tonsured and that the writer of Ivan's letter had this subject, and in general the role of clerics in worldly affairs, very much on his mind.[35] While one cannot be confident that it is the career of Filaret which is here referred to, there is sufficient chronological and textual evidence to permit such a hypothesis.

The verbosity and obscurity of the text of Ivan's first letter make any judgments about its origins based upon close reading extremely difficult; much is still to be done in this regard. It appears, however, that it would be fruitful to attempt such analysis within a context determined by the working hypotheses that the letter was written in the late 1620's or early 1630's by Semen Shakhovskoi.

The Second Version of Kurbskii's First Letter

I have spoken above of a second version of Kurbskii's first letter, which was apparently used in the composition of the second version of Ivan's first letter, and of the later Kurbskii letters. Whether this version of Kurbskii's letter, found only in later copies, was indeed a second version, rather than the original, is difficult to establish, but it seems that the preponderance of the textual information supports this conclusion. In spite of occasional preferable readings found in the second version (see App. III, notes 44, 68) and of its similarity to the first epistle to Vas'ian (see Chap. 2), which apparently was produced at roughly the same time as the first version, there are weighty reasons for considering the second version a later reworking of the first. Principal among these are observations based upon the passages which appear only in the second version. These passages are nowhere referred to in the short version of Ivan's response, but are alluded to in the long version.[36] Moreover, it is most unlikely that the editorial process which stands between the two versions would have led to the exclusion of precisely the words which were borrowed, for the second version, from the "Afterword" of Ivan Fedorov's L'viv *Apostol* (N.B. 1574).[37] It is, of course, possible that the author of the first version was also the editor of the second, and that, remembering the source of these words, he excluded them so as to eliminate an anachronism. In any case, it appears that the process of editing was roughly contemporaneous with the production of the second version of Ivan's first letter.[38]

The Second Version of Ivan's First Letter

It is the second, or "full," version of Ivan's first letter which is most familiar to modern readers; this is the source of most popular conceptions about Ivan and his political philosophy. Yet it appears from close examination of the relationship of this text to the rest of the *Correspondence,* and particularly to the first version of the same letter, that it cannot be associated with Ivan, with his time, or even, perhaps, with the author of the first version.

We noted in Chapter 1 that the second version is, on the basis of the manuscript evidence, to be considered apart from the earliest stages of the growth of the *Correspondence.* It was not stressed in the previous discussion, however, that a rather sharp line may be drawn between the first and second versions of the letter on the basis of textual comparison.

The most obvious difference between the two versions is the radical revision in the order of argument. While the first version makes no attempt to follow the sequence of Kurbskii's first letter in refuting its arguments, the second adheres slavishly to the order of Kurbskii's letter, adding at the same time a number of citations from it as points d'appui for extended discussion. As a part of the same painstaking and thorough editorial revision, the author of the second version corrected or expanded a number of the biblical citations found in his original, and enriched the text with extensive digressions dealing with Byzantine and Old Testament history, together with some biographical information about Ivan.[39]

The nature of these additions and digressions indicates that the "full" version is not simply a reworking of the "abbreviated" by the same author. One finds here, for example, numerous superfluous elaborations and explications of passages of the earlier version.[40] Would the author of the first version have found these necessary? In addition, a number of passages, ostensibly elaborations of arguments of the first version, indicate that the author of the second simply misunderstood the text of the first. Could the author misunderstand his own text?[41]

Another particularly striking example of the kind of dissonance that divides the two versions, in spite of the obvious dependence of the second upon the first, is pointed out in Fennell's meticulous notes. The second version contains two contradictory characterizations of Kurbskii's father: in one place he is accused of treachery; later Ivan speaks of the "high esteem ... and honor" which he enjoyed.[42] This contradiction is easily explained: the first comment is found in the first version, and copied in the second, but the latter observation is found only in the second version. It is unlikely that a single author would permit such a contradiction in a matter so important to Ivan's argument that Kurbskii's treachery was congenital. But some writer other than the author of the first version, who originally established this theme, might, while copying the earlier argument, fail to make it a part of his own thinking, and consequently write the contradictory characterization of Kurbskii's father in another sentence.

In the second version, even more than in the first, there occur strikingly incongruous arguments against suggestions which Kurbskii never made—indeed could not make. Thus, a long *cento* from works on Byzantine history, and some original passages, are introduced as part of an attack on separatism and in defense of highly centralized government (Fennell, *Corresp.*, pp. 50–56). Although these arguments may not be out of place in the 1560's, Kurbskii can in no way be linked (independent of the *Correspondence* and *History*) with separatist groups—if such existed in his time. In the mid-seventeenth century, however, when the centralist and absolutist monarchy was rapidly increasing its control over all spheres of Muscovite life, they might be considered entirely topical arguments.

The same comment applies to the incongruous statements which Ivan makes about the patrimonial estates (*votchiny*) of boyar families. As Fennell and others have pointed out, Ivan is mistaken about the "scattering about" of patrimonial estates in the 1550's: in fact they were being limited and service lands introduced in their place.[43] Now Ivan simply could not have made a mistake like this. In the mid-seventeenth century, however, when the very lands granted contingent upon service (*pomestiia*) in Ivan's time had become in effect *votchiny* through custom and the concessions of weak rulers during the Time of Troubles, and when the great landed families were struggling against the bureaucracy for their rights to these lands, a writer whose sense of the past was obscured by the controversies of his time might well put these words into Ivan's mouth.[44]

We should normally conclude, from such observations, that the second version of Ivan's letter was certainly not written by him, and perhaps not even by the author of the first version of the same letter. On the other hand, it should be noted that the language and contents of the second version are in general very similar to those of the original text, and that the date and convoys of the earliest copies of the second version do not necessarily set it apart from the time and environment characteristic of copies of the first. The two versions were apparently written within a few years of each other, and, if by two authors, by men of very similar education and views. In addition, although the evidence adduced above concerning the anachronisms and inaccuracies of the text seems to show that the second version has even less claim that the first to be considered Ivan's, or a sixteenth-century text, it is possible that the seeming differences in author's attitude between the versions can be explained by assuming that Shakhovskoi returned to his text some years after he wrote the first version and somewhat imperfectly reestablished himself in the role of Ivan.

In either case, it is with this letter, in whichever version, that the assumed participation of Shakhovskoi in the creation of the *Correspondence* comes to an end. He died in 1654, apparently before the remaining letters were written; they are the product of a different circle and a later time, to which we now turn.

The Final Phase

By all criteria, the later letters of both Kurbskii and Ivan stand apart from the first exchange. All of the earliest manuscripts containing these later letters appeared within a very short period of time, some four decades after the earliest copies of Ivan's first letter (in both versions). It is in this closely related group of texts that the "polonisms" of Kurbskii's later style appear—as does a radical change in Ivan's style. All of these copies, finally, are found in an environment very typical of the period and apparent place of their manufacture: the "convoy" here reflects the interest in history-writing which was characteristic of the "*prikaz* milieu" in the latter years of Aleksei Mikhailovich's reign.[45] In this respect, too, there is very little to distinguish Ivan's second letter from Kurbskii's later letters: the former is found together with a copy of the "Titulary" produced for the tsar in the *Posol'skii prikaz* in 1673; the latter occur alongside translations of Guagnini and Stryjkowski, probably made in the same office.[46]

In spite of these similar general features, it cannot be assumed that the later letters of Kurbskii (together with the *History*), which probably were written by the same person at approximately the same time, can be joined with the second letter of Ivan, as we have joined their respective first letters. The style is clearly different; and there are significant distinctions which must be made with regard to environment.[47] It may well be, however, that Ivan's second letter was written before, rather than after, Kurbskii's second, and that the latter was written at the same time as the other Kurbskii letters. This is indicated by the general chronology of the manuscripts, by the fact that Ivan never mentions Kurbskii's second letter, and by the fact that the writer of Kurbskii's third letter (which is always found with the second) resorts to what seems to be a device in saying that he never sent the second letter and is forwarding it together with the third.[48] That such was the sequence of writing may also account for the confused mention of "my first letter" in these later texts.[49] Similarly, we may explain the confused chronology of the fourth letter and Kurbskii's command to Ivan to write no more[50]—by positing that the later Kurbskii letters were written by someone who had at his disposal copies of the early part of the *Correspondence* like those found in the late manuscripts (in which Kurbskii's letter has no date), together with Ivan's second letter, and that this person set out to "fill in" Kurbskii's half of the *Correspondence*.

Although the correctness of these observations cannot be conclusively demonstrated, we may, for the sake of convenience, examine the remaining letters in the suggested order.

Ivan's Second Letter

In its two extant copies (see Chap. 1, Table 1) this letter is found in an environment which cannot be linked with the earlier letters, and it stands apart from all other parts of the *Correspondence* by virtue of its style, which is a Slavonic heavily influenced by the *prikaz* style.

The only known seventeenth-century copy is found in a manuscript which also contains the well-known "Titulary" (*Tituliarnik*) composed apparently in 1673 by Artamon Sergeevich Matveev or under his supervision. Matveev rose from somewhat obscure origins to become one of the most influential men in Aleksei Mikhailovich's court (the tsar's second wife had been Matveev's ward) and was, during the years when our manuscript presumably was produced, Chancellor for Foreign Affairs, as well as Minister for Ukrainian Affairs. At the same time, he took an active part in the writing of a number of major historical compilations prepared at the tsar's request.[51] After Aleksei Mikhailovich's death (1676), Matveev was exiled as a result of the intrigues of his political enemies (the charge—*chernoknizhie*, the possession of certain dangerous books—was apparently never specified).[52]

Ivan's second letter is clearly not an answer to Kurbskii's second, but rather a paraphrase of the second version of Ivan's first letter, which the writer must have had at his disposal.[53] It was supposedly written during the same campaign of 1577 which produced the letters discussed in Chapter 3, but this presumption raises a number of difficult questions: why did Ivan, who had numerous opportunities in the intervening twelve years to send letters to Kurbskii, choose this occasion to recapitulate an old letter? Did he take the expanded version of that old letter with him on the campaign? Did he also take along Kurbskii's letter, to which he refers?

The numerous oddities and errors contained in the letter have been pointed out by Professor Fennell: the tsar's title contains some questionable features; Ivan mentions his three daughters, the longest-lived of whom died, at the age of three, a quarter-century before the presumed date of this letter; the account of the Staritskii affair is incorrect; Ivan states erroneously that Kurbskii had chosen Valmiera as his "place of exile," and that he was there in 1577; Ivan's own reign is wrongly dated (!).[54] Ivan could not have made such mistakes.

Someone writing about the time of the earliest known copy, however (ca. 1675), might easily have confused dates and events which had occurred more than a century before, and which he knew from incomplete, corrupt, and tendentious chronicles. The evidence at hand indicates that Ivan's second letter is the work of such an author.

The Later Letters of Kurbskii

Kurbskii's later letters[55] form, with the *History*, a distinct group of texts whose style is homogeneous and different from that of all other letters of either Kurbskii or Ivan. They are found only in the latest group of manuscripts—the so-called "Kurbskii Collections"—in six closely related copies (see Table 3). In terms of "literary time," it appears that all of these texts were written after the second version of Kurbskii's first letter, and after Ivan's second letter.[56] They are in a number of ways closely related to the *History*.[57]

Kurbskii's first letter is found in these manuscripts as well—but in its second version, which, as we have seen, is distinguished from the first by some minor corruptions and the addition of a few short passages, including the one apparently taken from the L'viv *Apostol*.[58] The version of Ivan's first letter found here is rather corrupt; its variants represent an attempt to make sense of a copy of the second version in which the folios were out of order.[59]

TABLE 3. Seventeenth-Century Manuscripts of Kurbskii's Later Letters

No.	Date	Owner	HIST	KI	T	GI
639	1675–1684[a]		X	X		
[623]	1677[b]	V. V. Golitsyn	X	X	?[c]	?[c]
136	2nd half 17th c.		X	X	X	X
1582	1679	B. Khitrovo	X	X		
181/60	Before 1690	F. I. Divov	X	X	X	X
1494	2nd half 17th c.		X	X	X	X

No.	Date	Owner	KII	KIII-	KL	GUAG	STRY
639	1675–1684[a]		X	X			
[623]	1677[b]	V. V. Golitsyn	X	X	?[c]	?[c]	?[c]
136	2nd half 17th c.		X	X			
1582	1679	B. Khitrovo	X	X	X[d]		
181/60	Before 1690	F. I. Divov	X	X	X	X	X
1494	2nd half 17th c.		X	X	X	X	X

[a] On the question of the dating, see Chap. 1, n. 1, MS 639.

[b] The brackets indicate that what is being considered here is the protograph of the extant MS 623. Cf. Chap. 1, n. 1, MS 623.

[c] There is apparently no detailed description of MS 623 in print. We have it on Lur'e's good authority that it contains the same works as MSS 1494 and 181/60 (*Poslaniia*, p. 548) but since, as he indicates elsewhere (p. 549), the translation of Stryjkowski is dated in the text 1682, there is some question whether the translation, or indeed the other works here indicated by question marks, were present in the 1677 copy.

[d] Some letters are missing. (Cf. Leonid, *Opisanie*, III: 231.)

The remainder of the very consistent "package" in which the later letters are found is made up of a number of late seventeenth-century items of historical and geographical interest.[60] Examination of this convoy, and the contemporary marginal notes indicating ownership, reveals that they also form a close cluster around a very specific milieu—the cultured circles of the upper *prikaz* bureaucracy of that time.

It appears that we may follow Lur'e in dividing these manuscripts into two groups: those which contain the translations from Guagnini and Stryjkowski and those which do not.[61] It seems as well, from the printed variants, that the letters in the manuscripts which do not contain these translations are textually closer to the assumed protograph, and somewhat earlier in time.[62]

The owners' inscriptions found in three of these manuscripts are of considerable interest. The oldest known manuscript (of which we have only an eighteenth-century copy, MS 623), was "written in the home of the boyar Prince Vasilii Vasil'evich Golitsyn" in 1677.[63] Golitsyn is of course the well-known "westernizer," a well-educated nobleman who was de facto head of the government during the reign of Sofiia.[64]

The other two copies belonged to individuals who were apparently close to Golitsyn—to Bogdan Khitrovo, who also had a long and successful career in the service of the Romanovs and was apparently particularly friendly with Golitsyn, and to Fedor Ivanovich Divov, who was apparently the son of a servitor of Golitsyn's, Ivan Divov. The younger Divov may have received his copy from Golitsyn, whom he accompanied to the latter's place of exile in 1689 (7198), the very year in which Divov recorded his name in MS 181/60.[65]

Summing up, then, the evidence which is to be gleaned from the manuscript descriptions, we may note once again that all of the manuscripts which contain Kurbskii's later letters are nearly identical in contents, closely clustered in time, and, in all cases where a seventeenth-century owner can be identified, associated with the highest circles of the noble bureaucracy, in particular with V. V. Golitsyn.

The Contents of Kurbskii's Later Letters

Turning now to the analysis of the contents of these letters, we must remark immediately that there is very little of substance in them that might be used as a basis of judgments about their origin. They contain for the most part rhetorical elaborations upon themes which appear in the first letters, recriminations against Ivan's actions, and translations. A number of details, however, require comment.

The text of Kurbskii's second letter, which is clearly intended as a response to the "full" version of Ivan's first, is short; its message is, essentially, that Kurbskii has received Ivan's letter, that he finds it boorish, but has little to add to his own first letter. The well-known "polonisms" aside, there should be little doubt that this letter can hardly have been written in 1565. Kurbskii's introductory criticisms of Ivan's rhetoric (especially the implied expectations that a tsar should write verse [!] and be better educated than a soldier); the mention of scholars learned in rhetoric and dialectics in Lithuania; the chivalric code referred to at the end; the expression "Holy Russia"[66]—all of these are clearly anachronisms in the mid-sixteenth century, for Lithuanian as well as Muscovite territory. More striking are Kurbskii's statements about himself: that he had been wronged and driven out of Muscovy, and had learned Slavonic in Lithuania "in my old age."[67] He was, as we have seen, neither wronged nor driven away; he defected for personal gain. Moreover, he was probably only thirty-five or thirty-six at the time of presumed writing—and he had supposedly written a perfectly fluent letter in Slavonic to Ivan but a few weeks after his defection, hardly time enough even for him to learn a new language!

All of these problems are of course eliminated if we accept the evidence of the manuscript tradition and the conclusions of the foregoing chapters: this letter was written around 1675, by a writer with an understanding of the cultural flowering of the Lithuanian territories in the latter sixteenth and early seventeenth centuries, who imposed the rhetorical and chivalric standards of his own time upon the past, and who had an understandably imperfect sense of Kurbskii's curriculum vitae.

Although the remaining Kurbskii letters are much less specific in their contents, and contain no such anachronistic *realia*, they too contain the inappropriate "polonisms" found in the second letter, and a number of textual paradoxes.[68] But the most striking feature of the last letters is the verbatim inclusion of two (numbers II and IV) of Cicero's *Paradoxa stoicorum* (Fennell, *Corresp.*, pp. 218–227). This text is apparently the first known translation of any of Cicero's works into Slavonic,[69] and it is highly improbable that it appeared in 1579 (the accepted date of Kurbskii's letter) or, for that matter, at any time in the sixteenth century. Even in Poland, which anticipated both Lithuania and Muscovy in the discovery of Cicero, the first Ciceronian translations appeared only at the end of the sixteenth century;[70] there is no evidence of the circulation of the major western editions of Cicero's works in Muscovy before roughly the middle of the seventeenth century.[71] It was probably from such an edition that the present translation was made.

Such a conclusion is supported by the intuitive assumption that the selection of the *Paradoxa*, which are among Cicero's lesser works, would be made in the context of his other works and by an author who knew Cicero's reputation as statesman and orator. Much more substantial support is provided by a close comparison of the Slavonic translation with various sixteenth- and seventeenth-century editions of the *Paradoxa*. A number of scholars[72] have noted that Kurbskii's translation, while on the whole slavish and literal, departs occasionally from the Latin. But this is true only if one takes a sixteenth-century edition as standard (as Kuntsevich did). There is, however, a Latin edition which corresponds *exactly* to Kurbskii's text—the well-known edition of Choüet, published in Geneva in 1633.[73] In this edition we find not only the minor variants which set Kurbskii's translation apart from the standard texts, but a number of other similarities, such as marginal notes which were apparently incorporated in the translation.[74] That it was precisely this edition which served as the original for our translation can be definitively established only after examination of all editions of Cicero's *Paradoxa*, but until some edition at least as similar to our text as the Choüet edition is located, it may be considered that Kurbskii's third letter relied upon it.

Indeed, the larger question of the sources of the numerous translations found throughout the *Correspondence* should be reconsidered in the context of the popular seventeenth-century editions of classical authors which made these texts available, for the first time, in Muscovy. Many of the works cited in the *Correspondence* are known not to have been translated into Slavonic until the seventeenth century (if at all in the pre-Petrine period), although they became common in major collections around 1650.[75] The identification of these sources and the examination of the possibility that Kurbskii's translations occasionally rely upon Latin, rather than Greek—even in the case of familiar patristic literature—are matters that invite close study by specialists.

But it appears that further study can only confirm the conclusion indicated by all of our textual and other evidence: these later letters, like the first exchange, could not have appeared in the sixteenth century, and were not written by Ivan and Kurbskii.

But if this be the case, what evidence is there to support the hypothesis that the letters were written by some other specific individual or individuals, and in another time and place? There being so little in the text of the letters that might indicate their origin, one must rely, in the first instance, upon the evidence of the extant manuscripts, whose origin, dates, convoys, and owners' inscriptions all point to a single environment—the Romanov court, around the time of the death of Aleksei Mikhailovich.

It is this court, or its chancelleries, which seems the most probable milieu in which the second letter of Ivan and the later Kurbskii works may have been produced. One need hardly recapitulate the similarities between the domestic and foreign political concerns of this court and those aspects of Ivan's reign which are most vividly portrayed in the later letters and *History*. The drawn-out struggle for the same Livonian cities for which Ivan had fought and the renewed struggle of the *arriviste* bureaucrats against the old Muscovite aristocracy (culminating in the annulment of the system of *mestnichestvo* in 1682) made the reign of Ivan topical and symbolic to sophisticated Muscovites of this period.

Aleksei himself, it should be noted, was fascinated by the biography of his forebear and apparently fully aware of the parallels between Ivan and himself. As an observant Swedish diplomat remarked at the time, "The tsar is so engrossed by the reading of works on the history of [Ivan] and his wars, that he must want to follow in his footsteps." And, elsewhere, "The tsar, vain and barbarously cruel, and thus capable of anything, is obliged to find pleasure in tales from the history of Ivan Vasil'evich and his tyranny."[76]

The tsar's noble courtiers knew of his interest, although their attitude toward Ivan was probably rather different—more like, and very probably identical with, that attributed to Kurbskii. For these later letters, and the *History*, seem to have been written in precisely the environment so clearly indicated by the history of the earliest manuscripts.

Indeed, if we but permit ourselves to trust the clear indications of the manuscript evidence, we may construct an entirely plausible hypothesis concerning the origin of these letters. Ivan's second letter, it will be remembered, is found in a single seventeenth-century copy, together with the "Titulary" prepared in 1673 by Artamon Matveev. Matveev possessed, in addition to his political and administrative talents, considerable erudition and was a facile writer, as his "petitions" show.[77] It is clear, moreover, from these same "petitions" that Matveev was familiar with Kurbskii's and perhaps Ivan's first letter—but not, apparently, with the later letters.[78] Now Matveev's library, of which we possess an inventory,[79] was apparently not rich in Muscovite manuscripts, and it is doubtful that Kurbskii's first letter was available in Matveev's time in numerous copies— especially in Moscow. Indeed, we may assume that, in addition to the copies now known, most of which were in northern monasteries, the copy whose existence we may most confidently hypothesize would have been in the possession of the Shakhovskoi family.

There is an episode of some interest which may have made the Shakhovskoi family archive indirectly accessible to Matveev. At the very time when the "Titulary" was being prepared, one of Matveev's closest collaborators, the editor/scribe Ivan Vereshchagin, fled Moscow for unknown reasons and was later located at the Shakhovskoi family estate in Galich. Aleksei Mikhailovich sent an order to Fedor Semenovich Shakhovskoi (Semen's son), demanding that Vereshchagin be returned immediately, and the runaway was back at work with Matveev in the *Posol'skii prikaz* by the end of 1673. It is quite likely that the highly literate Vereshchagin became acquainted with the Kurbskii/Shakhovskoi letter (in the second version) during his sojourn in Galich and that he brought a copy of it with him to Moscow, and to Matveev.[80]

It is also possible that he brought a copy of Ivan's first letter—in the second version—and that he, or Matveev, or someone in their circle, produced the paraphrastic synopsis of it which is Ivan's second letter. The mixed Slavonic and plain style of this letter, together with the purely biblical citations (both Ivan's earlier letter and the later letters of Kurbskii cite numerous nonbiblical texts), are very similar to the style of Matveev's "petitions," and its imperious bombast is altogether in keeping with the views of the non-noble bureaucrat who was—in the name of the all-powerful sovereign— the most powerful man in Muscovy.

During the period of Matveev's greatest influence, the individual whose name was found in the earliest known manuscript of Kurbskii's later letters—Vasilii Golitsyn—was enduring a period of relative eclipse, which was to end with the death of Aleksei Mikhailovich and the exile of Matveev in 1676.[81] Golitsyn was, of course, a man of the old aristocracy, proud of his heritage, concerned about the place of the hereditary aristocracy in the increasingly bureaucratic absolutist state—a man, in short, who would find the views expressed in Ivan's letters unacceptable. Kurbskii's ideas, however—or more precisely those expressed in the later letters—would seem to be very much like his own.

Indeed they may be his. Golitsyn definitely knew Latin, and in his home he had one of Muscovy's finest libraries (including editions of many of the authors cited in the later letters and two editions of Cicero)[82] and, presumably, some of Matveev's own books, which he had appropriated from the library of the *Posol'skii prikaz*.[83] And it was in Golitsyn's house that the great-grandsons of Andrei Kurbskii, Iakov and Aleksandr, found "inexpressible kindness" after they had immigrated to Muscovy.[84]

Did Golitsyn himself write these letters? There is no conclusive evidence that he did. He left, apparently, no Slavonic writings, although we have a number of his letters, and there seems to be no hint, in the voluminous literature devoted to him and his time, of any secret publicistic activities. But he, like Matveev in the case of Ivan's second letter, stands so close to the presumed moment of creation of these texts that we may accept, as a first hypothesis, that they were composed "in his circle," among the talented and westernized nobles who were associated with the upper *prikaz* milieu. In any case, it is here that the search must begin.

Is this such a shocking conclusion, after all? It corresponds perfectly with the chronological information about the manuscripts and with the general linguistic features of these later texts. The contemporary concerns and historical and cultural interests of these individuals are well known, and they show a logical parallelism. And they owned, or wrote, most of the earliest copies of our texts. Certainly such a conclusion is more plausible than the assumption that Golitsyn and his friends, interested in Kurbskii, had somehow acquired copies of his writings, of which no other pre-Petrine copies survive, which were apparently unknown before this period, and which, in any case, could hardly have been written before 1620.

All of the preceding indicates that, under normal conditions of evidential argument and proof, we should tentatively conclude that the most probable period for the composition of the later letters of both Ivan and Kurbskii is the beginning of the last quarter of the seventeenth century, and the most probable milieu that of the cultured upper bureaucracy. Ivan's second letter was probably written first (i.e., before Kurbskii's second letter) by someone whose objective was the justification of the autocracy as it was emerging under Aleksei Mikhailovich; the Kurbskii letters were probably written shortly thereafter, by some (perhaps secret) critic of the Romanovs and their rule. As such, these texts are valuable monuments of Muscovite political thought in the latter seventeenth century and worthy of considerable further study.

Afterword

The numerous interdependent conclusions from this review of the evidence concerning the history of the *Correspondence* have been summarized in the Introduction and detailed in the various chapters. It is in keeping with the methodological premises which have underlain our argument throughout that we conclude with a few words concerning the relative probability of these conclusions and some thoughts about further study of the problems raised in the body of the book.

Our main conclusion, that the *Correspondence* was written neither by Ivan nor by Kurbskii, nor indeed in their time, is supported by a number of compatible conclusions of high probability and should itself be considered to be of the highest probability. By their nature, the possible arguments here have not permitted us to consider this finding conclusive, and each of the supporting conclusions upon which it depends must, and doubtless will, be examined carefully.

The chronological grouping of copies of the various portions of the *Correspondence* to which we have repeatedly referred seems essentially acceptable, in view of the relatively large number of copies already accounted for, but its progressive refinement has provided numerous helpful lines of investigation, and as new copies and better means of dating are found, it will need correction. It should be pointed out that the importance of these groupings to our main arguments should decrease as other conclusions are confirmed or rejected, although this chronological evidence must remain compatible with all other elements of the present argument.

Many of the arguments seem to provide conclusions of very high probability, while others require greater caution. It seems most probable that the relationships of Kurbskii's first letter to the texts of Isaiah and Khvorostinin, and the relationship between the first and second versions of Ivan's first letter, are as indicated in our text; the question whether all of Kurbskii's later letters were written after Ivan's second remains open, as does the particularly vexing problem whether the second version of Kurbskii's first letter (as found in the latest manuscripts) does not in fact reflect some very early version of the letter. This matter should be resolved along with that of the complete stemma of the extant manuscripts and their assumed protographs, about which we have been able to reach only tentative conclusions. There seems to be little question, however, that the second version of Kurbskii's first letter, which includes the borrowing from the L'viv *Apostol*, and the second version of Ivan's first letter, which apparently reflects some readings found only in the second version of Kurbskii's letter, were composed after 1574, the date of the *Apostol*.

Within the context of currently accepted methods of attribution of sixteenth- and seventeenth-century works, it appears that our attribution to Semen Shakhovskoi of Kurbskii's first letter may be considered a matter of high probability. It is likewise highly probable that the letter in original form ended with the word *Amin'*, and that it was the author who added the postscript.

Shakhovskoi's authorship of the first version of Ivan's first letter remains a more tentative conclusion, although for the moment there seems to be no more likely candidate. Whether the second version of Ivan's first letter was written by the same author remains an open question

While the evidence is quite unequivocal and consistent in leading us to the upper bureaucracy of the last quarter of the seventeenth century as the milieu in which the remaining letters and Kurbskii's *History* were written, it provides no single candidate who may be considered a "most probable" author.

Some New Directions in the Study of the Correspondence

It would be folly to assume that even the best-substantiated of the conclusions sketched above represents a line of inquiry that has been exhausted. Much remains to be done, even within the limited topical and logical framework here elaborated; many possibilities for entirely new approaches are manifestly still unexplored. Since such possibilities are perhaps not immediately apparent, it is the final task of this book to indicate some of them.

First, of course, is the thorough reexamination of all the relevant manuscript collections with regard to every aspect of their creation (one might, it seems, limit this process to seventeenth-century collections). Particularly important will be any paleographical observations that will permit us to link manuscripts with each other, with any of the individuals who have come under scrutiny above, and with particular *scriptoria*.

A second task, more time-consuming but equally important, will involve the collation of all copies of the basic stages of the *Correspondence* (together with comparison of other texts common to our manuscripts) with the aim both of establishing critical texts for the various versions of our letters and of determining a stemma for the *Correspondence* as a whole. This work, alas, cannot be done from the printed editions, which were prepared from copies chosen on the basis of certain misapprehensions.[1] It should be facilitated, however, by the apparent fact that we possess many of the most important links in the chain, that is, that we have not lost as much of the early manuscript tradition as has been previously assumed.[2]

Thirdly, a most thorough linguistic and literary analysis of all parts of the *Correspondence* is in order. This analysis must now proceed not within the context of late sixteenth-century literary Slavonic (studies in this frame have produced highly unsatisfactory results) but along the lines of juxtaposition of the various letters with the Slavonic of both the Khvorostinin-Shakhovskoi and the Khitrovo-Golitsyn generations and with the "literary plain style" of the middle and late seventeenth century.

A number of possibilities appear with regard to the sources used by the various authors. Previous attempts to establish such sources have foundered upon the chronological limits which they set themselves: it is truly impossible to find most of the relevant sources in texts of the mid-sixteenth century, and quite logical to assume, as so many have, that the sources have been lost. Within the chronological boundaries suggested above, however, many of the problems of Ivan's and Kurbskii's sources are easy to resolve,[3] and a study of seventeenth-century chronographs, translations, and collections of didactic and patristic literature will undoubtedly prove fruitful.[4]

Several interesting aspects of Muscovite cultural history in the mid-seventeenth century will have to be considered in the further elucidation of the relationship between the earlier (the first letters of both correspondents) and later portions of the *Correspondence*. The questions of the role of Shakhovskoi's sons as intermediaries between these periods, of the location of the earliest manuscripts, and of their use by various individuals require painstaking consideration. One must ask whether the authors of the later letters considered the earlier letters genuine, and how they perceived Kurbskii and his role. Extensive searching will seemingly be required to determine the origin of the apparently authentic "Lithuanian letters" and the means by which they came into the possession of the compilers of the late "Kurbskii collections." Some adequate explanation of the origin and significance of the Teterin and Polubenskii letters must be found. It seems that all of these problems may find acceptable solutions within the new, seventeenth-century context.

Finally, it should now be possible, particularly in regard to the latter stages of the composition of the *Correspondence*, to establish the participation of certain known literary figures of the late seventeenth century, about whose activities abundant source materials are available.

To this point we have been discussing prospects which are essentially the logical extensions of the methods employed in this preliminary study. There are a number of associated problems, consciously avoided here, whose study must proceed pari passu with the further elucidation of the textual history of the *Correspondence*.

First among these is the reexamination of the whole of the literature traditionally attributed to Ivan and Kurbskii. The general remarks made in Chapter 3 about the *Correspondence* apply equally to the majority of these works: there are no sixteenth-century copies; these texts are linguistically and stylistically suspect; they are not found in expected collections or groupings; they contain anachronisms and other oddities. Indeed, the question of the functional literacy of Ivan and Kurbskii remains an open one.

Of far greater significance than the specific new lines of inquiry into the archeographic problems of Ivan's and Kurbskii's legacy are the logical and conceptual adjustments which will have to be made in order to accommodate and stimulate new findings. For if even the most modest (and most probable) of the conclusions put forward above are to be accepted, in however modified form, we shall find ourselves obliged to revise our conceptions of sixteenth- and seventeenth-century political thought and literary forms, of Ivan's personality, and of the nature of his reign.

It is to be hoped that the conclusions now at hand, and those which may appear as a result of new research, will permit us to understand far more satisfactorily the cultural and intellectual response of seventeenth-century Muscovite society to the growth and strengthening of the absolutist monarchy.

Appendices

Appendix I

A. DE VISU *DESCRIPTION OF MANUSCRIPTS CONTAINING THE* CORRESPONDENCE

I examined these manuscripts while working in Moscow and Leningrad in 1968–69 on my dissertation about seventeenth-century Russian *turcica*, the texts of which are often found together with the *Correspondence*.[1] Since I was not studying the *Correspondence*, in some cases—for example, MSS 1551 and 2350—I ignored information relevant to it.[2] To a certain extent, errors of omission and commission may be attributed to inexperience—my work with old Russian manuscripts has been limited to months, which gives me pause when disagreeing with the observations of experienced scholars. Previous descriptions should be consulted in conjunction with mine, since I include full information only where none exists in print and otherwise stress material of specific relevance to this book or merely correct and supplement existing descriptions.

I have carefully noted physical facts about each manuscript—changes in hand and paper, watermarks, pagination—but have not always gone beyond previous descriptions in the examination of contents to be certain that a given work is indeed what it is said to be, to determine redactions, and so on. As a novice in the analysis of handwriting, I have probably left a great deal undone, but by and large the refinement of paleography for dating and determination of provenance of old Russian manuscripts has yet to be accomplished.

The watermark information here is quite complete, and the dating based on it is probably as accurate as one may expect, given the present reference works. There is every reason to believe that future watermark publications will allow more precise dating, as in too many cases now one is forced to rely on knowledge of approximately when a particular type of mark was found in paper in Muscovy rather than on identification of the mark with one of known date. Where I have identified a mark with one in an album,

I assume a potential error in dating of at least plus or minus five years. The absence of any identification indicates that I was unable to find the mark in an album or felt that it was of too common and undifferentiated a type to try. I have attempted to describe how closely a given mark matches a published one; my terms range in order of increasing certainty from "of the type" (merely for the purpose of visualization), through "similar," to "variant" or "likeness" with appropriate modifiers. Strict identity cannot be unquestionably established using the present reproductions found in albums.[3]

In my remarks after each description, I attempt to summarize important facts that pertain to the argumentation in this book and to note the possible date, unity of time and place of copying, and connections of the manuscript, where this information may not be explicit in the descriptions. In at least one case, MSS 1573 and 2524, the manuscripts are so closely interconnected that the two descriptions must be used together; in other cases, I have noted manuscripts which should be studied together with the ones I describe. Unfortunately we are still far from being able to place and establish connections among the most important Russian *sborniki* of the seventeenth century. However, I am persuaded that given the proper preliminary study— a careful classification of the numerous manuscripts containing works such as "The Kazan' History," the "Journey of Trifon Korobeinikov," the "Extracts from the Kizilbash Books," and the "Tale of the Two Embassies," to name a few, would be a first step—it may be discovered that the missing links between one manuscript and the next are fewer than is presently assumed and that the provenance of a given redaction or a whole *sbornik* may be determined with some confidence.

GBL, *fond* 205, Collection of the Society of Russian History and Antiquities (OIDR) No. 197
Sixteenth, seventeenth, and eighteenth centuries, 4°, 103 fols.
   Description. [Pavel Stroev], *Biblioteka Imperatorskogo Obshchestva istorii i drevnostei rossiiskikh* (Moscow, 1845), pp. 81–82.
   Watermarks. Fols. 2, 5, 8, 14, 15, two variants of a hand or glove with a ruffled cuff and a crown over the fingers. Generally a mark of the sixteenth century.
   Fol. 17, one-handled pot with unclear letters.
   Fol. 35ff., two-handled pot with letters IM; the top is a pyramid-shaped device topped by a crescent. Of the type No. 940 (1633) in A. A. Geraklitov, *Filigrani XVII veka na bumage rukopisnykh i pechatnykh dokumentov russkogo proiskhozhdeniia* (Moscow, 1963), which has only the letter M.
   Fols. 40–57, large two-handled pot with a small lily on the neck and a leaping rabbit (?); on the base, letters I/LL. No. 3675 (mid-seventeenth century) in Edward Heawood, *Watermarks Mainly of the Seventeenth and Eighteenth Centuries* (Hilversum, 1950), is an excellent likeness *but* for the letters.
   Fols. 58ff., small oval with a cross inside it. Similar to Geraklitov, *Filigrani*, No. 355 (1656).
   Fols. 76, 81 (mixed with the preceding), foolscap, type IV.
   Fol. 85 (new paper begins fol. 83?), top of a different foolscap, type IV.
   Fols. 86ff., two variants of the arms of the Seven Provinces, one over cursive letters AJ (fol. 91); apparently one with a countermark H(?)AR

(fol. 88). Heawood, *Watermarks*, No. 3144 (n.d.—1680's?) depicts an arms of the Seven Provinces over cursive AJ.

Fols. 92, 95, arms of Amsterdam, apparently over cursive AJ, with countermark CDG. S. A. Klepikov, "Bumaga s filigran'iu 'gerb goroda Amsterdama'," *ZOR* XX (1958), lists such a mark as No. 38 (1721).

Fol. 99, different arms of Amsterdam.

Inscriptions. Fols. 1–16, "leta 7173-go dal . . . zhivonachal'nye . . ."

Fol. 86 (in nineteenth-century [?] hand), "sbornik v kotorom . . . chastia istorii Kazanskago tsarstva."

Fols. 86v–98, "Siia kniga Suzdal'skago uezdu sela Ivanova . . . Ivanova syna Shipina (?) kuplena v Khlynove 1751 godu."

Fol. 103v (in the hand of the final work in the MS), "svoieiu rukoiu 1731 godu."

Handwriting. Changes in hand generally coincide with changes in paper and occur at the breaks between individual works on fols. 17, 35, 40, 58, 86, 92, and 99. The hand of the first two portions of the MS is sixteenth century, the middle of the MS (to fol. 86) seventeenth century, and the final portion eighteenth century.

Contents. See Stroev's description for a complete listing. Of particular interest is the first letter of Kurbskii to Ivan, a unique copy that begins on fol. 35 and ends with "amin'" on fol. 39, leaving a space and fol. 39v blank. As Stroev notes, this gathering occupied fols. 314–318 in another MS (the numbering is probably from the eighteenth century); one notes also under these numbers what may be the original foliation, beginning with fol. 32 (on present fol. 35). The first redaction of the "Tale of the Two Embassies," also in a distinct gathering, follows the Kurbskii letter. The final work in the MS, the "Petition of Polozov," has been published in a different variant in *Pravoslavnyi palestinskii sbornik*, X, 3, pp. 45–50, by P. A. Syrku.

Remarks. At the beginning of the MS is a table of contents compiled by Stroev in 1843; one cannot be certain whether the present composition is the result of his choice or whether he found the MS as it now stands. While the component parts are discrete, it is probably more than a coincidence that the Kurbskii letter and the "Tale of the Two Embassies" in the first redaction appear together here, since they do so in other manuscripts. At one time, "The Kazan' History" was connected with 197.

The unique and important copy of the Kurbskii letter seems to be contemporary with the other earliest manuscripts of its first version. Although the watermark on its paper has not been published, marks of similar design but with different letters are found on paper used in Muscovy early in the 1630's.

GBL, *fond* 310, Collection of V. M. Undol'skii No. 603
First half of the seventeenth century, 8°, vi + 330 fols.

Descriptions. GBL, Otdel rukopisei, "Opisanie sobraniia V. M. Undol'skogo (No. 580–1422)," typescript (Moscow, 1937–1938), pp. 38–39; Undol'skii, *Rukopisi*, appendix, pp. 44–45.

Watermarks. Fols. 3–86, 183–218, one-handled pot with letters I/OO. No. 807 (1634) in K. Ia. Tromonin, *Iz"iasnenie znakov, vidimykh v pischei bumage* (Moscow, 1844), is a good likeness.

Fols. 88–182, two-handled pot with letters IG.

Fols. 219–265, two-handled pot with letters PD. Any of Geraklitov, *Filigrani*, Nos. 761–770 (1626–1631) and 773–775 (1631–1633) are good likenesses.

Fols. 270, 272, 284, two-handled pot with "grapes" on top and letters PDY.

Fols. 285, 287, two-handled pot of somewhat unusual design with letters MF. Possibly a variant of Tromonin, *Iz"iasnenie*, No. 966 (ca. 1595).

Fol. 318, pot that is probably a variant of the preceding, even though only M is visible (there is a space for another letter), and there is a slight difference in the top.

Fol. 329, top for a large pot differing from the preceding ones.

Inscriptions. Fol. vi, which was apparently the back cover paper before restoration of the MS, "13 marta 1854 g. ot A. Sergeev(a) . . . 3 r." There are various eighteenth-century marginal notations of the type "zri" throughout the MS.

Contents. Fol. 1 (seventeenth-century *skoropis'* that varies somewhat in style—e.g., note the shifts on fols. 32v and 44v), *Syn tserkovnyi*, "Skazanie nuzhneishikh obychaev nauki pravoslavnyia khristiianskiia very." On fol. 19v, one portion of the work has chapter numbering "10". This work is apparently found also in MS 4469.

Fol. 47, "Vospominanie ot chasti sviatyia gory afonskiia kakoi a rechena byst' sviataia gora afon"skaia i koi radi del tak prozvasia."

(Half of fol. 58, all of 58v, 59, 59v and ii, between 59 and 60, are blank; ii verso is somewhat dirty. On fols. 52v and 59v are signatures "7" and "8".)

Fol. 60, chronicle-style notes about Russian metropolitans, beginning with Filip and ending with the thirty-ninth Metropolitan Makarii; apparently the beginning of the work is missing. A pencilled reference at the end of the text refers to the location of another copy, GIM, Uvarov Collection, No. 222(743)(694), beginning on fol. 188.

(Fol. 86v is blank and dirty.)

Fol. 87 (apparent change in hand, but very similar to the preceding; more extensive use of cinnabar begins here; change in paper. Signatures visible in this section include fol. 103 = 3, fol. 111 = 4, with continuation of this numeration on verso sides of the last folio of each gathering from fol. 150v = 8 through fol. 205v = 15. Presumably these numbers began with fol. 87 = 1. A second set of numbers, which may have been consecutive throughout the MS from the beginning, includes fol. 87 = 12(?), fol. 103 = 14 . . . fol. 143 = 19 . . . , the last number in the series being fol. 206 = 27), account of the miraculous salvation of Moscow in 1521 from a Tatar raid; begins: "Znamenie uzhasno i preslavno, kako spasen byst' grad Moskva ot nashestviia bezbozhnykh tatar . . ."

Fol. 125, "Chin i ukaz byvaemyi na ezhe ot sratsyn obrashchaiushchikhsia kh nashei vere khristiian'stei istinnei. Prezhde prikhodit' sratsynin . . . ," numbered as "Chapter 75."

Fol. 129v, "Prokliatie latynskim eresem izhe kto zhelaet istinnoe sviatoe kreshchenie poluchiti . . ." These two rituals appear together in a number of collections.

(A shift of hand occurs on fol. 135, with a gradual change back, the hand at the end of the work apparently the same as that in the first part of the MS; half of fol. 162 and all of 162v are blank, with the latter somewhat smudged.)

Fol. 163, "Tale about the White Cowl" in the first extended redaction, eighth group, according to the classification of N. N. Rozov, "Povest' o novgorodskom belom klobuke kak pamiatnik obshcherusskoi publitsistiki XV veka," *TODRL* IX:212.

(Part of fol. 218v is blank as is all of the following fol. iii.)

Fol. 219 (different seventeenth-century *skoropis'*; change in paper. Apparently this section had separate signatures added by someone other than the copyist, beginning with "1", as fol. 242 = 4(?) and fol. 250 = 5), "Tale of the Two Embassies," in the first redaction according to M. D. Kagan, *TODRL* XI:241; she provides variants from this copy in her published text.

(Part of fol. 250 and all of 250v are blank.)

Fol. 251, Kurbskii's first letter to Ivan in the first variant.

(Fol. iv, following fol. 258, is blank on both sides with the verso slightly smudged.)

Fol. 259 (different seventeenth-century *skoropis'*), account of the defeat of the Tatars in 1572, in the first full redaction. The beginning and ending correspond to the text published by V. I. Buganov, "Povest' o pobede nad krymskimi tatarami v 1572 godu," *Arkheograficheskii ezhegodnik za 1961 god* (Moscow, 1962), pp. 269–272, where Buganov was apparently unaware of this copy. The variants here seem to group this copy with that in MS Central State Archive of Ancient Acts (TsGADA), *fond* 181, No. 130.

(Fol. v, following fol. 265, is wholly blank and its verso slightly dirty.)

Fol. 266 (markedly different seventeenth-century *skoropis'*; change in paper, with the first folio of this new gathering being very dirty. New signatures begin here with fol. 273v = 1, fol. 274 = 2 ... through fol. 317 = 7), "Povest' sviatago i blazhennago izhe Khrista radi urodivago Andreia i uchenika ego Epifaniia o boliarine. V nedeliu za utra se mimo ide boliarin nekii . . ."

(While the same hand continues throughout, beginning with fol. 327 the bottom margins are much larger than previously; fol. 330v is blank.)

Remarks. Three portions of the manuscript may be distinguished: fols. 1–218, 219–265, and 266–330. Despite some internal breaks, the first of these was clearly copied in one place at one time and like the second probably dates to the early 1630's. The general similarity in hand of the second section with that in the first suggests that both may have been done in the same scriptorium at the same time, but the third section of the MS is distinct, clearly having been copied earlier. Some folios may have been lost, since at the time of the recent restoration, the MS was in poor condition.

GBL, *fond* 178, Museum Collection No. 4469
Second quarter of the seventeenth century, 4°, 653 fols.

Descriptions. Sochineniia I. Peresvetova, ed. A. A. Zimin (Moscow-Leningrad, 1956), pp. 83–85; GBL, Otdel rukopisei, "Muzeinoe sobranie, f. 178—russkaia (i slavianskaia) chast'. Opis'," II (MSS Nos. 640.2 and 3006–4500), typescript (Moscow, 1968), pp. 530–534.

Watermarks. I have described these in *Kritika,* VI (1970): 98–99. The best identifications, which are less than satisfactory, are with marks on paper used in the late 1630's.

Inscriptions. Fol. 653v, "Siia kniga tserkvi Kozmy i Domiana, chto v nizhnikh" (the GBL description reads the last word "nizhnem (?)"). Also on fol. 653, *proby pera* including the names "Semen Ivanov" and "gospodin Ivan Mikhailovich," which could be referring to Shakhovskoi and Katyrev-Rostovskii, respectively.

Contents (based on the listing in the GBL description).

Fol. 1, table of contents listing the twenty-five "chapters" which follow.

Fol. 12, the "Complete Version" of the works of Peresvetov, published from this copy by Zimin in *Sochineniia*, where this portion of the MS is described in detail. The "Large Petition" appears separately (see below). Includes "chapters" "1" and "2".

Fol. 75, Kurbskii's letter to Vas'ian, preceded by the appended note beginning "Vymete." "3".

Fol. 78, Kurbskii's first letter to Ivan in the first version.

Fol. 81v, Teterin to Morozov.

Fol. 82v, *gramota Polubenskogo.*

Fol. 83v, Peresvetov's "Large Petition."

Fol. 100v, "O sviatom grade Ierusalime," apparently from the "Journey of Trifon Korobeinikov." "4".

Fol. 104v, "Imena prosodiiam" and explanation (*tolkovanie*) of the word "amin'."

Fol. 105, the "Journey of Trifon Korobeinikov." "5".

Fol. 145, "Chin, kako podobaet kadilo chtiti." "6".

Fol. 146, "Skazanie prepodobnago ... Agapiia, chto radi ostavliaiut rody i doma svoia i zhenu i deti i vzem krest idut vo sled Gospoda ..." "7"

Fol. 154v, "Extracts from the Kizilbash Books," apparently in the Normal Version, Group A, according to my classification. See Appendix I, pt. b, below. "8".

Fol. 173v, "Kniga, glagolemaia syn tserkovnyi," also found in MS 603. "9".

Fol. 208, "Vedati podobaet o sviatei 50-tsy." "10".

Fol. 209, "Sv. Epifaniia ot Panarii, o srede i o piattse i o 50-tsy." "11".

Fol. 210, "O tom zhe blazhennago i velikago Afanasiia ot sochtaniia." "12".

Fol. 211, "Postnyi sii ustav na useknovenie chestnyia glavy ... krestitelia Gospodnia Ioanna." "13".

Fol. 214v, "Dostoit vedati i o sem, iako vo sviatuiu, velikuiu nedeliu paskhi ne podobaet prinositi k tserkvi miasnykh chastei ..." "14".

Fol. 217, the Answers of Afanasii of Alexandria to the Prince of Antioch "16".

Fol. 264v, St. John the Damascene on the Trinity and about Faith. "17".

Fol. 266, "Izlozheniia v"krattse o vere po voprosheniiu" by Anastasii of Antioch and Kirill of Alexandria. "18".

Fol. 268, questions and answers about the Trinity, by Kirill of Jerusalem. "19".

Fol. 270, "Skazanie o skuf'e," "20"; "Kako podobaet krestitisia," "O poklonenii na vostok," and "O khlebtse, prechistyia Bogoroditsy."

Fol. 272v, "Kanon na sv. Paskhu" and explanation of it. "21".

Fol. 285v, "Iz knigi blazhennago Afonasiia, arkhiepiskopa Aleksandrii-skogo, voprosy." "22".

Fol. 290v, "Tropnik" of Pope Innocent, in the translation by Fedor Kas'ianov Gozvinskii of the year 7117 (= 1608/9). "23".

Fol. 374, the *Stoglav.* "24".

Fol. 569, "Vera i protivlenie krestivshikhsia iiudei vo Afrakii, i v Kar-fagene", "25"; begins, "Byvshee znamenie, pache zhe chiudo vo dnekh nashikh izvolisia mne greshnomu Iosifu, novokreshchennomu ot iiudei ..."

Remarks. The manuscript was copied in one place at one time, probably by a single scribe. The best watermark identifications date it to the late 1630's, but more reliable data might push this date back somewhat, which would support the fact that the copies of Peresvetov and Kurbskii found here contain some of the best readings.

GIM, Collection of A. S. Uvarov Nos. 1386(116), 1453(108), 1442(113), 1581(330) [one manuscript in four separate bindings]
Mid-seventeenth century, 4°, 321 + 45 + 149 + 57 fols.
Descriptions. Leonid, *Opisanie*, III: 76–79, 106, 103–104, 230; *Poslaniia*, p. 545.
Watermarks.
(*In 1386[116]*)
Fols. 1–5, 105, 150ff., 278, 296, lily on squarish shield under a crown; over the letters ID. No. 2165 (1639) in E. Laucevičius, *Popierius Lietuvoje XV–XVIII a.* (Vilnius, 1967), is similar, but the letters may be LD.
Fols. 6, 13, two different but unidentifiable sets of pillars.
Fol. 17, letters?
Fol. 19, large two-handled pot with letters P/HI(?) and with three flowers and a crescent as decoration on the top.
Fol. 25, house topped by a cross with a snake entwined around it.
Fols. 31, 36, 38, lily on squarish shield under a crown; over letters HP(?).
Fols. 39, 40, 45, 46ff., different lily on a more elaborate shield. The lily is of cruder design with narrower petals than the preceding one; the crown-like top of the shield is unusual, with a trefoil in the center. Attached to the bottom of the shield is a projection resembling a bell.
Fols. 64ff., 263, 282, foolscap of unspecified type, with countermark PR (possibly PB or RR?). Similar is No. 237A (1639) in S. A. Klepikov, "Bumaga s filigran'iu 'golova shuta (foolscap)'," *ZOR* XXVI (1963).
Fols. 96ff., two-handled pot with letters C(?)D (possibly OD).
Fols. 110ff., one-handled pot of medium size with a lily on the base and letters I/OO.
Fols. 129, 130, lily?
Fols. 134, 147, one-handled pot with a somewhat unusual top and a "heart-shaped" projection on the bottom (containing a small off-center flower) instead of the usual flat-bottomed base. On the pot, letters IG(?)S/__G. A distinctive mark in all respects.
Fols. 143, 173, arms of Moisburg: a crown-topped shield containing a large ligature MB (which resembles M and the number 3). Laucevičius, *Popierius*, No. 3239 (1637) is clearly a variant of this; the same mark or a very close variant is in MS GPB, Pogodin Collection No. 1576, beginning on fol. 108.
Fol. 188, one-handled pot of medium size with letters MD(?)/O. The top row of letters is unusual, as the M seems to be missing the right vertical and the D the vertical; possibly the letter is merely a distorted large M.
Fol. 196, pillars topped by grapes; between the pillars, letters AD.
Fols. 205, 212ff., two variants of a bend over the letters SIM. Geraklitov, *Filigrani*, No. 241 (1642) is a good likeness.
Fols. 238, 239, two variants of a lily on a curving shield under a crown, one over letters SI and the other over IS.
Fols. 293ff., lily on a somewhat distorted squarish shield over letters IP (or IR).
Fols. 314ff., two variants of a coat of arms divided into four quadrants. In three are standing panthers (or lions) and in the fourth (upper left) parallel lines between which are the letters COD/IV.

(*In 1453[108]*)
Three marks: a lily on a shield under a crown; over the letters ID. On the center petal of the lily is a small loop.

A coat of arms with panthers and letters as above.

A lily on a shield under a crown; over letters IV.

(*In 1442[113]*)
A lily on a squarish shield.

A lily on a fluted shield, with a serpentine device attached to the bottom and bracketed by letters GD(?). Similar to Tromonin, *Iz"iasnenie*, No. 1325 (1647).

A coat of arms with panthers and letters as above—the dominant mark here.

(*In 1581[330]*)
Fols. 4, 7, the same arms with the "panthers."

Fol. 11, lily on a squarish shield under a crown; over letters PI ID (or PI PD).

Fol. 26, a similar lily and shield, over letters MIL (or MLI).

Fol. 46, another lily and shield, over letters ID, with a device on the center petal of the lily—the same mark as in 1453(108). This mark or a close variant of it is also in MS GBL, Collection of Lukashevich and Markevich No. 10.

Unnumbered folio preceding binding paper, one-handled pot with letters D/IV. The top is not visible, but the mark seems to be one of those depicted by Geraklitov, *Filigrani*, Nos. 588–600 (1626–1633).

Inscriptions. On fol. 1 of 1386(116) is a mid-seventeenth-century inscription neatly centered in cinnabar letters but not in the same hand as that of the MS: "Siia glagolemaia kniga letapisets kniazia Ivana Fedorovicha Khvorostinina Iaroslavskago."

Pagination. The gatherings are all numbered beginning with 1386(116); this numbering enables one to reestablish the order of the four parts as I have done here. The end of the last part is missing, as the text breaks off at the bottom of fol. 57v in 1581(330).

Handwriting. Most of the MS is the work of one copyist, although two or three changes in style occur in 1453(108). The beginnings of major new sections of the MS are decorated by cut-outs from headings in printed books, the initials from books, or pasted-on initials rather crudely drawn in imitation of the printed ones.

Contents. The manuscript was probably envisaged by its compiler as a compilation like a "Book of Degrees" (*Stepennaia kniga*). In 1386(116) is a lengthy account of Russian history, at least part of which seems to be based on the *Stepennaia kniga*. The account of the reign of Ivan IV (labeled "Degree 17") is clearly a condensed account of the text published in *PSRL*, Vol. XXI, pt. 1. Following this, in 1453(108), is "Degree 18," the "Life" of Tsar Fedor Ivanovich written by Patriarch Iov; in 1442(113) is "The Kazan' History," divided into seventy-seven chapters. The last part of the MS contains Kurbskii's letter to Ivan in the first variant and Ivan's reply in the "Chronograph variant." The title of the Kurbskii letter indicates it is "Chapter 72" and the title for Ivan's letter includes "Chapter 79." Ivan's letter breaks off on fol. 57v with the words, "iako Dimofil nepshchuet blagago o vsekh Boga ne byti chelovekoliubiva nizhe sobe trebovati miluiushchago ili spasaiushchago no i sviashchennik," which correspond to the text at the top of p. 68 in *Poslaniia*.

Remarks. The variety and types of watermarks should eventually allow fairly precise dating of this MS, which, given the existing evidence, probably was written ca. 1640. Although it belonged to Prince I. F. Khvorostinin (son of the boyar Fedor Khvorostinin, d. 1608), it is impossible to tell what role, if any, he had in its composition. The present division and binding of the MS is apparently the work of I. P. Sakharov, who owned it before Count Uvarov.

GIM, Collection of A. S. Uvarov Nos. 1584(168) and 1321(103)
[one manuscript bound in two parts]
Second quarter of the seventeenth century, 4°, 44 + 56 fols.
Descriptions. Leonid, *Opisanie,* III: 232–234 and 17–21; Zimin, *Sochineniia,* pp. 85–86.
Watermarks.
(*In 1584[168]*)
A single watermark throughout, a two-handled pot with a flower growing out of the top and a "cross and heart" device on the side. The two, possibly three, variants of this mark are similar to Geraklitov, *Filigrani,* No. 908, and Heawood, *Watermarks,* No. 3671, both of which are found on paper used in 1633.
(*In 1321[103]*)
Fols. 3–48, the same mark as in the preceding portion of the MS.
Fols. 49ff., alternation of two different marks (could one be the other half of the other?), one of them resembling vaguely the mark Briquet terms "mons"—three protrusions from a line, the center one being very elongated; the other mark is a standing female (?) figure with a fluted headdress and a staff in each hand topped by leaves or a fluted design. Around the lower part of the figure, which is quite faint, is something resembling a wreath.
Pagination. As Zimin indicates (*Sochineniia,* p. 85, n. 3), 1584(168) has eighteenth-century foliation, in Arabic numerals, 147–190; these numbers, written in ink, continue as 191–245 in the second part of the MS. Some signatures are visible: fol. 16(205)v = 11, fol. 33(221)v = 13.
Handwriting. In 1321(103), one gathering, fols. 2–8, seems to have been copied in a different hand, leaving a space on fol. 8v before continuation of the text. The hand of this gathering is that of 1584(168); otherwise, fol. 1 and fols. 9–56 of 1321(193) are in a single band, with a shift in style on fol. 49.
Contents. The manuscript contains in order the following works: the so-called "Pecherskii sbornik" of works connected with Kurbskii, including the letter to Vas'ian with its appended note ("Vymete"), the first letter to Ivan in the first version, Teterin to Morozov, and the *gramota Polubenskogo*; the "Large Petition" of Peresvetov; the remaining works of Peresvetov in the complete version, Museum variant (best represented by the copy in 4469). The Peresvetov complex apparently derives from a copy that lacked the ending, as the final work, the "Tale about the Emperor Constantine," breaks off with the words "ne dostoit tsariu Kon'stian'tinu na inoplemen-nikov khoditi" at the bottom of fol. 56(245). Fol. 56(245)v is blank, which would seem to indicate that Zimin errs (*Sochineniia,* p. 85, n. 3) where he indicates that the end of the manuscript is missing. As he notes, a small cinnabar mark has been placed at the end of the final line (to warn the reader that the text is defective?).
Remarks. As both the handwriting and watermarks indicate, the manu-

script was probably copied in the 1630's. When it was numbered in the eighteenth century (apparently by the same reader who added the marginalia noted by Zimin, *Sochineniia*, p. 86, n. 4), it contained an additional 146 folios at the beginning. The signatures indicate that prior to that time there had been only four additional gatherings at the beginning of the MS.

This MS should be studied in conjunction with two others which seem to have direct links with it. One of these, GPB Q.IV.172, may be connected merely by coincidence. According to the description by S. F. Platonov in *RIB* XIII: xvii–xviii, it preserves the foliation 124–146 in pencil and was at one time owned by P. M. Stroev and by I. P. Sakharov, who owned the Uvarov MS described here. Q.IV.172 is in quarto and apparently is an assemblage of fragments dating to various periods, all of them later than the Uvarov MS. The first portion of Q.IV.172 belonged at one time to Patriarch Adrian and contains I. A. Khvorostinin's account of the *smuta* as published from this copy in *RIB*, Vol. XIII, cols. 525–558; the second portion contains Chapter 168 from the Chronograph, second redaction, dealing with the *smuta*. The third portion, which formerly was part of MS 1311 (see below), contains the apocryphal correspondence between the sultan and Emperor Leopold.

MS 1584(168) and 1321(103) must be compared with MS Uvarov Collection No. 1363(16), where I have discovered a copy of the complete version of the works of Peresvetov, less the "Large Petition," that seems identical with the version found here. At the end of the copy in 1363(16), which was made between 1637 and 1640, a contemporary hand noted (fol. 526v): "list nedopisan ili malo bol'shi." Clearly 1363(16) had a common protograph with the copy in 1321(103) or used the latter as its source. MS 1363(16) contains many other interesting works, among them a Chronograph, the earliest copy of the "historical" tale about the seizure of Azov. and a copy of the "Extracts from the Kizilbash Books." As I have indicated elsewhere (*Kritika* VI: 88–89), another manuscript containing the latter two works and very closely connected with 1363(16) in time and place of copying is GIM, Collection of the Synodal Library No. 409, which also will have to be taken into account when the manuscript traditions of works attributed to Kurbskii are subjected to further scrutiny.

GIM, Museum Collection No. 1551
First half of the seventeenth century, 4°, 71 fols.
   Description. Zimin, *Sochineniia*, App. II (by M. D. Kagan), p. 369.
   Watermarks. Fols. 1ff., one-handled pot with letters oo/MC. Undoubtedly a close variant of Geraklitov, *Filigrani*, No. 567 (1628–1630) or one of the other marks in his group ranging from No. 560 (1622) through No. 573 (1631–1633).
   Fols. 66ff., two-handled pot with letters IB; on the base right under the bottom of the pot is a small circle. A close variant of Geraklitov, No. 782 (1628–1630), or the similar marks Nos. 778–781 (1625–1630) and 783–785 (1628–1633). For both watermarks my choices for the closest likenesses happen to be found in the same book, a *Triod' postnaia* printed in Moscow in 1630.
   Pagination. Arabic foliation includes fol. 6 = 65, fol. 7 = 66, etc. The first folio of the MS is relatively clean, but the last very dirty and damaged, which suggests that the present MS is the end of what was once a larger one.
   Handwriting. The same *skoropis'* throughout.

Contents. Fols. 1–4v, "Farewell epistle" of Metropolitan Kiprian (d. 1406), with some variants from that published in *PSRL* XI:195–197.

Fols. 4v–5v, the "appendix" to the above epistle: "Po konets zhe takovye gramoty pisano filosofskii." The ending differs from that in *PSRL* XI: (fol. 5) "no o mnogomilostive Khriste Bozhe nash blagodatiiu svoeiu v mire i v pokoianii // ispravi zhivot nash i pomilui nas. Amin'." After a space, the text ends with the same "afterword" as in the printed text.

Fols. 6–9v, Kurbskii's first letter to Ivan in the first version, with the heading, "Gramota kniazia Andreia Kurbskovo k tsariu i velikomu kniaziu Ivanu Vasil'evichiu vsea Rusii." It has the usual beginning but ends, "Pisano v Volmere . . . pache zhe Bogu mi pomogaiushchu."

Fols. 10–33v, Ivan's reply, apparently in the "abbreviated version" (this should be checked). The heading and beginning are: "Leta 7072-go tsarevo gosudarevo poslanie vo vse ego rosiiskoe tsarstvo na izmennikov ego na kniazia Andreia Kurbskovo s tovaryshchi o ikh izmenakh. Bog nash troitsa izhe prezhe vek sii i nyne est' . . ." The ending is: "i umolchal, voznepshcheval esi bezzakonie, iako budu tebe podoben, oblichiu tia i predstavliu pred litsem tvoim grekhi tvoia. Razumei te zhe siia zabyvaiush-chei Boga da ne kogda pokhitit i ne budet izbavliaiai. Dan otvet vselennei Rosiistei tsarstvuiushchago preslavnago grada Moskvy stepenei chestnago poroga krepkaia upoved' i slovo to leta ot sozdaniia miru 7072-go, iiulia v 5 den'."

Fols. 31–33v, Kurbskii's letter to Vas'ian, with the heading: "Leta 7072-go, Spisok s gramoty kniazia Ondreia Kurbskovo, Iz Litvy v Pechery k startsu Vas'ianu Muromtsovu." The work begins: "V prechestnuiu obitel' prechistye Bogoroditsy Pecherskago monastyria gospodinu startsu Vas'ianu, Andrei Kurbskoi radovatisia posylal esmi k igumenu i k vam cheloveka svoevo biti chelom . . ."

Fols. 34–35v, Teterin to Morozov, with heading and beginning: "Leta 7072-go, Timokhi Teterina iz Litvy. Gospodinu Mikhailu Iakovlevichiu, Timokha Tet(e)rin da Makarko Sarygozin chelom b'iu . . ."

Fols. 35v–41, a letter allegedly sent by Ivan IV to the King of Poland, Stefan Bathory, October 1, 1679. I did not examine the text closely, but the beginning in a partial copy which has been provided me reads: "Gramota gosudaria tsaria i velikogo kniazia Ivana Vasil'evicha vsea Rusii k Stepanu koroliu Pol'skomu. Bog nash troitsa, izhe prezhe vek syi otets i syn i sviatyi dukh, ni nachala imyi, nizhe kontsa imat' byti i prebyvaia nyne i prisno i vo veki vekom v tri litsa . . . my, velikii gosudar' . . . Ivan Vasil'evich . . . Stefanu bozhieiu milostiiu velikomu gosudariu koroliu Polskomu . . . my tvoiu gramotu vychli i vrazumeli gorazdo. I vzial esi velerechivye usta i ziiaiushchiia nepodobiiu khristiianskomu, a takiia esmia ukorizny i pokhvaly ne slykhali ni ot turetskovo, ni ot tsysaria, ni ot inykh gosudarei. A gde ty, v kotoroi zemli byl, i v tekh zemliakh bolshi tovo tebe vedomo, i nigde togo, chtob gosudar' gosudariu tak pisal, kak ty k nam pisal. A zhil esi v derzhave besermenskoi, a vera latynskaia polukhristiianstvo. A pany tvoi veruiut ikonobornuiu eres' liutorskuiu . . ." The ending is: "A my nadezhu svoiu i voliu i zhivot svoi polozhili na vsemogushchago boga . . . Pisano v nashei otchine vo grade Pskove leta ot sozdaniia miru 7088-go oktiabria v 1 den' indikta 8, gosudarstviia nashego 45-go a tsarstv nashikh Rosiiskago 32, Kazanskogo 28, Astrakhanskovo 25."

One notes the similarity of the opening to that in the first letter of Ivan to Kurbskii; the suggestions about Bathory's having lived in Turkish

(Muslim) territory are parallel to those in the letter to Bathory of 1581 (published in *Poslaniia*; note commentary of Lur'e on pp. 513–515). However the text of this letter apparently remains to be published. On the basis of this one copy one should be cautious in declaring it a "new" *sochinenie Groznogo*. There is no clear evidence from what we know based on the contemporary documents that Ivan sent such a letter; it is possible that he had already left Pskov by October 1 and was on his way back to Moscow. See, for example, N. N. Bantysh-Kamenskii, "Perepiska mezhdu Rossieiu i Pol'sheiu po 1700 god. Ch. I, 1487–1584" (*Chteniia*, 1860, bk. 4, sec. 2, pp. 157–158); compare *Poslaniia*, pp. 660–661, where it seems clear that this letter was unknown to Lur'e. The letter to which this would seem to be a reply—Bathory's declaration of war sent from Vilnius in July with his ambassador Lopacinski—was parodied as a polemical "pamphlet" that appeared in contemporary German and Czech editions (K. Estreicher, *Bibliografia polska*, vol. XII [pt. III, vol. 1], [Krakow, 1891], pp. 405–407). Such a pamphlet might have been the basis for the composition of the letter here attributed to Ivan, if in fact it is not genuine but appeared at a later date.

Fols. 41v–59, "Tale of the Two Embassies" in the transitional redaction according to the classification of M. D. Kagan.

Fols. 59–70, "Poslanie nekoego inoka k svoim roditelem," a work which I have been unable to identify. It begins: "Iz preslovushchiia i Bogom snabdimyia chestnyia i velikiia obiteli imiarek sushchee vo bogospasaemom grade imiarek bogoliubivomu i v vere blagochestiia tsvetushchemu blagorodrodnomu [*sic*] i smirenno mudromu . . ."

Fols. 70–end, "Slovesa vostavliatel'na k pokaianiiu," a work attributed to Maksim Grek beginning "Po chto vo zlykh prebyvaem i preziraem dobroe, po chto liubim sie ot nikh zhe pogibaem i ne zhelaem izbavleniia . . ." Since fol. 71v, the last one in the MS, is so dirty and damaged, it is impossible to tell whether the work ends there.

Remarks. Unfortunately, when looking at 1551 I failed to realize how important it may be in the manuscript tradition of the *Correspondence*. It may contain the earliest copy of the "abbreviated version" of Ivan's first letter; the Kurbskii letter to Vas'ian is also of interest because Vas'ian Muromtsev is explicitly named as the addressee. The copy of an apparently hitherto unknown letter of Ivan to Bathory demands close study. On the basis of watermarks, a date of ca. 1630 for the MS seems appropriate.

GIM, Museum Collection No. 2524
Mid-seventeenth century, 4°, 323 fols.

Descriptions. N. M. Petrovskii, "Novyi spisok puteshestviia F. A. Kotova," *Izvestiia ORIaS*, vol. XV, bk. 4 (1910), pp. 287–288; *Poslaniia*, p. 554.

Watermarks. Fols. 1, 158–165, 176–177, 242–245 (a slight variant?), foolscap, type IV, with letters LM bracketing the "stem" that attaches the trefoil. This is probably a variant of Geraklitov, *Filigrani*, No. 1331 (1656), where details of the face are different but the overall resemblance good. His drawings are too sloppy to assure identification on the basis of details.

Fols. 7–8, 13, 17, 64, 67, 78–85, 111–116, 124–140, 153, 167–169, several variants of a foolscap of the type depicted by Klepikov, *ZOR* XXVI, No. 257 (1650). One of these marks, which are of very crude and presumably unstable design, may well be a variant of the Klepikov mark.

Fols. 11, 12 (the paper begins on fol. 9), fragment of some letter.

Fols. 20–40, 87–101, 218, 219, 229, three or four variants of a plain, medium-sized lily.

Fols. 54, 61, 63, 68, 186–189, 253, 258, 268, 287–288, two variants of a house with an off-center door; attached to the roof a cross entwined by a snake. Generally a mark of the mid-seventeenth century. Another, more distinct, variant occurs on fols. 178–182, 194–197, 200–207, 252, 254, 257, 259, 269.

Fols. 121, 122, bend.

Fols. 208, 210, arms of Berne (bear on a shield, with letters WR attached underneath), and countermark PC on fol. 209. S. A. Klepikov, *Filigrani i shtempeli na bumage russkogo i inostrannogo proizvodstva XVII–XX veka* (Moscow, 1959), No. 1286 (1650–1651) is similar. This mark or a close variant of it is found in MS GPB, Pogodin Collection No. 1405 (fols. 9, 10), which has other connections with 2524 (see below), in the first portion of GIM, Uvarov Collection No. 1844(756)(720), where the hand is similar to that in part of MS 1573, and in TsGADA, *fond* 89, Turetskie dela, 1646 g., No. 3, which has been misfiled and dates to 1649. In the latter case, the the countermark reads C and "reversed" P, as given in Klepikov, *Filigrani*, No. 948 (1650–1651); however, since Klepikov finds the two marks in a single *fond* and apparently the same documents in the archive, it would seem that the two marks are a variant pair.

Fols. 248, 249, 251 (the bottom of the mark is missing since the following folios have been cut out), bend similar to Heawood, *Watermarks*, No. 128 (1646) and somewhat similar to Tromonin, *Iz"iasnenie*, No. 437 (1659). These identifications require particular caution, since too few bends are attested in albums and are often too poorly drawn.

Fols. 260–261, 266–267, somewhat unusual two-handled pot with a plant growing out of the top leading to a trefoil flower. The mark is larger than the two-handled pots common at the start of the second quarter of the seventeenth century.

Fols. 295–314, foolscap, type II.

Fol. 318, crude ligature HVF.

Fols. 315–321, cross of Lorraine (intertwined letters C around a cross under a crown) in two variants, bracketed by letters IC. Generally a watermark of the mid-seventeenth century.

Binding papers, Cyrillic RF and countermark KI, with the date 1827 at the point where the two halves of the full sheet join.

Inscriptions. On the right half of the front binding paper, in eighteenth-century handwriting, "letopisets."

Fols. 1–6, along the bottoms of the pages, "Kniga kholmogorskogo sobora protopopa Iova Ivanova." The absence of the expected "siia" at the beginning of the inscription supports other evidence for the loss of one folio at the beginning of the MS. Iov Ivanov was a priest in the Church of the Epiphany (in Kholmogory?), became *kliuchar'* of the Cathedral of the Transfiguration in Kholmogory in 1701, and subsequently was *protopop* in the cathedral between 1715 and his death in 1727. See A. Golubtsov, "Chinovniki kholmogorskogo Preobrazhenskogo sobora," *Chteniia*, 1903, bk. 4, sec. i, first pagination, pp. 251, 265, 271.

Fol. 6v, "Kniga letopisets i inye povesti pritiazhanie Nikolaevskago sviashchennika Aleksiia Venediktova syna Zolotareva keleinaia." The inscription dates prior to 1682, when A. V. Zolotarev was priest in the Church of St. Nicholas in the Lower *Posad* of Kholmogory. In October

1682, he was made *kliuchar'* of the main cathedral in the city (Iov Ivanov succeeded him), and his brother Kalinnik, later *protopop* of the cathedral in Archangel, succeeded him as priest in the church of St. Nicholas. As *kliuchar'* of the cathedral, A. V. Zolotarev apparently wrote or supervised the compilation of the *chinovnik*, the record of the activities connected with the church; judging from the *chinovnik*, his literary interests included contemporary versification. His daughter was married to the compiler of the "Dvina Chronicle." Both Zolotarev and his brother were important figures in the administrative hierarchy established by Afanasii, the Archbishop of Kholmogory in the last two decades of the seventeenth century. See Golubtsov, *Chteniia*, 1903, pp. xxix–xxxiii, 37; A. A. Titov, *Letopis' dvinskaia* (Moscow, 1889), p. iii.

Fol. 143, in a different hand from the text, a marginal gloss of "liturgiiu" for "sluzhbu" in the text.

Fol. 323, "1689-g mesiatsa marta 22 chisla."

Pagination. The present foliation in Arabic numbers clearly has been added over an earlier one to correct for the loss of the first folio; hence, fol. 1 formerly was fol. 2, etc.

Handwriting. Despite some slight shifts in hand which will be noted below, at least through fol. 231 the MS is probably the work of a single copyist. The handwriting in this part of the MS resembles that in parts of 1573, GPB, Pogodin Collection No. 1405, and F.XVII.15. Photographic comparison of the most similar portions in the first two with 2524 reveals that the hands are not the same, but tentatively it seems possible to indicate that they belong to one school of copyists or one scriptorium. As indicated below, the number of lines per page in some portions of 2524 is revealing of breaks which occurred in the copying.

Contents. Fols. 1–12, a short chronicle of Russian events from Riurik to the election of Mikhail Fedorovich, with a final article on his death in 1645 One should note the following:

1. Changes in paper, the use of cinnabar, the number of lines per page, marginal additions in the hand of the copyist, textual breaks, etc., all show that this is an "author's text." In particular there are the following breaks: one folio prior to fol. 1 has been lost—presumably after Iov Ivanov inscribed the MS—so that the text begins with the fragmentary "Vasil'evich Kazan' vzial"; fol. 1 is a separate insertion, and further seams occur between fols. 4 and 5, 6 and 7, 7 and 8 (where a folio has been lost), three lines up on fol. 8, and between 8 and 9.

2. Two of the component parts of the work, brought together here at the time this copy was made, can be traced readily to their immediate sources. All of fol. 1 following the fragmentary opening line is an extract from the "Short Chronicle of the Dvina *Voevody*," corresponding, with the exception of one variant, to the text of this "Short Chronicle" as appended to the unique copy of the *Kholmogorskaia letopis'* in GPB, Pogodin Collection No. 1405, beginning on fol. 446. Beginning three lines up on fol. 8 of 2524 is a *povest'* about the *smuta*, inserted at this point apparently because the text beginning on fol. 9 represents a copy of the bulk of this tale as found in the *gramota* from the Tsar to princes Fionmarkon and Ruliak, which begins later in the MS on fol. 173v. The portion of text between the bottom of fol. 8 and the bottom of fol. 8v seems to have been squeezed into the available space to give the tale its logical beginning: "i pri ego derzhave po vrazh'iu deistvu . . ."—which corresponds to the text near the top of the second

column on p. 5 of *Akty istoricheskie,* vol. III (St Petersburg, 1841), published from 1573.

3. A second copy of this chronicle, clearly later in date and probably removed by one intermediary copy, is in MS BAN No. 16.7.15, beginning on fol. 82. In the BAN MS, as here, the following two works are the "Legendary Correspondence" between the Sultan and Ivan IV and the "Tale of the Two Embassies." This coincidence of convoy, and, more strikingly, the close grouping of the variants between the two copies of these works demonstrate a very close relationship.

4. More important for this book is the connection between 2524 and 1573 as confirmed by this short chronicle, which is combined with a fragment of another one (on fols. 73v–76—see below) in 1573 beginning on fol. 11. Paleographic and textual features detailed below in the description of 1573 prove to my satisfaction that the copyist of this portion of 1573 *must have used* 2524.

(Most of fol. 12 and all of fol. 12v are blank.)

Fol. 13 (change in paper), "Legendary Correspondence" between the Sultan and Ivan IV, as published by M. D. Kagan, *TODRL* XIII:266–272. The variants in this copy coincide with those in 1573 and BAN 16.7.15, which she used for variants to the published text.

(Most of fol. 24v is blank.)

Fol. 25, the "Tale of the Two Embassies" in the first redaction, with variants close to those in 1573. See M. D. Kagan, *TODRL* XI:244–254. Omitted are the final lines (p. 254), "Sozdan byst' . . ."

(Fols. 44 and 45 are blank.)

Fol. 46 (a slight shift in hand; beginning of a new gathering), Kurbskii's first letter to Ivan in the first version. The final portion beginning "Slyshakh . . ." has a separate heading, "Kurbskago ko gosudariu" (fol. 49v).

Fol. 50, Ivan's reply in the "Abbreviated version."

Fol. 72v, three short extracts which may simply be "filler" for some blank space but may, when traced, prove significant for establishing connections of the MS and in particular Ivan's letter: "Tsaria Vasiliia Makidonianina k synu ego L'vu premudromu. Ne vsia glagolem, kaia vedaem . . ." and two more aphorisms; "Ot poslaniia k drugu. Pro chto druzhe oskorbliaeshsia ne razsuzhdaia. Pomysli druzhe gde nyne tsarstvo erosalimskoe . . .," followed by other similar examples to demonstrate the ephemeral nature of material gains and glory; "Ot prorochestva. Ashche ni napast' ni venets, ashche ni borenie . . ."

Fol. 73v, a portion from a short chronicle, beginning "V leta 7079-go v prikhod krymskago tsaria Devlet Kireia, Moskva vsia pogorela . . ." The bulk of the text deals with events in 1584, ending with "Pri tom zhe posle litovskom Lve, tovo zhe d'ni posol byl u gosudaria s utra." Apparently the text is connected with what M. N. Tikhomirov termed the "Bezdninskii letopisets" (*Kratkie zametki o letopisnykh proizvedeniiakh v rukopisnykh sobraniiakh Moskvy* [Moscow, 1962], p. 10) because of the unique information in it regarding the activity of *dumnyi dvorianin* Mikhail Andreevich Bezdnin. Tikhomirov noted the existence of similar material in MS 1573, where this chronicle extract from 2524 was used.

(Half of fol. 76 is blank.)

Fol. 76v, Kurbskii's letter to Vas'ian, prefaced by the text beginning "Vymete . . ."

(Coinciding with the beginning of a new gathering, fol. 78, is a sudden change from 18-line to 14-line pages without any break in text; most of fol. 8ov is blank.)

Fol. 81, two *pamiati* of 1626 regarding the death and burial of Igumen Adrian of the Poshekhonskii Andreianov *pustyn'* on the River Ukhra; published from the copy in MS 1573 as No. 141 in *AI*, III.

(Most of fol. 85 and all of fol. 85v are blank.)

Fol. 86 (shift in hand, the style here being precisely that of earlier portions of the MS—e.g., beginning on fol. 2; a new gathering begins here), "Journey of Trifon Korobeinikov" in a copy where apparently one of the gatherings has been bound in the wrong order. The text begins in the middle of the description of the journey to Jerusalem: "putem khodiat na Damask grad i ottole do Damaska khodu 3 dni a khodiat na osliatakh . . ." The actual beginning of the work is on fol. 90: "Po prikazu tsaria i velikago kniazia Ivana Vasil'evicha . . . i pri syne ego Feodore Ivanoviche . . . po blago-sloveniiu Dionisiia mitropolita . . ."

(Fol. 145v is blank.)

Fol. 146, "Extracts from the Kizilbash Books" in a defective copy of what I term the Normal Version, Group B. See App. I, pt. b.

Fol. 168, *gramota* of Patriarch Filaret to Iona, Igumen of the Antonievo-Siiskii Monastery, dated December 9, 1625.

Fol. 173v (change in style, probably due to great cramping of the previous hand, with the writing becoming larger as the work progresses; no cinnabar is used here), *gramota* of Tsar Mikhail Fedorovich to the "Megapolinsk" princes Fionmarkon and Ruliak, published from the copy in 1573, in *AI*, III: 4–7. I have not compared the text of this copy with the extract from the *gramota* as found in the short chronicle mentioned above. However, paleographic details (the identity in hand and number of lines per page and the absence of cinnabar) suggest that the emendation of the chronicle occurred precisely at the time the *gramota* was copied. The text ends on fol. 176v, with the following fol. 177 blank; apparently something unusual happened in the MS at this point, since there is a break in the normal sequence of 8-folio gatherings.

Fol. 178 (change in paper and hand, but the hand of fol. 2 passim returns on fol. 189), account about the journey of Fedot Kotov to Persia. The beginning of this copy (through fol. 182) is published by Petrovskii (*Izvestiia ORIuS*, vol. XV, bk. 4, pp. 287–288), who then gives variants for the remainder of the text against the copy published earlier by Pogodin. For some reason, N. A. Kuznetsova did not use 2524 in her edition, *Khozhenie kuptsa Fedota Kotova v Persiiu* (Moscow, 1958). The variants in 2524 seem to group it more closely with the Pogodin copy than with the one used by Kuznetsova as her basic text.

(Fol. 231v is blank.)

Fol. 232 (change in hand), "Tale about Dinar, Queen of Iberia."

(Fol. 241v is blank.)

Fol. 242, "Slovo sviatykh otets o startse, kako khote uvedati mudrost' bozhiiu i glagoly euangelskiia," in the second redaction, first group, according to the scheme of N. N. Durnovo, "Legenda o zakliuchennom bese v vizantii-skoi i starinnoi russkoi literature," *Drevnosti. Trudy Slavianskoi kommissii Imperatorskogo Moskovskogo arkheologicheskogo obshchestva*, IV, 1 (1907), p. 105. Durnovo did not use this copy but published the text of this version on pp. 106–111.

(Between fols. 251 and 252 five folios have been cut out of the MS.)

Fol. 252 (change in hand and paper), "Slovo o ikonakh is prologa"; begins, "Afanasii velikii arkhiepiskop aleksandriiskii povedashe chiudo . . ."

Fol. 255, "Slovo o Feodore kuptse izhe vzimaia zlato u zhidovina dast poruchnika obraz Khristov zhe nad vraty musieiu utvoren"; begins,"V Konstiantine grade biashe kupets bogat imenem Feodor . . ."

(Fol. 259v is blank.)

Fol. 260 (change in paper), "O molchanii na trapeze"; begins, "Reche avva Isak igumen skitskii . . ."

Fol. 261, "Ioanna Damaskina o izhe v vere usopshim v subbotu miaso-pustnuiu."

Fol. 261v, "Lestvechnik. Ne lepo est' videnie lisitsa v kokoshekh . . . ," followed by other short extracts from the church fathers.

(Most of fol. 263v is blank.)

Fol. 264, "Poslanie Grigoriia Bogoslova k velikomu Vasiliiu. Ustav monastyrskoi."

Fol. 265, "K Polikarpu chernoriztsu Pecherskago monastyria, poslanie episkopa Simona vladimir'skago i suzhdal'skago."

Fol. 269v, "Nachenshu ubo zdat Evseviiu episkopu tserkov' v Pilusii posla k Sidoru pustynniku prosia blagosloveniia, otpisa emu sitse."

Fol. 270, "Povest' i blagoslovenie preosviashchennago Makariia mitro-polita vsea Rusii o sviatem duse synu i sosluzhebniku nashego smireniia Piminu arkhiepiskopu velikago Novagrada i Pskova"; followed by a second similar work whose title I did not note.

(A change in hand occurred on fol. 273; fols. 276 and 277 are blank.)

Fol. 278 (change in hand), "Skazanie o Mikhailove tsarstvii i o poslednikh dnekh"; begins, "Egda zhe vo poslednee vremia o iskhode po sedmo tysiashchnykh letekh . . ."

Fol. 292 (change in hand), "Knigi obikhodnye Kirilova monastyria"; begins, "Leta 7101-go marta v 31 den' Kirilova monastyria igumen Mark . . ." The final entry in this, which I did not note, may provide additional material for the dating of the MS.

(Most of fol. 313v is blank; 314 has a religious inscription at the top; 314v is blank.)

Fol. 315 (change in paper and hand), "Izhe ot iunosti vo blagochestii vospitannomu i v nakazanii bozhestvennykh dokhmat so vozrast"shemu vsiakogo china . . ."; ends on 317v, "ubo veliko i vysoko aggelom ravnitsia, brak zhe chistota bez grekha, blud zhe v muku v vo."

(Fol. 318 blank.)

Fol. 318v, "Tretiia sedmitsa, Egda byvaet chelovek trekh sedmits . . ."; similar texts through "shestaia sedmitsa" on fol. 321v fill the verso of each folio, leaving the recto blank. Following blank fol. 322, on 322v the text begins: "Egda ubo chelovek prispeet ot rozheniia svoego v 70 let ili 80 ili viashche sego prikhodit . . ."

(Fol. 323 is blank but for the inscription already noted.)

Fol. 323v, "Zdravstvu gospodne moi o khriste na mnogie leta i so obder-zhatel'nym tvoim domom."

Remarks. See the remarks for 1573 below.

GPB, Pogodin Collection No. 1311

Primarily second half of the seventeenth century, 4°, viii + 698 pp.

Description. Ia. S. Lur'e, *TODRL* X:306–307.

Watermarks (by *page* number).

P. 1, foolscap, type IV.

Pp. 3–33, foolscap, type IV with countermark PB.

Pp. 39–49, 603(?), pillars of medium size with letters _ _B. In design similar to Heawood, *Watermarks*, No. 3496 (1662), but his letters CAB are not the letters here.

Pp. 53–73, sphere with various parallel horizontal and diagonal lines; at the top of the bisecting line, a star, and at the bottom a small circle. A mark common to the middle or second half of the sixteenth century.

Pp. 81ff. (especially clear on p. 255), coat of arms: squarish shield with crown at top; divided into quadrants. In two diagonally opposed ones are horizontal lines; in the other two, two vertical rows of small diamonds.

Pp. 259–319, crudely drawn arms of Amsterdam with countermark NIM in a rectangular frame.

Pp. 321, 331ff., two variants of a double-headed eagle, similar to that in I. Kamanin and O. Vytvyts'ka, *Vodiani znaky na paperi ukraiins'kykh dokumentiv XVI–XVII vv. (1566–1651)* (Kiev, 1923), No. 679 (1679).

Pp. 353, 367, 371, 375, 381 (mixed with the preceding mark), ALL MOD PAPIER of the type in Tromonin, *Iz"iasnenie*, No. 1355 (1697).

Pp. 385, 390, arms of the Seven Provinces over cursive letters AJ; with countermark CDG. W. A. Churchill, *Watermarks in Paper in Holland, England, France, etc., in the XVII and XVIII Centuries and Their Interconnection* (Amsterdam, 1935), No. 110 (1654) is such a mark, but with differences in detail in the main mark and in the shape of the letters in the countermark.

Pp. 405–567, a somewhat withered lily on an angular variant of the usual squarish shield, surmounted by a crown that has a prominent lily as its center decoration; the mark over an off-center MI (or IM). On p. 409 a variant of the mark has a peculiar trefoil suspended under the lily and the letters connected by a horizontal line (which could render them LM).

Pp. 571ff. (variant on p. 595), unusual foolscap which does not fit the normal types given by Klepikov, *ZOR* XXVI. Heawood, *Watermarks*, Nos. 2058 and 2059 (both 1673) are somewhat of the type.

P. 609, fragment of some combination of letters.

P. 613, foolscap, type IV.

P. 617, large one-handled pot with letters C/CH (or C/CR; in either case, the "C's" resemble upside down "G's"). A zigzag line decorates the inside of the curved top of the base.

P. 621, foolscap, type IV.

Pp. 625, 635, foolscap, type I, with countermark NLM in a rectangular frame. Klepikov, *ZOR* XXVI, No. 200 (168–) is such a mark.

P. 637ff., letters IW, probably as a countermark to and mixed with a circular arms, bisected vertically and containing a branch(?) on one side and half of a two-headed eagle on the other. Between the inner and outer circles at the top is a cross; around the ring they form is the word SCHENBERO. This arms is similar to Kamanin and Vytvyts'ka, *Vodiani znaky*, No. 1084 (1685, 1688, 1691), where no countermark is given. C. M. Briquet, *Les Filigranes* (Geneva, 1907), No. 934 is a mirror image of the main mark for the sixteenth century, but he notes that variants exist for a long period into the seventeenth century.

Inscriptions. P. iv (in the hand of M. P. Pogodin, as was pointed out to me by N. N. Rozov of GPB, who kindly assisted me in deciphering this inscription), "u S. P. Pobedonostseva 1845 . . . v, r. 15."

Pp. i, 698, various *proby pera*, including some in hands appearing later in the texts of the manuscript; for example, on p. i, "v leto ot sozdaniia mira 5530-go marta v 23 den' vo tsar", which is almost identical with and in the same hand as the opening line of the text on p. 259.

P. 3, a substitution alphabet, reproduced later on p. 503 in the same hand and with the corresponding Cyrillic letters. Under this is an eighteenth-century inscription, "kniga ruka bogoslovskaia i zhitie Aleksandra Osheven-skago".

Pagination. The manuscript is numbered by folios on the bottoms of pages, with the blank pages being assigned roman numerals, and by pages at the top. There are no signatures, but the "chapter" numbers given on p. 1 in the table of contents appear also on the first pages of the appropriate works.

Contents.
P. 1 (in late seventeenth-century *poluustav*), Table of Contents that reads:

(Pp. 2 and 4 are blank; p. 3, where new paper begins, contains only the inscriptions noted above.)

P. 5 (combination of *poluustav* and *skoropis'*), a set of paschal tables, the "ruka bogoslovskaia" of the contents, where the frames for some of the tables are in the form of a hand.

(Pp. 33–34 are blank; pp. 34 and 35, where new paper begins, are dirty.)

P. 35 (*skoropis'*), "Skazanie o sviatei knize sei glagolemei sluzhebnik . . . ," a copy of the introduction to the *Sluzhebnik* of 1651, printed in the *pechatnyi dvor* between May 13 and July 18. See A. S. Zernova, *Knigi kirillovskoi pechati, izdannye v Moskve v XVI–XVII vekakh. Svodnyi katalog* (Moscow, 1958), No. 231, p. 73. This introduction is reprinted in full from the 1651 edition by Pavel Stroev, *Opisanie staropechatnykh knig slavianskikh sluzhash-chee dopolneniem k opisaniiam bibliotek grafa F. A. Tolstova i kuptsa I. N. Tsarskago* (Moscow, 1841), pp. 128–137.

P. 47, "O chine edinoglasia pishet v toi zhe knige. Egda glagoletsia psaltir . . ." This and presumably the following work are based on the printed *Sluzhebnik*.

P. 49, "O chersvykh prosforakh, iako ne podobaet nad cherstvymi prosforami sluzhiti bozhestvennyia liturgii. Bliudi ubo o iereia i o sam . . ."

P. 50 (the hand is slightly smaller, but probably the same), "Ishkod, glava 12. I nuzhdakhu egiptiane otpustiti liudi skoro ot zemli. Vina sego

biashe iako uzhe desiat' iazv liutykh, zane otpushchenie ierusalimia iz raboty
svoeia preterpesha." Following this brief introduction to the twelve afflictions
visited on Egypt as described in 12 Exodus is a list of the afflictions written
in a substitution alphabet which had not, to the best of my knowledge, been
deciphered before now. There are also words and fragments of prayers in
this same hand and *tainopis'* on pp. 44, 45, 48, and 569. Given the similarity
of some of the letters to Cyrillic, the indication of the probable contents of
the long passage on p. 50, the short parallel Greek and Russian text in the
tainopis' on p. 48 ("Gospodi Iisuse Khriste Bozhe nash, pomilui nas" =
"Kirie Iisusu Khriste oteos imon eleison imas"), and the fact that the texts
are stressed, one can decipher the following alphabet:

а	б	в	г	д	е	ж	з	и	і	к	л
ꚃ	Ꙁ.б	ᴠᴠ	ʪ	Ꙋ	ꙅ	ю	ꙅ	н	ı	ɣ	ʌ

м	н	о	п	р	с	т	у	ф	θ	х	ω	ꙝ
ꙏ	и	≡	ᴎ	ꙍ	=	ꭓ	ꙡ	ꙿℇ	ꙮ	ꙭ	оо	ꙩꙩ

ц	ч	ш	щ	ъ(ь)	ы	ѣ	ю	я
ᵘ⁄₂	ꭥ.ꭥ	ꙏꙏ	ꙏꙏ⁄₂	ꙫ.ꙫ	ꙫ.ꙫ	ꙅ	ꙩ	ꭥ

P. 51 (late sixteenth-century *poluustav*; different paper that is somewhat
smaller than that in the rest of the MS), "3" (chapter number inserted by
the compiler of the contents on p. 1), "Glava 24. Kniga sviatago Ioanna
Damaskina filosofskaa, osmikh chiastekh slovo. Po bozhiiu obrazia s"zdan-
nom ia chelovekia . . ."

(Most of p. 74 and all of 75, which begins new paper, are blank.)

P. 76, ink drawing of St. Aleksandr Oshevenskii, labeled as such by the
skoropis' in which the prayer to him on p. 77 is copied.

(P. 78 is blank.)

P. 79 (late seventeenth- or early eighteenth-century *skoropis'*), "4"
"Mesiatsa apriliia v 20 den' prestavlenie prepodobnago ottsa nashego
Aleksandra kargopol'skogo novago chiudotvortsa igumena Oshevneva
monastyria . . ."

P. 97, the "Life" of St. Aleksandr Oshevenskii, founder of the monastery
named for him fifty kilometers north of Kargopol'. The heading begins:
"Mesiatsia apriliia v 20 den', zhitie i podvizi prepodobnago ottsa nashego
Aleksandra, sostavlshago prechestin' monastyr' nad rekoiu Chiuriugoiu vo
oblasti grada Kargopolia, bliz dyshushchago moria okiiana. Spisano iero-
monakhom Feodosiem toia zhe obiteli . . ."

(Hand changes near the bottom of p. 237 to *poluustav*; most of p. 254
and all of pp. 255–258 are blank.)

P. 259 (seventeenth-century *skoropis'*; different paper. The work begins with a very elaborate cinnabar initial), "5" "V leto ot sozdaniia mira 5539-go marta v 23 den', vo tsarstvo Tiveriia kesaria velikago Rima . . ."

(The hand changes on p. 274; p. 316 is blank but for a note by the copyist that he mistakenly skipped it; p. 400 is blank.)

P. 401 (*poluustav*; different paper), "6" "Nachalo gramote grecheskoi i ruskoi," a work by the Bulgarian monk Khrabr about the creation of the Cyrillic alphabet. Numerous variants are known in old Russian manuscripts, often in convoy with many of the grammatical works which follow here. The text here is apparently that published by K. Kuev, *Chernorizets Khrab"r* (Sofia, 1967), pp. 256–257, and by I. V. Iagich (Jagić), "Rassuzhdeniia iuzhnoslavianskoi i russkoi stariny o tserkovno-slavianskom iazyke," in *Issledovaniia po russkomu iazyku*, I (St. Petersburg, 1895): 635–636. Neither Kuev nor Jagić used 1311, but Jagić describes in detail (pp. 978–980) a manuscript that is strikingly similar in convoy (Collection of the Cathedral of Sancta Sophia in Novgorod, No. 318[1568], now presumably in GPB) and publishes many of the works found in 1311. I have compared only headings and opening words, but am reasonably confident that the published texts I refer to are the ones listed here for 1311.

P. 402 (change of hand to *skoropis*'), "Predislovie o bukovnitse" (Jagić, pp. 636–637).

P. 403, "Napisanie . . . o bukve" (pp. 637–644).

P. 409, "Imena znameniiu knizhnago pisaniia" (pp. 645–646).

P. 413, "Napisanie . . . o gramote" (pp. 648–673).

P. 452, "Prostopisannyia bukvy" (pp. 606–607).

P. 455, Maksim Grek's "O gramotiki" (pp. 601–605).

P. 463 (preceded apparently by a separate work for which I do not have the heading), "Damaskin . . . o padeniiakh" (pp. 771–778).

P. 475, "Ioanna Damaskina skazanie o osmi chastekh slova" (pp. 759–760), presumably followed by other separate works for which I failed to note headings.

P. 499, "Poslanie laodikiiskoe" of Fedor Kuritsyn. This copy, of the "grammatical type," second group, first series, was used in variants to the text published by N. A. Kazakova and Ia. S. Lur'e, *Antifeodal'nye ereticheskie dvizheniia na Rusi XIV-nachala XVI veka* (Moscow-Leningrad, 1955), pp. 272–276.

P. 503, a substitution alphabet, with corresponding Cyrillic letters, in part similar to the "poluslovnitsa" alphabet pictured by L. V. Cherepnin, *Russkaia paleografiia*, p. 264. The hand of the copyist here is apparently that of p. 50 where the previously mentioned *tainopis*' is found.

P. 504, "In prevod, vopros: Chego radi mnogi bukvy . . ." (Jagić, pp. 696–698).

P. 509, "Skazanie o bozhestvennom pisanii sviatykh knig, kako podobaet pisati sviatoe i posrednee i otpadshee, i chto pisati pod vzmetom i chego ne podobaet pokryvati" (pp. 724–730 or 1012–1018 ?). At the end (p. 561) in the hand of the copyist: "Spisano v pustyni sviatago Nila ubogim Shcherbakom [glossed 'Momisareg' = 'Gerasimom'] zhe molit pomianutisia." On this attribution in other MSS and for others of these grammatical works, see Jagić, pp. 730, 971, 1018, and his index of names, s.v. "Gerasim Palka."

P. 561, "Pouchenie ot bozhestvenykh pisanii . . . ponezhe podobaet nelenostno tshchanie imeti o sviatom pisanii velie prilezhanie s iziashchnym uprazhneniem."

(Most of p. 564 and all of 565–568 are blank.)

P. 569 (seventeenth-century *skoropis'*), "Pred kondaki i ikos ashche khoshcheshi. . . . 4 kondaki i ikosy so pokhvaloiu presviatei Bogorodits[y]. Kondak 1, glas 8. Izbrannoi voevode pobeditel'naia iako izbavlyia ot zol blagodarstvennaia . . ." This fills half the page; the remainder contains various *proby pera,* apparently by the same copyist (in the same black ink) but using various scripts, including *poluustav, viaz',* and the *tainopis'* as found previously on p. 50. Among the inscriptions in *viaz'* is "Prepodobnuiu ottsu nashemu Kirilu"; in *poluustav* is a line that repeats in part the one in *tainopis'* on p. 48: "Kirie Iisusu Khriste oteos imon. Ukaz v sviatoe tri eleison imas."

P. 570 (different *skoropis'*), heading for the "Life" of St. Martinian (d. 1448), second Igumen of the Ferapontov Monastery near Beloozero.

P. 571 (new *skoropis',* but with cinnabar headings and cinnabar corrections in the text done by the same copyist who used cinnabar on p. 569; change in paper beginning with p. 569 or 571 [my notes are unclear]), "Kondak 1, gla[. . .], Izbrannoi ot vsekh rodov bozhiei materi i tsaritse voskhodiashchei ot zemli k nebesnym . . . ," a collection of thirteen *kondaki* and twelve *ikosy* (chants or songs for church use).

P. 587 (seventeenth-century *skoropis'*), "Poklonenie na vsiak den' monakhu po pravile, egda dolzhno est', spati . . ."

(Half of p. 594, and all of 595–604 are blank; between pp. 600 and 601, ten folios have been cut out.)

P. 605, "8" "Chin diiakanskiia sluzhby v tserkvi. Nachalo 9-go chasa molitvami sviatykh otets nashikh . . ."

(Pp. 616–620 are blank; between pp. 616 and 617 at least six folios have been cut out.)

P. 621 (seventeenth-century *skoropis'*; change in paper), Ivan's first letter to Kurbskii in the "full" version, breaking off before the end (the text corresponds to that on p. 67 of *Poslaniia*) with the words: "ashche bo na torzhishchekh ikh videvshe rabavladets i startsu, iunoshu ili syna ottsu."

(Pp. 695–697), which form part of the final gathering of the letter, are blank.)

Remarks. With the exception of the portion of the manuscript beginning on p. 51, which clearly is of much earlier date, the bulk of 1311 probably was copied in the second half—possibly toward the end—of the seventeenth century. Presumably most of it was done in the Oshevenskii Monastery north of Kargopol'; the table of contents, listing the present works with the exclusion of items seven and nine, which have been replaced by other works, undoubtedly was drawn up after 1673. Patriarch Pitirim, whose testament was one of the two items now lost, died in that year. Instead of the "Spisok s gramoty turetskoi v Rim" (item nine), the manuscript now contains Ivan's letter in a copy that seems to be contemporary with the rest of the MS and which probably was in the Oshevenskii Monastery, as the *proby pera* at the beginning and end of the MS suggest that it was brought together in its present form where some of the texts were copied. The isolation of Ivan's letter, as it appears here in a separate gathering without any of the other connected works, certainly need not be taken as the "best proof" (*nailuchshim dokazatel'stvom*) that the epistle was sent to the "whole Russian tsardom" (*vsemu Rossiiskomu tsarstvu*) (Lur'e, *TODRL* X: 309). The missing "Copy of a Turkish Letter to Rome"—the apocryphal correspondence between the Sultan and the Emperor Leopold of the "legendary cycle" of *gramoty* in MS 43—is now to be found in MS GPB

Q.IV.172, beginning on fol. 17. Proof of this is the fact that on fol. 22 of Q.IV.172 in the same unique *tainopis'* discussed above is an inscription (which M. D. Kagan-Tarkovskaia has graciously communicated to me) that reads: "vsekh sorok tri tetrati raz[n ?]ykh." For more on Q.IV.172, see the remarks above under MS 1584/1321.

GPB, Collection of M. P. Pogodin No. 1567
Sixteenth and seventeenth centuries, 4°, viii + 104 fols.
    Descriptions. Bychkov, *Opisanie*, pp. 55–59; *Poslaniia*, pp. 533–540.
    Watermarks. Fols. 3–47, one-handled pot with letters E/DC, a mark probably of the 1620's or early 1630's. See my drawing and remarks in *Kritika* VI:99–101.
    Fols. 55–93, two variants of a hand (or glove) with a ruffle around the wrist and a crown over the fingers. N. P. Likhachev, *Paleograficheskoe znachenie bumazhnykh vodianykh znakov* (St. Petersburg, 1899), No. 1746 (1551) is a good likeness; there are variants given by both Likhachev and Briquet for the second half, especially the third quarter, of the sixteenth century.
    Fols. 95–102, unusual two-handled pot topped by grapes.
    Fols. 107–end, no mark.
    Pagination. There are two foliations, the old one of Stroev, where the sheets he inserted for the contents and to separate the individual parts of the manuscript are numbered consecutively with the remaining folios, and the new one, where his pages are assigned roman numerals. The old numbers are referred to here as in previous descriptions. Prior to Stroev's acquisition of the MS, at least the first portion of it was part of a larger compilation. There are arabic numbers, largely erased but faintly visible under the new foliation; in general they are much larger (e.g., one of the clearer cases is present fol. 45 = 260). In the first portion of the MS the following signatures are visible: fol. 2 = 1, fol. 12 = 2, fol. 27 = 3.
    Handwriting. Distinct changes in hand, coinciding with changes in paper, occur on fols. 55, 95, and 107; on fols. 76–80, there are corrections in a hand differing from that of the text.
    Contents. Bychkov provides a complete listing. The first portion of the MS contains in sequence Kurbskii's letter to Vas'ian (without the "preface" beginning "Vymete"), the first version of Kurbskii's first letter to Ivan (in which the final portion beginning "Slyshakh" is set off by a space and a cinnabar letter as though it were an independent work), Teterin to Morozov the *gramota Polubenskogo*, and the "full" version of Ivan's first letter to Kurbskii (lacking the ending). The other sections of the MS—copied apparently in the sixteenth century—include three letters dating from the time of Ivan IV (two of them associated with the priest Syl'vestr), the epistle of Spiridon-Savva, and fragments connected with the coronation of Ivan (notably an account of Monomakh's acquisition of the regalia, found in this variant in MS 1615). On Spiridon-Savva and the final work, see R. P. Dmitrieva, *Skazanie o kniaziakh vladimirskikh* (Moscow-Leningrad, 1955), pp. 54–55, 58–59, and 159–170, where the epistle is used in variants to the published text.
    Remarks. Since Stroev compiled a table of contents and had the MS bound in Tver' in 1832, we cannot tell when the four separate parts first came together. At one time, at least the portion containing the Kurbskii-Ivan works belonged to a larger compilation, although presumably any other

works found in convoy with them elsewhere, if here, would have followed Ivan's letter, assuming that signatures are a reliable indicator. Watermarks indicate that the first portion of the MS should not be dated as early as 1612 (*Poslaniia*, p. 537) but rather as much as two decades later.

GPB, Collection of M. P. Pogodin No. 1573
Mid-seventeenth century, 4°, 179 fols.
   Descriptions. Bychkov, *Opisanie*, pp. 139–146; *Poslaniia*, p. 554.
   Watermarks. Through fol. 119, two variants of a foolscap, type IV.
Fols. 120–end, two variants of a lily on a squarish shield under a crown. None of the watermarks could be satisfactorily identified, but the types seem to be from the mid-seventeenth century.
   Handwriting. Specific changes are noted below; however, it should be stressed that Bychkov's separation of the MS on the basis of apparent changes in hand is erroneous. Some of the changes merely represent the return of an earlier hand, while others may be only temporary aberrations in the style of a single copyist. The copyist of portions of the text is apparently the one who later added cinnabar headings in other portions. The one clear break in the manuscript occurs between fols. 119 and 120, but even here the cinnabar headings of the last portion may connect it with the first.
   Contents. Fols. 1–10v (apparently a single gathering; one seventeenth-century *skoropis'*), under the sheet later pasted over fol. 1 is a fragment of text from the "Extracts from the Kizilbash Books" in which the variants seem to coincide with those of the text in 2524 (see Appendix I, pt. b). On fols. 1v–10v is a genealogy of Russian princes through the sons of Ivan IV. As with other works in the MS, see Bychkov for details of headings and opening lines.
   (Fol. 10v is smudged; a mildew line at the bottom matches one on fol. 19, suggesting a former break in binding, with the intervening gathering bound out of line.)
   Fol. 11 (change in hand; fols. 11–18 form a separate gathering. In the middle of fol 14, yet another seventeenth-century *skoropis'* begins), a short chronicle of Russian events from Riurik to the accession of Boris Godunov. This text is a combination of the two short chronicles in 2524, on fols. 1–8 and 73v–76. The compiler of 1573 used the first extract as his basic text, including in it information found in the second extract but deleting entirely the *povest'* about the *smuta*, in the process contracting the information on the election of Boris, and using the entry on the earthquake in Nizhnii Novgorod as the basis for a separate tale appended at the end of the chronicle. Paleographic and textual evidence argues that 1573 used 2524, not a protograph, and probably not an intervening copy. The portions of the text which correspond reproduce one another verbatim, and the seams noted in 2524 have been smoothed over in 1573. However, where 1573 inserted under the year 7079 (1571) the entry from fol. 73v of 2524, the "V leta 7079-go" of the latter became "Togo zhe godu," since the year had already been noted in the preceding entry. Similarly, one notes a reverse case, where "Togo zhe leta" on fol. 74v of 2524, referring to the previously-mentioned 7092 (1584), becomes in 1573 "V leta 7092-go," since the copyist inserted the article in the wrong chronological order, following an article for 7105 (1597). On fol. 14v (see Fig. 2) there are three significant additions of information not in the first part of 2524, from which the text of 1573 is otherwise an exact copy, but from the second fragment on fols. 73v–76. In 2524, the entries

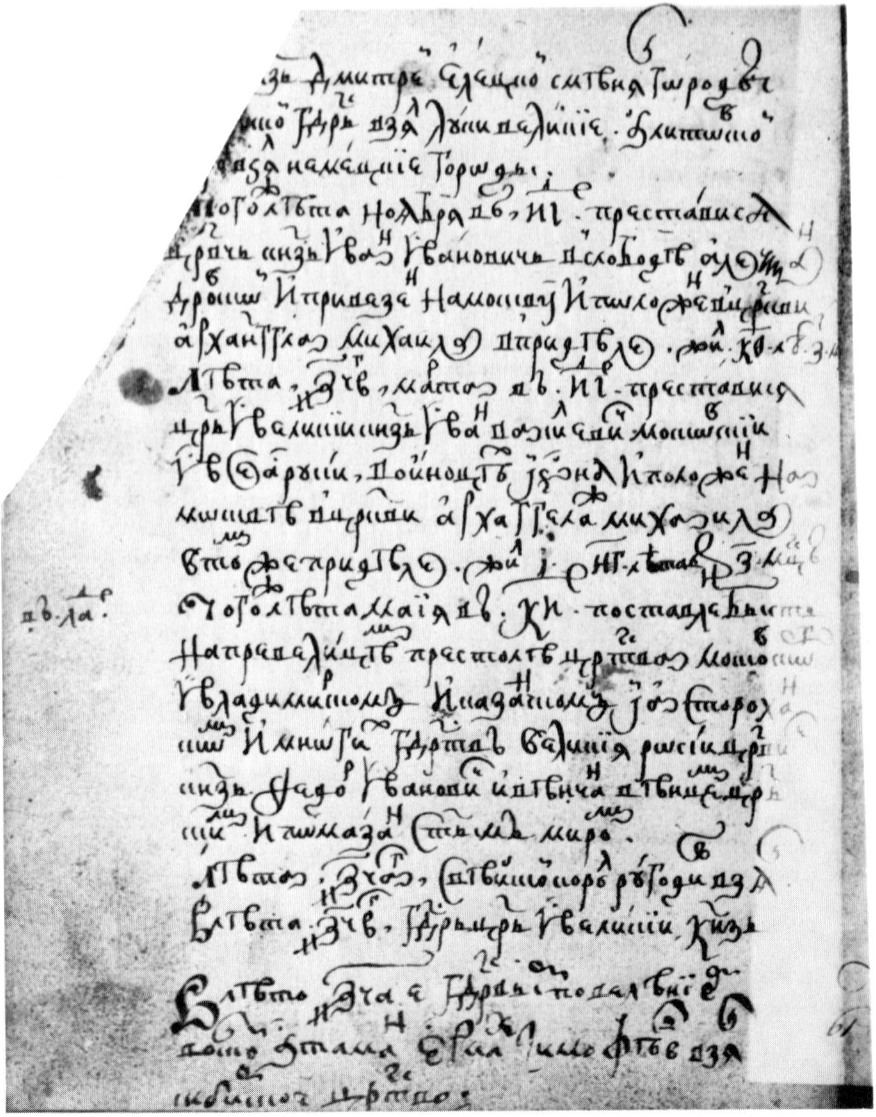

Fig. 2. Folio 14v of MS Pogodin 1573.

on the deaths of Ivan Ivanovich in 1580 and his father Tsar Ivan IV in 1584 end in similar fashion: "i polozhen v tserkvi arkhanggela Mikhaila v pridele" and "i polozhen na Moskve v tserkvi arkhanggela zhe Mikhaila v tom zhe pridele." After copying these words, 1573 added in the first case, "Zhil 29 let 7 mesiats" and in the second, "Zhil 53 let 7 mesiats." There is no change in hand, but the first of the additions runs past the normal margin and the second is squeezed in around the *vynosnye bukvy* of the next line. Moreover, in the next entry, where the basic text of 2524 as reproduced in 1573 gives May 29 as the day of Fedor Ivanovich's coronation, the same copyist noted an alternative date in the margin, "v 31 den'." Clearly the additions were done after the page had been copied following the first part of 2524, at which time the copyist looked again at the text he had in hand from fols. 73v–76, noted some information on these events which added to or differed from that which he had copied, and inserted it in the available space. He did not otherwise use the entries on these events in the second fragment in 2524, since the remainder of the information was repetitious. On fol. 14v, an entry added later in the seventeenth century in the bottom margin regarding the conquest of Siberia is also of some interest.

(Most of fol. 16v is blank.)

Fol. 17 (change in ink but probably not copyist), account of the earthquake in Nizhnii Novgorod, incorporating much of the material from the entry for the year 7105 (1597) in the chronicle of 2524, but adding various accounts of other earthquakes and natural disasters to form a separate tale.

(Most of fol. 18v is blank.)

Fols. 19–83 (return to the hand of fols. 1–10v, with the exception that the cinnabar headings in this portion are in a different hand, apparently that which begins on fol. 14. Similar cinnabar headings continue through fol. 91 and possibly also in the section beginning on fol. 120), the same sequence of works found in 2524 beginning on fol. 13 and continuing through fol. 85, with the following exceptions: in 1573 the short items following the first letter of Ivan on fols. 72v–76 are absent (including the chronicle extract, for obvious reasons). In all cases, the variants in 1573 and 2524 are very close, but do not necessarily indicate that one copied from the other—both MSS may have used a common source.

(Fol. 83 is glued to the end of the preceding gathering; clearly there is a physical break between fols. 83 and 84.)

Fol. 83v (with the exception of the first page of text, added by Stroev to replace a missing or damaged folio, the work, beginning with fol. 84, is in a hand similar to and probably the same as the preceding), tale told by the archdeacon Varlaam of the Vatoped Monastery on Mt. Athos about the false patriarch Pakhomii. A unique copy?

Fol. 88v (the hand clearly is that of the portion of manuscript prior to fol. 83), "Spisok s pravoslavnago spiska Isaina." On this text and its importance, see above, Chap. 2. At one time the work was "Glava 7." Other works in the MS had similar chapter headings noted in the margin, but they have been erased and are illegible.

Fol. 92 (change in hand to one similar to but not the same as that beginning on fol. 11; beginning of a new gathering), *gramota* of Tsar Mikhail Fedorovich to "Megapolinsk" princes Fionmarkon and Ruliak in 1613, published from this copy in *AI*, III: 4–7.

(Fol. 97v is blank.)

Fol. 98 (change in hand to that found in the middle of fol. 14 and in the cinnabar headings as noted above), letter of Mikhail Fedorovich to King Louis XIII in 1613, missing its ending. Bychkov notes that it differs some-what from the one published by V. N. Berkh, *Tsarstvovanie tsaria Mikhaila Fedorovicha i vzgliad na mezhdutsarstvie*, pt. II (St. Petersburg, 1832), pp. 116–159, sent to King Louis two years later. The *gramota* contains an extended account of the *smuta*; comparison of this account in the Berkh version with that in the *gramota* to Fionmarkon and Ruliak reveals a close textual connection between the two. The latter seems to be a severe con-traction of the former, produced by extracting whole paragraphs and piecing them together. Further study of these texts is required—including the second copy of the *gramota* to King Louis in F.XVII.15. On the identity of the Megapolinsk princes and Franco-Russian relations at the beginning of Mikhail Fedorovich's reign, see Givi Zhordaniia, *Ocherki iz istorii franko-russkikh otnoshenii kontsa XVI i pervoi poloviny XVII vv.*, pt. 1, Tiflis, 1959, Essay 5.

(Fols. 115 and 116 are a single sheet of paper, which indicates that the loss of the ending of one work and the beginning of the next resulted from the loss of at least two folios in the center of the gathering.)

Fol. 116 (shift in style but probably no change in copyist; on fols. 117–117v, the hand seems to be that of the text on fol. 92ff., but by fol. 118v the hand is clearly that of the *gramota* to Louis), letter of Patriarch Ioasaf dated September 14, 1634, about the removal of Suzdal' archbishop Iosif Kurt-sevich and his exile to the Solovetskii Monastery; lacking the beginning.

(Half of fol. 119 and all of 119v are blank and the latter smudged.)

Fol. 120 (change in hand; the text contains some cinnabar corrections. Signatures begin here with fol. 120 = 68 and end with fol. 176 = 76[?]), "dokonchal'naia gramota" of Władysław, King of Poland, dated April 23, 1635, confirming the peace treaty with Moscow.

(Fol. 173v is blank.)

Fol. 174, description of the ceremonies in Moscow on the arrival of the Polish embassy in February 1635, to confirm the peace treaty. Published from this copy in *AI*, III: 332–335. According to this account, the Poles left on March 23; two days later Shakhovskoi was sent after them to conduct further negotiations, as he relates in his *Domashnie zapiski*.

Remarks. MSS 1573 and 2524 have the same provenance and were copied in the middle of the seventeenth century. Judging from watermarks, 2524 is to be dated ca. 1650; while the portion of 1573 beginning on fol. 120 may somewhat antedate that, the remainder of the manuscript undoubtedly was compiled after 2524, using it and probably some of its sources. The evidence for this in the short chronicle discussed above is unequivocal: both the small textual and paleographic features and the fact that in reproducing an extended portion of the convoy of 2524, 1573 consciously omitted material used earlier.

The work was done in the region near Kholmogory, a fact established by the inscriptions in 2524 and the Dvina chronicle information, with its connections to the text found with the *Kholmogorskaia letopis'*. Moreover, the convoy links both MSS to the Solovetskii Monastery and 2524 to the Antonievo-Siiskii Monastery, the two major cultural centers in the region at mid-century. Additional evidence points to the latter: BAN 32.8.5, which contains a copy of Ivan's letter very similar to that of 1573 and 2524, textually is very close to another MS known to have been in the Siiskii Monastery; furthermore, the monastery had been the place of exile of

Filaret Romanov during the reign of Boris Godunov. A fourth manuscript, probably later in date, but connected with 1573 and 2524 in the same northern milieu, is F.XVII.15.

For this book the provenance and contents of these manuscripts are extremely important: Shakhovskoi was in exile in this northern region very near the time when 1573 and 2524 were copied, and their convoys point to a connection with him and to one of the sources from which the first Kurbskii letter was composed.

The manuscripts are also of interest because of the creative literary activity they evidence. It is rare that we have two stages of the editorial process on a work such as the short chronicle here represented in copies of what one might term the "author's text." Study of this chronicle in connection with the *gramoty* containing accounts about the *smuta* may provide new material for the history of mid-seventeenth-century Russian literature.

GPB, Collection of M. P. Pogodin No. 1615
Second quarter of the seventeenth century, 4°, 250 fols.
  Description. Bychkov, *Opisanie*, pp. 454–457.
  Watermarks. Throughout, a two-handled pot with letters G/LS, in two main and other minor close variants. One variant is continuous in the section fols. 71–93.

Fols. 6, 44–46, 67, 68, two variants of a two-handled pot with letters CB.
Fol. 248, pillars with letters MC between them. Of the type Geraklitov, *Filigrani*, No. 1126 (1636–1637), where the letters are CM.

  Inscriptions. Fols. 1–54, 57, "Kniga glagolemoia pokolipsis goroda Venevy sobornoi tserkvi popa [An]dreia a po(d)pisal svoeiu rukoiu. Siia kniga glagolemoia [poko]lip"sis goroda Venevy sobornoi tserkvi po[pa] Andreia Vasil'eva." "syna." As noted by Bychkov, p. 456, one initial folio and several others are missing. The separate "syna" on fol. 57, in a different hand, probably carries over from an inscription in a now lost section that preceded fol. 1.

There are various eighteenth-century marginal notations throughout, including the repetition several times of the opening words from the riddle: "Stoit more na piati stol"pekh. Tsar' reche, 'More, ty, more, potikha moia'; a tsaritsa reche, 'More, ty, more, pogibel' moia.'" By curious coincidence, in a similar fashion but different hand, these lines find their way onto the pages of MS GPB O.XVII.17, which contains the writings of Isaiah of Kam'ianets' in Podillia. Among the other eighteenth-century inscriptions is, "Vse presvetleishaia derzhavneishaia velikaia gosudarnia imperatritsa Anna Ioannovna samoderzhitsa vserosiskaia v nyneshnem 730 godu."

Fol. 250v (in eighteenth-century[?] hand), "gramota ot tsaria turlkago [*sic* = turskago?] tsariu ot Boga preproslavlennumu."

  Pagination. Although trimming has eliminated many of the signatures, one can distinguish in the hand of the copyist consecutive numbering from fol. 94 = 20 through fol. 214 = 36. Assuming eight folios to a gathering, in the original MS there must have been about 152 folios prior to fol. 94. Faint foliation in pencil can be distinguished under the present foliation in ink. Fol. 16 was "1" (according to the penciled numbers), fols. 58–70 were "13"–"25", fol. 3 was "27", fol. 4 was "28", etc. Beginning with fol. 71, the penciled numbers follow the order and magnitude of the present numbers.

Fols. 58–70 are somewhat smaller than those on either side of them. This is probably the result of damage to the pages and then rebinding of them out of line from the others. The manuscript is in fragile condition, with water stains and repairs on the inner edges of many folios. Comparison of the shape of the water stains on fols. 58–70 with those elsewhere in the MS suggests that when the staining occurred, these folios were at the end of the MS next to folios with similar stains and not in their present position. Following fol. 70, a portion of the MS is missing, as the texts on fol. 70v and fol. 71 lack ending and beginning respectively.

Handwriting. 1615 is possibly the work of a single copyist, but breaks in hand occur at the following points: fol. 58, where the hand is larger and the margins smaller than in the preceding 57 fols.; fol. 62 at the beginning of the "Tale of the Two Embassies"; fol. 66, where the hand that preceded fol. 62 resumes.

Contents. Bychkov gives these in extenso; here I list only the beginning and concluding works.

Fol. 1, various religious works, including primarily an "Apokolipsis sviatago Ioanna Teologa," which contains at the end on fol. 57, following a space for a miniature, the line from which Bychkov dated the MS: "Napisana siia kniga Pokolipsiia leta 7140-go godu." Immediately following this is the beginning of the next work in the same hand with no distinctive break in style. To me this suggests the possibility that the date was merely copied in along with the rest of the text and is not necessarily the date of the copy in 1615.

Fol. 58, Kurbskii's first letter to Ivan in the first version.

Fol. 62, "Tale of the Two Embassies," in the second redaction according to M. D. Kagan, *TODRL* XI:242. This copy comes from a defective text, as it begins in the middle of Ishchein's embassy with the words, "i Tsaregradskago, tsar' dumu dumav z gnevom otvet velel dati . . ." Sugorskii's embassy begins on fol. 63v and breaks off at the bottom of fol. 70v with the words, "da tsysarskoi tsar' poslal poltarasta tysiachi sasliiakh(?) i na korablekh na pomoshch' i turskikh liudei bozhiim izvole."

Fol. 71, fragment, lacking the beginning, from the homily of Gregory the Theologian about drunkenness; followed by a long series of selections from the Church fathers and other religious works.

. . .

Fol. 224v, "O shapki Manamakhove. Ot velikogo i blazhennago kniazia Vladimera, izhe prosvetil zemliu sviatym kreshcheniem . . ." This text is also in MS 1567.

Fol. 226v, "Siia azbuki istolkovanyia sviatymi ottsy, i sviatymi apostoly i sviatymi proroki slozheny." A series of ten "azbuki."

Fol. 241v, account of an earthquake in Italy and Turkey in 1500. Printed in *Novgorodskie letopisi* (St. Petersburg, 1879), pp. 71–73.

Fol. 244, conclusion of the third parable of Solomon, and an account concerning his wisdom and the judgment of two men by his father David.

Fol. 244v, homily of Kirill the Philosopher, beginning, "Brat moi Varflomeiu priidi ko mne aki pchela tsvetu . . ."

Fol. 246v, "Slovo o nekoem chelovetse. Nekii chelovek voin udolets ezdia po poliu . . ."

Fol. 249v, homily from the *Pchela* about evil women, beginning, "Nichto zhe podobna zloi zhene . . ."

Remarks. Although I question Bychkov's dating to 1632, in any case the

MS surely was copied in the 1630's in one scriptorium. Given the breaks which set off fols. 58–70, containing the Kurbskii letter and the "Tale of the Two Embassies," it is difficult to draw firm conclusions about the original convoy. The inscription at the end of the MS suggests the possibility that the "Legendary Correspondence" between the sultan and Ivan was once part of the convoy, although since the second half of the inscription is the opening lines from the Kurbskii letter, the first half may simply be a distortion of a title including Kurbskii's name.

GPB, Collection of the Russian Archaeological Society No. 43
Seventeenth century, 4°, i + 73 fols.

Descriptions. D. I. Prozorovskii, *Opis' drevnikh rukopisei, khraniashchikhsia v muzee Imperatorskogo Russkogo arkheologicheskogo obshchestva* (St. Petersburg, 1879), pp. 66–69; A. I. Sobolevskii, *Perevodnaia literatura,* p. 242 and passim; M. D. Kagan, "Legendarnyi tsikl gramot turetskogo sultana k evropeiskim gosudariam—publitsisticheskoe proizvedenie vtoroi poloviny XVII v.," *TODRL* XV:228, 240 and passim.

Watermarks. Fols. 1, 6, 7, 9–14, 15, 17, 20, foolscap, type IV, without any countermark. Possibly the mark on fols. 15, 17, and 20 is a slight variant on somewhat different paper.

Fols. 22, 24, 25, 27 (paper ends fol. 28), a different foolscap, type IV, with a somewhat unusual shape where the ruff normally joins at the back of the collar.

Fols. 29, 31, 32, 34, another foolscap, type IV. While that on fols. 29/34 undoubtedly is a variant of the mark on 31/32, the "4" under the former is crooked and the trefoil of circles missing.

Fols. 35, 36, 37, 42, three circles, tangential in a vertical row; the bottom one set on a rectangular box with letters RGI (or RGL).

Fols. 43, 44, 46, 47, pillars with crude letters MC.

Fols. 45, 48, different pillars with letters TI. Pillars of this and the preceding type are most common in Russian manuscripts from the second quarter of the seventeenth century.

Fols. 51, 53, 56, 58, 60, 63, two variants of a one-handled (?—if any) pot with letters M/LC.

Fols. 65–72, squarish shield containing a lily; surmounted by a crown. Apparently over letters, which are faint but may be one of the following combinations: TA, FA, EA.

Inscriptions. At the bottom of fol. 73v in green ink is a former classification number for the MS: "ruk. 241/925." On fol. 42v, what one might term *proby pera* read: (in eighteenth-century hand) "Iaryzhatskoi[?] chin byl chrit[?] 437 let"; (in seventeenth-century hand) "i prosviashche."

Pagination. Signatures and foliation are noted below. For determining the breaks in the manuscript, it is of some use to note the following connected folios which form centers of gatherings: 3/4, 11/12, 18/19, 24/25, 39/40. There is physical evidence of a break between fols. 7 and 8, and another between fols. 14 and 15. Fol. 21 is pasted to the preceding folio but apparently belongs with the following one, the final folio of the previous gathering apparently having been lost. In the second portion of the MS (beginning on fol. 43) presumably one gathering at the beginning and an undetermined number at the end have been lost.

Contents. Fol. 1 (seventeenth-century *skoropis'*—what I would term "*prikaz-style*"; fol. 1 has signature "1", apparently written by the copyist), account of the coronation of Michał Wiśniowiecki as Polish king in September 1669, translated from German and Dutch pamphlets or newspapers (*kuranty*) on October 13. Sobolevskii, *Perevodnaia literatura*, p. 242, gives headings and opening lines for this and the following account of the same event, a translation from German dated October 24. The heading for the second work (which begins at the top of fol. 8) is crowded onto the bottom of fol. 7v in a different hand from that of the text which precedes and follows; this heading reads: "Perevod s nemetskago pisma oktiabria 1-go chisla. Perevedeno v nyneshnem vo 178-m godu oktiabria v 24 den'."

(Fol. 10v is blank; fols. 8–14 have contemporary[?] foliation 1–7.)

Fol. 11, apocryphal correspondence between the Sultan and the Habsburg Emperor Leopold, dated 1663; published from this copy by M. D. Kagan, *TODRL* XV:247–249. At the end on fol. 14v, separated from the preceding text by a space, is precisely the same heading as that inserted at the bottom of fol. 7v. Kagan's inclusion of this heading in her published text is probably erroneous; it undoubtedly belongs with a work which normally would have followed in the next gathering. Such headings in the Muscovite *kuranty* invariably come at the beginning, not the end; possibly here there was some confusion in copying or binding, whereby the preceding account about the Polish coronation actually followed the legendary correspondence. Kagan takes issue with Sobolevskii, who listed this correspondence as a translation; it appears, however, that Sobolevskii was correct, at least for the sultan's letter. Details about this and similar cases mentioned below will be found in my dissertation, but one might note here a published pamphlet (presumably a slightly altered version of an earlier one) containing a very similar letter in German: *Schrecklicher und Gantz grausamer Absage-Brief Welchen Der Tuerckische Kaiser An den Roemischen Kaiser ueberschicket. In diesem 1683. Jahr.*

(On fol. 14v is the seventeenth-century notation "odna tetrat'"; fols. 15 and 15v are blank, but for a signature "41"; paper change begins with fol. 15 ?)

Fol. 16 (unusual small seventeenth-century *skoropis'* by a copyist who ignored the scoring of the pages and ran well over his right margins), "Legendary Correspondence" between Ivan IV and the Sultan in a defective copy containing only part of the letter of the Sultan; used in variants to publication of the text by M. D. Kagan, *TODRL* XIII:266–269. The variants in this copy do not group it closely with the copies in 1573 and 2524. The text ends on the top of fol. 18.

Fol. 18, Kurbskii's first letter to Ivan in the first version but a very mangled copy that derives from an early protograph and is extremely important (see App. II). The text ends at the bottom of fol. 19v.

Fol. 20, "Otpiska Timokhi Teterina iz Litvy v Iur'ev livonskoi k boiarinu . . . Morozovu," a fragment corresponding to lines 1–16 in Kuntsevich, col. 489.

(Part of fol. 20, all of 20v, the following unnumbered folio, and 21 are blank, but for a signature "42" on fol. 21, written by the same copyist who numbered fol. 15 as "41".)

Fol. 22 (different seventeenth-century *skoropis'*; change in paper), "Large" epistle of the sultan to the Polish king, allegedly written in 1637; published from this copy by M. D. Kagan, *TODRL* XV:240–243. As with the correspondence between the sultan and the emperor, the heading of this apocryphal letter correctly terms the Russian text a translation. Clearly the letter has a common source with a published pamphlet: *A Vaunting, Daring and a Menacing Letter, Sent from Sultan Morat to the great Turke, from his Court at Constantinople, by his Embassadour Gobam, to Vladislaus King of Poland, &c.* . . . (London, Printed by I. Okes, 1638).

Fol. 25v, apocryphal letter from the sultan to the German princes, dated 1663; published from this copy by M. D. Kagan, *TODRL* XV:245–246. The original, from which this letter is clearly a translation, is very similar to the following pamphlet: *Des Tuerckischen Kaeysers der gantzen Chriheit und aller die sich Christen nennen ewigen abgesagten Erbfeinds-Brieff So er durch den Legaten dem Roemischen Kaeyser zugesendet haben sol. Im Jahr 1663.*

Fol. 27 (beginning in the middle of the page immediately following the preceding work but in a different *skoropis'*), account of the entrance of Jan Sobieski into Krakow and the burial of Jan Kazimierz and Michał Wiśniowiecki in January 1676. After a short introduction, the work is divided into thirty-one short numbered paragraphs. Sobolevskii, *Perevodnaia literatura*, pp. 242–243, gives the heading and beginning of the work.

(Half of fol. 29v is blank.)

Fol. 30 (change in hand back to that of fols. 22–27), description of signs in the heavens over Hungary in 1671 predicting a victorious league between Poland, the Empire, and Muscovy against the Turks. This translated pamphlet is listed in Sobolevskii, *Perevodnaia literatura*, pp. 247–248, with reference to two published variants. The version in 43 seems to represent a variant later than either of these. In the original pamphlet, the text was accompanied by a picture in which the various parts of the phenomenon were labeled in the Latin alphabet. In the presumed first version of the Russian translation, where referred to in the text these letters were simply transcribed phonetically. Then they were changed to follow the Cyrillic alphabet; here, having lost all meaning, they have been eliminated entirely.

Fol. 31, two articles apparently deriving from *kuranty*, dealing with a miraculous occurrence in Germany and events involving the Poles and the Turks in the Ukraine. The headings and beginnings are in Sobolevskii, *Perevodnaia literatura*, pp. 244–245.

Fol. 32, translation from a German printed pamphlet concerning a prophecy of misfortunes to befall Poland, some of them at the hands of the Turks. Details about this unique copy are in Sobolevskii, *Perevodnaia literatura*, pp. 245–246. Although I have not seen the German text, probably the original of this work is the 1662 edition referred to in the title of the following: *Des Königreichs Pohlen Sonder- und Wunderbare Prophezeyung So Anno 1595 von einem Gottesfürchtigen Manne aus Cracau geschehen. Anno 1662 gedruckt, und nun dem curieusen Liebhaber zu Gefallen wieder nach- gedruckt mit angehängten Weissagungen der Sect. D. Lutheri.* Gedruckt zu Bresslau, Im Jahr Chr. 1698.

Fol. 35v (beginning with the title of the new work near the bottom of the page, a different seventeenth-century *skoropis'*; the "cinnabar" capitals of this and the following work seem to have been added in red pencil or crayon), correspondence allegedly exchanged between the Cossacks and the Sultan in 1678; published from this copy by M. D. Kagan, "Russkaia versiia 70-kh godov XVII v. perepiski zaporozhskikh kazakov s turetskim sultanom," *TODRL* XIV:311. The indication of the heading that this is a translation from Polish is probably accurate. See my "On the Origin of the 'Corre- spondence' between the Sultan and the Cossacks," *Recenzija: A Review of*

Soviet Ukrainian Scholarly Publications (Cambridge, Mass.), vol. I, no. 2 (1971), 3–46.

Fol. 36v (slight shift in hand), translation of an account about the burial of the Polish kings (see above, beginning fol. 27) and the coronation of Jan Sobieski in January 1676. Sobolevskii, *Perevodnaia literatura*, p. 243, quotes details from another MS. One variant is noteworthy—instead of the "V nyneshnem vo 184-m godu" of the other MS, here one reads "v proshlom," which dates this variant after 1676. The source for the work may well have been a printed pamphlet.

(On fol. 39 there is a change in hand or perhaps merely a shift by the same copyist without any break in text.)

Fol. 41v, an account deriving apparently from *kuranty* and datelined The Hague, August 17, 1680, concerning a prophecy by two old men in Spain about various calamities to culminate in 1695 with the Final Judgment. The opening lines are in Sobolevskii, *Perevodnaia literatura*, pp. 248–249.

(Much of fol. 42v is blank but for the *proby pera* noted above.)

Fol. 43 (*poluustav*, first half of the seventeenth century; change in paper. Contemporary signatures begin with "2" on fol. 43 and continue through "4" on fol. 64v; later, "5" was added on fol. 73v. Modern foliation in pencil begins with "1" on fol. 43), portions of a chronicle of Lithuanian history missing both the beginning and the ending. The first entries deal with the reign of Skirmont and the last with that of Vitovt. Prozorovskii, *Opis'*, pp. 68–69, provides a list of the chapter headings.

Remarks. There is a clear division in the manuscript between the portion up to fol. 43 and that which begins there and represents a manuscript copied earlier in the seventeenth century. In the first portion, the component parts seem to be fols. 1–14, 15–20, and 22–42, but the paper in the first two of these sections is very similar and the second and third sections at an early stage seem to have been connected, as indicated by the signatures. Despite clear lines of demarcation, I am inclined to think that fols. 1–42 came together in the present form at a fairly early date, which might mean soon after 1680, the date of the last extract from the *kuranty*.

The contents suggest that this compilation is the work of someone associated with the *Posol'skii prikaz*, where the *kuranty* were produced and kept. Moreover, the convoy of "legendary correspondence" and accounts of miraculous happenings just might indicate that the person who included a gathering containing the Kurbskii letter knew something more about its origins and real nature than anyone else has known until now.

GPB, F. XVII. 15

Seventeenth century, 2°, xv + 371 fols.

Descriptions. Sibirskie letopisi, publ. by the Arkheograficheskaia kommissiia (St. Petersburg, 1907), pp. x–xvi; *Povest' o prikhozhenii Stefana Batoriia na grad Pskov*, ed. V. I. Malyshev (Moscow-Leningrad, 1952), pp. 117–119, 124.

Watermarks (N.B.: These should be rechecked).

Fols. 7ff., Strasburg bend (lily over bend) with letters WP under the bar of the bend; attached to the bottom is a device with a "4" over some letter or letters.

Fol. 10, foolscap, type II, with countermark FB. Could Laucevičius, *Popierius*, No. 2637 (1662) with countermark *E*B be related? Followed by a different foolscap.

Fol. 27, arms of the Seven Provinces.

Fols. 28, 332, foolscap, type IV, over letters CLP. Klepikov, *ZOR* XXVI, No. 42 (1663) is such a mark.

Fol. 32, foolscap, type IV, with countermark GB on the left half of the sheet. Listed as No. 85 (1665, 1671) in Klepikov, *ZOR* XXVI.

Fol. 60, indistinct coat of arms over a banner with letters on it.

Fols. 68, 308ff., lily on a squarish shield under a crown; over letters PR.

Fols. 198, 338, two-headed eagle with a single crown; over monogram DVL.

Fols. 207, 251(?), ALLE MODE PAPPIER. Should be checked against Laucevičius, *Popierius*, Nos. 17 and 18 (1666, 1668).

Fol. 208, unclear arms depicting a quadruped on a shield topped by a large crown.

Fol. 356, letter "B" on a fluted shield.

Fol. 363, one-handled pot with letters P/DP; probably a variant of Geraklitov, *Filigrani*, No. 554 (1622).

Inscriptions. Fol. 1, "Iz sobranii Petra Frolova 1820, goda."

Fol. 135ff. (seventeenth-century hand), "Siia kniga diaka Dmitreia Stefanova syna Volottskova[?]."

Contents (see the description in *Sibirskie letopisi* for further details). Fols. 1–23, various short works, including "Skazanie . . . o kadile" and "O skufii popovskoi," which are apparently also in 4469; the tale of the twelve dreams of Mamer; "O razmeshenii iazyk i liudei divnikh" and various similar "definitions" from mythology or ancient history; the monk Khrabr's account of the creation of the Cyrillic alphabet, published from this copy by K. Kuev, *Chernorizets Khrab"r* (Sofia, 1967), pp. 343–345.

(Fol. 23v and the following folio are blank.)

Fol. 24 (paper change?; shift but probably not change in hand; gatherings numbered beginning with "1"), "Vypiska iz istoriia kievskago . . . ," beginning with the year 2244 and ending with the coronation of Ivan IV.

Fol. 38v, "Tale about the White Cowl" in the first extended redaction, according to N. N. Rozov, "Povest' o novgorodskom belom klobuke . . . ," *TODRL* IX:214.

Fol. 54v, "O prishestvii poslov k velikomu kniaziu Aleksandru Nevskomu."

Fol. 56v, Kurbskii's first letter to Ivan, apparently in the first version (this should be checked).

(Ends fol. 58; 58v and three following folios are blank.)

Fol. 59 (possible change in hand, but similar to the preceding and apparently of the same "school" as the hand in 2524), table of contents for "The Kazan' History," followed by the foreword on fols. 64 and 64v, a blank folio and the text beginning on fol. 65. Ends on fol. 191v with Chapter 79.

Fol. 192, a chronicle extract including largely Dvina information, with entries for the years 7061 (1553) through 7066 (1558). Apparently these entries do not overlap with those in the "Short Chronicle of the Dvina *voevody*" as extracted in 2524. The information found independently in these two variants, judging from my incomplete notes on F. XVII.15, is combined in the Dvina Chronicle text as published by N. I. Novikov in *DRV*, pt. xviii (Moscow, 1791), pp. 11–15.

Fol. 194, "O vziatii tsarstva Sibirskogo," the "Stroganov version" of the tale about Ermak's campaign in the short redaction according to N. A.

Dvoretskaia, "Arkheograficheskii obzor spiskov povestei o pokhode Ermaka," *TODRL* XIII:478. Variants from this copy were used in the publication of the text in *Sibirskie letopisi*, pp. 97–104.

(Followed by two blank folios.)

Fol. 198, "Tale of the Two Embassies" in the transitional redaction according to M. D. Kagan, *TODRL* XI:243. The two short *gramoty* found at the end of the first redaction are absent and the work concludes "i nariad u nikh otluchili. Amin'."

(Followed by two blank folios.)

Fol. 206, table of contents for the tale of the siege of Pskov by Stefan Bathory, which begins on fol. 209; in the fourth variant of the basic redaction, which, according to Malyshev, *Povest' o prikhozhenii*, p. 119, must have been written at the very end of the seventeenth century, judging from style and language.

(Followed by one blank folio.)

Fol. 255 (shift in hand), "Journey of Trifon Korobeinikov," in the full redaction with interpolations from the Gospels. The names and numbers are often miscopied, and the chapter on the passage through the Red Sea is missing. Similar to the copies in MSS GIM, Uvarov Collection No. 699 and GBL, Collection of the OIDR No. 113. See *Pravoslavnyi palestinskii sbornik*, IX, 3, pp. xlvi, lv, lx.

Fol. 279v, "Povest' o Ioanne Bolshem Kolpake."

(One blank folio follows fol. 280.)

Fol. 281, the *Skazanie* of Avraamii Palitsyn in the later of the two variants but an imperfect copy including only the first twenty-six of the seventy-nine chapters.

(A change of hand on fol. 321v is temporary; the original hand returns.)

Fol. 328, letter of Tsar Mikhail Fedorovich to Louis XIII. I have not compared this with the version in 1573.

Fol. 340, account of a Turkish expedition in 1614/1615 against the Poles.

Fol. 340v, account about the arrival of Filaret in Moscow in 1619.

(Followed by two blank folios.)

Fol. 341, "Postavlennaia gramota" of Patriarch Ieremii establishing the Russian patriarchate.

Fol. 344, account of Filaret's installation as Patriarch in 1619, with added notes on the installation of Germogen in 1606, Iosif in 1642, and Nikon in 1652. The concluding lines suggest that the work was composed before 1666

Fol. 352v, "Extracts from the Kizilbash Books," in the "normal version, Group B"; a significant variant in the opening line connects this copy closely with that in 2524. See Appendix I, pt. b.

Fol. 364, "Rospis' kitaiskomu gosudarstvu . . .," published from this copy by N. F. Demidova and V. S. Miasnikov, *Pervye russkie diplomaty v Kitae* (Moscow-Leningrad, 1966), pp. 41–55. This version of the "Rospis'" is found in many Chronographs; the copy in F.XVII.15 is apparently very close to one in MS GBL, Undol'skii Collection No. 761, which also contains a portion of the "Tale of the Two Embassies" in the first redaction.

Remarks. Estimates of the date of F.XVII.15 range from the middle of the seventeenth to the beginning of the eighteenth centuries. Highly tentative watermark data suggest the third quarter of the seventeenth century, with the final pages having been written on a remnant of earlier paper. Despite some indications of breaks (notably between fols. 23 and 24), probably the MS is the product of a single scriptorium and was copied at one time. Both content and hand suggest close ties with 1573 and 2524. Textually and paleographically the MS deserves closer examination, as my work on it was hurried and incomplete.

GPB, Collection of A. A. Titov No. 2350 (Shelf list No. 1121)
Second half of the seventeenth century, 4°, ii + 778 + fol. 345A + 33 blank fols.

Descriptions. GPB, *Kratkii otchet Rukopisnogo otdela za 1914–1938 gg.*, p. 58 (the number is given as 2250, but this must be an error); M. A. Salmina, "'O prichinakh gibeli tsarstv', sochinenie nachala XVII veka," *TODRL* X:336; Zimin, *Sochineniia*, App. II (by M. D. Kagan), p. 367; *Poslaniia*, pp. 560–562.

Watermarks. Fols. 1–218, various foolscaps, type IV, apparently none the same as the ones later in the MS.

Fols. 219–272$_{ii}$, paschal lamb on a shield under a crown.

Fols. 274ff. (including 347, 410, 578–601), unusual foolscap with countermark NRD.

Fols. 297, 394ff. (the main mark to about 470), 602ff., foolscap, also of unclassified type, similar to Laucevičius, *Popierius*, No. 2614 (1668).

Fols. 310ff., 477ff., 720, foolscap, type IV.

Fols. 350 (old numbering = one of the blanks following new f. 343), 658ff., 741ff., foolscap, type I, countermark E(or F)B(or R).

Fol. 650, foolscap, type IV.

Salmina notes a "very deformed foolscap with letters MR," presumably in the section 274ff.; however I have not seen these letters. My results should be rechecked.

Inscriptions. Fol. ii, "1881, iiunia (?) 10or.," apparently Titov's notation of date of purchase and cost of the MS. GPB acquired it in 1915.

Fol. 778, various *proby pera*, including "Siiu knigu chtpr (= ?) pop Aleksandr 1912-g."

Pagination. There are two sets of folio numbers: the old ones at the top include the blanks; the new ones at the bottom, which I follow here, number only the pages containing text.

Contents. Fol. 1 (seventeenth-century *poluustav*), the "Skazanie" of Avraamii Palitsyn, this copy not used in the edition by O. A. Derzhavina, *Skazanie Avraamiia Palitsyna* (Moscow-Leningrad, 1955).

(Following the ending on fol. 218 is one blank folio.)

Fol. 219 (change in hand and paper; the folio is dirty), a portion of a chronicle or chronograph beginning, "ot Adama zhe do potopa let 2042 a ot potopa do rozdeleniia iazyk let 529 . . ."; the final item deals with St. Savva and the last date mentioned is 6605 (1097).

(Fols. 272$_i$ and 272$_{ii}$ are blank; 272$_{ii}$, the end of a gathering, is smudged on the verso side.)

Fol. 274 (change in hand—*poluustav* tending toward *skoropis'*; change in paper. This portion of the MS has signatures fol. 281 = 2[?], fol. 289 = 3, fol. 297 = 4), "On the Reasons for the Destruction of Empires," published by Salmina, *TODRL* X where this copy, in the First Group, was used for the opening paragraphs of the text. Following the ending on fol. 300v is a work that appears in convoy with it elsewhere, a parable about the ingratitude of a man who had been saved from misfortune—a variant of a tale in the *Gesta Romanorum* (see Bychkov, *Opisanie*, p. 317).

(Following the ending of fol. 308 are three blank folios; fol. 309 contains only a late religious inscription.)

Fol. 310 (change in paper and hand—*skoropis'* of the second half of the seventeenth century), "Tale of the Two Embassies" in the second redaction according to M. D. Kagan, but with some important variants. Between the ending of Kvashnin's embassy and the short *gramoty* which follow (fol. 324) is a section of *tainopis'*, presumably identifying the copyist. It reads (with the Cyrillic numbers rendered as arabic numbers and beginning with the concluding words of the preceding text):

i vyshli poslany na Petrov den' togo zhe godu i gishmia kto
1. 1,1. 1. 2,6. 1,7. 9,1,10. 4,4. 40,60."
100,100,100. 60,40. 1. 20,10. 40,30. 100,100,". 20,200,80,100. 200,200.
30,8. 4,1. 40,30,30. a. 9,1,sy. 2 so. 1. istoritseiu suguba s
chetveritseiu suguboia i 10. ritsu u 3.e. gubshi s prikladnoi. 5.ritsi
tso i navershai zhe vosmeritseiu.

In the fourth line, I may have made two mistakes in copying: 30,8 should probably be 30,10 and the *sy* probably reads *s*" (where " represents a hard sign). Normal substitution of letters for numbers yields: "Avaii kir tralos tumerais Vasilei," which makes little sense in Russian or Greek. A correct interpretation may reveal more than is now known of the origin of the "Tale."
(Fol. 325v is blank.)
Fol. 326, "Tale about the Taking of Constantinople," beginning "V leto 6961-go vlastvuiushchi turki bezbozhnomu Magmetu." Apparently the version of the tale published in the appendix to *PSRL*, vol., XXII, pt. 1, beginning on p. 444, it breaks off in the middle (fol. 343) with the words: "i toi nas izbavit ot vrag nashikh i vsia sushchaia na nas vrazhia soveshchaniia razhdenet. Sitsevymi s inymi mnogimi be ukrepliaia narod. I tako sviatiteli i so vsemi."
(Fol. 343v and the following fourteen folios are blank but for two *proby pera*.)
Fol. 346 (signatures in this portion of the MS include fol. 354 = 2[?], fol. 362 = 3 through fol. 410 = 9, fol. 419 = 11), the first letter of Ivan to Kurbskii. I made no notes on this copy, which was not used in *Poslaniia*. In response to an inquiry from me, GPB graciously provided the following information. The copy is imperfect, breaking off roughly in the middle at a point corresponding to the text in *Poslaniia*, p. 105, line 13; it is a poor, late copy, differing from most of the known ones by a "stylistic" editing, but basically corresponding to the version of the letter found in the "Kurbskii Collections."
Fol. 392v, letter of Ivan to Igumen Koz'ma of the Kirillo-Belozerskii Monastery, used in variants to the edition in *Poslaniia*, where the MS is dated 1679.
(Between fols. 436 and 437 are five blank folios.)
Fol. 437 (in this section there are signatures, fol. 445 = 2, fol. 453 = 3), tale about the defeat of Mamai in 1380, in the first group, first variant of the extended redaction, but with elements of the second variant, according to N. S. Demkova, "Zaimstvovaniia iz 'Zadonshchiny' v tekstakh rasprostranennoi redaktsii 'Skazaniia o mamaevom poboishche'," *Slovo o polku Igoreve i pamiatniki kulikovskogo tsikla. K voprosu o vremeni napisaniia 'Slova'* (Moscow-Leningrad, 1966), p. 422.
(Fol. 493 is blank; signatures begin fol. 493 = 1 through fol. 549 = 8, followed by several different numberings: fol. 552 = ?, fol. 562 = 2, fol. 568 = 1, fol. 578 = 3, fol. 594 = 5; fol. 610 = 2, fol. 618 = 3.)

Fol. 493v (change in hand), "The Kazan' History." G. N. Moiseeva lists a copy of the second redaction, first group, in MS Titov Collection No. 1121, fols. 608v–662v, which she describes as being in 2° (*Kazanskaia istoriia* [Moscow-Leningrad, 1954], p. 29). It is not clear what copy she refers to, since No. 1121 in the numbering of Titov's own description of his MSS does not contain the *History*. A later hand added the chapter number "88" at the beginning of the work.

Fol. 648 (change of hand), the "Tale about Dinar, Queen of Iberia," numbered as chapter 89 by a later hand.

(Fol. 657 is blank but for an inscription.)

Fol. 658 (change in hand and paper), epistle of the Novgorod archbishop Vasilii to the bishop of Tver' Feodor concerning paradise; in various published versions, including *PSRL* VI : 87–89.

(Half of fol. 665, all of 665v and the following folio are blank.)

Fol. 666, merchant petition of 1646 to Tsar Aleksei Mikhailovich asking that he restrict the privileges of foreign traders. Published in *AAE*, vol. IV, no. 13. As the closing lines indicate ("takova chelobitnaia syskana v posol'skom prikaze v nyneshnem vo 175-m godu maiia v 9 den'"), the petition in this copy is to be associated with the following work.

Fol. 695v, the "Novotorgovyi ustav" of 1667. Published in *Pamiatniki russkogo prava*, VII (Moscow, 1963): 303–328.

(One folio has been torn out between fols. 740 and 741.)

Fol. 741 (new, eighteenth-century[?] hand; change in paper), letters of Ivan to King Johann III of Sweden, followed by the "answer of the boyars" to the Polish ambassador Kryjski in 1578 regarding Ivan's lineage from Prus. This copy of the letters, published in *Poslaniia*, pp. 334–350, belongs to the first of three groups.

Remarks. Watermark and handwriting breaks indicate that the MS is in at least three parts: fols. 1–218, 219–272₁₁, and 273–end. Since at various points the copyists left a number of blank pages, it is reasonable to assume that the letters to the King of Sweden were added on the end after the rest of the MS was copied to fill such a series of blanks.

A number of questions need to be answered about 2350. First is the question of identity. The manuscript is variously referred to by the number in the *okhrannyi katalog*, 1121, and the current number in the collection, 2350. Yet Moiseeva's reference to a MS, Titov Collection No. 1121 does not seem to mean this one; moreover, Likhachev published two short seventeenth-century letters, which I have not seen, from Titov Collection No. 1121 (see Golubev, *TODRL* XVII : 391). Titov's detailed description of part of his collection includes a No. 1121, but apparently this is not the manuscript in question.

Specifically with regard to the letter from Ivan to Kurbskii, the mystery of why this copy was not even mentioned in *Poslaniia*, while the following work and one later in the same MS were taken into account, is not satisfactorily explained by the fact that the copy is defective.

Finally, the question of date needs to be reexamined. 1667 is certainly a *terminus a quo* for the portion of the manuscript beginning on fol. 273, but not necessarily the date of copying, as one might conclude from the phrase "v nyneshnem vo 175-m godu" in the petition of the merchants. In his separate publication of the letter to Koz'ma and again in *Poslaniia*, Likhachev dates the MS 1679, but I did not see the evidence for this, and the *Kratkii otchet* similarly gives a date 1668–1679. Imperfect watermark data suggest the third quarter of the seventeenth century.

BAN, No. 32.8.5
Second half of the seventeenth century, 2°, 583 fols.

Descriptions. Opisanie Rukopisnogo otdela Biblioteki Akademii nauk SSSR,
III, 1, 2nd ed. (Moscow-Leningrad, 1959), pp. 517–523; *Poslaniia*, p. 554.

Watermarks. Fols. 3–133, foolscap, type IV.

Fols. 134ff., different foolscap, type IV.

Fols. 196–200, foolscap, type IV, with countermark PL. Klepikov,
ZOR XXVI, No. 227, lists two such marks. The one he takes from
Geraklitov, *Filigrani*, No. 1338 (1659), is not notably similar to the one here;
the other mark dates to the 1680's.

Fols. 201–321, 338–411, 413, 414, 416–456, 465–488, arms of Amsterdam
over the letters HG, with countermark IB on the left side of the sheet. The
crown over the arms is decorated with large flourishes.

Fols. 322–337, 412, 415, arms of the Seven Provinces over a ligature
GVH, with countermark CDG on the left half of the sheet.

Fols. 457–464, arms of Amsterdam, with countermark GP on the left
half of the sheet. S. A. Klepikov, "Bumaga s filigran'iu 'gerb goroda
Amsterdama' (Dopolnenie)," *ZOR* XXVI (1963), no. 8(88a) (1713), lists
an arms with this countermark on the right half of the sheet.

Fols. 489–496, foolscap, type IV.

Fols. 497–502, 531ff., arms of Amsterdam, with countermark DH on the
right half of the sheet.

Fols. 521ff., arms of Amsterdam with upside-down countermark MPB
on the right half of the sheet. Churchill, *Watermarks*, No. 8 (1668) is similar.

Inscriptions. Fols. 1–24, an inscription indicating ownership by Patriarch
Adrian (d. 1700).

On the inside of the front cover, partially legible inscriptions (in red pencil ?)
". . . Ivan Al . . . Fedot . . . Ivan . . . vich . . .," and in clear *skoropis'* of the
second half of the seventeenth century, "Nikita Ivanovich Romanov-Iur'ev."

Pagination. Beginning on fol. 201, signatures start with "1".

Handwriting. The *skoropis'* of fols. 1–198, described in *Opisanie*, p. 518,
is probably of the mid-seventeenth century. In the remainder of the MS,
the hand somewhat resembles that in BAN No. 45.13.12, and breaks occur
on fols. 492 and 568v.

Contents. The first portion of 32.8.5 contains the end of a "Book of
Degrees" (*Stepennaia kniga*), beginning with the seventeenth degree less
some of the initial folios. Inserted in this is Ivan's first letter to Kurbskii in
the "abbreviated" version. With this significant exception, most of the
remainder of the first portion of the MS is identical with MS BAN,
Archangel Collection S.131, which is a "Book of Degrees" with various
additions from Chronographs, the Miliutin Menolog (or its source), and
other sources. Beginning on fol. 201, there is a clear break in 32.8.5, with
this second portion containing the end of the Nikon Chronicle, the Life of
Fedor Ivanovich by Patriarch Iov, the *Novyi letopisets*, and a genealogy of
Russian princes.

Remarks. The description in *Opisanie* is thorough; my only reservation
about it is the implication that the manuscript once belonged to the cousin
of Tsar Mikhail Fedorovich, the boyar Nikita Ivanovich Romanov-Iur'ev
(d. 1655). If the MS dates to the *end* of the century (*Opisanie* gives the date
"XVII v.(kon.)"), clearly this would be impossible, although it could be a
copy from one of his MSS. The evidence of paper and binding does not
exclude an earlier date.

What is somewhat more certain is the connection of the MS with the northern milieu where 1573 and 2524 were produced. The variants in the letter of Ivan group it very closely with the copies in these two manuscripts, and the textual connections with BAN, Archangel Collection S.131, a manuscript given by the Igumen Feodosii to the Antonievo-Siiskii Monastery in the middle of the century and containing information through 1647, suggest a connection of 32.8.5 with the same monastery.

The manuscript may have been pieced together from two separate parts and bound after it came into the possession of Patriarch Adrian. Probably at one time the first portion included the text of the "Book of Degrees" up to Degree 17, although this may have been in a separate binding, which would explain its loss.

B. THE WRITINGS ABOUT THE TRANSLATION OF THE SAVIOR'S ROBE TO MOSCOW IN 1625: MATERIALS FOR FURTHER STUDY

In June 1624, the Muscovite ambassadors in Persia, Vasilii Gavriilovich Korob'in and Ostafii Kuvshinov, reported that the Shah was sending as a gift to Tsar Mikhail Fedorovich and Patriarch Filaret Christ's robe, which the Shah alleged to have taken while on campaign in Georgia.[1] Filaret immediately began to inquire about the origin and authenticity of the relic. While it became clear from the testimony of various Eastern Orthodox clergy that such a relic had actually been in Georgia, the only firm evidence for the authenticity of the gift was the word of the Shah himself.[2] As Filaret advised the Tsar after receiving the gift in March 1625, its authenticity should be tested, because "under it [on the box it came in] are described in Latin writing the Crucifixion and the other Passions of Christ. The Latins are heretics, and that relic, which they call the robe of Christ, was sent by a ruler of another faith Abbas Shah, and it is dangerous to accept this relic as authentic without true evidence."[3]

True evidence consisted of miracles. By March 26 several miraculous healings attributed to the robe had been reported, convincing Filaret that it should be declared genuine and installed in the Cathedral of the Dormition. The Metropolitan of Krutitsa, Kiprian, was ordered to compose a service in commemoration of the installation, to be celebrated henceforth on March 27.[4] Late in the year a service was printed and distributed along with letters of the Patriarch which described the arrival of the relic and the miracles attributed to it.[5]

Seventeenth-century writings about the robe and its translation to Moscow are numerous, among them three works attributed to Shakhovskoi and a fourth found in collections containing the Correspondence. The following preliminary listing and classification should facilitate further study of this material.[6]

I. Works about the Robe Attributed to Shakhovskoi

A. Letter to Shah Abbas thanking him for the relic and attempting to persuade him to convert to Orthodoxy; written at the request of Filaret in May 1625 (before May 26, when the Persian ambassador left Moscow). It is found in three collections of Shakhovskoi's writings: GBL, fond 173, Collection of the Moscow Theological Academy (= MDA), Nos. 27(213) and 28(214);[7] GIM, Collection of the Synodal Library, No. 327 (865).[8]

B. A service in verse commemorating the Installation, possibly written at the request of Kiprian, who is not known to us as an author but who clearly had the opportunity to become acquainted with Shakhovskoi's literary talents and might well have turned to him when instructed by Filaret to write a service. Judging from the opening words of Shakhovskoi's work however ("Griadite vernii, zhivonosnoi rize Spasove poklonimsia . . ."), it is not the same as the printed service of 1625 (see below, section IV.A).[9] copies of the Shakhovskoi service are in MSS MDA Nos. 27(213) and 28(214).

C. A Slavonic *povest'* about the translation of the relic, entitled: "Povest' preslavna, skazuema o prenesenii mogochiudesnyia rizy Spasa Khristova ot Persid v tsarstvuiushchii grad Moskvu . . . Spisano duksom Semionom Shakhovskim . . ." It begins: "Praveden i istinen Gospod' nash Isus Khristos, toi biashe samoprevechnoe Bozhie Slovo . . ." In addition to copies in MDA Nos. 27(213) and 28(214), it is found in the following MSS: GIM, Collection of the Resurrection Monastery No. 90;[10] Collection of the Aleksandro-Svirskii Monastery No. 21(56);[11] GPB, Pogodin Collection No. 1610;[12] and apparently also GIM, Collection of the Chudov Monastery No. 280;[13] GPB, Collection of the Society of Lovers of Ancient Literature (= OLDP) No. Q.CLXX(2052).[14] The same work, but possibly in slightly different variants, seems to be that in GIM, Collection of the Synodal Library No. 850, and GBL, Collection of N. S. Tikhonravov, No. 266.[15] In the former it is termed "Slovo na prinesenie" and the latter "Skazanie o prinesenii." Two other MSS contain a "Skazanie" that may be the same work: GBL, Bol'shakov Collection No. 422;[16] BAN No. 45.5.30.[17] A Slavonic homily ("Skazanie pokhvalno na polozhenie . . .") begins with words nearly identical to those of the Shakhovskoi tale. The single known manuscript contains also the "Extracts from the Kizilbash Books": GIM, Collection of the Resurrection Monastery No. 140 *bum.*[18]

II. Extracts from the Kizilbash Books (Vypisano iz kizylbashskikh otpisok)

This is a plain-style narrative of the events from the receipt of the first information about the relic until the official recognition of its authenticity; in one version of the work, there is an additional section recounting miracles that occurred following the installation of the relic in the cathedral. It seems clear from the original version of the tale, which has been preserved in the archive, that it was an official compilation by the Diplomatic Chancellery from various sources, some of which have survived independently.[19] The first version of "Extracts," which I term the "normal" version, was only one of several official accounts concerning the relic. It quotes a summary account that was sent around with the relic while it was being tested for miraculous powers; another account, apparently specifically regarding the miracles, was read at the time the relic was publicly declared genuine. A fourth narrative, about the arrival of the relic and its miracles, which incorporates all of "Extracts," is the "long" version discussed below.

While it is tempting to connect Shakhovskoi with the composition of "Extracts," no conclusive evidence supports such an association. His literary talents and erudition were employed in the letter to the Shah, but there is no reason to believe they were required in the rather mechanical task of compiling the plain-style narrative. He may have used the narrative, however, as a source when compiling his Slavonic tale.

A. The Normal Version. Most of the copies we possess of "Extracts" seem to belong to this group; their distinctive feature is that the ending coincides with that of the archival original ("emu zhe slava vo veki, amin'").[20] Among the copies of the Normal Version, although only examination of the hitherto unpublished texts can confirm this, one should probably distinguish two groups. Group A contains a version of the tale presumably most closely connected with the archival text, and Group B a version found in manuscripts containing the Russian Chronograph in the third redaction, second group (according to the classification of A. N. Popov) and copies made using this Chronograph version.

Group A. In addition to the archival copy, two other complete copies of the text are available in print, as they were used in variants to the publication in *DR*: GPB, O.XVII.15;[21] GBL, Collection of the Rumiantsev Museum No. CLVII.[22] The heading and beginning of the archival original is the basic text against which I note significant variants in the remaining copies "Vypisano is kizylbashskikh otpisok gosudarevykh poslannikov Vasil'ia Korob'ina da d'iaka Ostaf'ia Kuvshinova i iz rosprosu ierusalimskogo kelaria Onikeia o Srachitse Gospoda nashego Isusa Khrista." "V proshlom vo 132-m godu iiunia v 27-i den' pisali ko Gosudariu . . ."

The following four manuscripts probably contain texts of the Normal Version: GIM, Uvarov Collection No. 1852(187)(423),[23] with the date "iiulia" rather than "iiunia" and missing the heading, the work beginning simply "V proshlom . . ." Both of these features are common to the Long Version of "Extracts."

GBL, Museum Collection No. 4469,[24] with variants in the heading, as given in the unpublished catalogue of the collection, "moskovskogo gosudaria" instead of "gosudarevykh", and "iiulia" instead of "iiunia." An approximation of the text's length suggests that it is roughly the same as the defective one in 2524.

GIM, Uvarov Collection No. 1894(848),[25] the heading omitting "ierusalimskago."

GBL, Undol'skii Collection No. 397,[26] with the date "20" instead of "27" and "pisano" instead of "pisali."

Group B. While apparently this group contains a text that is essentially the same as that in Group A, there are distinctive headings and one key variant in the opening line ("V leto 7132 g." instead of "V proshlom vo 132 godu"). Presumably quoting from his own copy of the Chronograph, third redaction, second group (now in GBL, *fond* 236, Collection of A. N. Popov?), which may be the oldest copy of this version of the Chronograph and bears an inscription written in Sol' Vychegodsk in 1646, Popov gives the following heading: 'O prislanii k Moskve k gosudariu . . . Mikhailu Fedorovichu . . . i ko ottsu ego . . . patriarkhu Filaretu Nikitichiu . . . iz Kizylbash ot tsaria Abbasa shakha srachitsy khristovy, i gde on eia vzial."[27] The text begins, "V leto 7132 iiunia v 27 den' pisali ko gosudariu . . ."; separate headings follow for later sections of the work. A sentence which introduces a section of Gospel quotations about the robe (col. 778) becomes in slightly altered form a distinct heading: "Vypiski iz Evangeliia tolkovagol dlia svidetel'stva o onoi Khristovoi Srachitse ili Khitone," with the text beginning, "i togda voini igemonovi emshe Iisusa." Group A texts include between the heading and the beginning citation of the place in the Gospel According to St. Matthew where the passage occurs. The final heading is: "O prikhode poslov kizylbashskikh k Moskve," where the text then begins, "i 133 goda fevralia v 25 den' Kizylbashskie posly . . ." This corresponds to col. 781, but Group A lacks the heading.

Other copies of Group B include GPB, F.IV.90, F.IV.129, F.IV.250, F.IV.109, and GBL, Undol'skii Collection No. 723, all of which Popov lists; BAN, No. 33.10.6;[28] possibly the version in a Chronograph once in the Collection of the Archbishop's Residence in Petrozavodsk No. 68(155),[29] and in GIM, Khludov Collection No. 184, a manuscript containing various materials from chronographs and chronicles.[30]

The variant in the opening line, "v leto," and the break caused by the heading "Vypiski iz Evangeliia" lead me to group with these chronograph copies the following, although it is possible that here the texts combine features of both groups:

GIM, Museum Collection No. 2524 (see Appendix I, pt. a). Variants in the heading (which is that of Group A) include, "startsa grechina" instead of "kelaria"; the text begins, "v leto 7132-go godu iiunia v 22 den'." The variants of 2524 do not follow consistently those of any one of the published copies; furthermore, this copy derives from a defective protograph (apparently a MS in 8°, in which the concluding folios were out of order and from which some folios had been lost). Beginning with the miracle about the girl Marina (col. 789), the text reads (fol. 164): "Devitsa Marina skazala v rosprose, ona oderzhima byla chernoiu bolezn'iu // i serdechnoiu, izletaia i iazykom posle togo* dni gorazdo stalo tiazhelo. Kostromskie chetverti d'iak Afonasei Andronikov ..." After "posle togo" the text is that found at the end of the first full paragraph on col. 791; it then skips the next miracle entirely and continues with the one beginning on col. 792. There are further omissions and changes in the order of the text. The asterisk (*) above marks where the copyist of the manuscript inserted a mark and noted in the margin: "opis' spravittsa s ynym perevodom" (fol. 164v).

In GPB, Pogodin Collection No. 1573, the "Extracts" are found in only one fragment, concealed under a folio that has been pasted over it. The present fol. 1 consists of two pieces of paper pasted together, the top one having been added in the nineteenth century when Stroev had the manuscript bound. Underneath, on the recto side of the sheet whose verso is the present fol. 1v, is a final page of a copy from the "Extracts." The hand of the text is that of the work which begins on fol. 1v and of the works connected with Kurbskii that follow later in the MS; but the text has been crossed out in cinnabar, possibly by the copyist who added the cinnabar headings to the manuscript. The text tapers to end with the words, "i prines ee v Gruzinskuiu zemliu i mnogie ot nee chiudesa sotvorishasia," which come in the middle of the letter of Nektarii (col. 778) just before the line that forms the heading in the copies of Group B ("Vypiski iz Evangeliia ..."). Although I could not read clearly all the words of this fragment, the variants in it seem to be closer to those in 2524 than in any of the other copies for which I have this portion of the text, which in itself seems adequate reason to assign 1573 to Group B. Moreover, it is a reasonable hypothesis that the copyist stopped where he did—at a point which does not seem entirely logical from the standpoint of content—because he encountered a new cinnabar heading at that point suggesting the beginning of a section of purely religious interest. As demonstrated in Appendix I, pt. a, 1573 and 2524 were copied in close succession in the same scriptorium; judging from the marginal notation on fol. 164v of 2524, this scriptorium must have possessed, in addition to the copy from which 2524 was made, another copy of "Extracts." That the heading of Group A appears with the text of Group B in 2524 is further evidence in support of this. If the assumption is correct that the copyist of 1573 stopped at a cinnabar heading, then he may have had in hand the protograph for 2524, as in that MS there is no such cinnabar heading, although the actual Gospel quotation which follows is set off by a cinnabar capital at the top of a new folio. Contraction of the longer work would be consistent with the editorial techniques applied in 1573, but I hesitate to call this fragment a "short redaction," because it seems to be unique and textually falls within the group of 2524.

GPB, F.XVII.15, a copy with the Group A heading but the Group B opening and the significant variant that ties it even more closely with 2524, the date "22" instead of "27". On the other connections of F.XVII.15 with 1573 and 2524, see Appendix I, pt. a.

GIM, Uvarov Collection No. 1363(16).[31] Instead of the normal heading, this copy has, "Gl. 107. Povest' o srachitse velikago Boga i Spasa nashego Iisusa Khrista," with the text beginning "V leto . . ." Unfortunately I do not know the ending, but an approximation of its length indicates that this copy clearly cannot contain the Long Version and in fact may be somewhat shorter than the Normal Version (a defective text?). Although the manuscript seems to have been copied in the same scriptorium as GIM, Collection of the Synodal Library No. 409, the evidence of headings and opening lines indicates that the versions of "Extracts" in the two MSS differ. Because of the connections between 1363(16) and 1321(103)/1584(168) of the same collection noted in Appendix I, pt. a, this copy of "Extracts" may hold important clues to the manuscript history of the *Correspondence*.

GPB, Pogodin Collection No. 1580.[32] As described by Bychkov, this copy contains the interesting and indicative variant of an added line at the beginning of the heading: "Povest' o srachitse . . . Isusa Khrista, i svidetel'stvovannoe pisanie. Vypisano . . ." The text begins "V leto . . ." and presumably ends with "amin'," as Bychkov cites from the published version the column numbers corresponding to those for the Normal Version.

B. The Long Version. I know only one MS that definitely contains this version: GPB, Collection of Count Viazemskii, Q. XXXV.[33] The editors of *DR* chose this copy as their basic text. As noted above, it lacks the heading and gives the first date as "iiulia." Following "amin'" the text continues at great length, describing the miracles effected by the relic upon those who visited the cathedral and prayed to it there. The last of these miracles was reported to Patriarch Filaret on July 1, 1625; at this point the text breaks off, as the copy is defective. The Long Version includes a total of fifty miracles, counting those that occurred prior to the acceptance of the relic's authenticity. In comparison, the letter of the Archbishop of Tver' to the Koliazin Monastery[34] indicates that Filaret sent him a description of seventy-one miracles that occurred between March 23, 1625, and January 1626, most of which antedated September 1. Since the figures seem compatible, the suggestion is inescapable that the Long Version represents an account such as the one which Filaret sent to Tver'.

C. Copies for Which the Redaction Is Uncertain. GPB, Q.XVII.22,[35] used in variants in *DR*. In a MS containing various formerly separate parts (which suggests the likelihood that the ending of the work simply was lost), this copy ends with the transitional sentence just prior to the Gospel quotations in the letter of Nektarii, which becomes in Group B the separate heading noted above: "I vypisano sie iz Evangeliia dlia svidetelstva o Khristove srachitse i o khitone." The near coincidence of this break with that in 1573 does offer as an alternative explanation for the latter that it came from a text similar to that in Q.XVII.22, although the variants between this MS and 1573 are not as close as between 1573 and 2524.

GIM, Collection of the Synodal Library No. 409.[36] This copy apparently derives from a defective one, since the verso side of fol. 144 on which it ends is blank, and the ending (= col. 785) reads: "da s tem zhe poslom persidtskim Abas shakh prislal k velikomu gosudariu sviateishemu Filaretu Nikitichiu patriarkhu moskovskomu i vsea Rusii chast' srachitsy Gospoda nashego Isusa Khrista." As with Q.XVII.22, the heading and opening words suggest that it belongs in Group A of the Normal Version.

GIM, Collection of the Resurrection Monastery No. 140 *bum.* Following this copy of the "Extracts" is the homily mentioned above (section I.C); together the two works comprise the entire MS. In view of the number of folios and the headings, this might be a second copy of the Long Version. The initial heading is: "Skazanie o rize Gospodni, ezhe est' sviatago khitona chast', kako i v koe vremia prinesena byst' v tsarstvuiushchii grad Moskvu. Vypisano . . ." Stroev notes[37] that following the *Skazanie* is a section entitled "Leta 7133, rospis' chiudesem chestnyia i slavnyia i mnogotselebnyia srachitsy, ezhe est' sviatago khitona chast' . . ." The first miracle with which this section begins was not the first of the miracles in the Normal Version (col. 789); perhaps here some textual changes enabled the copyist to set off the miracles with a separate heading.

Collection of the Antonievo-Siiskii Monastery No. 277.[38] This copy may be similar to the preceding one, as the description indicates that the work is a *skazanie* and *vypiska* (cf. the above heading). The vague information of the description suggests that this text is not as long as the preceding one— possibly the separate section of miracles is missing.

III. Miscellaneous

A. A very condensed account of the presentation by the Persian ambassador, the decision to "test" the relic, and the installation of it in the cathedral. This work, published by Popov from a chronograph, GPB, Pogodin Collection No. 1451,[39] has clear textual connections with "Extracts," especially cols. 781–782, 795–796, where much of the text is identical. The text begins at the seam noted for Group B in the Normal Version: "O prinesenii Khristovy srachitsy. V leto 7133 fevralia v 25 den' prishel vo tsarstvuiushchii grad Moskvu . . ."

B. Very close to the preceding, except for some additions—several headings dividing the work into its component parts and a sentence summarizing the miracles—is another account in a chronograph, published by Popov from GPB, Pogodin Collection No. 1465.[40] Following the "amin'," however, is an appended work entitled "O khristove srachitse, o obretenii eia skazanie vkrattse," which begins, "Obretena zhe byst' siia sviatynia v Gruzinskoi zemli." A marginal notation gives the source for this: "Vypisano iz rozprosu Ierusalimskago kelaria Ioanikeia." Clearly both the tale in 1465 and that in 1451 derive from a fuller version of the "Extracts," probably the Normal Version, Group B.

C. A short account of the translation of the relic found in the *Novyi letopisets*[41] is significant for the information it provides not found in other accounts. It has the heading, "O prinesenii srachitsy Gospodni v tsarstvuiush-chii grad Moskvu i o mnogorazlichnem istselenii k boliashchim," and begins, "Pisal ko gosudariu. . . . Mikhailu Fedorovichiu . . ." In very condensed fashion, it follows the events recounted in the Normal Version, but clearly its author used another source. He refers to the Persian ambassador as Rusin Bek (cf. Rusam Bek, in "Extracts") and names a second ambassador Murat Bek ("Extracts" referred at an earlier point to a merchant Mameselei); the reception of the ambassador took place in the Granovitaia Palata (not mentioned in "Extracts," but found in the *dvortsovye razriady*); Ioanikei is mentioned as being from Serbia (not in "Extracts"); this account alone relates that the relic was divided and Kiprian instructed to compose a service. The account in *Novyi letopisets* probably was based on one similar to the "Extracts" kept at the Patriarch's court, where it has been suggested that the chronicle was compiled.[42] The additional details, especially the final two, tie the account even more closely to the circle of the Patriarch.

D. A brief Slavonic account of the translation of the relic, with heading and beginning: "O rize gospodni. I prizre Gospod' s vysoty svoeia na krotkago svoego i vernago slugu na blagochestivago tsaria . . ." This is appended to a copy of the Chronograph, 1617 redaction, dated 1647 and owned by Popov, who published the tale.[43]

E. In BAN, Collection of N. K. Nikol'skii No. 45, a "Skazanie o srachitse . . ." beginning, "Kako vo Ierusalime raspinali Gospoda nashego Isusa Khrista iiudei, togda obrali s nego rizy i srachitsu . . ."[44] Judging from the heading and opening lines, this account may have nothing in common with any of the others; however, since apparently this portion of the MS contains an inscription in the hand of the copyist dated May 3, 1625, this work may be the earliest dated manuscript account about the relic.

F. Perhaps related to the preceding is a work in a late MS, BAN, No. 38.2.47:[45] "Skazanie izvestno o rize . . . ," beginning "Egda prebezakonnyi iudei raspiasha gospoda . . ."

G. GPB, Pogodin Collection No. 1936, may contain simply an imperfect and late copy of "Extracts." Missing the first folios, it begins in the middle of the account of Ioanikei with the words, "sestra reche, nacha brata svoemu biti chelom, chtob eia podaril toiu srachitseiu . . ." Apparently this short text covers events described in the Normal Version, but Bychkov notes that it is not the same as the text in *DR*.[46] Also it differs from the one published by Popov (item C above) and the one in the *Prolog* for July 10.

H. A tale similar to the preceding, published by Brailovskii from MS TsGADA, *fond* 381, Collection of the Moscow Synodal Typography No. 446.[47] Brailovskii's comparison relies on Bychkov's description of the preceding manuscript. Judging from the content, the account must have been compiled later in the seventeenth century than the official "Extracts."

I. The *Prolog* text may be that in BAN, Archangel Collection D. 233,[48] entitled, "Mesiatsa iiulia v 10 den', o prinesenii bogotelesnyia rizy . . . v tsarstvuiushchii grad Moskvu," and beginning "Izhe krepostiiu nepobedimago Boga . . ." The manuscript was bound in 1661/1662 in the Antonievo-Siiskii Monastery.

J. A text apparently too short to be the Normal Version of "Extracts" but deriving from it (possibly one of the short Chronograph texts?), in GIM, Collection of the Synodal Library, No. 559.[49]

K. A brief work "O rize Gospodnei" in GBL, Collection of N. S. Tikhonravov No. 227.[50]

IV. Services

A. The printed service (*sluzhba na polozhenie rizy*), mentioned above in discussing the service by Shakhovskoi, is undated. However, its type and decoration place it in 1625,[51] and Filaret's letter to the Archbishop of Tver' in January 1626 is a *terminus ad quem*. This same service, reprinted in various Menologs, continued in use down to modern times. Its initial printing as a separate work, which makes it unique among seventeenth-century Moscow editions, was probably occasioned by the fact that the March volume in the complete *Sluzhebnaia Mineia* begun in 1619 and completed only in 1630 had been published already in the previous year.[52] The numerous seventeenth-century manuscript versions (e.g., GBL, Bol'shakov Collection Nos. 162 and 177) presumably reproduce the printed service.

B. Brailovskii mentions a service by Miletii Sirig, which is apparently of later origin judging from the title: "Sluzhba polozheniiu neshvennago khitona Khristova, prinesennago iz Persidy v Moskvu vo vremena blago-chestivago tsaria Mikhaila Feodorovicha."[53]

C. NOTES ON SEVENTEENTH-CENTURY TRANSLATIONS FROM THE POLISH KRONIKA OF ALEXANDER GUAGNINI

Since the appearance of A. I. Sobolevskii's monumental annotated bibliography of translated literature in Muscovy,[1] too few of the works he listed have been the subject of detailed study. Among the neglected items is Alexander Guagnini's "Description of European Sarmatia," published first in Latin in 1578 and extensively reworked and expanded in his Polish *Kronika* of 1611.[2] Various portions of Guagnini's work exist in Russian and Ukrainian translation and adaptation, but often the fragments extracted from Guagnini have not been recognized as such and are relegated to the category of works by anonymous authors. Although I hope to expand the following comments in a future article, it seems useful to discuss briefly here two such works, one of which is of particular significance for the study of the "Kurbskii Collections" of the second half of the seventeenth century.

The two works deal with the Ottoman Turks, one being a description of Ottoman mores and a resumé of Ottoman history, the other recounting the disastrous Tatar-Turkish campaign against Astrakhan' in 1569. The first of these accounts, noted by Sobolevskii under the title its manuscripts bear, "The Tale About the Turks" (*Povest' o turkakh*), is a translation of the final portion of Book Ten, Part Three, in the Polish edition of Guagnini. While the origins of this translation remain to be determined (it undoubtedly was done in the second half of the seventeenth century),[3] it is clear that Guagnini's original attracted the attention of those compiling larger historical works in Russia and the Ukraine. Both Panteleimon Kokhanovs'kyi—whose Ukrainian chronicle has often been mistakenly attributed to Feodosii Safonovich, the author of one of its sources—and Andrei Lyzlov, in his "History of the Scythians," extracted Guagnini's material on the Ottomans directly from the Polish edition.[4]

The "History of the Campaign of the Turkish and Tatar Army to Astrakhan'" (*Istoriia o prikhode turetskogo i tatarskogo voinstva pod Astrakhan'*), which appears in many of the manuscripts in the second group of "Kurbskii Collections" (in the classification of Lur'e, the first group),[5] is simply a translation *from Polish* of the section in Guagnini, Book Eight, Part Three, entitled "Astrachan krolestwo Tatarskie." The bulk of the material in the *Istoriia o prikhode* correctly has been traced to the account written by Andrzej Taranowski, the Polish ambassador who accompanied the Turks on the campaign. Guagnini's Latin edition contained a brief description of the campaign, but only in the Polish edition of 1611 was this account expanded with material from Taranowski.[6] That Taranowski's journal should have appeared in Guagnini 1611 but not Guagnini 1578 is not surprising, since its first publication in Polish was in the *Kronika* of Joachim Bielski (1597), a source for other additions to the original edition of Guagnini.[7] A comparison of texts reveals that the editor of 1611 spliced the two accounts, using parts of the introductory portion in the Latin edition, but then relying almost entirely on Taranowski for the remainder of "Astrachan krolestwo Tatarskie," and only occasionally emending from information in the Latin version. In the editorial process, references to Taranowski were systematically deleted, and many of his present tenses were changed to past tenses for consistency in the account that resulted. One need look no further than the opening paragraph of the *Istoriia o prikhode* and compare it with both the Polish and Latin versions of Guagnini to confirm that the Russian translation derives from the Polish text:

Istoriia (pp. 479–480):

Азов бо есть град Салтана турецкаго на брегу реки Дона у езера Меотскаго стоящий, к нему же егда приидоша оные свои потребныя запасы еже уготоваша себе на верблюдех . . . Потом паки уготоваше себе потребное еже возмогоша и идоша прямо в Астрахань. Над тем воинством турецким . . . Над татарским же воинством бе начальный Сулиз-бек казанский князь и Мустофа, всеж то воинство турское шествова польми пустыми чрез орды татар Нагайских и Черкас пятигорских, прийдоша ж под Астрахань в пятой день Августа утрудившеся. Тогда ж оное еже Салтан Селим турецкий послал собрание водное . . .

Guagnini 1611 (pp. 604–605):

A Azoph iest to Zamek Cesarza Tureckiego nad brzegiem rzeki Donu przy ieziorze Meotskim leżący. Do ktorego nim przyszli, onę żywność ktorą byli na wielbłądach . . . Potym naśpiżowawszy sobie znowu żywności co mogło, bydź iachali prosto pod Astrachan. Nad tym woyskiem Tureckim . . . Nad woyskiem Tatarskim był starszy Sulizbek, a drugi Azyiski Kniaź, y Mustapha. To woysko Tureckie szło wszystko polmi pustymi, przez Hordy Tatarow Nohayskich, y Cerkaskich Petyhorcow. Przybyli pod Astrachan 5. dnia Sierpnia strudzeni. A wtym ona ktorą Sołtan Zelim Cesarz Turecki wyprawił Armatę wodną . . .

Guagnini 1578 (fols. 4–4v):

Azoph autem in ostiis Tanais fluuii Turcica arx sita est, ad paludes Meotidis. Postea ad victum necessariis comparatis omnis equitatus Turcicus & Tartaricus, per campestria & Hordas Tartarorum Nahaicensium & Circassorum quinquemontanorum, taediosissimo itinere sub Astrachan 5. Septembris venerunt; 24 hebdomadis cum ineffabili famis & sitis angustia in via transactis . . .

The manuscript tradition of the *Istoriia o prikhode* is highly significant in view of what has been said above in Chap. 4 about the "Kurbskii Collections" and their possible connections with V. V. Golitsyn. The manuscript from which the *Istoriia* has been published (I do not know its present location) bears the title: "155 [read '185'] godu genvaria v 22-i den' pisana siia 7185 kniga v domu boiarina kniazia Vasil'ia Vasil'evicha Golitsina glagolemaia: siia kniga istoriia o prikhode turetskago i tatarskago voinstva pod Astrakhan' leta ot sozdaniia mira 7185 a ot Rozhdestva Khristova 1677." It is striking that one of the "Kurbskii Collections" containing among other items this work and a translation from Guagnini's material on

Ivan IV was also copied in the home of Golitsyn in 1677.[8] There is thus good evidence to suggest that the Polish edition of 1611 was the basis for all the translations from Guagnini found in these "Collections." This means that observations about the significance of the selection of these works by *edinomyshlenniki* of Kurbskii in Lithuania for inclusion in collections of his writings surely must be revised.[9]

Stemmata

Contents of Manuscripts

197	*4469*	*1584*	*43*	*603*	*1615*	*F.XVII.15*
KI[a]	PERE	VYM	COR	SYN	KI[a]	KI[a]
EMB[a]	VYM	PRE	KI[a]	KI[a]	EMB[b]	KAZ
(KAZ)	PRE	KI[a]	T	EMB[a]		DVINA[b]
	KI[a]	T				EMB★
	T	P				KOR
	P	PERE				LOUIS
	KOR					KIZ[b]
	KIZ[a]					
	SYN					

1551	*2524*	*1573*	*32.8.5*
KI[a]	DVINA[a]	(KIZ[b])	STEP
GI[a]	COR	DVINA[a]	GI[a]
PRE	EMB[a]	EMB[a]	
T	KI[a]	COR	
EMB★	GI[a]	KI[a]	
	VYM	GI[a]	
	PRE	VYM	
	KOR	PRE	
	KIZ[b]	ISAIAH	
	MEG	MEG	
		LOUIS	

1567	*230*	*1311*	*41*
PRE	KAZ	GI[b]	GI[b]
KI[a]	KI[a]		
T	T		
P	P		
GI[b]	GI[b]		

F.IV.165	1/91	1581
CHRON	STEP	STEP
KI^a	KI^a	KI^a
T	T	GI^c
GI^c	GI^c	

2350	181/60	1494	136	623	639	1582
GI^d	HIST	HIST	HIST	HIST	HIST	HIST
EMB^b	KI^b	KI^b	KI^b	KI^b	KI^b	KI^b
KAZ	T	T	T	(T)	KII-	KII-
	GI^d	GI^d	GI^d	(GI^d)		
	KII-	KII-	KII-	KII-		
	KL	KL	KL	KL		
	GUAG	GUAG		(GUAG)		
	STRY	STRY		(STRY)		

Key to Abbreviations

CHRON = "Chronograph"

COR = Apocryphal correspondence of Ivan with Sultan (see Kagan, *TODRL* XIII:247–272)

DVINA^{a,b} = Two variants of Dvina-region chronicles

EMB^{a,b,*} = First, second, and transitional versions of apocryphal embassies to Sultan (see Kagan, *TODRL* XI:218–254)

GI^a = "Abbreviated" version of Ivan's first letter

GI^b = "Full" version of Ivan's first letter

GI^c = "Chronograph" version of Ivan's first letter

GI^d = "Kurbskii Collection" version of Ivan's first letter

GUAG = Fragments of Guagnini's "Description of Muscovy"

HIST = Kurbskii's *History*

ISAIAH = Biographical notice of Isaiah

KAZ = "The Kazan' History"

KI^a = First version of Kurbskii's first letter

KI^b = Second version of Kurbskii's first letter

KII- = Kurbskii's other letters to Ivan

KIZ^{a,b} = "Normal" and "Chronograph" versions of "Extracts from the Kizilbash Books"

KL = Kurbskii letters to Lithuanian figures

KOR = "Journey of Trifon Korobeinikov"

LOUIS = Letter of Mikhail Fedorovich to Louis XIII

MEG = Letter of Mikhail Fedorovich to Megapolinsk princes

P = "Letter" of Polubenskii

PERE = "Works" of Ivan Peresvetov

PRE = Kurbskii's letter to Vas'ian

STEP = "Book of Degrees" (*Stepennaia kniga*)

STRY = Translated extracts from Stryjkowski's *Kronika*

SYN = *Syn tserkovnyi*

T = Teterin to Morozov

VYM = Note appended to PRE

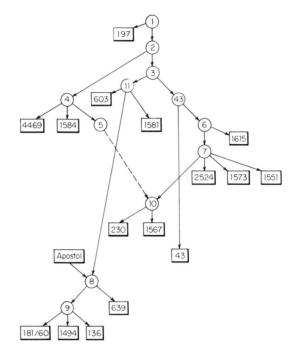

STEMMA A. Kurbskii's First Letter

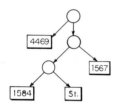

STEMMA B.
Polubenskii Letter

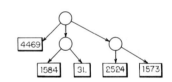

STEMMA C.
Vymete (The "Note")

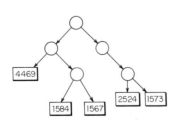

STEMMA D. *V prechistuiu*

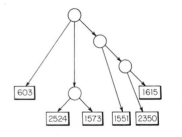

STEMMA E. Two Embassies

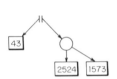

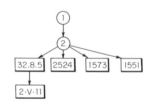

STEMMA F.
Correspondence

STEMMA G.
Ivan's First Letter, First Version

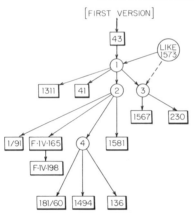

STEMMA H. Ivan's First Letter, Second Version

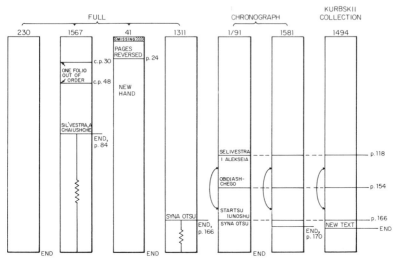

Ivan's First Letter, Second Version: Boundaries of Text

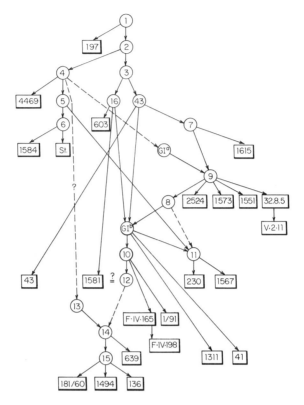

STEMMA I. Composite Stemma

Notes to Stemmata

STEMMA A. KURBSKII'S FIRST LETTER

1. Protograph of Kurbskii's first letter, with readings as in critical text (App. III) but ending with the word *Amin'*.

2. Very similar to 1; but with reversal of word order in phrase *I vozdal esi . . .* and addition of postscript, as in critical text.

3. Common protograph of 603 and (reconstructed) 43, 1581, and perhaps of 8 as indicated by common readings and in particular heading before *Slyshakh . . .*

4. Common protograph of 4469 and 1584.

5. Assumed source of collation in 1567 very much like 4469 and 1584, but apparently neither of these.

6. Protograph of 1615, 2524, 1573, 1551, and the basic text of 1567, as indicated by consistent common readings.

7. Common protograph of 2524, 1551, and 1573.

8. Protograph of second version of letter, with inclusion of citation from L'viv *Apostol*, etc.

9. Common protograph of "Kurbskii Collection" group.

10. The relationship between 5 and 10 is indicated by numerous common readings. 1567 seems to be a mixed text, sharing readings with two clearly different groups (i.e., descendants of 6 and 4469, 1584, etc. The absence of *iazytsekh* and the reading *dal'nokonnykh* link it with 1573, while a number of other readings associate it with the family of 4469. As we shall see, other evidence supports this conclusion. The establishment of the place of 43 (reconstructed) is complicated by gaps in the copy we have: it does share important features (esp. reversal of *ot Boga dannykh ti*) with the family of 6 and, as mentioned, with 603.

11. Common protograph of 603 and 1581. The relationship between 603 and 1581 is particularly close; consider the following readings:

603 and 1581	other MSS
прегоршаго/прегорша	прегорчающе [и т. д.]
погубляя	погубляя нас
сам ли	али ты
труды поты	поты и терпением
он бо весть	он бо есть
Князя Андрея же	[заглавия нет]
почитали	потакати

STEMMA B.   POLUBENSKII LETTER

This stemma is based upon only partial variant readings, as follows:

4469	1584	St.	1567
Вифляндской	=4469	=4469	Лифляндской
Шабликину	Шапкину	=1584	Шабликину
	человек твой	=1584	человек
	надобен		надобен
	лишь на пяти	лишена а	лише на пяте
	тетрадех.	тетрадей	кожа клеена.
	В ней...	в ней...	А тетрадей в ней...
	допытаюся	=1567	допытаешься
ты бы купил	он бы купил	ты бы купил	ты бы купил
допытаешься	домышляешься	допытался	допытаешься

Clearly a number of graphic representations would accommodate this limited material (from published texts and fragments in the appropriate descriptions), but this stemma has been preferred because of other evidence concerning the relationships among these manuscripts. "St." represents readings from an MS that belonged to Sakharov and from which he published this letter and *Vymete* in *Moskvitianin*, 1843, no. 9, pp. 147–148.

STEMMA C.   VYMETE ... (THE "NOTE")

The variants:

4469	1584	St.	1573 and 2524
положено под	положено	=4469	=1584
	писание		
в малой	мало писано	=1584	=4469
государское	церковное	царское	государское
царю	царю	царю	государю

These are in part contradictory readings: it has been assumed that the most important are *v maloi* and the evolution from the assumed original *tsarskoe* to the (normal) *gosudarskoe* and the incorrect *tserkovnoe*.

STEMMA D. V PRECHISTUIU

The variants are published in Kuntsevich and Bychkov, *Opisanie*. 1567 is clearly closest to 4469 but not a copy from it: it shares an important corruption (*prezrennykh* instead of *prezren bykh*) with 1584. A number of corruptions are found in 2524 and 1573, which are all but identical: perhaps more intermediate stages should be indicated.

STEMMA E. TWO EMBASSIES

Based upon Kagan's comments in *TODRL* XI:218–254, the important element being that 1615 is of a different recension than 2524, etc., containing elements not found elsewhere.

STEMMA F. CORRESPONDENCE

After Kagan, *TODRL* XIII:247–272.

STEMMA G. IVAN'S FIRST LETTER, FIRST VERSION

After Lur'e's variants in *Poslaniia*, p. 581, and his description of V.2.11, which he indicates to be a copy from 32.8.5 (ibid., p. 555). None of the other copies seems to depend upon any other: their common protograph apparently had some corruptions common to all texts. I have no text for 1551, but the heading (with date) indicates its similarity with 2524 and 1573.

STEMMA H. IVAN'S FIRST LETTER, SECOND VERSION

The protograph of 43 was apparently used as a source during the composition of the protograph of this text, as is indicated by the fact that texts cited in the second version, but not in the first, are missing from 43 (Fennell, *Corresp.*, 112: *Ne pregordye li tsarstva* . . .; ibid., p. 118: *Ne pretverdye li* . . .) and by a number of other observations about the protograph of 43.

Manuscript 43 contains a copy of KI which is mutilated almost beyond recognition, and seemingly useless for the study of the history of the text. Close examination, however, reveals a number of very significant features of this MS, which earn for it an important place in the reconstruction of the growth of the *Correspondence*. By all external indications (Wm. is Foolscap IV, hand mid-seventeenth century), 43 was produced sometime after midcentury, and would, were it not for the observations to follow, constitute an important exception to our chronological groupings. Analysis of this fragmentary and disordered text, however, shows that it is clearly a copy of a very early text of KI—the text, it seems, which was used (and abused) in the production of the protograph of the second version of GI. A number of features support this conclusion.

1. Textual variants taken from the text as it is indicate that 43 belongs to neither of the main groups of early MSS (4469, etc., or 1615, etc.), but that it is closest to 603 (with which in addition it shares some features of convoy) and 197 (with which it shares, in particular, the correct *sediai*).

2. 43 alone among known copies of KI shares a number of features with the assumed protograph of the second version of Ivan's letter, and is in general very close to the 1581 text of KI, which probably represents the version of KI which accompanied the second version of Ivan's letter.

3. Reconstruction of the protograph of 43 indicates that this protograph contained a text very much like that found in the Chronograph and Kurbskii collection MSS as published by Kuntsevich, which probably accompanied the protograph of the second version of GI. During the composition of GI[b],

this protograph was cannibalized for the purpose of providing lead sentences and quotations from the portions of Kurbskii's letter which had not been utilized in the writing of the first version of GI, and these passages were simply cut out of the text, cut into snippets, which were then arranged alongside the (presumably similarly dissected) text of the first version of GI, in the rearranged order, thus providing a kind of outline for the composition of GI[b]. At the same time, cuts were apparently made for the introduction of the passages found only in KI[b]. The copyist of 43 attempted to regather these snippets in order to make a fair copy of KI, but the puzzle was too complex for him, hence the *kasha* of 43. That such was the case may be seen from the following observations.

If one rearranges the text of 43 in original order, one produces a text which, by comparison with the Kuntsevich edition (hereafter cited by column and line, e.g., 1/4), has the following gaps: 1/16–18, 2/8–20; 3/4–7; 3/13–14; 3/15–28; 4/6–7; 4/12–13; 4/13–14; 4/25–26; 4/32–5/1; 5/27–6/4; 6/12–13; 6/17–18; 6/26–7/4. These lines, that is to say, are nowhere found in 43, in whatever order.

Now assuming that the original from which 43 was made once represented a text on five or six pages (i.e., parts of approximately six folios), we must attempt to find the beginning of such a page, if possible.

The first feature to strike the eye in the fragmented text is a certain repetition or parallelism of gaps and unbroken text at intervals of approximately 9/10 lines (as the text is published in *Poslaniia*, pp. 534–536). Thus the passage beginning *krov' moia . . .* is followed after 9 lines by a similarly unbroken passage beginning *iako malo i rozhdeshii . . .* much as the passage *budu besprestanno . . .* is followed at the same interval by a similarly long passage beginning *Asche i t'mami . . . .* A similar and very significant parallelism is observed between the places where cuts were presumably made for the additions found in the second version of Kurbskii's letter (KI[b]) and badly fragmented places in the text (*. . . i vozdal esi mi . . . / i sie ne vo edinom . . .* and *. . . Fedor Rostislavich . . . / soglasnim tvoim boiarom . . .*). By trial and error, the snippets may be arranged, assuming ca. 16 lines on a page and ca. 30 letters to a line, to produce the following reconstruction of the mutilated original which the copyist of 43 had at his disposal.

The original was unspoiled on 1v, where the Kurbskii letter began, and 5r, where it ended. The remaining pages had the following cuts and gaps (line numbers are given at the left; roman numerals indicate number of fragments in 43; first lines on pages always cited, even where missing in 43):

2r	2v
1: (I) *dushu za tia polagaiushchikh.*	1: (IX) *khotia uzhe . . .*
4: *. . . pravoslavnykh*/gap, 12 lines to end of page (*aki ne*)	4: *. . . v pravdu*/gap, 2 lines
6: possible editorial cut at *Chto provinili . . .* (cf. Fennell, *Corresp.*, p. 104)	6: (X)/*iako slovesa . . .*
15: possible editorial cut at *Ali ty bezsmerten . . .* (this text found in KI[a]; not used for additions to KI[b].)	15: *. . . ot tobe*/gap, two lines to end of page (*ponezhe gorest'iu eshche*)

3r

1: *dusha moia* . . . (text missing to line 5)

4: editorial cut for addition in KI[b] between *otognan bykh* and *i vozdal esi*

6: (IV)/*krov' moia iako voda* . . .

13–14: text transposed in 43: cut into lines?

15–16: missing in 43

4r

1: (VI) *ikh zhe sotvorikh* . . .

5: small gap

7: . . . *strashnogo suda*/gap, 1½ lines, part of which, *ne mni mia . . . osem* used as (VII), part, *do dni skonchaniia moego* lost

8: text begins,/*budu besprestanno* . . .

15: . . . *Rostislavicha. Ne mni*/gap, 1½ lines to end of page, caused by cut for addition in KI[b]

3v

1: *i nikogda zhe* . . .

4–5: . . . *sotvorikh*/fragments: *i sie ne* . . . moved, as (XI); *Dvoiu no* . . . retained as (II); gap (*mnogi* . . .)

6: (II con't)/*iako malo i* rozhdeshii

14: . . . *bitvakh*/one line missing

15–16: (III, V) *No tebe, tsariu* . . . used twice

4v

1: *aki uzhe pogibshikh* . . . , text missing to line 4

4: fragment (XIV) *razsechennye* . . . *prosiat* moved in 43

6: fragment (VIII) *zatochennye* . . . moved

7: fragment (XIII) *ot zemli k bogu* moved

8: fragment, *vopiem* used twice as XIV and XII

8: fragment, *den' i noshch'* omitted

8: text begins (XV) *ashche i t'mami* . . .

14–16: One- and two-word gaps from *laskatelem* . . . to end of page (*tvoei i telu*) caused by cut on other side of page.

With this reconstruction before us, we may seemingly recreate the copyist's decisions in reconstituting the text which has come to us in 43. Having copied the beginning of the letter as far as *pravoslavnykh* (i.e., fragment I), at which point his original had been cut for the purpose of the composition of GI[b] (cf. Fennell, *Corresp.*, pp. 44 and 104), the copyist found himself 4 or 5 lines into a page, but without textual clues to lead him to the following text (*i tshchasia* . . .) which had been cut into lead sentences for GI[b] (Fennell, *Corresp.*, pp. 104, 106, 112, 120). He therefore chose fragment II on 3v, which represented nearly a complete page, and began at approximately the same height on the page. He copied it as far as *bitvakh*, where it was probably cut, and located the bottom lines of the same page (III: *no tebe, tsariu* . . .). Having copied this line, he realized that the text found on the other side of fragment II (i.e., fragment IV; *krov' moia* . . .) was also a part of the listing of things which *ni vo chtozhe byst'*, and copied IV as far as *i skhozhakh*, transposing some lines of text. He then recopied fragment III as fragment V, forgetting to include the text found on the other side of this scrap (*no razvee* . . .).

He now found himself at the bottom of a page, which was obvious from the margins on the scrap which he had just copied, and set out to find a top-of-page scrap. He was aided in his search by the fact that the fragment

(VI) which he chose, the top of the original 4r, was textually obviously the correct choice. He then copied the bulk of 4r, omitting the ca. $1\frac{1}{2}$ lines excised at lines 7–8 (he later found a snippet from it which he used as VII) as far as the words *Rostislavicha. Ne mni/* at which point he realized that he needed ca. 2 lines to complete what was a page in his original. To fill out this page he used VII, which began with the same words *ne mni* . . . and VIII, a fragment from 4v, on the other side of the text he had just reconstructed.

He began again to look for the top of a page at this point, and located IX, which had been the top of 2v, the other side of which he had used at the beginning, but overlooked in his later work. He copied the whole page, piecing together the fragments presumably produced by the cutting of the text on 2r, with the exception of two lines which he could not locate. This however, left him short of the equivalent of a whole page, and he filled in with the tiny snippets XI–XIV. At this point only the text *asche i* . . . (XV) remained, and this he copied to the end, after which he went on to 5r, whose text was not mutilated.

Thus it appears that 43, in spite of its late date, is an important copy for the reconstruction of the textual history of the *Correspondence*: it is a copy of a text made from the snippets of a text of KI^a which had been cannibalized for the purposes of the editing of GI^b and KI^b.

That some text "like the 1573 copy of GI^a" was also used in the composition of the second version of this letter is apparent from the fact that the gap which is found in 1573 and apparently only there (Kuntsevich, col. 30, n. 7) is repeated in all copies of the second version. This gap may, of course, also appear in 1551 or 32.8.5, as Lur'e mentions a number of lacunae without indicating details, but in this case we would still be dealing with a text "like 1573." The rest of this stemma is based upon Lur'e's comments (*Poslaniia*, pp. 520–559) with the following qualifications: the Chronograph texts (2 and following) and especially 1581 are probably closer to the protograph of the second version than Lur'e originally indicated, although he remarked about the closeness of 1581 to the short version, and about its preferred readings in some cases (ibid., p. 545). But Lur'e was concerned with the "antagonistic" tradition of the "Kurbskii Collection" texts, and since the Chronograph texts are indeed closer to the latter than to the texts of 1567, 1311, etc., they may be closer to the protograph, or at least just as close. Indeed, the only real weakness of the Chronograph texts is the nerve-wracking transposition of passages (indicated in "Boundaries of Texts") at the textual level; the Chronograph texts—even those apparently later ones published by Kuntsevich—yield in many cases superior readings to those of the redaction preferred by Lur'e. A number of these are indicated in the variants in *Poslanii*, pp. 577–581; the following examples support this conclusion:

MS 41 (*Poslaniia*, pp. 57, 579)	Chron. (Kuntsevich, p. 91, col. 2; *Poslaniia*, p. 57)
глаголали	глаголаху
...сотвористе. Яко же в притчах...	...сотвористе, ниже мнисте, яко же ныне таковая *сотвористе*. Яко ж в притчах...
...приимет? Лице же свое драго показуеши...	...приимет? *Лице же свое* пишешь не явити нам до дне страшнаго суда Божия: *лице же свое* драго показуеши...
серы очи	закры очи

Cf. also:

| "Abbreviated" Version | MS 41 (*Poslaniia*, p. 59) | Chron. (Kuntsevich, cols. |

(Kuntsevich, col. 36)		99, 101)
смятших	сметевших	смятших
яве	явственно	яве
предстоя	стоя	предстоя
зияющую	[нет]	дыхающу
ону	сорну	ону
мужей онех	[нет]	мужей онех
Поликарпу	Поликарпа	Поликарпу
праведне	[нет]	праведне
просите	приемлете	просите

. . . and many others.

STEMMA I. COMPOSITE STEMMA

This chart combines the individual stemmata, including all presumed intermediate stages, as well as the information about convoys. It is presumed that further study of the manuscripts *de visu* will reduce the number of assumed protographs somewhat. Two additional comments are in order concerning the broken lines: (1) the protograph of the first version of Ivan's first letter (GI^a) was apparently produced from a copy of Kurbskii's letter which shared certain features with texts descended from 4 (*bezsoglasnym, ot Boga dannykh ti*) and not from 7 (*soglasnym, dannykh ti ot Boga*) and was accompanied by the other texts which 2524 and 1573 have in common with 4469 and 1584; (2) the relationship involving 1573, 32.8.5, the protograph of the second version of Ivan's first letter (GI^b), and 1567 was in fact probably more complex than indicated. If 1551, the text of which I have not had at my disposal, is in fact nearly identical to 1573 (including the absence of "iazytsekh" and the lacuna *i az bezsmerten byti ne*, Kuntsevich, col. 30, n. 7) then it may be = 8, and the sole source of the passages from GI^a which appear in GI^b, and of the latter's original heading. It is also possible that 1551 was copied from a copy of GI^a which was a part of a manuscript containing the rest of the convoy which 2524, 1573, 1567, and 230 share, and that 9 descends from 5 rather than 4.

The numbered circles represent hypothetical stages with the following features:

1–5 = Same numbers on stemma of Kurbskii's first letter.
  6   Assumed protograph of Polubenskii letter as shared by 1584 and St.
  7 = 6, stemma of Kurbskii's first letter.
  8 = text "like 1573" used in composition of protograph of GI^b and for collation in 1567 or its protograph, 11.
  9   Collection containing texts common to 1551, 2524, 1573, 8, 32.8.5, and common protographs of these texts.
GI^b = protograph of GI^b, see 1 in stemma of GI^b.
 10 = 2 in stemma of GI^b, i.e., collection containing "Chronograph" version of GI, plus KI^a like 603 (not like those descended from 9).
 11 = Protograph of 230 and 1567, bringing together GI^b in version also represented in 1311 and 41, but with KI as in group "like 1573," together with other texts from 4469/1584 group.
 12 = Defective copy of "Chronograph" type, common protograph of "Kurbskii Collection" type of GI. Perhaps = 1581; see "Boundaries of Texts."
 13   Text of KI^b, including citation from L'viv *Apostol*, but with basic features of 4469/1584/603 not 2524/1567/1573 type.
 14   Protograph of "Kurbskii Collection" type, perhaps = 639.
 15   Protograph of 181/60, 1494, and 136.
 16 = Protograph of 603, 1581, and 12.

Critical Text of Kurbskii's First Letter
(Based upon variant readings in the 11 manuscripts)

The main purpose of the following text is to indicate the relationships among the various groups of copies of the first version of Kurbskii's letter. It cannot be considered a definitive text; I have compiled the variants from the texts published by Kuntsevich (1573, 2524, 181/60, 1494, 639, 136) and Lur'e (1567) and from copies kindly made by Mr. Waugh (1584, 1581, 4469, 1615, 603, 43, 197) and have not had the opportunity to check them against the originals. A number of important texts, notably 1551, are not represented. I have not attempted to render all orthographic peculiarities nor have I standardized forms. I have chosen in most cases the readings of the first version, even where the second version provides a possibly superior reading.

Курбского*

Царю, от Бога[1] препрославленному, паче же[2] во православии пресветлу[3] явльшемуся,[4] ныне же, грех ради наших, супротивным[5] обретшемуся[6]. Разумеваяй да разумеет, совесть прокаженну имуще[7], якова же ни[8] в безбожных языцех[9] обретается. И болши сего глаголати о всем поряду не попустих моему языку[10]; но гонения[11] ради прегорчайшаго[12] от державы твоея, и[13] от многие горести сердца[14] потщуся мало изрещи ти[15].

Про[16] что, царю,[17] сильных во Израили побил еси, и[18] воевод, от Бога данных ти[19] на враги твоя[20], различными смертьми разторгал еси[21], и победоносную, святую кровь их[22] во церквах божиих пролиял еси,[23] и мученическими кровьми[24] праги церковныя обагрил еси, и на доброхотных твоих и душу за тя[25] полагающих неслыханные[26] от века[27] муки и смерти и гонения[28] умыслил еси[29], изменами[30] и чародействы[31] и иными неподобными[32] облыгая[33] православных, и тщася со усердием свет[34] во тьму прелагати и сладкое горькое[35] прозывати[36]? Что провинили пред[37] тобою[38] и чем[39] прогневали[40] тя християнские предстатели[41]? Не прегордые ли царства[42] разорили и подручныя тобе их во всем[43] сотворили[44], у них же преже в работе[45] были[46] праотцы наши? Не претвердые[47] ли грады германские[48] тщанием[49] разума их от Бога тебе данны быша[50]? Сия ли нам бедным воздал еси[51] всеродно погубляя[52] нас[53]? Али[54] безсмертен, царю, мнишися[55], и[56] в неизбытную[57] ересь прельщен[58], аки не хотя уже[59] предстати неумытному[60] судье[61], надежде христьянской[62], богоначальному[63] Иисусу, хотящему судити вселенней[64] в правду, паче же не обинуяся[65] пред гордым[66] гонителем[67] и хотяще[68] изтязати их до влас[69] прегрешения их, яко же словеса глаголют. Он есть, Христос мой, седяй[70] на престоле херувимстем[71] одесную силы величествия[72] во[73] превысоких, судитель[74] межу тобою и мною.

Коего зла и[75] гонения[76] от тебе не претерпех[77]! И коих бед[78] и напастей на мя не воздвигл[79] еси! И коих лжей и измен[80] на мя[81] не возвел еси! А вся[82] приключившая ми[83] ся от тобе[84] различныя беды поряду[85] за множество[86] их, не могу[87] изрещи, и понеже горестью еще душа объята бысть[88]. Но[89] вкупе вся реку: конечне[90] всего лишен бых[91], и от земли божия тобою туне отогнан бых[92]. И за благая моя воздал ми еси злая[93] и за возлюбление мое — непримирительную[94] ненависть. И[95] кровь моя, яко вода пролитая за тя[96], вопиет на тя к Богу моему[97]. Бог сердцам[98] зритель[99] — во уме моем прилежно смышлях и совесть мою свидетеля поставлях[100], и исках, и зрех[101], мысленне обращаяся[102], и не вем себе[103], и не наидох, в[104] чем пред тобою согреших[105]. Пред войском[106] твоим хожах и исхожах[107], и никоего[108] тебе безчестия приведох[109]; но развее[110] победы пресветлы[111] помощию ангела господня, во славу твою поставлях, и никогда же полков твоих хребтом[112] к чюжим обратих[113], но паче одоления преславна[114] на похвалу тобе сотворих[115].

И сие не во едином лете[116], ни в двою[117], но[118] в довольных летех потрудихся[119], многими[120] поты[121] и терпением; яко мало и рождешии[122] мене[123] зрех и жены моея не познавах[124], и отечества своего отстоях[125] но всегда в дальних и окольных[126] градех твоих, против врагов[127] твоих, ополчяхся[128] и претерпевах[129] естественныя болезни, имже господь мой, Иисус Христос, свидетель; паче же учащен[130] бых ранами от варварских рук в различных битвах[131] и сокрушенно уже[132] ранами[133] все тело имею[134]. Но тебе, царю, вся сия ни во что же бысть[135].

Но[136] хотех рещи вся поряду ратные мои дела[137], ихже сотворих[138] на похвалу твою[139], но сего ради не изрекох, зане лутчи[140] Бог весть: он бо есть[141] всим сим мздовоздаятель[142], и не токмо сим, но и за чяшу[143] студеные воды. И еще, царю, сказую ти и[144] х тому: уже[145] не узриши, мню, лица[146] моего до дня Страшнаго суда[147]. И не мни[148] мене молчаща[149] ти о сем: до дни[150] скончания живота[151] моего буду непрестанно[152] со слезами вопияти[153] на тя пребезначальной тройцы[154], в нея[155] же верую; и[156] призывая[157] в помощь херувимского Владыки[158] матерь, надежу мою и заступницу[159], владычицу богородицу, и всех святых, избранных божиих, и государя моего, князя Федора Ростиславичя[160].

Не мни[161], царю, ни помышляй нас суемудренными[162] мыслми аки уже погибших и избъенных[163] от тебе[164] неповинно заточенных[165] и прогнанных бес правды[166]. Не радуйся о сем, аки одолением тщим[167] хваляся: избиенные тобою[168] у престола господня стояще,[169] отомщения на тя просят, заточенные же и[170] прогнанные от тебе без правды от земля ко Богу вопием[171] день и нощь[172] на тя[173]. Аще и[174] тмами хвалишися в гордости своей, в привременном сем и[175] скоротекущем веке, умышляючи[176] на христьянский[177] род мучительныя сосуды, паче же наругающе[178] и попирающе[179] ангельский образ, и[180] согласующим[181] ти ласкателем и товарищем трапезы бесовские[182], согласным[183] твоим бояром, губителем[184] души твоей и телу, иже и детьми[185] своими, паче Кроновых жерцов[186], действуют. И о сем, даже и до сих. А писаньеце[187] сие, слезами измоченное[188], во гроб со собою повелю вложити[189], грядущи[190] с тобою на суд Бога моего, Иисуса[191]. Аминь[192].

Писано во граде в Волмере[193], государя моего[194], Августа Жигимонта короля, от него же надеюся[195] много пожалован быти и утешен[196] ото всех скорбей моих, милостию его господарскою, паче же Богу ми помогающу[197].

Слышах[198] от священных писаний, хотящая[199] от дьявола пущенну[200] быти на род христьянский[201] губителя[202], от блуда зачятаго, богоборнаго[203] антихриста, и видех[204] ныне сигклита[205], всем ведома[206], яко от преблуждения рожден[207] есть[208], иже днесь шепчет во уши ложная царю[209] и льет[210] кровь кристьянскую, яко воду, и выгубил уже сильных во Израили[211], аки согласник делом антихристу[212]: не пригоже у тебя быти таковым[213] потаковником[214], о царю! В законе господни в[215] первом писано: «моавитин и аммонитин в выблядок до десяти родов во церковь божию не входят,» и прочая[216].

VARIANTS

*. *Так* 4469, 1584; 197: Послание благоверному царю и великому князю Ивану Василевичю всеа Русии от Курбскаго из Литвы; 1615: Грамота князя Андрея Кур(б)скова; 43: Послание к царю и великому князю Ивану Васильевичю Всеа Росии бывшаго его боярина князь (так) Андрея Михаиловича Курпскаго, а писал сие писание из Волмера Полского города отехав к полскому королю; 603: К великому государю царю и великому князю Ивану Васильевичю всеа Русии самодержцу князь Ондрей Михаилович Курбский изменя в Литву отъехав так пишет; 1573, 2524: Лета 1564-го. Грамота Курбского к царю из Литвы; 1551: Лета 1564-го. Грамота князя Андрея Курбского к царю и великому князю Ивану Васильевичю всеа Русии; 1567: *нет*; 1581: Лист, присланный из Вифляндской земли из города Волмера от князя Ондрея Курбского Глава 72; 181/60, 1494, 639, 136: Эпистолиа первая князя Андрея Курбскаго, писана к царю и великому князю московскому прелютаго ради гонения его.

1. 1581: от Бога *нет*.
2. 1615: паче же да; 43: паче же и; 2524, 1567: же *нет*.
3. 197: пресветло; 1615: *нет*; 181/60, 639: пресветлому.
4. *Так* 197; 4469: явившеся; 1584, 1581: явльшуся; 1615: удивлющуся; 43: явивцюся; 603, 1573, 2524, 1567, 181/60, 1494, 639, 136: явившуся.
5. 197: сопротивне; 181/60, 1494, 639, 136: сопротив сим.
6. *Так только* 181/60, 1494, 136; *все другие* обретеся.
7. 197: прокажению имуща; 43: имея; 1581: преимуще.
8. 43, 603: и.
9. 1573, 2524, 1567: *нет*.
10. 197: Болша о сих не попустих моему языку глаголати вся поряду; 4469, 1584: И болши сего о сем глаголати поряду вся не попустих моему языку; 43: Но сего о сем вся поряду не попустих глаголат...; 1581: И болши сего вся поряду о сем глаголати не попусти языку моему; 181/60, 1494, 639, 136: И болши сего о сем всех [1494: всем] поряду глаголати не попустих моему языку.
11. 181/60, 1494, 639, 136: гонения же.
12. 1584: прегорчайщая; 1615: прегорчающе; 43: прегорчающего; 603: прегоршаго; 1581: прегорша; 1573, 2524: горчайшаго.
13. 43: твоея уклонихся; 181/60, 1494, 639, 136: и *нет*.
14. 4469, 1584: сердце.
15. 197, 1615, 1573, 2524 ти *нет*; 1615, 1573, 2524, 1567: изрещи (ти) царю; 43: и... ти *нет*.
16. 197, 1615, 43, 1581, 1573, 1567, 2524: По.
17. 1615: царю *нет*.
18. 4469: и *нет*.
19. 197: ти *нет*; 1567: от Бога *нет*; 1615, 43, 1573, 2524: данных ти от Бога.
20. 181/60, 1494, 639, 136: на враги твоя *нет*.
21. 603: растерзал еси; 43, 197: расторгнул еси; 181/60, 1494, 639, 136: различным смертем предал еси.
22. 1615: победною их святую кровь.
23. 181/60, 1494, 639, 136: божиих, во владыческих торжествах пролиял еси.
24. 181/60, 1494, 639, 136, 1615: мученическими их кровьми.
25. 1581: душу свою; 197: душа воя на тя.
26. 197: неслыхованные; 4469: неслышано; 1584: не слушал но; 1567: неслыханы.
27. 4469: от великия; 43, 181/60, 1494, 639, 136: от века *нет*.
28. 181/60, 1494, 639, 136: мучения и гонения и смерти.
29. 1615: смыслил еси.
30. 4469: измена.
31. 1567: чярдвани; 639: неродействы.
32. 1584: неподобно.

33. 181/60, 1494, 136: оболгающи; 639: оболгая.

34. 4469: все.

35. 1615, 1584: горьким; 603: за горькое.

36. 1615, 1584: призывати; 1573: сопрозывати; 197: и тщащеся преложити и тьму во свет прозвати и горькое сладко.

37. 1615: О чем правились пред; 197: Что согрешили пред; 1581: провиних.

38. 181/60, 1494, 639, 136: тобою о царю.

39. 4469, 1584: чим; 603: или чим.

40. 197: прогневаша; 1573: прогневили; 2524: прогневали *переправлено на* прогневили; 1581: прогневах.

41. 181/60, 1494, 639, 136: представателю.

42. 197: гордыя ли царства; 1615: прегордое ли царство.

43. 197, 1567: подручны тобе сих во всем; 181/60, 1494, 639, 136: подручных во всем тобе; 4469, 1584, 603: подручна; 1615: подручия тебе во всем.

44. 181/60, 1494, 639, 136: сотворили мужеством храбрости их у них.

45. 1615: в работех.

46. 181/60, 1494, 639, 136: быша.

47. 4469, 603, 1567: предтвердые.

48. 1567: ерманские; 1615: гермонские.

49. 197: тщанием *нет*.

50. *Так* 197, 1581; 4469, 1584, 603, 181/60, 1494, 639, 136: бысть; 1615, 1573, 2524, 1567: быста.

51. 1615: воздал еси злая возблагая всеродных погубляя.

52. 197: погубляеши.

53. 603, 1581: нас *нет*.

54. 197, 181/60, 1494, 136: Или; 603, 1581: Сам ли; 1615, 1573, 2524, 1567: Али ты.

55. 1615, 603, 1573, 2524: мнишися быти.

56. 181/60, 1494, 639, 136: или.

57. 1573, 2524: неизбытную.

58. 4469, 1567, 181/60, 1494, 639, 136: еси *нет*;

59. 4469: уде; 1584: уд.

60. 1615: не хотя у пред Спаса.

61. 4469, 1584: суду; 43: суду и.

62. 181/60, 1494, 639, 136: надежде христьянской *нет*.

63. 1567, 197: Богу начальному; 1615: кристьянскому богоначальному моему Иисусу.

64. 1615: всей вселенней; 1581: вселенную

65. 197: обинуюся.

66. 197, 1584, 1573, 1567, 2524: пред гордым.

67. 197, 181/60, 1494, 639, 136: мучителем.

68. 1573: хотяща; 1615, 603: хотящу; 181/60, 1494, 639, 136: паче же прегордым мучителем и не обинуяся истязати их и до.

69. 1567, 1573, 2524, 1615: до власти; 197: истязати до влас.

70. *Так только* 197; 43: сядяй; 181/60, 1494, 639, 136: седящий; *все другие:* седяще.

71. 4469, 1584, 181/60, 1494, 639, 136: херувимском.

72. 181/60, 1494, 639, 136: владычествия; 1581: превеличествия; 1615, 1573, 2524, 1567: силы *нет*.

73. 1584, 603: во *нет*.

74. 1615: светел; 43: он бо есть судитель ; 1581: судити.

75. 4469, 1615, 1581: и *нет*.

76. 1615: злаго гонения.

77. 43: приял есмь.

78. 197: и коих иже; 603: обид.

79. 1573, 181/60, 1494, 639, 136: подвигл; 197: подвигнул.

80. 4469: лжени и; 1573: коих же измен; 181/60, 1494, 639, 136: лжеплетений презлых.

81. 197: на мя *нет.*

82. 181/60, 1494, 639, 136: вся *нет.*

83. 1615, 603: ми *нет.*

84. 197: от тобе *нет.*

85. 1573, 2524: беды претерпех но за.

86. 181/60, 1494, 639, 136: множеством.

87. 4469, 181/60, 1494, 639, 136: могу ныне.

88. 181/60, 1494, 639, 136: горестью души моей объят бых; 1615: еще *нет.*

89. 1567, 4469: И; 603: но *нет*; 197: не.

90. 4469, 1584: конечне и; 197: конец не.

91. 1615, 197: бых *нет.*

92. 181/60, 1494, 639, 136; 1573, 1581: тобою *нет*; 1615: от тебя. 197: отогнан есмь. *Здесь во второй редакции прибавлено*: аки тобою понужден. Не испросих умиленными глаголы, не умолих тя многослезным рыданием, ни исходатай-ствовах от тебя некоея же милости архиерейскими чинми.

93. *Так только* 197; 1567: злая возблагая; 1581: злая за возблагая.; *Все другие списки*: И воздал мне еси злая за благая. *См. выше, прим.* 51.

94. 1615: непременительную; 603: непримерительную

95. 181/60, 1494, 639, 136, 1615: И *нет.*

96. 1573: за тя *нет.*

97. 1573, на тя *нет*; 1581: к Богу моему на тя.

98. 1615: Бог се царь.

99. 4469, 1584 зритель *нет*; 197: сердцу зрителю.

100. 181/60, 1494, 639, 136: смышлях и обличник совестный мои свидетеля на ся поставлях; 43, 4469, 1584: и совести моей свидетеля поставлях; 197: представлях.

101. 1615: зре; 603: зрих.

102. 603, 2524, 1573: зрех, мысленне обращаяся; 43: мысленно не обращая-ся; 181/60, 1494, 639, 136, 1567, 1615, 4469, 1584: и зрех мысленне и обращася; 197: мысленно обращахся.

103. 1573: и не вем себе *нет*; 4469, 1584: не вем себя; 197: не свем собя; 1581: не вем в себе.

104. 1494, 181/60, 639, 136, 1567: ни в чем.

105. 181/60, 1494, 639, 136, 1567: согрешивша. 197: виновата и согрешився.

106. 4469, 1584, 603, 1581: воинством.

107. 1615: и исхожах *нет.*

108. 1573, 43: николи же.

109. 4469: безчестна; 1567: приводях.

110. 181/60, 1494, 639, 136: токмо; 197: различные.

111. 1615: пресветлюю; 4469, 1584, 197: пресветлыя.

112. 1567: кристьян.

113. 197: твоих к чюжим полком хрептом обратих.

114. 181/60, 1494, 639, 136, 197: преславныя; 1615: на преславно.

115. *Так* 1567, 1615, 4469, 197; *другие списки*: сотворях.

116. 603: месте.

117. 181/60, 1494, 639, 136, 4469, 1584: во дву; 197: водво; 1581: не вдвух.

118. 1567, 1573: и; 43: но в давних; 197: но во многых.

119. 1615: трудихся.

120. 181/60, 1494, 639, 136: со многими; 43: многими... терпением *нет.*

121. 603, 1581: многими труды поты и терпением.

122. 181/60, 1494, 639, 136: рождшия; 1573: рождешия; 4469: рожения ми; 1584: роженный ми; 603: рожешия мя зрих; 1581: рождшая ми; 1615: мало из-рещи; 197: рожшия.

123. 181/60, 1494, 136, 639: мя.

124. 197, 1584, 603, 43, 1581: познах; *Вторая редакция*: терпением и всегда отчества своего отстоях и мало рождшия мя зрех и жены моея не познавав.

125. 4469, 1584, 197: остах.

126. *Так* 197; 1573: *переправлено другими чернилами из дальноконных*; 1567,

181/60, 1494, 639, 136: дальноконных; 4469: дальнюю окольных; 1584: в дальнеокольных; 603, 43, 1581: в дальних градех; 1615: в довольных ратех.

127. 4469, 197: враг.

128. 197: ополчевахся.

129. 1615: ополчихся никогда ж безумна бывал и претерпевал.

130. 43: уязвлен; 197: учащаем.

131. 1615: различных бедах.

132. 1584: уже на; 1581: уже ми ранами имею.

133. 181/60, 1494, 639, 136: язвами.

134. 1567: имея; 197, 1581: все тело мое; 43: и сокрушенно... имею *нет*.

135. 43: ни во что же быша; *Вторая редакция*: вся сия аки ничто же бысть но развие нестерпимую ярость и горчаишую ненависть, паче же разженные пещи, являешь к нам.

136. 181/60, 1494, 639, 136: И.

137. 4469, 603, 1581; 1584, 197: дела моя.

138. 1573, 603: сотворил.

139. 197, 1584: тебе; *Вторая редакция*: твою, силою Христа моего, но.

140. 1615, 1573, 2524, 1567: лутше един Бог.

141. 1573, 1615: он бо, Бог, есть *нет*; 43: Бог весть. Он бо есть всем сим; 1584: лутче Бог он Бог есть; 603, 1581: лутче Бог весть, он Бог весть всем сим; 197: лутче Бог весть, он бо есть. *Вторая редакция*: лутче Бог весть нежели человек. Он бо есть за все мздовоздаятель.

142. 603: воздатель; 1615: создатель; 1581: мзды воздатель.

143. 181/60, 1494, 639, 136: не токмо но и за чашу; 1615: не токмя семного и за чаша.

144. 1584, 603: и *нет*; 197: тебе к тому.

145. *Вторая редакция*: воды, а вем яко и сам их не невеси. И да будет ти, царю, ведомо к тому: уже.

146. 181/60, 1494, 639, 136: мню в мире лица; 197: мню *нет*; 603: уже мню не узриши лица.

147. *Вторая редакция*: до дня преславного явления Христа моего.

148. 181/60, 1494, 639, 136: и да не мни; 197: и не могу о сем молчати.

149. 1567, 603, 1615: молчяти.

150. 181/60, 1494, 639, 136: дни *нет*.

151. 197: жития; 181/60, 1494, 639, 136, 1615: живота *нет*; 43: и не мни... моего *нет*.

152. 1567: безпрестанно; 1615: безпрестани.

153. 181/60, 1494, 639, 136: вопияти со слезами; 197: вопити; 4469, 1584: вопия.

154. 1615: пребезначальную тройцею.

155. 4469, 1584, 603: в ня.

156. 603: и *нет*.

157. 181/60, 1494, 639, 136, 1573, 43, 197: призываю.

158. 1567: владыку.

159. 4469: владыку и матерь мою надежду; 1584: монастырь мою надежду Богородицу; 197: матерь надежду мою владычницу.

160. *Вторая редакция*: государя моего праотца князя Федора Ростиславича, иже целокупно тело имеет во множайших летех соблюдаемо, и благоухание паче аромат от гроба испущающе, и благодатию Святого Духа струи исцеления чудес источающе, яко же ты о том царю добро веси. Не мни.

161. 197: не мни *нет*.

162. 4469: с мудрыми; 603: суемудрыми; 197: и не мудрствуй.

163. 1615: помышляй на суде мудренными мысльми уже погибших избиенных

164. 1573, 197: от тебе *нет*.

165. 603: заточенных в темницах.

166. 1573: избиенных бес правды. Не радуйся о сем аки одоле от тебе неповинно; 197: избиенных от тебе неповинно без правды.

167. 4469, 1584, 603: тощим; 197: аки сим.

168. *Так только вторая редакция;* 197: разсеянные тобою; *остальные списки*: разсеченные.

169. 1567, 1615: стояше; 197: предстоят господня.

170. 603: заточенные же в темницы.

171. 1615, 4469, 1584, 603, 197: вопиют.

172. 197: день и нощь *нет*.

173. 181/60, 1494, 639, 136: на тя *нет*.

174. 4469, 1584, 603: и *нет*.

175. 603: и *нет*.

176. 197: умышляеши.

177. 1567, 1615, 4469: крестьянский.

178. 197: наругаешися. 43: помысляющи.

179. 603: попирающе и наругающе; 4469: и наругаяся потирающе; 1584: и наругаяся попирающа.

180. 197: и *нет*.

181. 181/60, 1494, 639, 136, 4469, 1584, 603: согласующе ; 1581: из согласующе

182. 197, 4469, 1584, 181/60, 1494, 639, 136, 1581: бесовские *нет*. 1581: бесом.

183. 197, 1584: безгласным; 4469: безсогласным; 639: бесособогласным; 181/60, 1494, 136: несогласным.

184. 1567: боярогубителем; 603, 197: бояром и губителем.

185. 603: иже действы; 197: и з детьми.

186. 1573: Ароновых жерцов; 197: кровных жерцов; 1584: кровенных жерцов; 1615: телу и жертвами своими, паче Кровых жерцов, действуют. *Вторая редакция:* иж тя подвижут на Афродитские дела и детьми... действуют.

187. 4469: даже до сих и писание; 603: А писание; 197: до здее и сие писание.

188. 4469, 1584: измоченно.

189. 1615: а сие писаниейца со слезами измочено во гроб свой повелю с собою вложити; 603: велю положити; 197: велю с собою положити; 1584: велю вложити.

190. 4469, 1584, 603, 1615: грядуще; 197: грядущими.

191. 1573, 2524, 181/60, 1494, 639, 136: Иисуса Христа.

192. *На этом слове кончается 197.* 43: Аминь. Под сим же посланием Князя Андрея Курбского по конце приписано сия словеса: Слышах.

193. 181/60, 1494, 639, 136: Писано Волмере граде; 1573: в Володимере; 1615: во граде Олмереа Лета [1564]; 1584: в Волмомере; 4469: во Владимере; 603: во Лвове; 1567: в Полмере.

194. 1567: господаря.

195. 1567: надеян; 1573, 1581: надеяся; 603: надеяхся.

196. 4469, 1584, 603, 1581: пожалован и утешен быти.

197. *На этом слове кончается 1551.* 2524, 1573: помогающу [1564].

198. 2524, 1573: *Заглавие:* Курбского ко государю. Слышах; 603, 1581: *Заглавие:* Князя Ондрея Курбского же. Слышах.

199. 1615: хотяще; 4469: хотяща; 603, 1581: хотя.

200. 1615: пущенну; 1584: попущенна.

201. 1615: народу кристьянскому.

202. 1567, 1573, 2524: прогубителя; 1615: погубителя.

203. 4469: богоборца; 603: богоборного *нет*.

204. 1615, 43: видев.

205. 1584: синклиста.

206. 1573: ведом; 603, 1581: ведомо.

207. 1584, 603: рожен; 1581: рожден *нет*.

208. 43: бысть.

209. 603, 181/60, 1494, 639, 136: шепчет ложное во уши; 1581: щепчес.

210. 1584: или есть; 43: пиет; 1581: льешь.

211. 181/60, 1494, 639, 136: сильных и благородных во Израили.

212. 1615, 2524, 1573, 1567: согласник *нет*; 603: яко согласии их демоном.

213. 43, 1567: таковым.

214. 181/60, 1494, 639, 136: пригоже таким потакати; 4469, 1584: потаковником *нет*. 603, 1581: таким почитати.

215. 4469, 1584: в *нет*.

216. 603: не входят до десяти родов во церковь а по десяти родех и вовеки; 1615: не входят и притсая[?] ко мне грамоту курскова.

Appendix IV
Texts

A. *KHVOROSTININ'S* *"FOREWORD"*
(From *LZAK za 1905 god* XVIII [1907], third pagination, pp. 38–39)

К читателю.

Возлюбленный мой брате любодушевный читателю! Аще кое узриши в моих слозех и словесех или в речеточьстве, Бога ради исправи поспешением своего учения, советом боголюбезных мудрец и не буди подвизатися на гнев, но аще что хощеши, не гордостию, но смирением исправляй, да некогда ты темже искушен будеши. Буди брата своего тяготу носити, воспоминающе блаженнаго Мартириа, како виде гнилаго и струпами слепшися; старец же виде и простре мантию свою, на рамо восприят, гнилаго нося. Хотяще уже внити в монастырь, взятся мнимый гнилый на небо, и виде его старец Христа Бога грядуща, возглашаше к нему: о Мартирие, ты мене зде не презрел, Аз тя во оном веце помилую, ты о мне зде умилися. Аз тя в небесном царствии прославлю. И тако невидим бысть. Аз убо, возлюбление, желатель бых рачению любомудрых издавна, многое учение преидох тщанием паче сверстник моих в роде моем, ни по гаданию ниже по любопрению, да сам мудрейший неких явлюся — буди далече от мене высителное сие беснование — но смирением хождахом, того ради и беды приемля многи, жалостию преходя. В ратех тиронствовах, в полцех воеводствовах, со враги брахся. Что реку или что возглаголю? Коея не приах беды? Но по Павла апостола словеси «беды от сродник, беды во градех», беды в наследиах, многи скорби от владык, множайшиж от властей, також и от церковник неученых, туне поставленых. Камень бех утроба моя, железа крепчайши сердце мое, не возвеселихся вином, ни услади мя брашно. Всяко пианьство противно бе нрава моего; видя нечестивых, истаяше сердце мое пианьства исполненым. Глаголаше ко мне языком, егож не прия свойство мое, чюже бе сребро и злато хотению моему. Не совратен бех от пути царьска, владыкам бе верен во мнозе и в мале и не совратихся от них ни на десно ни на шуие, никакож позыбахся от них, ни враг их не возвесели служением своим, праведно и нелестно и беззлобно сердце к ним стяжах, ни покленух в храминех своих, ни вымениах своих посмеяхся им, ниже поругавя им в ложницы своей на ложе моем владыкам моим. Якож имуще нецый, не умех лстивен быти никомуж, того ради никому угоден бых, не умех бо ковати кова на братию свою православныя христиане. Не прелсти мя честь и слава, не обузда мя к веселию, и не хотех злата и сребра лишшее, в лихву не дах сребро мое, не понудив рабы моя мучительством жити и быстрым быти на чюжая имения. И что еще безумне глаголю? Остаток понуждает беды моея сетования и плача глаголати. Бог убо сердца моего зритель и всякому благодеянию податель. Он бо есть Христос Господь мой всем Владыка и Бог, Иже седяй на престоле величествия своего в превысоких, всем богатый дарователь и всем сим, не токмо сим, но и за чашу студеныя воды. Той бо весть, коего злаго гонения не претерпех, коих напастей не претерпех, коего зла не возведоша на мя, коего лжееретичества и лжеизменных малодушеств не приложиша ми. Но вся сия безвинно претерпевая, хотех мало написати и вразумети ово от Греческих и Римских писм, овогда потребное предложити тщахся, и возбранен бых, от неученых невежд осудим бых, яко еретика вменяше мя. Странен бых во стране благодушных и бых в поношение и в стыд. О беда! о скорбь! како могу изрещи? в темницах того ради, во юзах, в терпении, во изгнании, в заточении! Коего лжезлоизменнаго слова на своих раменах не понесе? Хлеб бо яко пепел ядях и питие мое слезами растворях; ложе мое без сна прехождах, камень вменяшеся постела моя. Пространны быша пути моя отбегати от озлобления, злати быша стези к дарованию моему, но и вси сродницы и братия моя понуждаху мя к тому, яко и сродница моя не сотвориша ми о сем предкновения, но еще и в волю погагаша ми, да не видит око ея безвинно страждуща мя туне, но точию ми едино возбраняше — Христа моего закон образом креста, яко Того слава и держава со Отцем и святым Духом и во веки. Аминь.

B. *LETTERS OF SEMEN SHAKHOVSKOI*

To Prince D. M. Pozharskii
(From Golubev, *TODRL* XVII: 407–413)

Твое же, государь, писано словенъски по краегранесии
Аще умом своим вонмеши, тогда да увеси
Наше же убогое, не весма ти объявлено,
Занеже многими и безмерными грехи обременено.
5 Несть ползы во многогрешном нашем нарицании,
Аще не пребудем в добродетельном деянии.
Ваше же бы явно и славно было везде,
Чтоб враги царевы боялись во всякой орде.
Подобает паки светлым и благоплеменитым ражатися
10 И против сопостат мужественне вооружатися,
Без таковых бо земля крепко и славно не может стояти,
Вящи же всего всесилна бога достоит на помощь призывати.
Яко не силою бывает брань, но божиим поможением
И богоносных и чюдотворных отец к нему молением.
15 Занеже всего силнее бывает чистая к богу молитва,
И на невидимыя враги, аки некая изощренная бритва.
Ей, ей, тако неложно.
Без нея быти невозможно.
И еще ми много слово недостало рещи о твоем мужестве и храбръстве.
20 И о совершенной твоей добродетели к богу, и о душевном паки богатьстве,
И о божиих к нам великих щедротах, и о долгом терпении,
И о нешем к нему жестосердстве и всегдашнем неисправлении.
И хощем воспомянути твою к себе милость и рещи о своей скорби и недо-
    статце,
Не мощно бо великия ради нужды преминути сего въкратце.
25 И еще без лености хощу потружатися чернилом и пером
И убогою своею мыслию и недостаточным своим умом,
Понеже мысль моя разгорается во мне, аки пламень в пещи,

Нудит мя о всем твоем добродеянии доволне рещи,
Аще и без нас недостойных идет о тебе предобрая слава всюду,
30 Яко всегда имееши на враги мечь свой остр обоюду
Да неизлиха будет и наше малое сие к тебе, государю, прошение,
Понеже отняли есте тогда от всех поношение.
Что же рцем и что возглаголем, но воспомянем выше реченное слово.
Было же врагов наших зияние на нас, аки рыкание львово,
35 И мыслили во уме своем владети во веки землею Российскою,
Якоже поганыя богомерзкия тоурки и ныне владеют Палестинъскою
И господь бог совет их разорил
И гордость их до конца низложил.
А ведомо есть, стояли на нас, аки острыя ножи.
40 И паки господь бог не дал им того сотворити и по их умышлению не учини-
    лося,
И все великое государство на них врагов въкупе с вои собралося.
И дал нам бог вас крепких и нелестных по вере побарателей,
Что отгнали от нас таких злых и немилостивых наругателей
И что учинил такову славу и похвалу в нынешния роды,
45 Якоже вы избавили всех православных християн от конечныя тоя незгоды.
Неложно паки пред всем государством правда ваша изошла,
Якоже преже помянутая Июдив всего Израиля спасла,
Якоже тогда от единыя жены все асириане ужасилися
Такоже и наши враги от крепкаго вашего сражения смесилися.
50 И побегоша кожда их с страхом и трепетом и придоша неправе,
И не возмогоша урядитися к многокозненной своей справе,
И обьят их весь страх и трепет от вашего против их воополчения,
Паче же от божия и от пречистыя его матери и нашея заступницы поможе-
    ния.
А и ныне надеемся на божия его щедроты и пречистую царицу
55 И ея ради молить являет нам победителную свою десницу,
И на государевы праведныя молитвы, яже самому всесильному богу.
Да претъкнет их окаянных и богоборных нечестивую ногу,
И на вас крепких его государевых воин и неизменных воевод,
Да разсеяни будут с своим умышлением, аки древний исполин Неврод.
60 Понеже без вины хотят нашу православную веру на разорение.
Обаче рещи есть и наше пред богом велие и согрешение
Сего ради подобает о том бога молити и просити со слезами,
Понеже всегда за грехи наша смиряет нас всякими бедами.
Аще учнем ему с верою молитися, не предаст своего создания
65 И не презрит и ныне по-прежнему нашего к нему стенания.
Милостив и премилостив есть, утолит свой гнев и ярость
И даст нам над ними, над враги, по-прежнему велию радость.
Якоже и сам инде глаголет: «Обратитеся ко мне и обращуся к вам
И учиню вас страшны и грозны многим окрестным ордам,
70 Аще ли не послушаете мене, чюждия землю вашу поядят,
И жены ваша, и дети, и богатъство все пленом пленят».
И по сему его святому речению вся над нами за грехи наша збылося,
И великое государство во многих концах от них врагов разорилося.
Милуючи господь бог посылает на нас таковыя скорби и напсти,
75 Чтоб нам всем злых ради своих дел въконец от него не отпасти.
Свойственно бо есть християном в сем житии скорби и беды терпети
И к нему, своему творцу и богу, неуклонно всегда зрети
Аще бы не посылал на нас таковых бед, отпали б его вконец.
И никто тамо получил бы нетленный венец.
80 И никако же бы удерживалися от зла и шли б вси в муку вечную.
И ни един бы сподобиться внити в радость безконечную.
Сего ради премудрым своим промыслом и правдою все устрояет,
И аки коня браздою, тако и нас тацеми бедами от грех возражает.

Аще бы не тако нас возражал, и зверей бы дивиих горше были,
85 И паки бы вконец друг друга и брат брата не любили
Что же нас и так лютее и жестосердее ? Кое естество в безсловесных ?
И кто может исчести, колико бывает над нами смертей безвестнах ?
И зря над собой такови скорби и никако же от зла отвращаемся,
Но и паче друг на друга, аки враг на врага, завистию вооружаемся.
90 И милосердный господь, еще терпя нашим грехом, ждет нас на покаяние,
Того ради посылает на нас таких лютых врагов в наказание,
Некли приидем в чювьство и принесем к нему сердечную веору,
Да воздаст нам и во оном своем веце сторичную меру.
Аще ли и тем не накажемся, что нам будет от него, от своего творца,
95 Понеже никако же не можем смиритися преже конца.
Писано есть: «Отраднее будет Содому и Гоморе, неже тому роду».
Приличны же и мы к сему речению, поне забываем прежнюю свою незгоду
Сего ради не на тщету, но на ползу дает нам таковы казни
Чтоб нам жити пред ним, своим творцом, не без боязни,
100 Якоже негде пишет: «Ползует пелынь злопитающих утробы»,
Тако и мучением грешным ползя, зане возъбраняет от всякия злобы
Тем не люто нам прияти язва, люто по язве не наказатися,
Ей, подобает нам всем от злых своих дел отвращатися,
Да не сами себе будем враги и уготоваем вечныя муки,
105 И зде не впадем врагов наших нечестивых руки.
Положим же паки надежу на всемилостиваго в щедротах,
Он же избавил своего Израиля, бывъшаго во многих работах.
Его святая воля, что хощет, то по своей воли и сотворит,
Аще не захощет предати нас, то врагом нашим конечне возбранит
110 Ты же, государь, буди всегда чист душею своею и телом,
Понеже во оном веце всяк восприимет по злым и добрым делом,
И держи храбрость с мужеством и подание с тихостию,
И господь бог будет к тебе с великою своею милостию.
Обаче рещи, и так дела твои, аки труба вопиют всегда,
115 Не щадиши бо лица своего противу сопостат никогда.
К тому же присовокупил еси велие милосердие ко всем,
Всякаго приходящаго к тебе не оскорбляеши ни в чем,
Яко некая великая река неоскудно всех напояет,
Тако твоя прещедрая душа таковым подаянием всех утешает.
120 Ей, воистинну не имеем себе ныне такова благоутробна дятеля.
Да будет ти за то мъзда от всех творца и создателя
Зритель тебе господь, вси людие дивятся твоей велицей милости,
Никто же бо оскорблен бывает, приходя к твоей благонравно́й тихости,
Ты же, государь, во уме своем не скорби, ниже паки стужай,
125 Но на мъздовоздателя всю надежу свою и упование полагай,
Той бо воздаст ти во оном своем веце стократное воздаяние,
Зрит бо в сердцы твоем неоскудное ни тщеславное ко всем подаяние,
Якоже и сам глаголет: «Блаженни милостивии, яко тии помиловани будут».
А немилостивии и жестосердии вечных мук не избудут.
130 Ничто же есть вящи милости, та бо множество грехов прощает,
И не токмо до небеси, но и до самаго престола божия душу провожает.
И паки: велик человек милостив, и хвалится милость на суде,
Того ради слава твоя добрая и хвала идет ныне везде.
И уже не вем, како конец сказати твоей велицеи щедрости,
135 Яко помогаеши многим людем в конечной бедности,
Поминаючи божественное писание, яко «дающаго рука не оскудеет»,
А удержаваяй богатьство и ничто же себе успеет.
Того ради многое православие за тебя, за государя, молят бога и владыку,
Еже бо еси много православных прекормил и учинил славу и похвалу вели-
кую,
140 И ныне не пременил еси своего добраго обычая и нрава, всех утешаешь,

И всякаго приходящего к тебе никогда не оскорбляешь.
И не презрел еси, государь, и нашея тогда великия скудоты,
Прекормил еси нас с супружником нашим и с родшими от нас сироты.
И потом не въменил еси себе в тягость нашего же к тебе стужения,
145 И не видя от нас никоторого к себе рабъского послужения,
Пожаловал нас своею великою милостию и нищих нас не отпустил,
Но человеколюбец бог добрая тебе, государю, на ум положил,
И довольно время твоим великим жалованием и с червишками питалися,
И всегда поминаючи твое милосердие к себе утешалися.
150 Паче же плачю и рыдаю и горкими слезами землю омакая,
И к твоим государьским честным ногам главу свою подъклоняю,
Буди ми помощник и заступник в сей моей беде и напасти,
Чтоб ми бедному и с червишками вконец не пропасти.
И во веки бы за тебя, за государя своего, бога молити,
155 Чтоб тебе, государю, вся желанная от него получити.
Сам, государь, веси, напрасно стражу и погибаю,
Помощника и заступника себе в таковой сущей беде не обретаю.
Рад бы был, иж бы жив вошел во общую матерь землю,
Понеже на всяк день смертное биение от спекуляторей приемлю.
160 Но не мощно ми сего сотворити, что самому себя смерти предати,
И многогрешная душа своя и тело во ад низпослати.
И паки веси, государь, стою всегда не на лепом том позоре,
Аще бы не Христово имя, гонзнул бы живота въскоре,
Тем укупаю себе живота от того тления смертного,
165 Не хитро и не славно осудити и погубити мужа безъответнаго
А не имею милующаго ни ущедряющаго отнюд никого,
Мню же, яко всякому злато и сребро милее бывает всего,
Или рещи: немилосердие и презорство всех обдержит,
Отнюдь просто рещи: чюжая беда и напасть никому не болит.
170 И вержеи есмь, аки камень в море, никим изъвлеком,
Аще бог человеколюбец не пощадит праведным своим судом.
Разве вижу в твоем сердцы есть сияет истинный свет,
Поне бо даешь ми, государь, всегда благоутешный ответ.
И паки умилися сердце твое о нашем убожестве и сиротстве.
175 Но избран еси сосуд уродилься во своем благочестивом родстве,
И вижу, чтоб ми еси, государь, и помог, но не возмет твоя мощь,
А уже нам, грешным, в скорби сей и день, аки темная нощь.
И на том тебе, государю, много челом бью, падая на лице земли,
И ты, государь, душею своею и сердцем себе внемли.
180 И то тебе, государю, въменится в самую истинную правду,
И всегда помышляти таковое дело твоему разсудному измарагду.
Ничто же бо таковыя милости вящи у бога не бывает,
Кто в скорби и беде поне малым чим помогает.
Писано есть: «Аще не можешь помощи делом, и ты поне словом,
185 Яко утвердит кто непокриту храмину твердым кровом».
Аще ли, государь, не возможешь тем ныне помощи,
Не прогневайся, иже о чем тебе, государю, дерзнем изрещи.
Что же реку и что возглаголю и како еще дерзну к твоему величеству?
Не вем бо числа сказати твоему милосердному количеству.
190 Велик студ и зазор обдержит к тебе, государю, стужати,
Но презельныя ради скорби и беды не могу в себе молчати.
Понеже нужды ради весь страх и срам в сердцы отлагается
И кто на страсть не дерзает, той желаннаго своего не сподобляется.
Общая наша госпожа и всех томителныя свойства своего желает,
195 И для ради прироженнаго своего естества весь срам отлагает,
Яко некоторый гладный пес или волк на вся человеки шибается,
Подобно же тому и гладная утроба никого не срамляется
И паки: ничто есть тако зло всякому человеку, якоже глад,

Его же ради некогда взят бысть не един великий и преименитый град.
200 В лепоту реченно: глад уязвляет не менее меча,
От него же и самых крепких и сильных немощны бывают плеча,
И всякому человеку начало животу хлеб и вода, риза и покров.
Ей, ей, не мы глаголем, но сама наша великая нужа и кровь,
Аз же грешный за премногия грехи своя всего того пуст.
205 Но токмо мало нечто имею изо многогрешных своих уст.
Тем убогую свою душу и тело питаю и утешаюся на всяк день и час.
И еще не презре нас до конца своими щедротами всемилостивый спас.
И что было ваше жалованье, государей моих, то все изошло,
А ныне, государь, и сам веси по грехом по нашим понужное время пришло.
210 А се, государь, особная великая скорбь и беда за грех мой постигла
И без чернаго одеяния и без самоволнаго обещания до конца постригла.
А не имею милующаго ни ущедряющаго искренно в нынешнее время,
Зане, по апостольскому речению, уродилося все немилосердое семя,
И злым немилосердием и скупостию одержими, аки слепотою.
215 И самохотно гнушаемся душеспасителною нищетою.
Сего ради презираем есмь от всех, аки трава, ростящая в засени,
Поистинне нелепо рещи: от великая тоя печали подобен есмь стени,
Или яко дуб при пути повержен, от всех ногами попираем,
Такоже и аз грешный и недостойный от всех человек презираем,
220 Или яко некий сосуд непотребны изметаем бывает вон.
А ведомо есть, и всяко земное житие пар есть и сон.
И что ми о том много вещей к твоему благородию приводити,
Подобает же на всесилнаго бога вся надежа возложити.
Той всем нам надежа, и упование, и промысленник и кормитель,
225 И на вся видимыя враги наша непобедимый прогонитель.
И еще мышлю в сердцы моем, надеюся на тебя, государя моего милосердаго,
Вем бо тя верою к богу и правдою, аки адаманта твердаго.
Якоже и преже рех, не имею милующаго, ни ущедряющаго отнюд,
Вем бо паки, многих свела лютая скупость и немилосердие, в незазорный студ.
230 Не поминающе апостольскаго речения: «Не брашном брата своего погубляй,
Но егда в нужди и беде есть, тогда ему всячески помогай».
И паки пишет: «Брат от брата помогаем бывает,
Яко град тверд, а презирающии и немилующии и сами своим душам вечныя
      муки проуготовляют».
Ты же, государь, не внимай, не ревнуй таковому злому обычаю и нраву,
235 Да получишь себе не токмо зде, но и тамо у Христа бога вечную славу.
Еще молю твою премилостивую и многощедрую ко всем утробу,
Да не прежде времени предадимся бездушной вещи гробу.
Ущедри свое благонравное сердце и буди въместо бога,
Да сподобишися стати у самаго его небеснаго чертога.
240 И паки: укупи благородной души своей и телу спасение,
Да будеши имети у владыки Христа бога велие дерзновение,
Понеже всех добродетелей вящи у него вменяется
И у самаго его страшнаго и неприступнаго престола поставляется,
Иже кто в скорби и беде сущей другу своему поможет,
245 Той воздухи и облаки и солечныя луча пройти возможет,
Якоже и выше рех, стати у самаго его престола божия,
А мы, грешнии, плачемся, стоя у твоего государева подножия,
З горкими слезами и болезненным сердцем к тебе, государю вопием,
Понеже по грехом своим преданы есмы злым и немилостивым змием,
250 Иже на всяк день и час тянут сердце, аки клещами,
И злым умышлением измождавают жилы, аки огненными свещами,
Для ради своего тленнаго прибытка и кровавыя корысти,
Понеже извыкли, аки червь, древо православных християн грысти
Пожалуй, государь, что на искупление от того тления смертнаго,
255 Да сподобит тя господь бог со избранными своими венца нетленнаго,

И на препитание многогрешной души и телу и з горкими сиротами,
Да украсится душа твоя добрыми делы, аки драгими пестротами,
Как тебе, государю, вышняго промысл известит и пречистая его мати,
Да даст ти всегда силу и помощь враги цареви побеждати.
260 И молю тя, государя, в гнев не положити,
Ни в великую тягость и паки не позазрити,
Поне от нужды и от беды тако дерзаем
И твоему достойному величеству и добродею докучаем.
Аще бы не в таковей скорби и беде, не так бы тебе, государю, и скучали,
265 Разве бы милосердаго слова и сладкаго ответа от тебя ждали.
Вем бо, что уже тяжко ти, государю, от нас вменится,
Да зритель господь, что не к кому, кроме тебя, государя, приклонится.
Многи бо, аки аспиды глухия, затыкают своя слухи
И забывают, яко неимущих ради дает бог благорастворены воздухи.
270 Аще помилован еси государь от небеснаго царя, и земнаго
Сам помилован будеши. Не погуби самовластным изволением шесточислен-
    ного камени драгаго,
Пожалуй нас, грешных, и призри в конечной сей беде,
Да даст ти господь благая и полезная получити везде.
А мы должни за тебя, государя, его молить
275 Дондеже и душа в теле, чтоб тебе, государю, и до смерти правда творить.
Кто словом и делом последний невежа, въсе в его божией и всемогущей
    безсмертней деснице содержится,
И кто на него уповает, той во всем врагов своих не убоится.
Его святая воля буди, что хощет, то по своей воли и сотворит,
И за твою великую правду и кровь сугубо тя воздарит.
280 И аще ти, государю, будет и негоде, не вели ввергнути в подножие,
Зане царево и рождьшаго тя имянуется ту лице божие,
Тако же и свое честно брегий, яко славно и хвально во всех,
Понеже бо еси, государь, не бывал никогда побежден на бранех,
Паче же самаго бога и пречистыя его матери, общея нашея заступинцы,
285 Сам, государь веси, та посремляет вся законопреступницы,
Чтобы божию имени, его матери, купно и цареву не было бранно.
Веси паки и сам, что християньское имя от всех родов преизбранно.
Паки здравствуй, государь, о всещедром Христе,
И побеждай враги царевы о пречестнем его кресте,
290 Еже бо тем бывает на них победа и одоление,
И некли услышит господь наше к нему моление,
И чтоб вам, государем, дал бог на них, супостат наших, победу,
Отнюд просто рещи, не осталось бы их в земли нашей следу.
Мнози бо люди дивятся мужественному твоему храбръству.
295 И радуются, что бог тебя принес к великому государству,
Поне всегда против сопостат лица своего не щадишь,
К богу и царю и ко всем человеком правду творишь,
И сподобил тя владыко видети образ пречистыя царицы,
Та бо всегда подает победу на враги,
300 Потом же в светлости и радости лице царево,
Его же роди и воспита благоплодное чрево.
Тако же и свою рождьшую и супругу с чады,
Вси бо от бога и от вас чаем отрады.
Еще же и ближних своих приятелей и добродеев,
305 Да побиет врагов правда твоя, аки огнь сирских халдеев.
Потом же паки виде все православное множество,
Желали же видети твоего зрака и наше убожество.
Мнози бо паки жаждали видети в радости твоего лица,
Аки дети, долго не видючи своего отца.
310 Свидетель на то бог,
Иже возносит християнъский рог. Аминь.

To Tret'iak Vasil'ev
(From *VMOIDR*, bk. 9 [1851], *Smes'*, pp. 5–8)

1.

Братолюбному и благопотребному в человецех и превысокому в разуме и разсудителному божественных догмат, Третьяку Васильевичю радоватися. Писал еси к моему убожеству велми любително и унынию утешително, и аз недостаточный умом и всего блага лишенный прочтох е, и от скорби пременихся и не мало обвеселихся, благодарил благодавца Бога, еже благоразумию человека научающе и к любви наставляюще и все дарующе и благоискусными беседами учреждающе, яко мастми болезненная сердца помазающе. А напасти, государь мой, за грехи постизают мя, а иного не вем в себе ничесо же, един Господь свесть сердца и ум человеков; да у меня ж у беднаго сверх настоящие моей напасти вотчинишко подмосковное выгорело до основания, в ней же лучилося твоему благонравию любително мя посещати, и запасишка хлебные и всякие чем питался пригорело, а всего горее поведают ми, что и церковь божия моего ради окаянства сгорела ж, а иную вотчинишку отымают, а иную отняли. И от всех сих благодарю всещедраго Бога, яко биет милостивно и наказует, яко отец чадолюбивый, и вся человеколюбно строит оваго наказуючи, оваго милуючи и ко обращению от грех ожидаючи, и не даст никомужждо выше меры своея искуситися, всех равно милует, и всем вся дарует и ко спасению призывает. А на твоей великой и не сбытной любви и благоразумном утешителном писании много и премного чел бью. Бог ти воздаст за вся яже к моему окоянству любителное утешение. Еще спрошу твоего братолюбия, не вмени во тщету прошения нашего, пришли мне Бога ради Тоболской рыбки осенней осетриков и стерлядок и икрицы, елико ти возможно, а у вас то присный мой друже бывает не в дорогой цене.

2.

Благодателю моему и присвоенному духовною любовию государю моему Третьяку Васильевичу Сенка Шаховской радоватися приносит. Писанейцо государь твое и посылочка противу писания до меня дошла; и я на твоем жалованье много чел бью, а пространнее сего писати недоумеюся в своих великих напастех. В Усть-коле терпел многие смертоносные беды, и потом милость Государская взыскала, велено мне быть на Устюге; и я зря на свою неповинность ожидал милости божией и государскаго жалованья, что велят мне быть к Москве, а вместо таковаго чаяния подвинули меня подале, указал мне государь быть у Соли у Вычегоцкой. А беде своей конца не ведаю, тако ми судившу праведному и неумытному судии человеколюбцу Христу Богу нашему, за мое согрешение во изгнании и в заточении и в убожестве жизнь века сего скончавати. По сем любително по духовному союзу яко брату и другу много и премного чел бью.

3.

Премудра есть в пернатых пчела и сладостен плод ея, его же людие со тщанием насыщаютца и светло веселятца; такожде и яз друже мой насыщаюся твоих пресладких ми медоточных словес и весь радостен от печали бываю, и ко здравию себе прилагаю, обаче же сими твоими похвалами совесть свою обличаю. И сице реку по писанию твоему глаголя: яко созда нас Бог по образу своему и вся покори нам и дарова нам касатися мысленне поднебесным и подземным и почтены саном величества во всякой вещи; и сему позавидев богопротивный враг окраде праотца нашего первозданнаго Адама, и пошепта ему во ухо, и приведе его на преступление, яко быти ему повинну греху и смерти, вместо воздержания брашен приплоди ему лакомство, обаче же и всем нам рождшимся от него телоносен недуг пода, яко быти нам слабым и лакомым, вместо целомудрия блуда желаем, вместо смиренномудрия гордость стяжим, вместо любве вражду имеем, вместо похваления братоненавидение гоним и зависть, и иная богомерзская похотения в нас раждаетца лукаваго беса злохитрым замышлением, и многокозненнаго лаятелства его по отнадении славы божия не может язык человечь изрещи ниже ум вместити. Первое убо сотворена бысть от Бога в человецех правда, и потом воста от неприязни неправда и вниде в человеки, и в человецех же нача жити неправда и братися с правдою, и преможе кривда правду и прогони правду, и прияша человецы неправду а правду отвергоша. Яко же рече сын Божий ко Июдеем: яко свет рече приде в мир, и возлюбиша человецы паче тму неже свет; беша бо их дела зла, всяк бо рече делая злая ненавидит света и не приходит ко свету, да не обличатся дела его яко лукава суть. И быша мнози не творяше правды ни инем дающе; и остави их правда во своей воли жити, да погибнут яко же изволиша; и воста бо на девство блуд, воста скверна на чистоту, и лютость на кротость, и ненависть на любовь, несытство на пост, пьянство на трезвость, обида на смирение и прочая злая на благая. Тому убо последовах аз окаянный и побежден всеми сими слабостию своею; и сего ради по самохотию поруган бысть, от него и срама и бесчестия и безумия исполнихся и в плен ласкосердием отведохся; яко же Исав по навождению бесовску брашна ради первенства испадох, тако же аз безумный самоизволно в напасти впадох, и сбываетца на мне вся пророчествия древних велемудренных и духоносных мужей: яко разгневах Господа Бога своего, и сего ради навел на мя праведный судия Господь Бог мой вся клятвы сия; яже прокля во исходе Моисей люди непокоривия и жестосердыя. Пущу же яко о мне окаянном пророк глаголет: сия грешнику же рече Бог вскую ты поведаеши оправдания моя и восприемлеши завет мой усты твоими, ты же возненавиде наказание и отверже словеса моя вспять, аще видяше татя течаше с ним и с прелюбодеем участие свое полагаше, уста твоя умножиша злобу и язык твой сплеташе лщения, седя на брата своего клеветаше и на сына матере своея полагаше соблазн; сия сотворил еси и умолчах, вознепщевал еси беззаконие, яко буду тебе подобен, обличу тя и представлю пред лицем твоим грехи твоя. Да разумеют о мне окаянном вси языцы забывающие Бога, по истинне грешен есмь и законопреступен; и за сия вся моя согрешения наказует мя Господь и Бог мой милостивно. И о сем прекращу слово да не тяжестно будет ушесам прочитающим сия, ниже твоей премудрости учителем обращуся; но точию реку и твое благонравие хвалю и за вся твоя благая Творца и Господа благодарю; понеже подобен еси пчелней премудрости и сладостному и целителному плоду ея, им же мя веселиши друже мой. Да воздаст ти благодавец хотения твоя, его же просиши и молиши от него; понеже заповеди его сблюдаеши и дружелюбия не забываеши. О сих же возлюбленный учить: не заповедь рече нову пишу вам, но заповедь ветху юже иместе исперва, яко тма проходит и свет истинный уже сияет, глаголя себе во свете быти, а брата своего ненавидит, во тме есть доселе, а любяй брата своего во свете пребывает и соблазны несть в нем. И паки Единородный рече: любите друг друга, яко же Аз возлюбих вы, любяй же друга и творяй истинну грядет ко свету, да явютца дела его, яко о Бозе суть соделанна. По сем здравь и радостен со всем домом своим буди, а нас непотребных незабуди, а посылочка твоя Третьяк Васильевич до меня дошла и яз на твоем жалованье много челом бью; а что еси пожаловал впредь обещал, и в том твоя воля, как пожалуеш по доволу своему так и учиниш. А февраля в 3 день приехал с Москвы к Соли Степан Силич Шишкин, а поехал в Тоболеск с государскою богомолною грамотою, что его государя нашего Бог сочетал законному браку; а мне бедному сказал государскую милость, что велел меня государь от Ленские службы отставить, а до своего государева указу велел еще побыть у Соли, а что вперед дасть Бог того неведомо.

4.

Яже о Христе сочетанныя любви брату и другу Третьяку Васильевичю радоватися. Пиши Государь ко мне о своем здравии и благопребывании, а про мое и бед исполненное житьишко изволишь ведать, и моему окаянству всещедрый Бог милостию своею терпит у Соли Вычегодские, Июня по 19 число в живых вменен бых, а с мертвыми осужден бых. И как государь даст Бог поспеет путь зимней и ездоки из Тоболска к Москве будут; и ты Господа ради пришли ко мне осетрика два три осенних и стерлядок и икрицы осетрьи и стерляжьи с пудик. Сенка Шаховской челом бьет. А что государь за то даш денег; и о том ко мне пожалуй отпиши с тем, с которым рыбу пришлеш, и тому у меня и платеж будет, или заплатим тем что у нас лучится. По сем много и премного челом бью.

To Patriarch Filaret
(From Buslaev, *Khristomatiia*, cols. 1047–1048, Gorskii and Nevostruev, IV (sec. II, pt. 3), p. 698, and Leonid, "Svedenie," p. 246)

Великопреименитому государю святейшему Филарету Никитичю патри-арху Московскому и всея Русии, бьет челом и припадая молит твое благо-честие непотребный раб ваш Сенка Шаховской. Услыши, государь великий, мое многогрешное моление и воими учителю наш благий, призри милостивым си оком и приими мое теплое исповедание.

Прости мя, яко блуднаго, добрый наш учитель и пастырь, и отпусти ми, поне едину мою вину от множеств моих преступлений; умершу ми трем женам в маловременной године, и ни со единою доволно пожих, токмо очима своима видех я, со единою пожих тригодинное число, со второю полтора года, с третею девять на десеть недель и о сем опечалихся зело и во уныние впад, и в распаление духа приидох, понеже юн есмь и плотскаго сладострастия не могу одолети и за невоздержание плоти своея и удаляяся от различново многова блудодеяния, сочетался есмь браком з девицею сущею и жил с нею два года и детки, государь великий, даровал ми Бог с нею. Ныне бо лишен супружества моего и деток за премногое мое беззаконие, но ты, прехитрый врачю, исцели мя, не дай мне бедному от уныния впасти в руце дияволи! Аще ли великий государь наш и учитель, и не потребно учиних, аз нищий но за немощь, и за возраст юности моея, остави сие прегрешение...

To Archbishop Kiprian
(From Buslaev, *Khristomatiia*, cols. 1048–1050)

Великому господину и многомилостивому ко мне преосвященному Киприя-ну, архиепископу Сибирскому и Тоболскому, непотребный в человецех и обремененный многими напастми Сенка Шаховской челом бьет...

Наполнихся есмь горести, яко адово жилище суть каиново, восприях стена-ние находимых ради напастей на мя, болезнию лютою жегом есмь и в скудосте велицей пребываю и еще унынием многим обдержим за разлучение ради жены моея и ни откуду себе чаяс спасения, в такове напасти живуще. И на всяк день болезненно воздыхающе не токмо в Бозе упование имею и по Бозе тебя великого отца и учителя на помощь призываю и уповаю скорби своей от тебе отраду. Восприяти аще не отвратиш лица своего от моего грешнаго мо-ления, пощади великий господине мой и учитель, услыши мое многогрешное моление, призри милостивно и помощь подай, избави мя ходатайством своим от многа одержимаго уныния. Не о всех скорбных приключившихся мне на-пастех молю тя утешения; они же предрекох, но о единой вещи токмо, еже ми всегда вредит неослабно и уныние наводит и домишко пусто сотворяет сия ми скорбь лютеиши паче прочих...

Но ты, прехитрый врачю, исцели мя, уклони священный слух свой к моему многогрешному молению. И подвигнися, буди ходатай великому госу-дарю нашему святейшему Филарету Никитичю патриахру Московскому и всеа Русии, да подаст ми рабу своему свое щедрое милосердие...

C. DOMASHNIE ZAPISKI—*SHAKHOVSKOI'S AUTOBIOGRAPHICAL NOTES*
(From *Moskovskii vestnik*, 1830, pt. 5, pp. 61–70. N.B. immediately following the *zapiski* in the original manuscript was a defective copy of the third letter to Tret'iak Vasil'ev; it is reproduced ibid., pp. 70–73.)

В 7109 году [от сотворения мира или 1601 от Рождества Христова] приходил к Москве посол Литовской Лев Сапега с товарищи, а с ним многое честное панство, воеводы и воеводичи и старосты во дворянех о мирном поставленье.

7110 году. В начале на Семен день хлеб, мороз побил, и бысть по всей Русской земли глад велии, по дорогам люди помирали и волцы живых поедали.

Во 112 году. В начале сбежал с Москвы в Литву из Чудова монастыря диакон черной Галичанин Гришка Отрепьев с иными двумя чернецами, и пришед в Киев назвался царевичем Димитрием Углицким.

Во 113 году. Вначале пришел он с войском в Северские городы в Путивль с товарищи, и волею Божиею поддалися ему все городы, и тогоже году царя Бориса не стало скорою смертию апреля и 9-й день в полудню, а бояре и воеводы, князь Федор Иванович Мстиславский, в то время стояли под Кромами, и тогож лета июля в 20 день пришол ростига на Москву.

В 114 году. Противу Николина дни вешняго женился на Сендомирсковой дочери, и после Николина дни в десятый день того вора убили, и того лета июля в 9-й день сел на царство царь Василий Иванович Шуйской. И тогож лета на Преображение в день послали нас стольников и стряпчих пятнадцать человек со князем Михаилом с Кашиным на Северу под Елец на службу, и с тех мест учали на меня князя Семена приходить беды многия. Царь Василий велел меня с службы прислать к Москве за приставом, и не сказал мне никакия вины, велел сослать в Новгород в мор, и не допуская до Новагорода велел меня воротить и велел жить до указу в деревне.

Во 115 году. После Покрова пришли под Москву Северских городов люди под воеводством холопа князя Андрея Телятевскаго Ивашки Болотникова и их под Москвою Божиим промыслом побили. И тогож году пошли бояре и воеводы под Калугу весною и тоя же весны из под Калуги к Москве побежали, а на Тулу пришол из Путивла вор Петрушка, назвался царевичем.

Во 116 году. Царь Василий осадил Тулу, а меня пожаловал, велел взять к Москве.

Во 117 году. В осень царь Василий взял Тулу потопя водою, и тогож году на весну в Волхове князя Дмитрия Шуйскаго побили Литовские люди, и того же лета вор пришол под Москву со многими Литовскими и Русскими людьми, стал в Тушине. И тогож лета на Ходынке Литовские люди Русских людей побили, и я князь Семен на том бою был.

Во 118 году. Вначале пришел Петр Сапега под Троицу, а за ним пошол с Москвы князь Иван Шуйской, и был бой в Рахманцове, и князя Ивана Шуйскаго побили, и я князь Семен на том бою был, и с тех мест сели на Москве в осаде и тогож 118 году, я князь Семен да князь Андрей Мосальской, да князь Петр Бахтеяров, да Михайло Бутурлин отъехали в Тушино в великой мясоед, и тогож мясоеду после нас спустя две недели перед масленицою за неделю в субботу приходили на царя Василья многие дворяне с шумом и отъехали в Тушино Казарин и Бегичев с товарищи. И в том же во 118 году Тушинской вор сбежал в Калугу, а Литовские люди пошли все под Смоленск к королю, тогож году пошол гетман Жолкевской под Москву.

Во 119 году. Бояре и дворяне и вся земля королевичу крест целовали и в Москву Литовских людей пустили, а царя Василья постригли и в Литву отдали, а сидел на царстве четыре лета, и два месяца; и того же году Литовские люди Москву выжгли и высекли на страшной недели во вторник, и тово же 119 году весною пришли на Московское очищенье из Калуги князь Дмитрей Тимофеевичь Трубецкой, да с Рязани Прокопий Ляпунов; и тогож лета июля в день немецкие люди Новгород взяли, и я князь Семен на том Новгородском взятье был, и стояли под Москвою бояре полтора года, и взяли Москву на Дмитриев день во 121 году; а я князь Семен в то время был в Торопце, от бояр из под Москвы послан в походные воеводы, и того году на Сборное Воскресение государя царя и великаго князя Михайла Феодоровича всея Русии выбрали на Московское государство, а я князь Семен в то время приехал к Москве и выборные люди изо всех чинов на Кострому по нево государя поехали, а с Костромы с государем к Москве на Радунице приехали, и тогоже лета князя Дмитрия Мамстрюкова под Смоленск послали, и меня князя Семена послали с ним же, и мы в том походе Вязьму и Белую и Дорогобужь взяли.

Во 122 году. На Покров пресвятыя Богородицы я князь Семен с Белыя с разными людьми шел под Велиж, и в том походе ранен, и в том же 122 году тьмою Смоленск осадил, а на весну на светолй неделе во вторник на рубеж Гамов острожок пошол князь Иван Троекуров, а я был с ним же, и того году у меня князь Семена жены первыя не стало; и тойже весны ходил я князь Семен из Гамова под Мстиславль с разными людьми, и под Мстиславлем ранен и отписан к Москве.

Во 123 году. Послали нас с Пожарским на Северу противу Лисовскаго, и мы о том били челом, что заволочены с службы да на службу, и за то челобитье мимо всех нашей братьи меня сослали на Унжу, и вскоре пожаловал государь велел взять к Москве.

Во 125 году. Послал меня государь в Ядрин в воеводы.

Во 127 году. Пришол королевич Польской под Москву и приступил к Арбатским воротам, а воеводы были у Арбатских ворот князь Василий князь Семенов сын Куракин, а у Стретенских ворот Иван Морозов да Борис Давыдов, за Яузою князь Семен Прозоровской, да я князь Семен Шаховской, за Москвою рекою князь Иван Кавтырев, да князь Никита Борятинской, и тогож 127 году на весну послали на Тулу в большой полк от Крымских людей, князь Ивана Кавтырева, а в передовой полк князь Федора Куракина, а в сторожевой Ивана Салтыкова, на Рязань князя Семена Прозоровскаго, на Михайлов князя Ивана Засекина Салеха, в Пронск меня князя Семена, и тое весны у меня другия жены не стало после Светлова Воскресения вскоре, и тогоже лета в Июне пришол к Москве из Литвы митрополит Ростовской Филарет Никитичь и поставлен на патриаршество, а я князь Семен был в Пронску в то время.

Во 128 году. Из Троицкаго походу послан я князь Семен в Вязьму в товарищи князю Ивану Хованскому Белогузу, и того же лета на Филипово заговенье женился я князь Семен на нынешней своей княгине.

Во 130 году. Сослан я князь Семен в Тобольск в опалу в чужом деле, и того же году пожалован взят к Москве.

Во 134 году. Государь царь и великий князь Михайло Феодоровичь всея Русии зимою женился на государыне царице Евдокии Лукьяновне, и того же году на Преполовеньев день Москва выгорела, Китай и кремль, а государь в ту пору был у Троицы в походе.

Во 137 году. Послали в Сибирь воевод князя Петра Пронскова в Томск, а меня князя Семена в Енисейск, и тогоже году родился царевич, а нынешний государь царь и великий князь Алексей Михайловичь всея Русии, а с тою вестью пригнал гонец к нам на Верхотурье на Велик день, а из Сибири я князь Семен приехал к Москве во 140 году на Успеньев день, и тогоже числа пошол Михайло Шеин под Смоленск.

Во 142 году. На Покров святой Богородицы патриарха не стало и тогоже году декабря в 1-й день пошли бояре Мастрюков да Пожарской в Можайск, а я князь Семен послан с ним же, и тогож году весною был с Федором Шереметевым на посольство за Вязьмою на рубеже.

Во 143 году. На Благовещениев день послал меня государь князя Семена за Польскими и Литовскими послами за Песочинским с товарищи в погоню, а со мною был дворцовой дьяк Григорий Нечаев, изъехали их в цареве займище, и тут с ними о государевых делах говорили по наказу в Великую суботу; а к Москве приехал на святой неделе во вторник к Благовещенской обедне, и тут у руки были и список статейной посольства своего подали.

Во 145 году. В великой пост на первой неделе великаго поста в среду меня князя Семена в Литву послали посланником, а наместничество дано мне князю Семену Елатомское, а со мною тот же дворцовой дьяк Григорий Нечаев да три человека дворян Московских.

Во 146 году. Послали меня князя Семена на Крапивну в товарищи Ивану Шереметеву.

Во 147 году. На Терек послали меня князя Семена воеводою.

Во 151 году. Послали меня князя Семена во Тверь встречать королевича Датскаго на Рождество Христово, а были со мною князь Семеном стольники и жильцы и городы многие.

Во 152 году. В великой пост на первой неделе послан я князь Семен в Усть Колу в воеводы.

Во 153 году июля во 12 день. Государя царя Михайла Феодоровича всея Русии не стало.

Во 154 году. На Егорьев день вешний пришла в Колу государева грамота, велено меня князя Семена отослать на Устюг.

Во 155 году. Велено меня князя Семена отослать с Устюга к Соли Вычегодской на масленице в среду.

Во 157 году. Велено меня князя Семена от Соли отпустить в вотчину мою в Галичь; и того же году на Дмитриев день государь пожаловал велел мне быть к Москве, и того же году на мясопустной неделе послали в Сибирь в опалу в Томской город, а в Томской приехал в 158 году сентября в 10 день.

Appendix V

Genealogy and Curriculum Vitae of Semen Shakhovskoi

Genealogical Table of Iaroslavl' Princes

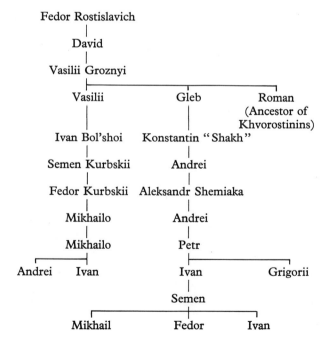

Curriculum Vitae of Semen Shakhovskoi

(Based upon Platonov, *Skazaniia*, with corrections from *RBS*, *DZ*, *DR*, *KR*, *DRV*, and *AMG*.)

1603/4   Signs receipt for his father's *oklad* of 10 rubles. L. M. Sukhotin, ed., *Chetvertchiki Smutnogo vremeni (1604–1617)* (Moscow, 1912), p. 26.

1606   Serves as *stol'nik*, in repression of the rising of Severskii cities (*RBS*). Punished, by Vasilii Shuiskii for crimes of his cousin, sent to Novgorod to prison but soon allowed to go to "the village" (near Galich?) (*DZ*).

1608   Called to Moscow; participated in battles of Khodynka and Rakhmantsov (*DZ*).

Beginning
of 1610   Joins *tushintsy*; in February goes to the camp of Sigismund (*DZ*).

1610   February/March: Granted lands by Sigismund (*Akty Zapadnoi Rossii*, IV: 321–322).

1611   July: "Present" at taking of Novgorod by Swedes.
Married first wife (Matrona?) (*DZ*).

1613   In "*opolchenie*" outside Moscow, sent by boyars to Toropets (region of his *pomestie* granted by Sigismund); participates in battles vs. Poles at Viaz'ma, Belaia, Dorogobuzh (*DZ*).
After October 1: Wounded in battle of Velizh and in battle for Mstislav (*DZ*).

1615   Death of first wife. Exiled to Unzha region for complaints about hard service; returned almost immediately (*DZ, RBS, AMG* I:131).

1615/1616   Listed as "*dvorianin*" (*AMG* I:146).

1616   Summer: *Voevoda* in Iadrin (*DR*).

1617–1618   In Iadrin (*KR, DZ*), marries second time (Anastasiia?).

1618   August: Called to Moscow for defense against Władysław (*DR*) (*KR*).

1619   March 12: Sent as head of "*polk*" to Pronsk (*DR, KR*).
After March: Death of second wife (*DZ*).
June 20: Returned to Moscow (*DZ, KR*).
Summer: Third marriage and death of third wife (Tat'iana?) (*DZ*).
November 14: Fourth marriage (*DZ*).

1620   Summer: Sent as *voevoda* to Viaz'ma (*DZ, KR*). Arrest and exile of members of Shakhovskoi family.

1621   March 21: Removed as *voevoda* in Viaz'ma (*DR, AMG* I:158–159).
ca. November: Fourth marriage dissolved by Filaret.

1622   Exiled to Tobol'sk, property confiscated (*DZ*). Returns to Moscow immediately. Letters to Kiprian and Filaret.

1624   May 12: In Moscow (*DR*).

1625   May: Writes letter to Shah Abbas for Filaret.
July: At the court (*DR*).

1627–1629   "*Boiarin*" (*DRV* IX:280).

1627–1632   *Voevoda* in Eniseisk (*DR, KR*).

1630   August: In Eniseisk Ostrog (*VMOIDR*, bk. IV, 1849, *Smes'*, p. 38).

1631   "*Boiarin*" (*DRV* IX:280).

1632   August: Returns to Moscow (*DZ*).

1633   October 1: Death of Filaret.

October 5: Shakhovskois pardoned.

December 1: Shakhovskoi sent with Pozharskii to Mozhaisk (*DZ*).

1634   Spring: Embassy with F. I. Sheremetev to Poland (*DZ*).

1635   March 25: Sent to border with message for Polish envoys (*DZ*).

1637   February 22–July: Embassy to Warsaw (*Chteniia*, 1862, bk. 4, sec. II, p. 91.).

July 25: At court for "angel's day" of Tsarevna Anna Mikhailovna (*RIB* X:100).

1638   April–November: Campaign against Crimeans (*DR*, *DRV* IX:280, *AMG* II:391).

1639   February: Imprisoned, then sent to Siberia, for false *mestnichanie* vs. Gagin (*DR*).

April 14: At the court for Easter (*RIB* X:180).

(It is possible that one of the two above reports refers to the other Semen Ivanovich Shakhovskoi. See Platonov, *Skazaniia*, 2nd ed., p. 301.)

1641   May 5–1642: *Voevoda* on the Terek (*DZ*, *DR*, *DRV* IX:281).

1643   December 29: Sent to Tver' to greet Prince Waldemar (*DZ*, *DR*).

Letter to Mikhail Fedorovich about marriage to Irina.

1644   April 4: Sent as *voevoda* to Kola Peninsula (*DZ*).

1645   March 9: *Voevoda* in Kola.

1646   April 23: Moved from Kola to Ustiug (*DZ*).

1647   April 25: Moved from Ustiug to Sol'vychegodsk, but still listed (*?DRV* IX:281) as *voevoda* in Kola.

1648   February: Letter to Tret'iak Vasil'ev from Sol'vychegodsk.

June 19: Letter to Tret'iak Vasil'ev from Sol'vychegodsk.

June 21: *Voevoda* in Sol'vychegodsk (Sergei Mironovich Solov'ev, *Istoriia Rossii s drevneishikh vremen*, V [Moscow, 1961]: 487)

Fall: Allowed to go home to Galich; then called to Moscow for new trial in Waldemar affair.

1649   January 4: Sentenced to death by *d'iak* of *posol'skii prikaz*, sentence commuted to exile in Tomsk.

September 10: Arrived in Tomsk (*DZ*).

1653   In Moscow, writes letter to Simon Azar'in.

1654   Death (*DRV* IX: 281).

1655   Sons quarreling over property (*AMG* II:475–476).

Abbreviations

AAE	*Akty, sobrannye v bibliotekakh i arkhivakh Rossiiskoi imperii Arkheograficheskoi ekspeditsiei Imperatorskoi Akademii nauk*, 4 vols. St. Petersburg, 1836.
AI	*Akty istoricheskie, sobrannye i izdannye Arkheograficheskoie kommissiei*, 5 vols. St. Petersburg, 1841–1842.
AMG	*Akty Moskovskogo gosudarstva, izdannye Imperatorskoi Akademiei nauk*, 3 vols. St. Petersburg, 1890–1901.
BAN	Biblioteka Akademii nauk SSSR (Leningrad).
Chteniia	*Chteniia v Imperatorskom Obshchestve istorii i drevnostei rossiiskikh pri Moskovskom universitete.*
DR	*Dvortsovye razriady, … izdannye II-m otdeleniem sobstvennoi Ego Imperatorskogo Velichestva kantseliarii*, 3 vols. in 4. St Petersburg, 1850–1854.
DRV	*Drevniaia rossiiskaia vivliofika*, ed. N. I. Novikov, 2nd ed. 20 pts. Moscow, 1788–1791.
DZ	[S. I. Shakhovskoi]. "Domashnie zapiski kniazia Semena Shakhovskogo," *Moskovskii vestnik*, 1830, pt. 5, pp. 61–73.
Fennell, Corresp.	J. L. I. Fennell, ed. and trans. *The Correspondence between Prince A. M. Kurbsky and Tsar Ivan IV of Russia 1564–1579*. Cambridge: The University Press, 1955.
Fennell, History	J. L. I. Fennell, ed. and trans. *Prince A. M. Kurbsky's History of Ivan IV*. Cambridge: The University Press, 1965.
GBL	Gosudarstvennaia ordena Lenina biblioteka SSSR imeni V. I. Lenina (Moscow).
GIM	Gosudarstvennyi istoricheskii muzei (Moscow).
Gorskii and Nevostruev	A. V. Gorskii and K. I. Nevostruev. *Opisanie slavianskikh rukopisei Moskovskoi sinodal'noi (patriarshei) biblioteki*, 6 vols. Moscow, 1855–1917.

GPB	Gosudarstvennaia ordena trudovogo krasnogo znameni Publichnaia biblioteka imeni M. E. Saltykova-Shchedrina (Leningrad).
Ist. zap.	*Istoricheskie zapiski.*
Ivanishev	N. D. Ivanishev, ed. and introd. *Zhizn' kniazia Andreia Mikhailovicha Kurbskogo v Litve i na Volnyi*, 2 vols. Kiev, 1849.
"*Jarlyk*"	Edward L. Keenan, "The *Jarlyk* of Axmed-xan to Ivan III: A New Reading," *International Journal of Slavic Linguistics and Poetics* XII (1969): 33–47.
KR	*Knigi razriadnye, . . . izdannye II-m otdeleniem sobstvenno Ego Imperatorskogo Velichestva kantseliarii*, 2 vols. St Petersburg, 1853.
Kuntsevich	G. Z. Kuntsevich, ed. *Sochineniia kniazia Kurbskogo*, vol. I: *Sochineniia original'nye*. St. Petersburg, 1914.
LZAK	*Letopis' zaniatii Arkheograficheskoi kommissii.*
ORIaS	*Otdelenie russkogo iazyka i slovesnosti Akademii nauk.*
PDP	*Pamiatniki drevnei pis'mennosti.*
Poslaniia	*Poslaniia Ivana Groznogo*, ed. D. S. Likhachev and Ia. S. Lur'e. Moscow-Leningrad, 1951.
PSRL	*Polnoe sobranie russkikh letopisei.*
RBS	*Russkii biograficheskii slovar'.*
RIB	*Russkaia istoricheskaia biblioteka.*
RIO	*Sbornik Russkogo istoricheskogo obshchestva.*
SEER	*The Slavonic and East European Review.*
SGGD	*Sobranie gosudarstvennykh gramot i dogovorov, khraniashchikhsia v Gosudarstvennoi kollegii inostrannykh del*, 5 vols. Moscow, 1813–1894.
TODRL	Akademiia nauk SSSR. Institut russkoi literatury. *Trudy Otdela drevnerusskoi literatury.*
TsGADA	Tsentral'nyi gosudarstvennyi arkhiv drevnikh aktov (Moscow).
Ustrialov	N. Ustrialov, ed. *Skazaniia kniazia Kurbskogo*, 3 eds. St. Petersburg, 1833, 1842, 1868.
VMOIDR	*Vremennik Imperatorskogo Moskovskogo obshchestva istorii i drevnostei rossiiskikh.*
ZhMNP	*Zhurnal Ministerstva narodnogo prosveshcheniia.*
Zimin, *Sochineniia*	*Sochineniia I. Peresvetova*, ed. A. A. Zimin. Moscow-Leningrad, 1956.
ZOR	Gosudarstvennaia ordena Lenina biblioteka SSSR imeni V. I. Lenina, *Zapiski Otdela rukopisei.*

Notes

INTRODUCTION

1. Epitomes of these letters have appeared in Russian readers for schools and gymnasia since the mid-nineteenth century. See, e.g., N. [K.] Gudzii, comp., *Khrestomatiia po drevnei russkoi literature XI–XVII vekov*, 5th ed. (Moscow, 1952), pp. 289–303. One might well ask whether early exposure to these texts, in an entirely unskeptical atmosphere, has not lowered the sensitivity of precisely the most diligent students to their numerous stylistic and contextual incongruities.

2. For a thoughtful review of the historiographical background, see S. F. Platonov, *Ivan Groznyi (1530–1584)* (Petersburg, 1923), chap. 1, or the same, with minor changes, as "Ivan Groznyi v russkoi istoriografii," *Russkoe proshloe*, bk. 1 (Petrograd-Moscow, 1923), pp. 3–12, translated in abridged form in Sidney Harcave, ed., *Readings in Russian History* (New York: Thomas Y. Crowell Co., 1962), I: 188–194. A somewhat more detailed account is given by I. U. Budovnits, "Ivan Groznyi v russkoi istoricheskoi literature," *Ist. zap.* XXI (1947): 271–330.

3. The best edition is that edited by J. L. I. Fennell, *The Correspondence between Prince A. M. Kurbsky and Tsar Ivan IV of Russia 1564–1579* (Cambridge: The University Press, 1963; hereafter cited as Fennell, *Corresp.*). This edition, while meticulously prepared and skillfully translated, was dependent upon the Kuntsevich and Lur'e editions. The publication of the letters of Ivan IV by Ia. S. Lur'e (*Poslaniia Ivana Groznogo*, ed. D. S. Likhachev and Ia. S. Lur'e [Moscow-Leningrad, 1951]; hereafter cited as *Poslaniia*) contains very good texts of Ivan's first (in both versions, see below) and second letters, and a somewhat less satisfactory text of Kurbskii's first, but the rest of the *Correspondence* is lacking. Kuntsevich's edition (*Sochineniia kniazia Kurbskogo*, vol. I: *Sochineniia original'nye* [St. Petersburg, 1914], also pub. as vol. XXXI of *RIB*; hereafter cited as Kuntsevich) while painstaking and thorough, was based upon very late, and in

some cases corrupt, texts of the *Correspondence*. The question of a systematic examination of the nature and provenance of works attributed to Ivan was raised, but in no sense resolved, in the early nineteenth century by I. N. Zhdanov ("Sochineniia tsaria Ivana Vasil'evicha," *Sochineniia I. N. Zhdanova*, I [St. Petersburg, 1904]: 84–90). An original but partial and inconclusive review of some problems of filiation of texts was made by P. V. Vil'koshevskii, "K voprosu o redaktsiiakh pervogo poslaniia Ivana Groznogo k kniaziu A. M. Kurbskomu," *LZAK za 1923–1925 gg*. XXXIII (1926):68–76. Here and below the following correspondences with Russian usage will be observed: *spisok* = copy; *rukopis'* = manuscript; *redaktsiia* = version; *sbornik* = manuscript or collection; on the question of "first" and "second" versions of Ivan's first letter, see below, Chap. 4.

4. See the unusually frank biography in *Entsiklopedicheskii slovar'*, pub. F. A. Brokgauz and I. A. Efron (St. Petersburg), vol. 35 (1902), s. v. "Ustrialov."

5. *Skazaniia kniazia Kurbskogo*, 2nd ed. (St. Petersburg, 1842), p. xli, (hereafter cited as Ustrialov).

6. Thus, he chose as the basis of his edition the manuscript of the Synodal Library, No. 136, which belongs to the late seventeenth century. For details, see below, Chap. I, n. I.

7. These criticisms are summarized by M. P. Petrovskii (M. P——skii) in *Kn. A. M. Kurbskii: istoriko-bibliograficheskie zametki po povodu poslednego izdaniia ego "Skazanii"* (Kazan', 1873); also pub. in *Uchenye zapiski Kazanskogo universiteta* (1873) pp. 711–760.

8. S. Gorskii, *Zhizn' i istoricheskoe znachenie kniazia Andreia Mikhailovicha Kurbskogo* (Kazan', 1858).

9. N. D. Ivanishev, ed. and introd. *Zhizn' kniazia Andreia Mikhailovicha Kurbskogo v Litve i na Volyni* (Kiev, 1849).

10 Kuntsevich's texts of Kurbskii's first letter and of the first version of Ivan's letter, for example, are still the best available. See Kuntsevich, cols. 1–8 and 10–50.

11. It was transferred to the archive of the *Arkheograficheskaia kommissiia* shortly before Kuntsevich's death, and later used by Vil'koshevskii. See *LZAK za 1923–1925 gg*. XXXIII (1926):6, and Vil'koshevskii, "K voprosu o redaktsiiakh . . .," ibid., p. 75, n. I.

12. Including MS 1567 and MS 41, from which Lur'e was able to reconstruct the integral text of the second version of Ivan's first letter (*Poslaniia*, pp. 520–544). For key to numbers of MSS., see List of Manuscripts Cited.

13. I.e., MS 1567 (*Poslaniia*, pp. 534–536). On MS 1567, see below, App. I, pt. a.

14. *Poslaniia*, pp. 520.

15. See App. I, pt. a.

16. It will become apparent that the terms "Kurbskii's first letter," "Ivan's second letter," etc., are perhaps not the most precise means of designating these texts. I have chosen, however, for the sake of convenience, to be consistent; the letters will be so designated throughout, and the formulas "Kurbskii writes . . . ," "Ivan says . . . ," will be used even after considerable doubts about the authorship of either Kurbskii or Ivan have been established.

CHAPTER 1

1. For detailed *de visu* descriptions, see App. I, pt. a. Manuscripts not

described there are here briefly characterized (for abbreviations, see list preceding notes).

TsGADA, *fond* 181, *delo* 60 (Old number *Gosudarstvennoe drevlekhranilishche*, V.2.18)
Collection of Kurbskii's works, dated by Lur'e "end of seventeenth century." In folio, 454 fols., cursive hand.
  Descriptions. Kuntsevich, p. v; *Poslaniia*, p. 547.
  Inscription. Indicates that MS was owned by F. I. Divov in 1689/1690.
  Contents. Kurbskii's *History*; his first letter (second version); the letter of Teterin to Morozov; Ivan's first letter; Kurbskii's later letters; excerpts from Guagnini's "Description of Muscovy"; the fourth chapter of Stryjkowski; two other fragments from Guagnini (the second the tale of the Turkish attack on Astrakhan' in 1569); and a number of translations of religious texts (Ustrialov, 2nd ed., p. 402).
  Remarks. Ivan/Kurbskii materials published from here in Kuntsevich.

GIM, Collection of the Synodal Library No. 136
Collection of Kurbskii's works, dated by Lur'e "second half of seventeenth century." In folio, 266 fols., cursive hand.
  Descriptions. Kuntsevich, p. v; Ustrialov, 2nd ed., pp. xxxvi and 402; *Poslaniia*, p. 548.
  Inscriptions. Two, indicating that MS belonged to Kirillo-Belozerskii Monastery and to Fedor Polikarpov.
  Contents. According to Lur'e, same contents as 181/60, not including the portions from Guagnini and Stryjkowski.
  Remarks. Texts published by Kuntsevich and Ustrialov.

GPB, Collection of M. P. Pogodin No. 1494
Collection of Kurbskii's works, dated by Lur'e "last quarter of seventeenth century." In folio, 405 fols., cursive hand.
  Descriptions. Kuntsevich, p. v; *Poslaniia*, p. 547.
  Contents. Same as 181/60.

GPB, New acquisitions No. 623/1938
Collection of Kurbskii's works, eighteenth century.
  Description. Gosudarstvennaia ordena trudovogo krasnogo znameni Publichnaia biblioteka im. M. E. Saltykova-Shchedrina, *Kratkii otchet Rukopisnogo otdela za 1914–1938 gg.*, ed. T. K. Ukhmylova and V. G. Geiman (Leningrad, 1940), p. 61.
  Inscription. Indicates that present copy made from a copy written in 1677 "in the home of the boyar Prince V. V. Golitsyn."

Archive of the Leningrad Section of the Institute of History, Collection of the *Arkheograficheskaia komissiia* No. 41
Collection of historical works, written in different hands on various papers. 4°, 499 fols.
  Descriptions. *Poslaniia*, pp. 540–541; N. P. Barsukov, *Rukopisi Arkheograficheskoi komissii* (St. Petersburg, 1882), pp. 26–27.
  Contents. See *Poslaniia*, p. 540. Only GI^b of *Correspondence*.
  Remarks. The text of GI^b here is confused (pages out of order) and poorly copied, but nonetheless superior to the versions which had been relied upon

before Lur'e's edition. The date of this manuscript is difficult to establish; Lur'e cites watermarks which might appear over a long time span.

BAN, Current acquisitions No. 230
Composite manuscript, second quarter of seventeenth century (ca. 1640?). 4°, 214 fols.
Descriptions. Ia. S. Lur'e, "Novye spiski 'Tsareva gosudareva poslaniia vo vse ego Rossiiskoe tsarstvo'," *TODRL* X (1954):306; *Opisanie Rukopis-nogo otdela Biblioteki Akademii nauk SSSR*, III, 1, 2nd ed. (Moscow-Leningrad, 1959), pp. 375–376.
Watermarks. Pots: in first part with letters RO; in second, c/GC.
Contents. First part: "The Kazan' History"; second part: Kurbskii's first letter (first version?); Teterin to Morozov; Polubenskii to Shablikin and Ogibalov; second version of Ivan's first letter.
Remarks. Lur'e notes the particular closeness of MS 230 to MS 1567, which he assumes to have had a common protograph with 230.

GIM, Collection of A. S. Uvarov No. 1582 (301)(224)
A "Kurbskii Collection," seventeenth century. In folio, 231 fols., cursive hand.
Descriptions. Archimandrite Leonid, *Sistematicheskoe opisanie slaviano-rossiiskikh rukopisei sobraniia Grafa A. S. Uvarova*, III (Moscow, 1894): 230–231; Pavel M. Stroev, *Rukopisi slavianskie i rossiiskie, prinadlezhashchie pochetnomu grazhdaninu i Arkheograficheskoi kommissii korrespondentu Ivanu Nikitichu Tsarskomu* (Moscow, 1848), pp. 191–192.
Inscription. Provides a *terminus ante quem* of March 12, 1679: "Leta 7187-go marta v 12 den' siia kniga boiarina i dvoretskogo i oruzheinichego Bogdana Matveevicha Khitrovo."
Contents (for details, see Leonid, *Opisanie*). *History*; all of Kurbskii's letters to Ivan; Kurbskii's other letters (two missing because of lost pages); translations from works of Chrysostom; fragment of the "History of the Eighth Council"; translations from Eusebius, bk. 3, chaps. 22 and 23 and bk. 5, chaps. 5, 17, and 18.

GBL, *fond* 299, Collection of N. S. Tikhonravov No. 639
A mixed collection, written in two cursive hands in 1684. In folio, 566 fols. Hand changes fols. 551/552.
Descriptions. Kuntsevich, p. v; G. P. Georgievskii, *Sobranie N. S. Tikhonravova* (Moscow, 1913), p. 111; O. A. Derzhavina, "*Velikoe zertsalo*" *i ego sud'ba na russkoi pochve* (Moscow, 1965), p. 156.
Date. 1684, in afterword to *Velikoe zertsalo*. But note that Derzhavina (p. 156) feels that this inscription applies only to the first 463 fols.
Contents (for details see Georgievskii). *Zertsalo velikoe* (*Speculum magnum*); *History*, fols. 464–551; Kurbskii's letters to Ivan, fols. 552–566. (It is obvious from the number of folios given by Georgievskii that he was mistaken in calling this text "The Correspondence of Ivan Groznyi and Andrei Kurbskii"; it must include only Kurbskii's letters.)
Remarks. From variant readings, one may assume that this copy represents the earliest text of the later Kurbskii letters, even if in a copy later than those derived from it.

2. Hereafter only numbers will be used to designate the various manuscripts discussed. For the full designations, see List of Manuscripts Cited.

3. *Poslaniia*, p. 572.

4. Kurbskii's first letter and Ivan's reply are dated in the text 1564. Karl Stählin (trans. and introd., *Der Briefwechsel Iwans des Schrecklichen mit dem Fürsten Kurbskii [1564–1579]* [Leipzig, 1921], p. 162) and Fennell (*Corresp.*, p. 180) deduce on not altogether conclusive grounds that Kurbskii's second letter was written in 1565. Ivan's second letter is dated in the text 1577, and Lur'e concludes that it was written in September of that year (*Poslaniia*, p. 649). Fennell assumes from textual evidence that Kurbskii's third letter was written in late 1578 (*Corresp.*, p. 199) and his fourth in 1579 (p. 228). Kurbskii's fifth letter is dated in the text 1579.

5. Kurbskii's *History*, itself a document of unproven provenance (see below, Chap. 3), was edited by Ustrialov (pp. 3–128) and Kuntsevich (cols. 161–354). Kuntsevich's edition was translated by Fennell (J. L. I. Fennell, trans. and ed., *Prince A. M. Kurbsky's History of Ivan IV* [Cambridge: The University Press, 1965]; hereafter cited as Fennell, *History*).

6. On the language of the *prikaz*, see B. Unbegaun, *La langue russe au XVIe siècle (1500–1550)* (Paris, 1935). The introduction and second paragraph of Ivan's letter maintain Slavonic style, but thereafter (beginning on p. 788 bot. in Fennell, *Corresp.*) plain style predominates, mixed (especially where Ivan is paraphrasing his first letter) with a very late Slavonic. Of particular interest are verb forms (*budet molvish'*, *ia pochal protiv vas stoiati*). The term "plain style" will be used throughout instead of the unfamiliar "*prikaz* style." What is meant is the late Muscovite version of the diplomatic chancellery language of Orthodox Slavic states in Eastern Europe in the post-Kievan period. This was a standard, stylized language, conservative and precise, and might be termed, by contrast with the literary language, "State Slavonic."

7. Indeed, on the basis of superficial study, it may be said that the later letters and the *History* are identical in style. On the Ukrainianisms in this style, see Norbert Damerau, *Russisches und Westrussisches bei Kurbskij* (Wiesbaden, 1963).

8. There can be no question about this: the words of Kurbskii's letter are often cited; see Fennell, *Corresp.*, p. 24, n. 2, p. 26, n. 1, and passim.

9. Ibid., p. 181, n. 3.

10. In fact there is really nothing significantly new in the second letter, by comparison with the first. For similarities of phrasing, note e.g. (pages as in Fennell, *Corresp.*) *rastlen razumom* . . . 188/26; *slovom* . . . *delom* . . . 190/46; Sitskii 190/96; *Oserdiasia* . . . *prirazili* 192/16; *dal'nokonnye grady* . . . 194/140; *Narodilsia* . . . *na tsarstve* 192/14, etc.

11. The references are indicated in Fennell's notes (*Corresp.*, pp. 200–247). Note especially the "affairs of Cronus and Aphrodite" (ibid., pp. 214–215). As Fennell appropriately remarks, Ivan, to whom Kurbskii is here responding directly, does not mention Aphrodite anywhere. Kurbskii does, but only in the second version of his first letter, which Fennell, following Kuntsevich, chose for his edition.

12. Recent interest in this problem has been stimulated by the programmatic article of D. S. Likhachev, "Izuchenie sostava sbornikov dlia vyiasneniia istorii teksta proizvedenii," *TODRL* XVIII (1962):3–12, recapitulated in his *Tekstologiia na materiale russkoi literatury X–XVII vv.* (Moscow-Leningrad, 1962), pp. 232–248.

13. See App. I, pt. b.

14. See App. I, pt. a, MSS 4469, 32.8.5, 1573, and Chap. 4, Table 3.

15. See App. III and App. II, Stemma A, for variants and explanation of symbols.

CHAPTER 2

1. These citations and allusions are conveniently indicated in Fennell, *Corresp.*, notes, passim, and in the "Commentaries" to Ivan's letters in *Poslaniia*, pp. 583–612 and 652–655.

2. See the stimulating contribution to the study of this form by my colleague Kirill Taranovski, "Formy obshcheslavianskogo i tserkovno-slavianskogo stikha v drevnerusskoi literature XI–XIII vv.," in Henry Kučera, ed., *American Contributions to the Sixth International Congress of Slavists, Prague, August 7–13, 1968*, I: *Linguistic Contributions* (The Hague–Paris, 1968): 377–394. I should like to thank Professor Taranovski for his thoughtful assistance in dealing with these texts. The further study of the *Correspondence* should benefit much from consideration within the context of liturgical literary traditions.

3. See, e.g., I. F. Golubev, "Dva neizvestnykh stikhotvornykh poslaniia pervoi poloviny XVII v.," *TODRL* XVII (1961): 404–413.

4. For this text, and a more extensive discussion of Isaiah's life in Muscovy than that which is to follow, see Edward L. Keenan, "Isaiah of Kamenets-Podol'sk: Learned Exile, Champion of Orthodoxy," forthcoming in *Studies in Eastern Orthodoxy in Honor of Georges Florovsky*.

5. See A. N. Murav'ev, *Snosheniia Rossii s vostokom po delam tserkovnym*, I (St. Petersburg, 1858): 104 (cited by Abramovich; see n. 6 below).

6. On Isaiah and his background see P. A. Syrku, "Iz istorii snoshenii russkikh s rumynami," *Izvestiia ORIaS*, vol. I (1896), bk. 3, pp. 495–542; Mikhailo Vozniak, *Istoriia ukrains'koi literatury*, vol. II, (L'viv, 1921), pp. 63–64, 117–119; K. V. Kharlampovich, *Malorossiiskoe vliianie na velikorusskuiu tserkovnuiu zhizn'*, I (Kazan', 1914): 4, 8, 11, etc.; D. I. Abramovich, *K literaturnoi deiatel'nosti mnikha Kamianchanina Isaii* (St. Petersburg, 1913) (*PDP*, CLXXXI). The chronology of Isaiah's life in Muscovy is known only in part; we find him in Vologda in July 1562, in Rostov in March 1566 and May 1567, in Moscow in March 1582, and in Rostov again in April 1591. This last date, found in a biographical note about Maksim Grek, is the last mention of Isaiah. See Sergei A. Belokurov, *O biblioteke moskovskikh gosudarei v XVI stoletii* (Moscow, 1898), app., pp. iii–vi.

7. A. V. Gorskii and K. I. Nevostruev, *Opisanie slavianskikh rukopisei Moskovskoi sinodal'noi (patriarshei) biblioteki*, vol. III (sec. II, pt. 2) (Moscow, 1859), p. 126; hereafter cited as Gorskii and Nevostruev.

8. Belokurov, *O biblioteke*, app., pp. iii–vi. See also Elie Denissoff, "Une biographie de Maxime le Grec par le métropolite Isaie Kopinski," *Orientalia Christiana Periodica* XXII (1956): 138–171.

9. Another text found in GPB, MS O.XVII.70, a "Note" (*listochek*) only partially published by Abramovich, has recently been published in facsimile by Mieczysław Gębarowicz, in his thoughtful study *Iwan Federow i jego działalność w latach 1569–1583 na tle epoki* (Warsaw, 1970; offprint from *Roczniki Biblioteczne*, 1969, nos. 1/2 and 3/4). Gebarowicz's interpretation of Isaiah's significance and of the "Note" (which he considered to have been a provocation, fabricated by ecclesiastical enemies of cultural relations with the Orthodox in Lithuania) are original and thought-provoking, although not entirely convincing. On Isaiah, see especially pp. 30–46. I

should like to thank John Simmons of All Souls College, Oxford, for bringing this study to my attention.

10. They were published from MS O.XVII.70 of the Public Library by Abramovich in *Mnikh Kamianchanin*. The manuscript is described in *Otchet Imperatorskoi publichnoi biblioteki za 1905 god* (St. Petersburg, 1912), pp. 133–135. Another manuscript is No. 53 of the St. Petersburg Theological Academy (A. Rodosskii, *Opisanie 432-kh rukopisei, prinadlezhashchikh S.-Peterburgskoi dukhovnoi akademii i sostavliaiushchikh ee pervoe po vremeni sobranie* [St. Petersburg, 1893], pp. 74–78).

11. Thus, the first two texts are dated 1567 and 1566, respectively; most of the texts are in standard late Slavonic, while the "Deposition" and the "Note" are for the most part in the "Lithuanian" recension of diplomatic plain style.

12. Note the rubrics: *Spisok s lista . . . do velikogo kniazia*; *V mestechku v Rostove . . . roku* (1566), etc.

13. See Abramovich's judgment, *Mnikh Kamianchanin*, p. x. Professor Ihor Ševčenko, who kindly read these texts at my request, shares this opinion.

14. Portions of these texts incorporate common liturgical formulae, but important phrases (*neumytnomu sud'e, do vlas pregreshenii ikh*, etc.) do not appear, judging from the notoriously deficient reference works, to come from any single source (*Simfoniia na Vetkhii i Novyi Zavet* [St. Petersburg, 1900]; I. I. Sreznevskii, *Opyt slovaria drevnerusskogo iazyka*, 3 vols. [St. Petersburg, 1893–1903]. Franz Miklosich, *Lexicon Paleoslovenico-Graeco-Latinum* [Vienna, 1862–1865], p. 466, lists *neumytnyi sudii* from a fifteenth-century Serbian manuscript). They were not identified by Kuntsevich, whose knowledge in such matters was considerable. Mine is not, and I have consulted with the Very Reverend Georges Florovsky of Princeton University and Professor John L. I. Fennell of Oxford, and with Ia. S. Lur'e of the Institute of Russian Literature of the Academy of Sciences of the USSR on the matter. None of these colleagues in their gracious responses indicated any common source—if such exists, it is arcane indeed.

15. It is perhaps noteworthy that Kurbskii's words *i tshchasia so userdiem svet vo t'mu prelagati i sladkoe gor'kim prozyvati*, which precede the identical passages by a few lines, are taken from the biblical Isaiah (5:20).

16. Compare Kurbskii's words, *Bog . . . est' vsim sim mzdovozdaiatel'*, with second paragraph of folio 178 in Abramovich, *Mnikh Kamianchanin*.

17. Leonid, *Opisanie*, III (Moscow, 1894): p. 76, and cf. p. 230. See also App. I, pt. a.

18. For details of its provenance, etc., see V. I. Savva, S. F. Platonov, and V. G. Druzhinin, eds., "Vnov' otkrytye polemicheskie sochineniia XVII veka protiv eretikov," *LZAK za 1905 god* XVIII (1907):33–106.

19. An additional observation should be made here, based upon the possible assumption that what I have called the second version of Kurbskii's first letter is in fact the original version. The second version (published as the basic text in Kuntsevich and Fennell, *Corresp.*) is found in the later groups of manuscripts and contains a number of minor apparent corruptions (see App. III). In spite of this, however, there are good reasons to consider this text closer to the original. (1) In spite of the grammatical and orthographic degeneration of the text in the late copies which contain it, the second version provides syntactically and stylistically superior readings in a number of places (Kuntsevich, col. 2, lines 13–19, where *muzhestvom khrabrosti ikh*,

not present in the first version, has a parallel in *tshchaniem razuma ikh*; col. 3, lines 4–6, where the second version is syntactically superior; col. 4, lines 15–20, where the order of the elements in the long sentence seems more logical in the second version). (2) The second version contains one parallel with the Epistle to Vas'ian which is not found in the first version—the citation from the L'viv *Apostol* (Kuntsevich, col. 3, lines 22–26; see below, Chap. 4, n. 36). It is generally agreed that these two texts were written by the same person at roughly the same time, and it may be assumed, since the Epistle to Vas'ian seems to antedate the Kurbskii letter, that the *Apostol* was available to the author in both cases, but paraphrased in the Epistle and cited verbatim in the Kurbskii letter. But since the Vas'ian letter is always accompanied by the first version, which does not have this passage, it may well be that the second version, in a copy now lost, was in fact the original version of this letter.

This might well have been Shakhovskoi's own copy—and the one which, after Vereshchagin's visit to the Shakhovskoi family estate in 1673 (see below Chap. 4) was reintegrated into the manuscript tradition, and now appears in all later copies. In view, however, of the uncertainties in this train of reasoning, and of the fact that the first version is clearly associated with the earliest stages of the development of the *Correspondence*, I have chosen to assume throughout that the version published by Lur'e (*Poslaniia*, pp. 534–536) is the first version. In any case, it seems to be the first version of the letter once it had been attributed to Kurbskii and put into a single package with the letter to Vas'ian, which may have been reattributed, through a change in the heading (the only indication of Kurbskii's authorship) at the same time.

20. See App. IV. For similar endings see, e.g., a series of religious letters published in V. G. Druzhinin, "Neskol'ko neizvestnykh literaturnykh pamiatnikov iz sbornika XVI-go veka," *LZAK za 1908 god* XXI (1909): 1–117.

21. See App. III and App. I, pt. a.

22. The headings, which vary from copy to copy, cannot of course be considered a part of the original text, nor did seventeenth-century copyists treat them as such. The hypothesis that the original letter ended with the *Amin'* is supported by the rubric introduced in MS 43 at this point: "And under this missive of Prince Andrei Kurbskii after the end are added these words," after which follows the postscript. See below, App. III, n. 192. Two other early manuscripts (603 and 1581) contain a separate heading for the text after the *Amin'*. Note also that the second letter of Kurbskii (Fennell, *Corresp.*, p. 184) ends with *Amin'*.

23. Published from MSS 2524, 1573, and 1567 by Kuntsevich, cols. 405–410. For a detailed discussion of some of the features of this text, see R. G. Skrynnikov, "Kurbskii i ego pis'ma v Pskovo-Pecherskii monastyr'," *TODRL* XVIII (1962): 99–116, and Nikolay Andreyev, "Kurbsky's Letters to Vas'yan Muromtsev," *SEER* XXXIII (1955): 414–436.

24. See App. II, notes to Stemma D.

25. Cf. the following passages in Kuntsevich: col. 3, lines 1–2, 12, 19–20; col. 4, lines 4–10, 20–24; col. 6, lines 22–24; and col. 409, lines 2–6; col. 406, line 9; col. 408, lines 26–27; col. 408, lines 16–21, 22–23; col. 408, line 30–col. 409, line 1, respectively.

26. For the interesting problem raised by the parallel between col. 406, lines 11–14, of the letter to Vas'ian and col. 3, lines 22–26, of the Kurbskii

letter, which we do not consider a part of the original text of the latter, see Chap. 4, n. 37.

27. Comment by A. V. Gorskii on MS 27 (213) of the Synodal Collection, cited in Archimandrite Leonid, "Svedenie o slavianskikh rukopisiakh . . . Sviato-Troitskoi Sergievoi Lavry . . . ," *Chteniia*, 1884, bk. 3, sec. ii, p. 245.

28. See above, Introduction, nn. 8 and 9, and biography of Kurbskii in *Russkii biograficheskii slovar'*.

29. The following sketch is based primarily upon the materials provided by Platonov in *Drevnerusskie skazaniia i povesti o smutnom vremeni XVII veka, kak istoricheskii istochnik* (St. Petersburg, 1888), pp. 231–250.

30. Isaak Massa, *Kratkoe izvestie o Moskovii nachala XVII v.* (Moscow, 1937), pp. 144–145.

31. Filaret mentions this, according to Platonov (*Skazaniia*, p. 191), and Khvorostinin denies his "drunkenness" in his "To the Reader" (see App. IV, pt. a).

32. There is no extensive biography of Shakhovskoi. Brief sketches may be found in *RBS*, vol. "Chaadaev-Shvitkov" (St. Petersburg, 1905), pp. 586–589; S. F. Platonov, *Sochineniia*, vol. II (St. Petersburg, 1913; reprint of 1888 edition of *Skazaniia*, with additional material on Shakhovskoi, pp. 451–452), passim; Golubev, *TODRL* XVII:397–399; Pavel M. Stroev, *Bibliologicheskii* [sic] *slovar' i chernovye k nemu materialy*, ed. A. F. Bychkov (St. Petersburg, 1882; also pub. as vol. XXIX, pt. 4, of *Sbornik ORIaS*, pp. 290–298.

33. Shakhovskoi was not tonsured in his exile, unlike many of his contemporaries, apparently because he was excommunicated. See below.

34. Shakhovskoi's works are listed in n. 60 below.

35. Golubev, *TODRL* XVII:399; Platonov, *Skazaniia*, pp. 236–237. See in particular his denunciation of Khvorostinin in Gorskii and Nevostruev, vol. IV (sec. II, pt. 3), p. 696.

36. There is some indication that he was earlier employed by Patriarch Jove in the writing of saints' vitae: V. [O.] Kliuchevskii, *Drevnerusskie zhitiia sviatykh kak istoricheskii istochnik* (Moscow, 1871), p. 319.

37. On this episode, one of the first "security cases" (*po slovu i delu gosudarevym*) see I. [I.] Polosin, "'Igra v tsaria' (Otgoloski Smuty v moskovskom bytu XVII veka)," *Izvestiia Tverskogo pedagogicheskogo instituta* (Tver' [Kalinin]), I (1926): 59–63.

38. Platonov, *Skazaniia*, p. 452.

39. We may assume that Shakhovskoi died by 1655, at which time we find his sons squabbling over his possessions. See *AMG*, II:475. A document in DRV indicates that he died in 1654. (IX:281).

40. Specimens of Isaiah's Slavonic may be found in Abramovich, *Mnikh Kamianchanin*, of Khvorostinin's in Savva, Platonov, and Druzhinin, *LZAK za 1905 god* XVIII:33–106; and of Shakhovskoi's in the literature cited in n. 60 below.

41. Golubev, *TODRL* XVII:411, lines 210–211. The letter to Dmitrii Pozharskii in which these lines occur was almost certainly written at the time of the exile of the Shakhovskois, as is seen from an apparent reference to the six cousins: "Ne pogubi samovlastnym izvoleniem shestochislennogo kameni dragogo, Pozhalui nas, greshnykh . . ." (ibid., lines 271–272). This text is reproduced in App. IV, pt. b.

42. See Maikov, *ZhMNP*, pt. 275 (June 1891), p. 776.

43. A. I. Nikol'skii, "Sofiia premudrost' Bozhiia," *Vestnik arkheologii i*

istorii, izdavaemyi Imperatorskim Arkheologicheskim institutom (St. Petersburg), XVII (1906):84.

44. See, e.g., the introduction to his collected works, where he writes: "ovogda mi sluchisia byti v velitse pechali i skorbi, i terpenii, ovogda zhe v zakliuchenii i vo izgnanii . . ." (Leonid, "Svedenie," p. 245), in addition to the other letters cited below, n. 60.

45. Kurbskii took a rather important part in the Polotsk campaign of 1563, and his appointment to Tartu in 1564 can hardly be considered a form of punishment or expression of lack of confidence. The closest thing to evidence that Ivan punished Kurbskii in any way is contained in instructions to Muscovite messengers in Lithuania in 1565: "and Kurbskii had begun to engage in treasonous matters against our sovereign," they were to say, "and our sovereign *had wanted* [*byl khotel*] to punish him" *RIO* 71:321.

46. See Fennell, *Corresp.*, p. 139, n. 6, documents in Ivanishev, II: 193–194, and R. G. Skrynnikov, *Nachalo oprichniny* (Leningrad, 1966), pp. 210–211. Kurbskii did not depart "in a terrible rush," and he was not obliged to leave his wife, son, armor, and "papers" behind (*Nachalo*, p. 210). According to his own later account, Kurbskii took with him—at the least— 300 gold pieces, a golden chain of the same value, a heavy gold bracelet, 30 ducats, a gold ring, 50 Thalers, at least three horses, and various other trinkets, in addition to twelve bags of odds and ends (*z rechmi drobnymi*). Clearly Kurbskii took what, and whom, he considered important to his later life abroad. See G. Z. Kuntsevich, "Akt Litovskoi metriki o begstve kniazia A. M. Kurbskogo," *Izvestiia ORIaS*, vol. XIX (1914), bk. 2, pp. 281–285.

47. For a discussion of the arguments which demonstrate that Kurbskii remained in Ivan's favor after the battle of Nevel', see Skrynnikov, *TODRL* XVIII:103. One cannot agree, however, that Kurbskii's appointment to the important frontier post of Tartu was a form of disgrace (ibid., p. 104).

48. . . . *rospis' tsenovaia . . . Shekhovskikh i Sheleshpal'shikh kniazei opal'nym zhivotom 130-go godu* (N. P. Likhachev, *Razriadnye d'iaki XVI veka* [St. Petersburg, 1888], app., p. 62).

49. There seems to be some confusion about the number of Kurbskii's brothers. The genealogical books (e.g. "Rodoslovnaia kniga Velikogo Rossiiskogo Gosudarstva Velikikh Kniazei, . . . i boiarskim i dvorianskim rodam . . . ," *VMOIDR*, bk. 10 [1851], p. 148) and other official documents (*Tysiachnaia kniga 1550 g. i Dvorovaia tetrad' 50-kh godov XVI v.* [Moscow, 1950], p. 57) list only one brother, Ivan, while Fennell (*Corresp.*, p. 265) and M. P. Petrovskii (*Uchenye zapiski* [1873], p. 721) assume the existence of a third brother, Roman, as well. Ustrialov makes the same assumption in his second edition, but corrects it in the third edition, with the remark that Karamzin had erroneously called Ivan "Roman" (Ustrialov, 3rd ed., p. viii). In all probability, Ivan was the only brother, and he died of wounds suffered in the Kazan' campaign of 1552. A number of scholars (e.g., Skrynnikov, *Nachalo*, p. 214) have assumed that the term *vserodno* in Kurbskii's letter is to be construed as applying to the *boiarstvo*, as a kind of brotherhood, but this is a very forced interpretation, unattested by other similar uses of *rod*, which is quite specifically associated with consanguinity. Kurbskii might have meant the Iaroslavl' princes (*rod Iaroslavskii*), but there is little evidence to suggest that the early punishments of individual boyars (i.e., before Kurbskii's flight) were selectively directed against any one princely clan. Indeed Kurbskii himself (or someone!) says in the *History*, "[Kurliatev was] . . . tonsured . . . with all his family [*vserodno*], i.e. with his wife and

small children at the breast, weeping and wailing" (Fennell, *History*, p. 182).

50. See his letter to Tret'iak Vasil'ev in *VMOIDR*, bk. 9 (1851), *Smes'*, p. 6, reproduced below in App. IV, pt. b. Shakhovskoi speaks of his military service: "i rabotakh im gosudarem na ratekh vsedushno ne shchadia golovy svoei, dazhe i do krovi podvizakhsia" (Gorskii and Nevostruev, vol. IV [sec. II, pt. 3], p. 700).

51. Golubev, *TODRL* XVII:410, lines 156–161; cf. p. 412, lines 236–237. See App. IV, pt. b.

52. Shakhovskoi was wounded during fighting near Velezh' and Mstislav in 1613–1615 (*RBS*, vol. "Chaadaev-Shvitkov," p. 588).

53. Ivanishev, I:xv–xviii.

54. F. [I.] Buslaev, comp., *Istoricheskaia khristomatiia tserkovno-slavian-skogo i drevne-russkogo iazykov* (Moscow, 1861), cols. 1047–1048, in which some passages are omitted out of prudery, and the missing passages in Gorskii and Nevostruev, vol. IV (sec. II, pt. 3), p. 698, and Leonid, "Svedenie," p. 246. The full text is given below in App. IV, pt. b.

55. Stroev, *Slovar'*, p. 291.

56. See below, Chap. 3.

57. Ivanishev, I:xix–xx.

58. See Platonov, *Skazaniia*, pp. 231–250, and literature cited there.

59. Two other items of a general nature require comment. Kurbskii speaks of the exploits of Muscovite *voevody* in winning "German" cites for Ivan, which allusion has been interpreted (e.g., Fennell, *Corresp.*, pp. 4–5) as a reference to the Baltic cities captured early in the Livonian war (1558–1560). But it should be remembered that in the seventeenth century many of the cities which the Muscovites contested with the Swedes (*Sveiskie nemtsy*) were called "German," including the very Velizh near which Shakhovskoi was wounded. See Petr Bartenev, ed., *Sobranie pisem tsaria Alekseia Mikhailovicha* (Moscow, 1856), pp. 54–55. A second allusion, one which has caused particular consternation among commentators on the first letter of Kurbskii, is the mention of the boyars who, "worse than the priests of Cronus, act through their children" (i.e., use their children; here I differ with Fennell's translation). It seems altogether reasonable to assume, on the basis of all other evidence, that this is a reference to the attempts to find a bride for Mikhail Fedorovich, which culminated later in the obscure case of Mariia Khlopova. She was betrothed to Mikhail Fedorovich, but never married him as a result of a tangled intrigue involving her parents and the Saltykovs, Boris and Mikhail. They apparently bribed palace doctors and perhaps employed mild poisons to insure that suspicions concerning her health would arise. The intrigues were successful, but in the end the Salty-kovs were exposed and punished. See *SGGD* III:257–268. In the second version of this letter, it is stated that Fedor Rostislavich of Smolensk was the ancestor of the writer. As it happens, since Prince Fedor was the pro-genitor of the Iaroslavl' line of princes, he was the ancestor of Kurbskii, Khvorostinin, and Shakhovskoi. See App. V, genealogical chart.

60. Although Semen Shakhovskoi is usually mentioned in surveys of both secular and religious literature, few of his numerous works have appeared in print, and there exists no general evaluation of his significance as a writer and thinker. Without extensive study of the relevant manuscript materials, it is difficult to establish which works attributed to him are in fact his. It appears from the printed materials that he may be credited with the following impressive bibliography.

(A) Historical works:

(1) *Povest' o ubienii tsarevicha Dimitriia*, published by Platonov in *RIB*, vol. XIII, cols. 837–859, from MSS 213/191 and 214/192 of the Moscow Theological Academy (now GBL, *fond* 173, nos. 27 and 29).

(2) *Povest' o nekoem mnise, kako poslasia ot Boga po tsaria Borisa . . .*, published from the same copies in *RIB*, vol. XIII, cols. 859–876 (these are in fact columns, called pages in the Index to *RIB*, XIII).

(3) A *Povest' o velikom pozhare moskovskom*, narrating the events surrounding the burning of Moscow in 1626. Unpublished, found in the same manuscripts, and apparently used in the composition of later "Chronograph" texts.

(4) A "chronicle," or perhaps a number of such compositions: Filaret (*Obzor russkoi dukhovnoi literatury*, I [Khar'kov, 1859]:218–219) mentions a *letopis' o tsariakh Ivane Vasil'eviche, Borise Godunove, Mikhaile Fedoroviche;* Ikonnikov (*Opyt russkoi istoriografii* [Kiev, 1891], vol. I, pt. 2, p. 891) mentions a *Khronika*; perhaps one of these is the *Letopisets* sent to the *Zapisnoi prikaz* by Shakhovskoi's relation, the widow Mar'ia in 1659 (Sergei A. Belokurov, "O Zapisnom prikaze ('Zapisyvati stepeni i grani tsarstvennye') 1657–1659 gg.," in his *Iz dukhovnoi zhizni moskovskogo obshchestva XVII v.* [Moscow, 1902], p. 64).

(5) It is quite possible that the "Tale" attributed to Prince I. M. Katyrev-Rostovskii should be added to this list. The most authoritative opinion concerning the authorship of the "Tale" is that of S. F. Platonov, who reversed his earlier view in 1917 ("Starye somneniia," *Sbornik v chest' professora M. K. Liubavskogo* [Moscow, 1917], pp. 172–190) and rejected the possibility that Katyrev-Rostovskii was the author. Although Platonov does not mention Shakhovskoi in this article, he gives evidence which would support such an attribution, which in fact had been made by Stroev (*Slovar'*, p. 289) and Berednikov ("Vypiska is doneseniia Bibliotekaria Imperatorskoi Akademii nauk Berednikova G. Nepremennomu Sekretariu ee Fusu, ot 26 iiulia 1835 goda," *ZhMNP*, pt. 8 [October 1835], p. 76) long before Platonov's original (1888) view became generally accepted. In particular, in reestablishing what he feels to have been the original text, Platonov points out that the true author was, by his own testimony, "of the Iaroslavl' line" (*rodu Eroslavshogo shhodatai*). An almost identical device is used to conceal Shakhovskoi's name in his letter to Korob'in (*rodu eroslavskogo iskhodatel'*, Gorskii and Nevostruev, vol. IV [sec. II, pt. 3], p. 697).

(6) An autobiographical sketch, labeled by the publisher (Pogodin?) *Domashnie zapiski*. Published in *Moskovskii vestnik*, 1830, pt. V, pp. 61–70. This is presumably the same text mentioned by Filaret (*Obzor*, p. 218). See below, App. IV, pt. c.

(B) Liturgical works

(7) "Slovo pokhval'noe trem moskovskim sviatitelem Petru, Alekseiu i Ione" (see Kliuchevskii, *Zhitiia*, p. 319; F. G. Spasskii, *Russkoe liturgicheskoe tvorchestvo* [Paris: YMCA Press, 1951], p. 263). According to Kliuchevskii, this work is found in the Miliutin Menolog. Another manuscript, MS 178 of the Moscow Theological Academy, is mentioned by Stroev (*Slovar'*, p. 298). See also a collection of Shakhovskoi's works in the collection of the Chudov Monastery, described by P. N. Petrov ("Knigokhranilishche Chudova monastyria," *PDP* 1871, IV (V), p. 182, no. 280).

(8) "Slovo Khrista radi iurodivym Prokopiiu i Ioannu, ustiuzhskim chudotvortsam" (see Kliuchevskii, *Zhitiia*, p. 319, and Spasskii, p. 263). A

manuscript copy is in the Undol'skii collection ([V. M. Undol'skii], *Slavianorusskie rukopisi V. M. Undol'skogo* ... [Moscow, 1870], cols. 249–250).

(9) Canons of Masses for the three Moscow *Sviatiteli* and the Miracle-Workers of Ustiug (Spasskii, pp. 263–264).

(10) Mass to Sofiia the Divine Wisdom. Published with an introduction from a number of manuscripts of the Synodal collection by A. Nikol'skii ("Sofiia premudrost' Bozhiia," pp. 69–102).

(11) "Akafist prepodobnomu Sergiiu," mentioned in Ilarii and Arsenii, "Opisanie slav'ianskikh rukopisei Sviato-Troitskoi, Sergievoi Lavry," *Chteniia,* 1879, bk. 2, 2nd pagination, p. 174.

(12) A number of prayers, found in the manuscripts cited above in (1). Spasskii (pp. 265, 309) attributes a number of other liturgical and religious works to Shakhovskoi.

(13) Service celebrating the installation of the Savior's robe. See App. I, pt. b.

(14) "Povest' preslavna o prenesenii rizy Gospodnei ..." see App. I, pt. b. (This tale, apparently, might also be classified under historical writings.)

(C) Letters

Dozens of Shakhovskoi's letters have been preserved. They are enumerated and described in Spasskii (pp. 264–265) and Stroev (*Slovar',* pp. 290–298), and published in excerpts in Gorskii and Nevostruev, vol. IV [sect. II, pt. 3] pp. 695–701) from MS 327(865) of the Synodal collection. Among the more important are:

(15) Letter (for Filaret) to Shah Abbas, May 1625.

(16) Letter to Filaret (ca. 1622 ?). Published in excerpts in Buslaev, *Khristomatiia,* col. 1048. For full text see App. IV, pt. b.

(17) Letters to Kiprian: (a) between Sept. 8, 1620, and Dec. 12, 1624. Text from Buslaev, *Khristomatiia,* cols. 1048–1050, reproduced in App. IV, pt. b; (b) two between Dec. 12, 1624, and Oct. 20, 1626, from the first of which portions are cited immediately below in this chapter.

(18) Two letters to Ivan Khvorostinin, one (Stroev, *Slovar',* p. 292) written apparently before the end of 1622 (the time of Khvorostinin's exile) and the other in 1624 or early 1625. Fragments of the first have been published by Platonov (*Skazaniia,* pp. 236–237).

(19) Four letters to Tret'iak Vasil'ev (monastic name, Savvatii) apparently written in the late 1640's. Published from MS of the Patriarchal library old number 307, in *VMOIDR,* bk. 9 (1851), *Smes',* pp. 5–8, and reproduced in App. IV, pt. b.

(20) A letter in verse, apparently addressed to Prince D. M. Pozharskii, published by Golubev (*TODRL* XVII:407–413), and reproduced in App. IV, pt. b.

(21) A letter to Aleksei Mikhailovich concerning the marriage of Irina Mikhailovna to Prince Waldemar. Published by Golubtsov ("Pamiatniki prenii o vere, voznikshikh po delu korolevicha Val'demara i Tsarevny Iriny Mikhailovny," *Chteniia,* 1892, bk. 2, sec. ii, pp. 158–165).

Among Shakhovskoi's other known correspondents were the *okol'nichii* Semen Gavriilovich Korob'in, Ivan Borisovich Cherkasskii, and one Varlaam, former *igumen* of the Bogoiavlenskii Monastery in Suzdal'.

A number of authors (A. I. Andreev, *Ocherki po istochnikovedeniiu Sibiri,* I [Moscow, 1960]: 20; S. V. Bakhrushin, *Nauchnye trudy,* III [Moscow, 1955]; 121, 192) have attributed to Shakhovskoi a brief geographical description of the basin of the Verkhniaia Tunguska, "Rospis' imainnaia rekam i novym zemlitsam, kniaztsom, s kotorykh gosudarev iasak zbiraettsa v Eniseeiskii ostrog . . ." (pub. by N. N. Stepanov in *Izvestiia Vsesoiuznogo geograficheskogo obshchestva* LXXXI (1949):298–299). This report, of interest to historians of Siberia, tells us nothing of Shakhovskoi, other than the fact that he was in Eniseisk in 1629–1630.

61. Gorskii and Nevostruev, vol. IV, (sec. II, pt. 3), p. 700.

62. *VMOIDR*, bk. 9 (1851), *Smes'*, p. 6.

63. Golubev, *TODRL* XVII:410, line 122, and 413, line 267, and App. IV, pt. b, below.

64. See above, n. 60 (5).

65. *RIB*, vol. XIII, col. 580.

66. Especially MS 1615. Compare A. F. Bychkov, *Opisanie tserkovno-slavianskikh i russkikh rukopisnykh sbornikov Imperatorskoi Publichnoi biblioteki*, pt. I (St. Petersburg, 1882), and [I. Ia. Porfir'ev], *Opisanie rukopisei Solovetskogo monastyria, nakhodiashchikhsia v biblioteke Kazanskoi dukhovnoi akademii*, pt. 2 (Kazan', 1885), pp. 553–559. This latter is the earliest text of the letters to Vas'ian (R. G. Skrynnikov, *TODRL* XVIII: 99–100). The three manuscripts that contain these letters are all of the mid- to late seventeenth century.

67. The other text is "Ioannu mnogouchennomu . . ." (Kuntsevich, cols. 361–376).

68. The arguments are summarized by Skrynnikov (*TODRL* XVIII: 101–103), who believes that it was written before Kurbskii's flight.

69. App. IV, pt. b.

70. See Shakhovskoi's curriculum vitae, App. V.

71. Skrynnikov, *Nachalo*, p. 206.

72. *Entsiklopedicheskii slovar'*, pub. by Brokgauz and Efron, half-vol. 82 (1892), pp. 932–933.

73. V. S. Sopikov, *Opyt rossiiskoi bibliografii*, 2nd ed. (St. Petersburg, 1904), p. 55.

74. See below, Chap. 4.

75. It would appear that one may provide an even more precise date for this letter, on the basis of an analysis of Shakhovskoi's other letters. These are found in the available manuscripts in apparent chronological order and indicate a certain evolution in Shakhovskoi's tone, although all of the letters are full of lamentation and requests for forgiveness or intercession. In the early Korob'in letter, written ca. 1622, Shakhovskoi is rather proud and angry, and does not mention his difficulties with Filaret concerning his uncanonical marriage. Later, however (cf. letters to Filaret and Kiprian), in 1624 and 1625, he seems a broken man, full of remorse and contrition— although he refuses to accept the original charges of complicity with his cousins. It would seem from this evolution—and particularly from the fact that there is no mention of the dissolution of his marriage in the Kurbskii letter—that the latter was written shortly after he was removed as *voevoda* in Viaz'ma (March 1621) but before his marriage was dissolved (late summer?) in the same year. This assumption is confirmed by the fact that in the Kurbskii letter the author speaks not only of his own misfortunes, but of the "strong in Israel" in general, and of the oppression of his whole family (*vserodno*). Such an assumption would also account for the fact that this letter is not found with the other letters which are all of later date, after his property was confiscated for the first time, etc. Finally, in Shakhovskoi's

apparent editing of Isaiah's text, he omitted the words *Dnes' az v temnitsy* . . . , which would indicate that he was out of prison (cf. the Korob'in letter where he thanks Korob'in for help while he was in prison).

CHAPTER 3

1. For a recent exposition of this view, see *Poslaniia*, pp. 470–471.

2. As may be seen from Lur'e's erudite commentaries to these letters, ibid., pp. 583–612, 652–655. See also I. Duichev, "Vizantiia i vizantiiskaia literatura v poslaniiakh Ivana Groznogo," *TODRL* XV (1958): 159–176.

3. Some of the texts falsely attributed to Ivan are discussed in I. N. Zhdanov, "Sochineniia," which is to my knowledge the closest approach to a skeptical view of Ivan's literary activities, but Zhdanov apparently had no doubts about the *Correspondence*. In 1956 S. M. Dubrovskii expressed some passing doubts about Ivan's writings, but in a context which was perhaps not directly relevant to our concerns here ("Protiv idealizatsii deiatel'nosti Ivana IV," *Voprosy istorii*, 1956, no. 8, p. 123).

4. This is not to minimize the importance and usefulness of many of the best studies of the text within the traditional context—such as those of Lur'e, Damerau, Nørretranders, Likhachev, et al.

5. Thus, we possess contemporary and in many cases autograph copies of many works written in the period and contemporary copies of most chronicles, including the great *Litsevoi svod*, not to mention hundreds of other manuscripts found in monastic collections. As to printed books, in which Muscovy was not rich, there are few if any well-attested editions which have not been preserved. For Ukrainian territory, in addition to the extensive *grodskie knigi* used in Ivanishev's compilation, we possess a vast amount of polemical, didactic, and other literature, in contemporary editions, in addition to the rich manuscript tradition. Moreover, for the early seventeenth century in Muscovite territory, where manuscripts, produced in mass quantities, assumed some of the functions which in the West were carried by the printed book (indeed many manuscripts were made from Kievan and other Western printed books), we possess thousands of manuscripts of every possible description.

6. While this is not the appropriate place for a full-scale study of this important question, it may be pointed out that we possess all of the last wills and testaments of the Grand Princes of Muscovy which are indicated in these inventories, in addition to very impressive runs of diplomatic documents (in contemporary copies) extending back into the 1470's, and many of the sundry treaties, charters, and other records which are mentioned. Moreover, as careful study of the later Muscovite chronicles reveals, many of those diplomatic documents which are now missing were probably lost not as the result of any calamity within the Grand Princely archive itself, but in a separate catastrophe that struck the place in which they were preserved after having been removed for the purposes of chronicle writing. For the inventories, see S. O. Shmidt, ed., *Opisi tsarskogo arkhiva XVI veka i arkhiva Posol'skogo prikaza 1614 goda* (Moscow, 1960).

7. I rely here upon Lur'e's research and a perusal of the printed descriptions of Ukrainian archives, e.g., N. I. Petrov, *Opisanie rukopisnykh sobranii nakhodiashchikhsia v gorode Kieve*, 3 vols. (Moscow, 1891, 1897, 1904); vol. III, p. 109—a nineteenth-century copy of Ivan's first letter.

8. The following editions have been checked in support of this statement: L. E. Berry and R. O. Crummey, *Rude and Barbarous Kingdom: Russia in the*

Accounts of Sixteenth-Century English Voyagers (Madison, 1968); Henrich Staden (Genrikh Shtaden), *O Moskve Ivana Groznogo*, ed. and intro. I. I. Polosin (Moscow, 1925); Jacques Margeret, *Estat de l'Empire de Russie et grande duché de Muscovie, 1590 jusques en 1606* (reprinted, Paris, 1860); E. A. Bond, ed., *Russia at the Close of the Sixteenth Century* (London, 1856); S. H. Baron, trans. and ed., *The Travels of Olearius in Seventeenth-century Russia* (Stanford: Stanford University Press, 1967). It is particularly interesting that Kurbskii is not even mentioned by the German agent in Polish service, Paul Oderborn, in his "Ioannis Basilidis Magni Moscoviae Ducis Vita." See I. [I.] Polosin, *Sotsial'no-politicheskaia istoriia Rossii XVI-nachala XVII v.* (Moscow, 1963), p. 193.

There is one source which mentions that Kurbskii wrote to Ivan after his defection: Franz Nienstadt's *Livländische Chronik*, ed. G. Tielemann, in *Monumenta Livoniae antiquae*, 2 (Riga and Leipzig, 1839): 67. Nienstadt's evidence in general has been questioned by Belokurov (*O Biblioteke*, pp. 246–280); there is no need to dwell upon this bit of information, since it is clear from the Nienstadt's account that, even if Kurbskii wrote some letters to Ivan, and Ivan to him, these letters cannot be the texts presently known as their *Correspondence*. The text:

> Der Knäse Andrey Kurpsche ward auch bey dem Grossfürsten dieses Handels halber verdächtig, als ob er mit dem Könige von Polen gegen ihn practisiret, dass er bey sich bechlossen hatte, ihn auch durch einen schmähligen Tod zu würgen; aber dieser kahm in der Nacht über die Mauren, und rettete sich zu dem Könige von Polen, welcher ihn zu Gnaden auffnahm, und ihme viele Güter in Littauwen verehrete. Der Knäse schrieb darauff dem Grossfursten seine unschuld uber, und dieser hätte ihn damahls gerne zurücke gehabt; aber er wollte nicht, sondern begehrete seine Frau, welche ihme in seiner Abwesenheit einen Sohn gebohren hatte, allein der Moscowiter wollte sie ihme nicht folgen lassen, gab aber dem Sohne des Vaters Güter wieder. So hoch achtete er sein Meriten, denn er war ein wackerer Kriegesmann, und in vielen Schlachten Feld-Obrister gewesen. Der Knäse nahm aber eine andere Frau in Littauwen, mit welcher er eine Tochter gehabt, und ist daselbst in Ruhe gestorben. Alexander König, der itzt noch ein Eltester in Riga ist, und sowohl bey dem Graffen Artze, als auch nachher bey dem Knäse Andrey Kurpsche gedienet hatte, erzehlete, dass der Knäse den Graffen offtmahls mit Schuffzen beklaget habe, weilen er unschuldig sey, und solch einen schmähligen Tod nicht verwircket habe. Ein Schreiber ward auch mit dem Graffen gerichtet und enthauptet.

9. See *Pamiatniki polemicheskoi literatury v Zapadnoi Rusi*, 3 vols. (St. Petersburg, 1878–1903), and Mykhailo Hrushevs'kyi, *Z istorii relihiinoi dumky na Ukraini* (Winnipeg, 1962). Cf. Kurbskii's later writings in Kuntsevich, cols. 411–484. It is worth noting here that Sobolevskii (*Perevod-naia literatura Moskovskoi Rusi XIV–XVII vekov. Bibliograficheskie materialy* [St. Petersburg, 1903], p. 196, no. 2) concluded that the works which Kurbskii wrote in Lithuania were not known in Muscovy until the end of the seventeenth century.

10. See his article, "Ivan Groznyi i pripiski k litsevym svodam ego vremeni," *Ist. zap.* XXIII (1947): 251–289, and Nikolay Andreyev, "Interpolations in the Sixteenth-Century Muscovite Chronicles," *SEER* XXXV (1956):95–115.

11. Thus, the first literate tsar was, by all accounts, Aleksei Mikhailovich—although his grandfather Filaret, de facto ruler for much of Mikhail Fedorovich's reign, was apparently literate, and even attempted at one point to learn Latin (Berry and Crummey, *Rude and Barbarous*, p. 331). Leaving aside

such members of the princely warrior class as Vassian Patrikeev, who "emigrated" to the other culture through voluntary or involuntary entry into the monastic state, it is difficult to name any lay authors not of the professional *d'iak* class before the Time of Troubles. Certainly the generation of Shakhovskoi and Khvorostinin was the first to produce a number of educated laymen of that class.

12. See above, Chap. I, n. 7.

13. For an urbane discussion of such matters, see D. S. Likhachev, *Poetika drevnerusskoi literatury* (Leningrad, 1967), pp. 84–108.

14. For a discussion of "genuineness" with regard to Ivan's official letters, see below.

15. A refinement of this judgement about the exclusive use of "plain style" would concern letters to members of the higher clergy and correspondence with Mt. Athos, etc., which was composed in Slavonic, probably in the chancellery of the Metropolitan. In later diplomatic correspondence with the Polish-Lithuanian court, some biblical citations were made in Slavonic, but these are always clearly marked. See Introduction to *RIO*, vol. 71.

16. *Poslaniia*, pp. 193–194.

17. It is true, of course, that in the heat of the polemical rhetoric which became so characteristic of Ukrainian literature in the last decades of the sixteenth century, the ponderous gentility of traditional Slavonic began to give way to acerbic and colloquial styles. (See the literature cited in note 9 above and, e.g., Isaiah's reference to the Metropolitan of Cyzicus as a *blekotlivaia baba*.) The *Correspondence* aside, it is not until the early seventeenth century, in the early literature of the Time of Troubles, that one generally encounters this kind of rhetoric.

18. The standard historical grammars of Russian are of little help in understanding the stylistic problems here, since they often fail to distinguish between shifts in stylistic and regional features on the one hand, and linguistic evolution on the other. The chronicles of the sixteenth century, which do contain both Slavonic and plain passages, are essentially Slavonic texts with long citations in plain style, which is an indication of citation from official documents. D. S. Likhachev is apparently speaking of these incongruities when he writes "[Ivan] was an astonishingly talented person. It seems that in writing nothing caused him difficulties. His speech flowed with complete freedom. And—what lexical variety, what a striking contamination of styles, what a disinclination to observe any literary conventions of his time whatsoever!" (*Poslaniia*, p. 461). One may agree entirely with these observations, as they apply summarily to the works attributed to Ivan, but the question of attribution remains open, and the description of the linguistic and stylistic features of these texts as extraordinary (without any exclamation point) is a part of the process of attribution, without which evaluation and appreciation are premature.

19. On this version of Slavonic see Damerau, *Russisches und Westrussisches*, passim.

20. I have in mind the established view that the last letter of Kurbskii was written in 1579 (Fennell, *Corresp.*, p. 247).

21. The argument has been advanced that it was Kurbskii's intention to impress Ivan with Western terms and in general with his newly acquired erudition. This is hardly acceptable: although the Ukrainian version of Slavonic acquired a certain chic in the seventeenth century due to the activities of Ukrainians in Muscovite cultural life, it can hardly have been

considered stylish in 1565, before the literary renaissance in the Ukraine had properly begun. Had Kurbskii wanted to engage in such oneupmanship, he would probably have chosen Latin.

22. See, for example, Belokurov (*O Biblioteke*, passim) and the observations of Fletcher (Berry and Crummey, *Rude and Barbarous*, passim).

23. It appears that Cicero was first translated into Polish by Stanisław Koszutski in Vilnius in 1576 (A. Anushkin, *Na zare knigopechataniia v Litve*, Vilnius, 1970, p. 81). The *Paradoxa stoicorum*—used in the later Kurbskii letters—apparently did not appear in Polish before the eighteenth century, as Prof. Kumaniecki of Warsaw has kindly informed me. It is highly unlikely that any such work would have appeared first in Muscovy in the sixteenth century. It was only much later that Latin authors began to be translated— often from Polish—in Muscovy. The anachronism of a number of the allusions and citations found both in the *Correspondence* and in other works attributed to Ivan and Kurbskii is correctly noted by Fennell (*Corresp.*, pp. 185, n. 2; 201, n. 10; 202, n. 1; 244, n. 1; etc.) and is clear from even a cursory comparison of the works cited with the evidence concerning the first appearance and translation of such works in Muscovy contained in Sobolevskii's still unsurpassed *Perevodnaia literatura* (see his information on Ambrosius, Augustine, M. Bielski, etc.).

24. See I. N. Golenishchev-Kutuzov, *Ital'ianskoe vozrozhdenie i slavianskie literatury XV–XVI vekov* (Moscow, 1963).

25. See, e.g., Akademiia nauk SSSR, Institut literatury, *Istoriia russkoi literatury*, vol. II, pt. 2, *Literatura 1590–1690 gg.* (Moscow-Leningrad, 1948), and J. Krzyżanowski, "Proza polska wieku XVI," in Polska Akademia Nauk, *Odrodzenie w Polsce*, IV (Warsaw, 1956): 259–312.

26. For an excellent general treatment of the Ukrainian cultural movement of the period see Mikhailo Hrushevs'kyi, *Kul'turno-natsional'nyi rukh na Ukraini v XVI–XVII vitsi*, 2nd ed. (n.p., 1919).

27. See Kharlampovich, *Malorossiiskoe*, vol. I.

28. For a thorough, somewhat controversial discussion of the introduction of printing in Muscovy, see E. Nemirovskii, *Vozniknovenie knigopechtaniia v Moskve: Ivan Fedorov* (Moscow, 1964).

29. Detailed biographical information may be found in Petrovskii, *Kn. A. M. Kurbskii*, Gorskii, *Zhizn'*, and Ivanishev.

30. Ivanishev, I: 197. A modification of Ivanishev's stern judgments about Kurbskii's behavior has been urged by Oswald Backus, who feels, after examination of documentary material not published by Ivanishev, that the latter's selection of materials for publication was one-sided. It is to be hoped that Professor Backus will continue his research into Kurbskii's later career, and that the appropriate archival materials will be published. See Oswald P. Backus, "A. M. Kurbsky in the Polish-Lithuanian State (1564–1683)," *Acta Baltico-Slavica* (Białystok), VI (1969): 29–50.

31. Here, too, one must, temporarily at least, exclude the evidence in Kurbskii's and Ivan's writings.

32. Belokurov, *O Biblioteke*, passim.

33. Ivan left no autographs, not even a signature. A signature has been preserved on Kurbskii's last will and testament, a tracing of which has graciously been provided me by Oswald P. Backus of the University of Kansas from the Central Library of the Lithuanian Academy of Sciences (see Fig. 3). Three comments are in order. First, the signature is in an exceedingly unpracticed hand, hardly that of a translator of Cicero, however

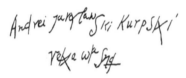

Fig. 3. Signature of Andrei Kurbskii on a testament dated September 14, 1582. From a tracing by Professor Oswald Backus from the original in the collection of the Library of the Lithuanian Academy of Sciences (Vilnius MAB, F-20, TA 103).

nonchalant about calligraphy. Second, a signature in Latin letters on an official document drawn up in cyrillic encourages the conclusion that the writer learned to make his signature only after his departure from Muscovy. Third, while the orthography of proper names was by no means stabilized in the sixteenth century, and the spelling "Kur*p*skii" is found in numerous texts, such a spelling is not to be expected, in his own signature, from the polyglot and etymologist who is projected by the *Correspondence*. Had Kurbskii possessed the erudition credited to him, he would have formed the proper adjectival form from the name of his native village, Kur*ba*, and not the analphabetic phonetic transcription we find on his testament.

In addition to the *Correspondence* and the *History*, a number of letters and translations have been attributed to Kurbskii, usually on the flimsiest of grounds. They may be grouped as follows.

(*A*) *Original works.* (1) Kurbskii has been credited by Il'ia Denisov (Elie Denissoff, "Une biographie de Maxime le Grec par Kourbski," *Orientalia Christiana Periodica* XX [1954]: 44–84) with a short biographical notice of Maksim the Greek. Denisov's attribution is not convincing, although his juxtaposition of this text with the Introduction to the *Novyi Margarit* and with the *History* (see below) reveals some telling similarities. The biographical notice might also have been compared with the "History of the Eighth Council," also attributed to Kurbskii. In fact this biographical note is probably a reworking of the short Introduction to Maksim's works written in 1591 by the same Isaiah whom we have discussed above. The final elucidation of the odd relationship between the works ascribed to Maksim and those attributed to Kurbskii must await a proper study of Maksim's literary heritage. That Kurbskii might have known Maksim, as most authorities claim, is of course possible, but that the author of the *History* did is questionable: he makes Maksim a contemporary of the Council of Ferrara (Kuntsevich, col. 475), which incongruity Denisov explains away: "Visiblement l'état de decrepitude du moine à 86 ans permet au jeune prince de le croire plus que centénnaire" (*Orientalia Christiana Periodica* XX: 61). (2) Ivanishev, apparently, was the first to attribute to Kurbskii a text entitled *Predislovie na knigu sloves zlatoustovykh, glagolemuiu Novyi Margarit*, published by Ivanishev (II: 303–316), Ustrialov (3rd ed., pp. 269–278), Arkhangel'skii (*Ocherki iz istorii zapadno-russkoi literatury XVI–XVII vv.* [Moscow, 1888], app., pp. 68–72), and in the study of Ferdinand Liewehr (*Kurbskijs "Novyj Margarit"*) (Prague, 1928). No proper attribution of this work has been undertaken. (3) Ustrialov, apparently, first attributed to Kurbskii the "History of the Eighth Council" published by him (2nd ed.,

pp. 3–147) and by Kuntsevich (cols. 473–484). This work is in all probability
a Muscovite revision and translation of the printed text attributed to the
"Klirik ostroz'kyi" (Ostroh, 1598; republished in *Pamiatniki polemicheskoi
literatury*, vol. III [1903], [*RIB* XIX: 433–476]) as is clear from the comparison of the texts performed in my seminar by Mr. Lubomyr Hajda, to be
published in a forthcoming Festschrift for O. Ohloblyn. (4) K. V. Kharlampovich ("Novaia bibliograficheskaia nakhodka," *Kievskaia starina* LXX
[1900]: 211–224) identified as belonging to Kurbskii a text entitled "Ot
drugoi dialektiki Ionna Spanderbergera [sic] o silogizme vytolkovano" by
analogy with a collection of the works of St. John the Damascene, which was
itself attributed to Kurbskii on very questionable grounds (A. N. Popov,
Opisanie rukopisei i katalog knig tserkovnoi pechati biblioteki A. I. Khludova
[Moscow, 1872], pp. 106, 115). It would appear that this text is a translation
of the printed version as is indicated by the fact that other copies of the same
text have been identified as such and from the association with the "Gram-
matika" of the Mamonich brothers (Ostroh, 1584), a copy of which is found
in one manuscript of the "Dialektika" (Chudov Monastery, No. 34) and
together with it in the library of the *Sinodal'naia tipografskaia biblioteka* as
described by A. N. Popov, *Chteniia*, 1881, bk. II, sec. iv, pp. 53–55. (5) The
History of the Grand Prince of Muscovy, see below, note 42.

(*B*) *Letters.* Numerous other letters have been attributed to Kurbskii.
They may be grouped as follows. (1) The letters to Lithuanian-Ukrainian
personages which are found together with the latter parts of the *Correspondence* and are published in Kuntsevich (cols. 411–472). These letters, in
the western recension of the Slavonic literary language, appear to be genuine,
i.e., to have been written to the persons indicated in the latter sixteenth
century, and they contain a number of factual details that are strongly
reminiscent of information to be found in documentary records of Kurbskii's
activities in Lithuania. They may indeed have been written by or for
Kurbskii, although this cannot be proved at this time. (2) A second group of
letters, also published in Kuntsevich (cols. 359–410), should be separated
from the letters in group (1). These texts are written not in the western, but
in the Muscovite version of Slavonic. Although they have been rather
intensively studied in recent years, their attribution apparently rests upon the
half-hearted comments of Stroev (*Rukopisi slavianskie i rossiiskie, prinadlezhashchie . . . Ivanu Nikitichu Tsarskomu* [Moscow, 1848], p. 577): *ne
Kurbskogo li?; i eto byt' mozhet Kurbskogo.* See Andreyev, *SEER* XXXIII
(1955): 414–436, and Skrynnikov, *TODRL* XVIII (1962): 99–116. The
texts are (as listed by Kuntsevich):

(a) "Ivanu mnogouchennomu otvet o pravoi vere" (Kuntsevich, cols. 361–376), a
   theological treatise which contains no personal or historical *realia* that would
   require attribution to Kurbskii. This letter appears only in the Solovetskii
   Monastery copy 683 (852) ([Porfir'ev], *Opisanie rukopisei Solovetskogo monastyria*, p. 554) This manuscript contains (b) and (c) as well, and is apparently
   (cf. variants in Kuntsevich) the earliest and best copy of all three letters.
(b) "Poslanie kniazia Andreia Kurbskogo o lozhnykh pisanii . . ." (Kuntsevich,
   cols. 377–382).
(c) "Poslanie k startsu Vas'ianu" (Kuntsevich, cols. 383–404), discussed above,
   Chap. 2. This letter and (b) are found in two other manuscripts: Beliaev 1549
   (A. Viktorov, *Sobranie rukopisei I. D. Beliaeva* [Moscow, 1881], p. 43) and

Uvarov 1971 (Tsarskii 461) (Leonid, *Opisanie*, IV: 363–364). The Uvarov copy, made in the eighteenth century, also contains KI.

(C) *Translations.* Kurbskii is credited with a number of translations, most notably of the works of SS. John Chrysostom and Damascene. The 1665 Moscow edition of the "Sermons" of Chrysostom indicated in a prefatory note that Kurbskii had translated sermons 44–47, but Aleksandr Vostokov (*Opisanie russkikh i slovenskikh rukopisei Rumiantsovskogo muzeuma* [St. Petersburg, 1842], p. 251) was more cautious. Since the translations found in the manuscript in question are different from those of the 1665 edition, the attribution remains conjectural.

Liewehr ("*Novyj Margarit*," pp. 1–16; see also his summary of the scholarly literature) and others seem confident that Kurbskii was the translator of the works contained in the *Novyi Margarit*; here, too, conclusive proof is lacking.

Some manuscripts containing translations from St. John the Damascene (Vostokov, *Opisanie*, pp. 251, 555–557); two other copies, one once owned by Piskarev and the other (1619?) in the Public Library in Leningrad, vaguely referred to by Viktorov and Obolenskii (see below), have been attributed to Kurbskii, particularly by Prince Mikhail Obolenskii ("O perevode kniazia Kurbskogo sochinenii Ioanna Damaskina," *Bibliograficheskie zapiski*, 1858, no. 12, cols. 355–366), who was quite certain, on the basis of similarities with "known works" of Kurbskii, that the translations were his.

This is not the place to go into the question of the attribution of these translations. Its solution will require a most careful philological and bibliographical study, one which will take into account all possible sources of the translated texts and approach the problem of attribution after a careful appraisal of the cultural and literary ambience in Muscovy and the Ukraine/Belorussia in both the sixteenth and seventeenth centuries.

On the works other than the *Correspondence* which are attributed to Ivan, see below.

34. Bjarne Nørretranders, *The Shaping of Czardom under Ivan Groznij* (Copenhagen, 1964). In fact, as Nørretranders points out (p. 66), it is only by applying certain preconceptions to the analysis of the letters of Kurbskii that one can come to any clear view of just what his views were, on the basis of these letters.

35. It is, as we have seen (Chap. 1, Table 1), always found in the company of these letters. The correspondences of content and, in some cases, of wording have been indicated by Fennell, in his notes to *History* (Index, s.v. *Correspondence*).

36. See Chap. 1, Table 2.

37. Sobolevskii, *Perevodnaia literatura*, p. 78. See also App. I, pt. c.

38. The basic contributions to the discussion of these puzzles are cited in Fennell's notes, *History*, passim. See also Skrynnikov, *Nachalo*, pp. 41–43.

39. L. V. Cherepnin, "'Smuta' i istoriografiia XVII veka," *Ist. zap.* XIV (1945): 81–128; D. S. Likhachev, *Chelovek v literature drevnei Rusi* (Moscow, 1958), chap. 1.

40. It will be recalled that all known seventeenth-century copies are found in Muscovite collections. The "westrussianisms" aside, the basic linguistic medium is Muscovite Slavonic. The enormous amount of historical,

and particularly biographical, information makes the possibility that the *History* was composed outside Muscovite territory very doubtful.

41. A. N. Grobovsky, *The "Chosen Council" of Ivan IV: A Reinterpretation* (Brooklyn, 1969).

42. Indeed, it should be said that the textual evidence, even that provided by the published versions, weighs so heavily in favor of a Lyzlov-to-Kurbskii borrowing that under normal conditions it might be considered conclusive, the traditional dates and attributions for these works notwithstanding. What comparison of these texts reveals is simply stated: over almost all of Kurbskii's Chapter Two (Fennell, *History*, pp. 26–68), and elsewhere in patches, the *History* follows the Lyzlov text most closely, indeed verbatim. These are the most detailed portions of what "Kurbskii" has to say about himself, and they are rather different in style from the other portions of the *History*, either those devoted to direct criticism of Ivan or to the listing of his victims. In the portions which the *History* has in common with Lyzlov's work, two editorial principles are observed: the author of the *History* in general shortens his original, leaving out, in particular, details (names, dates, etc.) concerning the campaigns in question, and various religious and patriotic excursions found in the Lyzlov text; and, second, he substitutes Polish words for Russian ones, not in all cases, but rather consistently. This second feature, coupled with the regular change of long lists of *voevody* containing Kurbskii's name to "I and my comrades," etc., seems to have been a part of the effort to create the impression that Kurbskii was the author. In fact, what is produced is a parody of the polonized language of Ukrainian emigrants to Muscovy in the later seventeenth century; that Kurbskii, writing what is essentially Muscovite Slavonic, would have "lapsed" into the use of such Polonisms as "dela" for "pushki" and "mesto" for "grad" is highly unlikely. In addition to the above observations, consider the following variants (L = 1787 edition of Lyzlov, K = Fennell, *History*): (1) In shortening, or changing the subject of a sentence from third-person forms (lists of names) or "oni" in L to "my," the author of *History* forgets to change verb forms to correspond, leaving the third-person plural: L/130: *Tiizhe . . . ustremishasia . . . preekhasha* = K 28: *My zh . . . ustremishasia . . . preekhasha*; L 131: *Potom pomozhe Bog khristianom . . . i izbisha ikh* = K 28: *potom pomog Bog nam khristianom . . . i izbisha ikh*; L 132: *Tiizhe . . . zaslonisha ego* = K 30: *poneshe my zaslonisha ego*(!) Such examples appear passim. (2) Author of *History* simply misreads original: L 130: *Tsar' tatarskii . . . pripasy potopi v perepravakh* = K 28: *tsar' tatarskii . . . kuli potopil i porokhov.* Cf. Fennell's note 1, *History*, p. 28. (3) Author of *History*, in converting Lyzlov's *versty* to miles, usually simply divides by five (instead of seven), but occasionally is mistaken (*pol-2* for 15, L 130/K 28); and in the case of small numbers, apparently unable to convert to yards/paces, he gives very approximate numbers or retains *versta* (L 141/K 40). (4) Abbreviations in *History* lead to non sequiturs and obscurities: e.g., L 135, where the preparations for the entry into Sviiazhsk are described, including the sending of a detachment into the town to greet the tsar when he approached. The entry is then described *I tako . . . priide voinstvo iako vo svoi domy.* K 32 omits the preparations, and *I tamo kh tomu priekhali . . . voistinu iako v svoi domy* makes little sense. Cf. L 146 bottom, = K 44; L 151, where Lyzlov lists animals useful for fur and meat while Kurbskii (50) omits some names of animals needed for meat but retains the reference to eating: *kuny . . . i belki i protchie zverie ko odezhdam i ko iadeniiu potrebnye.* These examples

could be multiplied: the relationship of these texts requires meticulous study on the basis of extant manuscripts.

43. See above, note 33.

44. I.e., MSS 136, 1582, 181/60, 1494, 623. See Chap. 1, n. 1.

45. Mikhailo Hrushevs'kyi, *Istoriia ukrains'koi literatury*, vol. 5 (New York: Knyhospilka, 1960), p. 252. The "History" was published in Ostroh in 1598. See I. Karataev, *Opisanie slaviano-russkikh knig, napechatannykh kirillovskimi bukvami*, vol. I, *S 1491 do 1652* (St. Petersburg, 1883) (*Sbornik ORIas*, XXXIV, No. 2), No. 155.

46. The proofs of this conclusion, consisting mostly of an analysis of the untranslated Ukrainian cognates found in the Great Russian text, have been systematically summarized by Lubomyr Hajda in the unpublished paper mentioned above, n. 33.

47. See n. 33. As we shall see in Chap. 4, there are several possibilities for transmission of these letters from Kurbskii's heirs to the very individuals who are associated with the latter portions of the *Correspondence*.

48. See, e.g., Kagan's studies and the article by V. N. Avtokratov, "'Rech' Ivana Groznogo 1550 goda' kak politicheskii pamflet kontsa XVII veka," *TODRL* XI (1955):255–279.

49. Cf. Zhdanov, *Sochineniia*, I:81–90.

50. It appears that there simply can be no question of this: these letters form normal chronological series, are written upon contemporary paper, and in many cases are duplicated by equally authentic copies in foreign archives.

51. Above, Chap. 1, n. 6.

52. Series of these documents have been published in *RIO*, vols. 35, 41, 71, 95, etc.

53. See, for example, *Akty sotsial'no-ekonomicheskoi istorii Severo-vostochnoi Rusi kontsa XIV—nachala XVI v.*, 3 vols. (Moscow, 1951–1964).

54. In particular, it should be noted that the use of this letter as an example of Ivan's supposedly "vulgar" style is questionable both for the fact that his participation cannot be definitively proven and because the famous comment that Elizabeth was a *poshlaia devitsa* should not be construed in the modern sense "base/common girl" but must be read "commoner" as opposed to true sovereign, and is therefore not "vulgar" in the way that other letters attributed to Ivan are. Cf. the contemporary translation, "a maide" (I. Tolstoi, *The First Forty Years of Intercourse between England and Russia* [St. Petersburg, 1875], pp. 110–115).

55. *RIO* 129:227–240. For other publications see *Poslaniia*, p. 560.

56. E.g., such expressions as *nashego poroga stepeni velichestvo = my*, *velikosil'naia zapoved'*, etc. (*RIO* 129:228 and passim; cf. ibid., p. 5).

57. *RIO* 71:498–499. Thus, Book Seven covers 1562–1569 in unbroken sequence, while these documents, in a book containing numerous blank pages, are dated 1567.

58. Shmidt, *Opisi*, p. 108.

59. See "*Jarlyk*," pp. 36–41.

60. *Poslaniia*, pp. 668–672.

61. *RIO* 35, passim.

62. Ibid., p. 102.

63. "Ot ego tsarskogo velichestva sovetu boiarina i voevody navyshshago i namestnika Volodimerskogo i derzhavtsy Galichskago i Lukhovskogo i Kineshemskogo . . . ," *Poslaniia*, p. 247.

64. See Jack M. Culpepper, "The Kremlin Executions of 1575 and the

Enthronement of Simeon Bekbulatovich," *Slavic Review* XXIV (Sept. 1965): 503–506.

65. See *RIB*, vol. XXII, "Introduction," and Zaozerskii, *Tsar' Aleksei Mikhailovich v svoem khoziaistve* (Petrograd, 1917), pp. 270–274,

66. Lur'e (*Poslaniia*, p. 569) considers the single extant copy to be contemporary, but note the term *chelobitnaia*, used twice in the heading. This form apparently appears only at the very end of the sixteenth century (S. S. Volkov, "Razvitie administrativno-delovoi terminologii v nachale XVII veka," in *Nachal'nyi etap formirovaniia russkogo natsional'nogo iazyka* [Leningrad, 1961], p. 155).

67. *Poslaniia*, p. 570.

68. Ibid. It is noteworthy that Popov's original belonged to the well-known courtier D. M. Golitsyn. See below, Chap. 4.

69. One assumes this from Lur'e's comments (*Poslaniia*, p. 570).

70. V. Novodvorskii, *Bor'ba za Livoniiu mezhdu Moskvoiu i Rech'iu Pospolitoiu (1570–1582)* (St. Petersburg, 1904), p. 49.

71. Ibid.

72. *Poslaniia*, p. 644.

73. Ibid., p. 507.

74. N. F. Beliashevskii, ed., "Donesenie kniazia Aleksandra Polubens-kogo," *Trudy desiatogo arkheologicheskogo s"ezda v Rige 1896*, III (Moscow, 1900): 127. Polubenskii's chronology is very confused, and from the fact that the *Sprawa* is entitled "Sprawa Je[g]o M[o]sci [sic] Pana Nowo-grockiego w Kiesi," a title he received in 1586, it may be presumed that it was written some considerable time after the fact.

75. *Poslaniia*, p. 655.

76. The literature on the letter is cited by D. S. Likhachev in his description of the manuscripts in *Poslaniia* (pp. 562–565) and in his article in *TODRL* VIII (1951): 247–286. Although Likhachev chooses MS 94 of the N. P. Likhachev collection (last quarter of the seventeenth century) as the basis of his edition, he gives evidence later that MS 332 of the same collection should be considered the first draft of the letter, and that, since 332 is a seventeenth-century manuscript, Ivan could not have written the letter. In MS 332 the long citations from the letters of Ilarion the Great are omitted, but are indicated in marginal notations, which appear to be instructions to a scribe to copy the appropriate citations from a collection of Ilarion's letters. Likhachev quotes the instructions, from which it is clear that, if they are followed, the letter as we have it in all other copies may be produced. But Likhachev, after originally assuming that MS 332 represented a copy of Ivan's draft with instructions to a copyist, finally concluded that it was a hastily made copy, from which a *paradnyi spisok* was to be made, and that to save time, the copyist left out the long citations from Ilarion's letter. This is ingenious, but illogical: why make a rough draft from a complete copy, and then send a copyist to copy portions, already in the assumed original, from Ilarion's works? There being no sixteenth-century copy (and apparently none definitely earlier than MS 332), we should assume that 332 was the draft, with instructions for copying the texts which complete the letter as we now have it.

77. *RIO* 71, passim.

78. See D. S. Likhachev, "Voprosy atributsii proizvedenii drevnerusskoi literatury," *TODRL* XVII (1961): 21: "ne sokhranilos' avtograf[a] dazhe Ivana Groznogo."

CHAPTER 4

1. See above, Chap. 2.

2. From the text published in Golubtsov, "Pamiatniki," p. 159.

3. See text in Chap. 2, above, lines 1–2, 116–119.

4. Above, Chap. 2.

5. Such were, apparently, the collections described in Stroev, *Slovar'*, pp. 291–298, those loaned to the *Zapisnoi prikaz* in 1658 by Shakhovskoi's son Fedor (see Belokurov, "O Zapisnom prikaze . . . ," pp. 63–65) and probably MSS 1573 and 2524. Shakhovskoi's view of his literary efforts is seen in the introduction to one of his collections, where he writes: "At times it happened that I was in great sorrow and grief, and suffering, at times even in prison and in exile, and I was visited then by God-loving men, with charity, because of my penury, and with conversations which were good for my spirit. And I had nothing to give them in return for their God-loving gift. And in the place of recompense, I set my hand to paper, and praised their God-given acts" (Leonid, "Svedenie," p. 245).

6. Thus, in the rhymed letter mentioned above (Golubev, *TODRL* XVII:407, lines 3–5, and App. IV, pt. b, below), whose addressee's name is concealed in an acronym, he writes: "Thy [name] Sire, is written in Slavonic in an acrostic [*kraegranesii*]. If you pay attention, then you will know it/As to our poor [name] it is not fully revealed to you/For it is encumbered with numerous and immeasurable sins/There is no use in our sinful appellation . . ." Elsewhere, he justifies an anagram: "I have written my name cryptically [*sokrovenno*] in order that my account not be dishonored and scorned because of my sins by those whom I know" (Stroev, *Slovar'*, p. 298). In still another place, Shakhovskoi employs a complex cypher as a means of disguising his name (L. V. Cherepnin, *Russkaia paleografiia* [Moscow, 1956], pp. 393–394). Finally, note should be taken of the many forms of his name (Senka Shakhovskoi, Semen Ivanov, Duks Simeon, Simon Voinov, etc.) which he used at various times.

7. The *terminus ante quem* of the year 1632 relies, of course, upon the dating note in MS 1615, which Mr. Waugh is inclined to question (App. I). Although the dates here given seem to fit well within the watermark dates of the first group of manuscripts, one cannot rely too heavily upon such dates, and the possibility that the postscript—and indeed the original letter—were written somewhat later may not be excluded. This possibility is supported by the letter to Mikhail Fedorovich of 1644, which is so similar to the first letter of Kurbskii. The acceptance of a later date would not change either the attribution or the explanation of the appearance of the postscript.

8. *Akty otnosiashchiesia k istorii Zapadnoi Rossii*, IV (Moscow, 1851):322 (March 2, 1610).

9. See "K rodislovnoi kn. A. M. Kurbskogo," *Chteniia*, 1895, bk. 3, pp. 2–3, where the report is published from the Archive of the Ministry of Justice by A. Ekzempliarskii. For the Tsar's commendation of Shakhovskoi's initiative, see *AMG* II:509.

10. *Akty, izdavaemye Vil'nenskoi Kommissiei dlia razbora drevnikh aktov*, XXXIV (Vilno, 1909):270–271.

11. Mikhail Semenovich had a long and varied career in the service of tsars Mikhail and Aleksei. He was a *stol'nik* from 1635, *dvorianin* from 1651, and *d'iak* of the *Moskovskii sudnyi prikaz* in 1661–63, in addition to his military service. See *DR*, Index of Names, p. 289.

12. Actually Kuntsevich, who first published the "abbreviated" version (Kuntsevich, cols. 10–50, even numbers only), made no such judgment other than to number it III, the "Chronograph" and "Kurbskii collection" texts being I and II, respectively. Vil'koshevskii, however (*LZAK za 1923–1925 gg.* XXXIII:75), concluded that the "abbreviated" version (which he called "version C") "emerged in its entirety from version B [the Chronograph version] . . . [and] was the work of the hands of a very late copyist, who had a pronounced tendency to shorten the letter." Following Kuntsevich, Stählin, Fennell, and Lur'e preferred the "full" version.

13. *Poslaniia*, pp. 557–558. Unfortunately, Lur'e was examining the relationship of the versions in the context of an assumed opposition between traditions "favorable" to Groznyi and the "antagonistic" traditions of the "Kurbskii Collections," and proceeded on the assumption (borrowed from Vil'koshevskii) that the "abbreviated" version could not be the original version, because it was clearly the "full" version which was referred to in Kurbskii's second letter. But this fact may be explained otherwise—that the "abbreviated" version appeared first, followed by the "full" which served in its turn as the basis of Kurbskii's second letter.

14. See Chap. 1, Tables 1 and 2.

15. Thus, in addition to the brief remarks to this effect by Lur'e (*Poslaniia*, p. 557) one should note the following variant readings:

"Abbreviated" Version (Kuntsevich)	"Full" Version (*Poslaniia*)
орел летанием (стб. 2, строка 22)	орел летаем (стр. 9)
венец жизни носити (16.17)	венец жизни наследити (12)
усрамишися (16.18)	страмишися (13)
отвержеся (16.18)	свержеся (13)
с Силиверстом (22.25)	[нет] (23)
побежден (24.19)	побиен (23)
се ли гордое (24.25)	Се горд (51)
достальных истребити (28.27)	достойных истребити (53)
Тако... тако... то (34.15 и след.)	Тако... како... то (18)
зияющу (36.9)	дыхающу (59)
несть (42.25)	ныне (61)
во учительстве (42.28)	в детстве (61)
. . . and many others.	

16. Here again one must consider two possible editorial processes: either the "full" version represents a cutting up and rearranging, without the loss of a single word (for an exception, see below) of the "abbreviated" version, plus the addition of an enormous amount of new material, or the "abbreviated" text represents excerpts from the "full" without additions, rearranged in an order which does not correspond to the order of Kurbskii's first letter. It should be intuitively apparent that the first is the more logical assumption: that a text like that of the "full" could be abbreviated radically, and the remaining excerpts arranged in random order (see below) in such a way that no words were lost and no transitional passages required for the sake of smoothness, is all but impossible. Assuming, on the other hand, that the "full" is the derivative text, the editorial process is clear: the original was dissected thematically, rearranged in the order of the first Kurbskii letter, and provided with transitions, elaborations, explanations, and considerable additional material. That such was the case is apparent from the following collation of the texts:

No. of passage	"Abbrev." col. of Kuntsevich	"Full" p. of Fennell, Corresp.	Contents	Notes
1	9–18	12–22	Introduction	"Full" contains numerous interpolations.
2	18	64–66	sil'nye vo Israile	"Full" contains interpolation not found in "Kurbskii Collections."
3	18	122–124	neumytnyi sud'ia	
4	20	108–110	predstateli khristianskie	
5	22	104	svet/t'ma	Four sentences.
6	22	40	Khto tia postavil . . .	Two sentences.
7	22–24	46–48	tsarstvovati/ sviashchenstvovati	
8	24	126	kako zhe sobaka . . .	Single sentence: order of 8 and 9 reversed in "full," sense better in "abbrev."
9	24–26	126–130	stanem zhe . . .	Paraphrase, change in order, see above. One sentence omitted in "full": Sikh vsekh prezrel esi.
10	28	58	Gore domu . . .	Three to four sentences; confusion in "full."
11	28	22	tako . . . podobno sluzhiti	One sentence.
12	28	62	dobrokhotnykh	
13	30	122	bessmerten ne mniusia	One sentence, corrupt in "full"; and in MS 1573 only of "abbrev."
14	30	40	uchitel'skii san	This theme taken up in "abbrev." after 9 and 8, but here (with 6) because of order of Kurbskii letter.
15	32	44	protiviatsia istine	This passage, but a few words in "abbrev.," serves, like 14, as stimulus in "full" to citation of adjoining verses of Bible, largely irrelevant.
16	32	34–36	Pastyriu podobaet ⎫	These two passages, obviously linked by parallel construction and context in "abbrev.," separated by long interpolations in "full."
17	34	40	Tsariam podobaet ⎭	
18	36–40	146–148	Dionisii/Polikarp	Confusion in "full." See below.
19	36–40	30–34	Kako, sobaka . . .	
20	40–46	150–156	vy zhe izmenniki . . .	
21	46–48	36–38	Zlodeev muchenniki . . .	
22	48–50	176–178	Conclusion	

The relationship of the editorial principles in the two versions is also revealed by a consideration of the placement of the common passages within the whole text of the "full" version:

Order in "abbrev."	Pages in "full"	Comment
1	12–22	Beginning
11	22	Adjoins 1
19	30–34	
16	34–36	Adjoins 14
21	36–38	Adjoins 16
17	40	
6	40	
14	40	See above
15	44	
7	46–48	
10	58	
12	62–64	
2	64	Adjoins 12
5	104	
4	108–110	
13	122	
3	122	Adjoins 13
9	126	
8	126	
18	146	
20	150	
22	176	

These figures reveal the differences in the structure of the two versions and clearly indicate the direction of borrowing, thus supporting all of the above. The "abbreviated" version, having chosen a thematic discussion of the issues raised in the Kurbskii letter, states a number of the main themes at the outset (passages 1, 2, 3, etc.) and then returns to further discussion of them, reverting again to the words of Kurbskii's letter (11, 12, 13, etc.). The "full" version, by contrast, is bound to a point-by-point refutation of Kurbskii's letter, and, because it is using the "abbreviated" version as its model, it rearranges the passages (1 adjoins 11, 2/12, 3/13). That this is so is confirmed by the fact that the passages of the "abbreviated" version are found not scattered at random in the "full" version, but grouped thematically (in violation of their order in the "abbreviated" version, but in accordance with the principle of following the Kurbskii letter) on a limited number of pages (*Poslaniia*, pp. 12–22, 30–48, 58–64, 104–110, 122–126, 146–148, 150–156, 176–end). To assume the reverse process—that the presumed editor of the "abbreviated" version chose snippets apparently at random, changed their order, but not a single word, and produced a smooth and thematically integral text—is to make of him not a "much later copyist with a pronounced tendency to abbreviate" but a wizard of linguistic and ideational collage. Equally telling is the comparison of the titles of the eight copies here considered (see Ia. S. Lur'e, *TODRL* X (1954):305–309), which may be graphically represented as follows:

2524	X	1311	Y
1573	X	41	[Y]
1551	X		
32.8.5	Y	1567	X
V.2.11	[Y]	230	X

where X represents *Tsarevo gosudarevo poslanie ...* , and Y stands for two slightly different versions, containing the full title *Velikii gosudar', tsar' i velikii kniaz' Ivan Vasil'evich vsea Rusi*. The brackets indicate that the heading is lost in 41, and assumed, in V.2.11, to be like 32.8.5. This relationship indicates that the "abbreviated" form came from no single version of the "full," and supports the other evidence that the "full" version was made from one copy of the "abbreviated" and collated with another (see App. III). It would seem, incidentally, that one may accept a rather simple explanation of the Carpus/Polycarpus tangle (*Poslaniia*, p. 608; Fennell, *Corresp.*, pp. 148–149, n.). The author of the original short version, remembering the legend about Carpus, thumbed through a text until he found it (Epistle VIII), then searched backwards in his text for a heading. For some reason, however, he skipped the heading of the letter to Demophilus that he was citing and recorded the preceding heading (Epistle VII, "Polycarpo Antistiti") and at the same time apparently acquired the information (from the notes of a printed edition?) to the effect that Polycarpus was Bishop of Smyrna (see *Sancti Dionysii Areopagitae operum omnium quae extant, et commentaribrum quibus illustrantur, Tomus I, ... cum adnotationibus Balthasaris Corderii* [Paris, 1644], pp. 771–780).

In the production of the full version, however, the author returned to his sources, copied the long texts from Dionysius which are found only in the long version (*Sancti Dionysii*, p. 780), and correctly included the name of Carpus, leaving, however, the "Polycarpus" in the text which he retained from the short version. These passages, it should be noted, were evidently translated from Greek (cf. notes in Fennell, *Corresp.*, pp. 158–173).

17. See App. II, "Contents of Manuscripts."

18. *Opisanie ... BAN*, III, 1, p. 518. But see Mr. Waugh's reservations, App. I, pt. a.

19. See App. I, pt. a.

20. See above, Chap. 1, Table 2.

21. See App. I, pt. a.

22. See App. I, pt. b.

23. See his autobiographical notes published as "Domashnie zapiski" in *Moskovskii vestnik*, 1830, pt. 5, pp. 61–73, reproduced below in App. IV, pt. c.

24. See App. I, pt. a, MS 4469.

25. Fennell, *Corresp.*, pp. 12, 14, 22, respectively.

26. On *vedoma da est'* and *pochen*, see "*Jarlyk.*" That *pochen ot* was an oddity is indicated by the difficulties scribes had with this passage (see Kuntsevich, cols. 1 and 2, line 26 in each). Lur'e (*Poslaniia*, p. 586) calls the use of *pisanie zhe tvoe ...* a "parody" of the diplomatic style.

27. See Chap. 1, Table 2. Compare, in particular, the close: "Dana vo vselennei Rossiistei tsarstvuiushchego, pravoslavnogo grada Moskvy,

stepeni chestnogo poroga krepkaia zapoved' i slovo to" (Fennell, *Corresp.*, p. 178) with the close of the genuine documents published in *RIO*, vol. 71, passim. This unusual close seems to be composed of three calques from turkic diplomatic style, the last of which (*i slovo to*) belongs at the beginning, not at the end, of diplomatic documents, Muscovite or Tatar. See *"Jarlyk."*

28. Compare Fennell, *Corresp.*, p. 186, and Kagan, *TODRL* XI:244.

29. Lur'e, who construes the relationship of the versions differently, remarks on the absence of secular themes in the "abbreviated" version, which, in his view, "is a collection of Biblical citations" (*Poslaniia*, p. 557).

30. It was apparently Platonov who first observed this (*Skazaniia*, p. 302). His view is repeated in *RBS* and Ikonnikov (*Opyt*, II:1848). See for example Shakhovskoi's historical tales in *RIB*, vol. XIII, cols. 837–876. There is one minor textual coincidence between Shakhovskoi's Mass to Sofia the Divine Wisdom and Ivan's first letter which is of some interest. In the Mass, Shakhovskoi speaks of the "premudrost' . . . toiu tsarie tsarstvuiut i sil'nye derzhat zemliu i mudrye pishut pravdu" (Nikol'skii, "Sofiia premudrost' Bozhiia," p. 86), which corresponds to the perhaps ironical words of the introduction of Ivan's letter: "Sviatyi Dukh . . . imzhe tsari tsarstvuiut i silnii pishut pravdu" (*Poslaniia*, p. 9).

31. This view is widely accepted in the literature and is based primarily upon the letters to Lithuanian figures published in Kuntsevich, cols. 361–472.

32. See text of letter, lines 97–100.

33. *Poslaniia*, p. 129. It should be pointed out that Ivan's "Testament" (itself a document of uncertain provenance, found in a single nineteenth-century copy) takes a diametrically opposed view. Ivan admonished his sons to "learn every craft [*delo*], the divine, the priestly [*sviashchennicheskoe*], the monastic, the military, the juridical . . ." (*Poslaniia*, p. 525).

34. This sentence is not entirely clear. Lur'e and Fennell construe it as cited, but it appears from variants that it was originally intended to be read: "Many who even in recent years have been shorn—including those of the great council (even the first among them)—did not dare to do this, although they were returned to their former dignity" (see Fennell, *Corresp.*, pp. 32–33; *Poslaniia*, pp. 291, 588; Kuntsevich, col. 22). In this case, one would construe the addition in the second version as a remark favorable to Filaret and assume that it was written at a time when the writer enjoyed the Patriarch's grace.

35. Fennell, *Corresp.*, pp. 32, 46, 58, 84, 86, and in general passages which refer to Sil'vestr.

36. Thus the words added in line 21 (App. IV), *muzhestvom khrabrosti ikh*, find an echo in Ivan's words (*Poslaniia*, p. 46).

37. Thus the words *Ne isprosikh . . . chinmi* (App. III, n. 68) coincide verbatim with the text on fol. 262 *verso* of the *Apostol* (Houghton Library, Harvard, Kilgour A) and end precisely at the point where the second citation from Isaiah begins (*Vosdal esi . . .*). That the borrowing occurred the other way round seems highly improbable—could Fedorov, in whose narrative the given words fit perfectly, have borrowed precisely and only those words which distinguish two versions of Kurbskii's letter, and have inserted them in the middle of a sentence?

38. App. II, notes to Stemma H.

39. For the details of this process, see above, n. 16.

40. Such can be found almost at random: see, e.g., passages 14 and 15 in n. 16, above.

41. See examples cited in n. 15. A special category of oddity is presented by two passages in which the author of the second version apparently misunderstood his text of Kurbskii's letter or perhaps was working from a defective text. Both occur in the introduction of Kurbskii's letter: neither is contained in the first version of Ivan's letter. The first concerns Kurbskii's expression *v pravoslavii presvetlu iavl'shemusia*, which is corrupt in all early copies of the second version and correct only in MS 1/91. The second has to do with the expression *nyne zhe suprotivnym obretshemusia. Razumevaiai da razumeet, sovest' prokazhennu imushche* . . . From the numerous references to this phrase where its sense is misapplied (Fennell, *Corresp.*, pp. 44, 90, 100, 102), it appears that, although the thought is once correctly interpreted (ibid., p. 24) and repeated once from the text of the first version (p. 38), the author of the second version somehow tended to misuse it.

42. Cf. Fennell, *Corresp.*, pp. 134 and 62.

43. See Fennell's note (ibid., pp. 88–89) and the literature there cited.

44. See M. N. Pokrovskii, *Izbrannye Sochineniia*, vol. I (Moscow, 1966), Chap. 8.

45. On history-writing in this environment see Belokurov, "O Zapisnom prikaze" and his *O Posol'skom prikaze* (Moscow, 1906); I. M. Kudriavtsev, "'Izdatel'skaia' deiatel'nost' Posol'skogo prikaza," *Kniga: Issledovaniia i materialy*, VIII (Moscow, 1963): 179–244.

46. On these translations see, respectively, Sobolevskii, *Perevodnaia literatura*, pp. 76–78, and A. I. Rogov, *Russko-pol'skie kul'turnye sviazi v epokhu Vozrozhdeniia (Stryikovskii i ego Khronika)* (Moscow, 1966). See also App. I, pt. c.

47. See Chap. 1.

48. Fennell, *Corresp.*, pp. 214–216.

49. Cf. Fennell's notes, pp. 217, 228.

50. Ibid., p. 216. The suggestion that Kurbskii's second and third letters were written at the same time is further supported by the very close similarity in wording in a number of places, e.g., ibid., p. 198, cf. p. 180.

51. L. Shchepot'ev, *Blizhnii boiarin Artamon Sergeevich Matveev kak kul'turnyi politicheskii deiatel' XVII veka.* (St. Petersburg, 1906).

52. Kudriavtsev, *Kniga*, VIII:197.

53. See Chap. 1, n. 10. That it was the second version is indicated by the mention of the Sitskii/Prozorovskii case, not mentioned in the first version. Cf. *Poslaniia*, pp. 589, 209.

54. Fennell, *Corresp.*, notes to pp. 187–197. Fennell points out (p. 187, n. 10) that Siberia was first subjected to Muscovy in 1581, but Ivan did apparently use the title *vsea Sibirskiia zemli i Severnie strany povelitel'* in 1577, the date given in this letter (*RIO*, vol. 129, *Pamiatniki diplomaticheskikh snoshenii Moskovskogo gosudarstva s Shvedskim gosudarstvom*, vol. I [1556–1586] [St. Petersburg, 1910], pp. 348–350 et passim). What is questionable in Ivan's second letter, which was obviously written by someone who knew his historical titulature, is the order of the titles, which differs from the order consistently used in genuine documents of the same time (ibid.) and contains the irregular *zemli Lifliantskoi nemetskogo chinu.*

55. See Fennell's note, *Corresp.*, p. 288.

56. The mention of the "aphrodisiacal deeds" is found only in the second version of Kurbskii's first letter: see App. III, n. 186. See also notes 1 and 2, Fennell, *Corresp.*, p. 214.

57. Above, Chap. 3, n. 35.

58. See above, n. 37.

59. The relationship among the three types of text may be graphically indicated thus:

A (1567, etc.)	B (Chronograph)	C ("Kurbskii Collections")
1. Beginning to *Sil'vestr* (Fennell, *Corresp.*, p. 118)	= A (Kuntsevich, p. 24)	= A
2. *Adashev* to *obidiashchego* (Fennell, p. 154)	*voskhititi* to *iunoshu* (Kuntsevich, p. 82) i.e., = A. 3.	= B
3. *voskhititi* to *iunoshu* (Fennell, p. 154)	= A.2	End of common text and short closing passage.
4. *syna* to end of text	= A.4	

It is apparent that the copyist of this last version, found in the manuscripts containing the latter Kurbskii letters, abandoned his effort to make sense of the disordered text at the second nonsensical "seam," added a few words of his own, and copied the end of his original (cf. *Poslaniia*, pp. 552–553, and Vil'koshevskii, *LZAK za 1923–1925 gg*, XXXIII:73). The relationships here indicated have to do only with the extant copies of the text and the origin of the C version; on the possible primacy of the so-called "Chronograph" version, see above, n. 15.

60. Notably the works of Guagnini and Stryjkowski. See App. II, "Contents of Manuscripts."

61. *Poslaniia*, p. 546.

62. This is particularly true of MS 639 (T = Tikhonravov in Kuntsevich's notes), which for the later letters consistently contains the best readings (Kuntsevich, col. 127/n. 1; 128/14, 16; 145/10; 146/16; and passim). Of special interest are the variants in 639 for the passages translated from Cicero: here the glosses in the margins of 639 seem to reveal a correction or redaction of the text against a Latin original (138/13; 139/9; 144/22: text— *okromnykh*; margin: *uedinen = privatorum*; 144/24: text—*izmennikom*; margin: *izgnantsom = exulasse*). In a number of places only 639 has a correct translation (142/7: *insanum = neistovym*; 143/6: *vozhem = duce*; 142/9: *contemptione = prezireniem*; 145/9: *cum telo = so oruzhiem*). Elsewhere 639 contains in its text words corresponding to the Latin which are found in no other copy (143/9; 143/13, etc.). Note that 639 contains an early copy of the *Velikoe zertsalo*, which was translated in the *Posol'skii prikaz* in 1675 (Kudriavtsev, *Kniga* VIII:222).

63. GPB, *Kratkii otchet Rukopisnogo otdela za 1914–1938*, p. 61.

64. On Golitsyn, see the study of N. N. Danilov, published in two parts in *Jahrbücher für Geschichte Osteuropas*, 1936, I:1–33 ("V. V. Golicyn bis zum Staatsstreich vom Mai 1682") and *Jahrbücher* 1937, IV:539–596 ("Vasilij Vasil'evič Golicyn [1682–1714]").

65. See, for example, the friendly note from Khitrovo to Golitsyn in *VMOIDR*, bk. VII (1850), Smes', p. 70, which indicates that the women of the two families were also friendly.

Divov, then *voevoda* in Vologda, was charged with accompanying Golitsyn from Vologda to Iarensk in the late fall of that year. Golitsyn spent five days in Vologda (October 2–7, 1689) and arrived in Iarensk on January 6, 1690. It seems quite likely that Golitsyn, who was traveling with a company of one hundred men and twenty-five wagons, might have given Divov a copy of the manuscript during this period, and that Divov would inscribe his copy with the date immediately after receiving it. Cf. *Rozysknye dela o Fedore Shaklovitom i ego soobshchnikakh*, vol. III (St. Petersburg, 1888), cols. 35–36, 41, 79, 83, 114.

66. This expression is used only in the *History* and the third letter (Fennell, *Corresp.*, p. 214). Nørretranders (*Shaping*, p. 49) repeats A. Solovjev's observation that this expression was not used elsewhere in sixteenth-century texts and cites a number of scholars' explanations of this anachronism.

67. Fennell, *Corresp.*, p. 182. Cf. Fennell's note, p. 183.

68. In particular the confusing references to "my first letter" with obvious reference to the second, etc. Cf. Fennell, *Corresp.*, nn. to pp. 199, 217, 228.

69. No Slavonic translation is listed in Sobolevskii, *Perevodnaia literatura*.

70. See Chap. 3, n. 23, above.

71. Copies of western editions of Cicero are found in the numerous mid-seventeenth-century libraries described in Belokurov, *O biblioteke*. It appears that the *Paradoxa* have never been fully translated into Russian.

72. Fennell, *Corresp.*, pp. 218–227; Ustrialov, 3rd ed., pp. 205–209, 358.

73. *M. Tulli Ciceronis Opera Omnia*. Genevae, 1633, Apud Petrum et Iacobum Chouët.

74. The Chouët edition of 1633 coincides with the Kurbskii translation in all variants which distinguish different versions of the *Paradoxa*. Moreover, it provides, in its marginalia, the information which has been added to Kurbskii's text (the reference to Claudius, the addition of the name of Claudius' friend Cornificius) and is apparently found in no one Latin edition of the sixteenth century. It would seem that, until we find a text which permits us to resolve the few differences which remain between Kurbskii's translation and the 1633 edition, the latter or an edition much like it may be considered the original from which the translation was made. The following list indicates the general characteristics which separate the editions available to me and identify Kurbskii's original. The final elucidation of this important matter will require a thorough search among sixteenth- and seventeenth-century editions.

KEY (Copies B–H in the Houghton Library, Harvard University)

A   *Mar. Tul. Ciceronis Paradoxa . . . cum annotationibus Barpt. Latomi*. Parisiis Apud Ioannem Roigny, 1541 (as cited by Kuntsevich, cols. 137–142).

B   *Ciceronis De Officiis Libri Tres . . .* [Venetiis, 1555, Apud Paulum Manutium Aldi F.].

C   *Ciceronis De Officiis Libri III . . . Cum annotationibus Pauli Manutii . . .* Venetiis, Aldus, 1564.

D   *M. T. Ciceronis, De officiis libri tres . . .* [Viennae Pannoniae, in aedibus Hieronymi Vietoris, & Ioannis Singrenii sociorum . . . 1512] (the Paradoxa apparently printed separately: [*M. T. C. Paradoxa*] . . . [Impressum Viennae Austriae per Hieronymum Vietorem & Ioannem Singrenium . . . 1514]).

E   *M. Tullii Ciceronis Philosophica*. Parisiis. Ex officina Roberti Stephani, 1538 (vol. IV of *M. T. Ciceronis Opera*).

F   *M. Tulli Ciceronis Paradoxa Stoicorum* . . ., ed. Otto Plasberg, fasc. 1, Leipzig, B. G. Teubner, 1908.
G   *M. T. Cic. De officiis libri tres* . . . *Cum annotationibus Pauli Manutii* . . ., Lugduni, apud Antonium Gryphium, 1585.
H   *M. T. Cic. Officiorum. lib. III* . . . [Venetiis, in aedibus Aldi, et Andreae Asulani soceri, 1517].

The significant variants as they appear in a number of editions are as follows:

Paradox II

(1) Chouët, *virtutem praesidio munitus* = Kurbskii's *velikikh dobrot pomoshchmi vooruzhen*; A, D, E, F do not contain *munitus*.

(2) Chouët, *ne unum quidem diem* = Kurbskii, *a ni edinogo dnia voistinnu*; E and F do not contain *ne*.

(3) Chouët, *exsilium terribilis* = *izgnanie est' strashno*; A, E, and F do not contain *terribilis*.

(4) Chouët, *et id ipsum quod habes* = *i to samoe, chto maesh'*; E and F do not have *quod habes*.

(5) *respirare* = *otdokhnuti*; A, D, E, F, and G have *suspirare*.

(6) *debet* = *podobaet*; E and F read *decet*, A has *potest*.

Paradox IV

(1) Chouët, *num civitas erat* = *grad li byl*; A, C, D, E, F, and G, have *non civitas erat*.

(2) Chouët, *quae tum nulla erat* = *ikhzhe nikako zhe togda*; A, D, E, F, and H read *quae nulla erat*.

(3) Chouët, *consilia, quibus Resp. invicta stat* = *sovety, imizhe obshchina nepreodolima stoit*; A, E, and F have *consiliis stare te invitissimo*; D reads *consilia, si meo Respu. cum meis curis.*

(4) Chouët, *ergo ego semper civis eram* = *togo radi iaz vsegda grazhdaninom bykh*; *eram* is missing in D, E, and F.

(5) Chouët, *et me exsulem, tuo nomine, appellas* = *i mene izgnannikom, tvoim imenem, naritsaesh*; *exsulem* is missing in A, E, and F (cf. Fennell, *Corresp.*, p. 225, n. 5).

(6) Chouët, *iubeant, non eris tu exsul? Non appellatur inimicus, qui* . . . = *pokazuiut, ne budeshi li ty izmennikom? Egda naritsaettsa supostatom, iazhe* . . .; A, E, and F have *iubeant, non appellet inimicus* (cf. Fennell, *Corresp.*, p. 275, n. 9).

(7) Chouët, *qui templa deorum occupaverit* = *iazhe tserkov' bogov obladal*; in D and F *deorum* is omitted.

(8) Chouët (marginal note) *porto* = *pristannishche* (cf. Fennell, *Corresp.*, p. 226, n. 1) A, B, C, E, F, and G have *oporto* or *operto*. D and H have *portu*.

(9) The information from Chouët marginal notes g, p. 584 (= Kurbskii heading, Kuntsevich, col. 141) and e, col. 585 (= Kuntsevich, col. 145, l. 22) is not found in many other texts, although Cornificius is found in A, and the marginal note "Contra Clodium" in B, C, and G.

75. The selection of authors and works cited in the *Correspondence* and related works is of considerable importance to the eventual attribution of authorship, and should be carefully studied. In particular, it is noteworthy that a number of authors cited in the later Kurbskii writings, some of whom are rather unusual for sixteenth-century Muscovite libraries, are represented in the inventory of books taken into the library of the *Posol'skii prikaz* from the library of Artamon Matveev and appropriated later by Vasilii Golitsyn (Belokurov, *O biblioteke*, pp. 69–74).

A partial listing:

	KI	GI	KIII-	HIST	KL	PP	Notes
St. Ambrose		F 34			X	XM	No known translation (F 35)
St. Athanasius		F 36			X	XMG	Cf. F 36, n. 5
St. Augustine			F 244		X	M	F 244, n. 1
St. Basil				F 266	X		
Cicero			F 216			M	
Dionysius		F 142		F 88	X	X	
St. Gregory		F 106		F 234	X	X	G
Chrysostom		F 34	F 246	F 266	X	MG	
Damascene			F 238		X	X	
Metaphrastes			F 235	F 234	X		(Life of St. Nicholas). No translation into Slavic before 17th c. (F 234)
Kallistos					X	X	

Abbreviations: F = Fennell editions of *Correspondence* and *History*.
PP = Indicated in inventory of *Posol'skii prikaz* 1696 as given in Belokurov, *O biblioteke*, pp. 66–80.
M = Listed among the books belonging to Artamon Matveev, in Belokurov, *O biblioteke*, pp. 69–74.
G = Listed (?) among books belonging to V. V. Golitsyn in *Rozysknye dela o Fedore Shaklovitom*, IV: cols. 31–33.
KL = Letters of Kurbskii to Lithuanian personages.

76. Zaozerskii, *Tsar' Aleksei Mikhailovich*, p. 269.

77. N. Novikov, ed., *Istoriia o nevinnom zatochenii blizhnego boiarina Artamona Sergeevicha Matveeva* . . . (St. Petersburg, 1776).

78. In addition to the parallels noted by Kudriavtsev (*Kniga* VIII:197) compare Novikov, *Istoriia*, p. 138, with Ivan's first letter (Fennell, *Corresp.*, p. 20), p. 263 with Kurbskii's *pred voiskom . . . ne obratikh*, and p. 114 with Kurbskii's *ne pretverdye li grady* . . .

79. Belokurov, *O biblioteke*, pp. 69–74.

80. Kudriavtsev, *Kniga* VIII:239–240.

81. N. N. Danilov, "Golicyn," pt. I, pp. 7–10.

82. For Golitsyn's books, see *Rozysknye dela o Fedore Shaklovitom*, vol. IV, Index, s.v. "knigi."

83. Belokurov, *O biblioteke*, p. 74.

84. Indeed it appears that Golitsyn was the godfather for Iakov Kurbskii, who was closely associated with him later and who used the patronymic "Vasil'evich," probably as his brother Aleksandr used "Borisovich," from the name of his godfather Boris Alekseevich Golitsyn, Vasilii's cousin. Cf. *Rozysknye dela o Fedore Shaklovitom*, vol. III, cols. 231, 633, 1007, and Ustrialov, 2nd ed., p. xxvii, n. b.

AFTERWORD

1. See above, Introduction, n. 6.

2. See the tentative stemma in App. II.

3. See, e.g., Lur'e's comments in *Poslaniia*, pp. 585–586, 589.

4. This is particularly true of Bible translations. In a careful study of the biblical passages of the first version of Ivan's first letter for my seminar, Thomas Owen found, without the opportunity of comparison with manuscript or printed redactions of the early seventeenth century, a strong likelihood that these were indeed the texts from which Ivan's citations were taken. Cf. Vil'koshevskii, *LZAK za 1923–1925 gg*. XXXIII:73.

APPENDIX 1, PART A

1. I am grateful to my sponsor, the Inter-University Committee on Travel Grants, my host, Leningrad State University, and the various institutions and repositories in the Soviet Union which made possible this research, and to the Harvard Russian Research Center for support during the current academic year.

2. For full identification of manuscript numbers, see the List of Manuscripts Cited.

3. For further information on the problem of identification, the existing reference works, and the reliability of watermark information in present manuscript descriptions, see my "Soviet Watermark Studies—Achievements and Prospects," *Kritika*, VI (1970):78–111. Regarding my citations of folios on which the watermarks appear, note that in some cases I cite where a given paper begins or ends, not necessarily only the location of the mark.

APPENDIX 1, PART B

1. The best account of these events of 1624–1625 is in S. A. Belokurov, "Delo o prisylke shakhom Abbasom rizy Gospodnei tsariu Mikhailu Feodorovichu v 1625 godu," *Sbornik Moskovskogo glavnogo arkhiva Ministerstva inostrannykh del*, V (1893):1–48, where he publishes the relevant archival records.

2. Among those who testified about the previous history of the relic were the cellarius of the Monastery of the New Savior, the Greek Ioanikei, the Greek archbishop Nektarii, and the archbishop Feodosii from Jerusalem. The latter's testimony, included in the draft copy of the official account of the translation of the relic, was deleted from the final version, presumably because it unequivocally denied that the Shah had the robe. For some years afterward there was a question as to whether, in fact, the Georgians retained possession of the relic. See ibid., pp. 14–15, 43–47, and vii.

3. Ibid., p. 25.

4. The information about Kiprian is apparently found only in the *Novyi letopisets* (*PSRL* XIV:151–152).

5. Such a letter is cited by the Archbishop of Tver', writing to Igumen Evfimii of the Koliazin Monastery in January 1626 (*AAE*, vol. II, no. 168, pp. 245–247). What may be the same *gramota*, but mistakenly attributed to the Patriarch and dated March 27, 1626, is mentioned by Viktorov, *Opisi*, p. 284.

6. Cf. the single previous (but very incomplete) effort at such a classification by S. Brailovskii, "Novyi variant povesti o rize Gospoda nashego Iisusa Khrista," *Bibliograf*, 1889, no. 1 (1890), pp. 17–21.

7. See above, Chap. 2, n. 60, regarding other works by Shakhovskoi in these MSS, which are described by Leonid, "Svedenie," pp. 244–251, and by Stroev, *Slovar'*, pp. 291–297, where he refers to them by the old numeration as Nos. 191 and 192.

8. Gorskii and Nevostruev, vol. IV (sec. II, pt. 3), p. 699.

9. Spasskii, *Russkoe liturgicheskoe tvorchestvo*, p. 66, using evidence that is not entirely clear, concludes that Kiprian did write a service, and apparently sees no reason to identify it with the one attributed to Shakhovskoi.

10. Leonid, "Opisanie slaviano-russkikh rukopisei . . . Voskresenskogo . . . monastyria . . . ," *Chteniia*, 1871, bk. 1, sec. v, p. 52. The quotations are from Leonid's description of No. 27 (213) cited in n. 7.

11. Viktorov, *Opisi*, p. 179. I do not know the present location of the MS.

12. Bychkov, *Opisanie*, p. 307.

13. See P. N. Petrov, *PDP*, 1879, vol. IV (V), p. 182, which mentions an unspecified account about the robe, lacking the beginning, in this collection of the "Works" of Shakhovskoi.

14. Kh. Loparev, *Opisanie rukopisei Imperatorskogo Obshchestva liubitelei drevnei pis'mennosti*, pt. II (St. Petersburg, 1893), p. 238. The opening lines are those given above, but the title lacks the attribution to Shakhovskoi. Loparev cites the publication of the official account about the robe (see sec. II) in *Dvortsovye razriady*, vol. II, cols. 767–822, but it is not clear that he compared the texts as he did with the quite different text in the 1878 edition of the *Prolog*. The OLDP copy may be fragmentary, occupying only part of a total eight folios.

15. For the Synodal MS (not described by Gorskii and Nevostruev), see Stroev, *Slovar'*, p. 423, and Belokurov, *Sbornik*, p. ix, n. The Tikhonravov manuscript, from which Belokurov quotes several of the opening and closing lines (to the best of my knowledge, the longest published extracts from the Shakhovskoi work) is described by G. P. Georgievskii, *Sobranie N. S. Tikhonravova, I. Rukopisi*, (Moscow, 1912), pp. 46–47. Preceding the "Skazanie" in the same binding is a copy of the printed service of 1625.

16. G. P. Georgievskii, *Rukopisi T. F. Bol'shakova, khraniashchiesia v Imperatorskom Moskovskom i Rumiantsovskom muzee* (Petrograd, 1915), p. 361.

17. *Opisanie . . . BAN*, IV, 1, pp. 290–291.

18. Described by Stroev, *Slovar'*, pp. 422, 403, under the old number 82/391; also by Leonid, "Opisanie . . . Voskresenskogo," p. 52, as No. 89.

19. Belokurov published the clean corrected copy of the account and noted variants from the draft copy of part of it which has also been preserved; the documents are apparently at present in TsGADA, *fond* 77, Relations with Persia. It may be significant that the draft copy stops at a logical "seam" in the work, just before the letter of testimony sent to the Diplomatic Chancellery by Archbishop Nektarii. Belokurov notes that there are various watermarks on the paper of these archival copies, including one which Tromonin, *Iz"iasnenie*, dates 1638. This should be checked, as there is every reason to believe that the account was compiled in 1625 very shortly after the events it describes—in fact even begun before the last of them was recorded. Belokurov publishes as an appendix the complete *otpiska* of Korob'in and Kuvshinov, from which "Extracts" borrowed only a portion, and notes that the original testimony of the cellarius Ioanikei has been preserved separately. See Belokurov, *Sbornik*, pp. ix–xi, 16, and 37–43.

20. This corresponds to the text at the top of col. 796 in *DR*, vol. II. It is customary and more convenient to cite the column numbers in this version of "Extracts" as I do subsequently; the text has only slight variants from that in the archival original.

21. Described by K. Kalaidovich and P. Stroev, *Obstoiatel'noe opisanie*

slaviano-rossiiskikh rukopisei . . . *grafa Fedora Andreevicha Tolstova* (Moscow, 1825), sec. III, no. 35.

22. Described by A. Vostokov, *Opisanie russkikh i slovenskikh rukopisei Rumiantsovskogo muzeuma* (St. Petersburg, 1842), pp. 208–209.

23. Leonid, *Opisanie*, IV, p. 182.

24. Described above in App. I, pt. a.

25. Leonid, *Opisanie*, IV, pp. 271–272.

26. Undol'skii, *Rukopisi*, col. 263.

27. On the manuscript, see Andrei Popov, *Obzor khronografov russkoi redaktsii*, II (Moscow, 1869): 173 and passim; the citations are from his *Izbornik slavianskikh i russkikh sochinenii i statei, vnesennykh v khronografy russkoi redaktsii* (Moscow, 1869), p. 279.

28. *Opisanie . . . BAN*, III, 1, 2nd ed., p. 279.

29. Viktorov, *Opisi*, p. 301. The present location of the MS is unknown to me.

30. See M. N. Tikhomirov, "Maloizvestnye letopisnye pamiatniki," *Istoricheskii arkhiv*, VII (Moscow-Leningrad, 1951):218.

31. Leonid, *Opisanie*, III, p. 50.

32. Bychkov, *Opisanie*, p. 54.

33. See *Opisanie rukopisei kniazia Pavla Petrovicha Viazemskogo* (St. Petersburg, 1902), p. 196, where one notes among the inscriptions by the owner a complaint that parts of the manuscript were stolen when it was borrowed to prepare the edition of "Extracts."

34. See above, n. 5.

35. Described in Kalaidovich and Stroev, *Opisanie . . . Tolstova*, sec. II, no. 140.

36. See A. Orlov, *Istoricheskie i poeticheskie povesti ob Azove. Tekst* (Moscow, 1906), pp. 3–4; *Kritika*, VI:88–89.

37. Stroev, *Slovar'*, p. 403.

38. Viktorov, *Opisi*, p. 108; the present location of the MS is unknown to me. No. 227 also included the printed service discussed in sec. IV.A below. Another text about which we know nothing, but possibly containing the "Extracts," is in the Academy of Sciences Institute of Russian Literature (Pushkinskii dom), Collection of V. N. Peretts No. 10; see V. I. Malyshev, comp., *Drevnerusskie rukopisi Pushkinskogo doma (obzor fondov)* (Moscow-Leningrad, 1965), p. 70.

39. A. Popov, *Izbornik*, pp. 390–391.

40. Ibid., pp. 425–427.

41. *PSRL*, XIV:151–152. Two other chronicle accounts should be noted: in the Mazurin Chronicle, *PSRL*, XXXI:159, and the *Letopisets 1619–1691 gg.*, ibid., p. 180. The former seems based on a contemporary account such as "Extracts" and indicates March 27 as the day of veneration; the latter, which mentions July 10, clearly is based on later sources.

42. See L. V. Cherepnin, *Ist. zap.*, XIV, passim.

43. A. Popov, *Izbornik*, pp. 207–208.

44. *Opisanie . . . BAN*, IV, 1, p. 131.

45. Ibid., p. 308.

46. Bychkov, *Opisanie*, pp. 478 and 537.

47. Brailovskii, "Novyi variant," pp. 20–21. His suggestion that the account about the robe provided by Ioanikei may derive from a Greek original merits further study.

48. *Opisanie . . . BAN*, III, 2, p. 233; Viktorov, *Opisi*, p. 92; Stroev, *Slovar'* p. 403, where the heading and opening lines are cited.

49. See Belokurov, *Sbornik*, p. ix, n.; the MS is not described in Gorskii and Nevostruev.

50. Georgievskii, *Sobranie N. S. Tikhonravova*, p. 36.

51. On this basis, A. S. Zernova, *Knigi kirillovskoi pechati, izdannye v Moskve v XVI–XVII vekakh. Svodnyi katalog* (Moscow, 1958), No. 60, p. 33, lists the printed service between the last dated Moscow edition of 1625 and the first of 1626.

52. See ibid., No. 50. The next complete printing of the Menolog occurred in the 1640's. In this edition, the service about the robe appears in the July volume for the tenth of the month, with a preface explaining why the date has been changed from March: "Prelozhen zhe byst' sii prazdnik prazdno-vati iz marta mesiatsa, 27 chisla, v 10 den' mesiatsa iiulia poveleniem blagochestivago i khristoliubivago gosudaria . . . Aleksiia Mikhailovicha . . . i po blagosloveniiu . . . Iosifa patriarkha . . . seia radi viny zanezhe vo sviatei chetyredesiatnitse ne let' byti Zlatoustove sluzhbe i posta razreshati krome blagoveshcheniia presviatyia Bogoroditsy . . ." (*Mineia sluzhebnaia*, for the month of July (Moscow, 1646), fols. 137v = iv-2; copy in BAN, No. 555 *sp*). The book was printed between September 23, 1645, and June 1, 1646; peculiarities in pagination suggest that the decision to include the given service was made when the book was nearing completion. Cf. Zernova, *Knigi*, No. 186. Subsequent printings of the complete *Mineia* (1690–1691, 1692–1693, 1711) contain the identical service for July 10, but without the preface. One should note that Spasskii's remarks on the change in date need correction (*Russkoe liturgicheskoe tvorchestvo*, p. 72, nn. 4 and 6).

53. Brailovskii, "Novyi variant," p. 18, n. 1.

APPENDIX 1, PART C

1. A. I. Sobolevskii, *Perevodnaia literatura*.

2. The works of Guagnini (Gwagnin), which include various portions of the "Description" published separately, are listed by K. Estreicher, *Bibliografia polska*, vol. XVII (pt. III, vol. 6) (Krakow, 1899), pp. 480 passim. The Latin edition, *Sarmatiae Evropeae Descriptio . . .* [Krakow, 1578], was republished in Speyer in 1581 with supplementary materials but without changes in the text. The Polish edition, *Kronika Sarmacyey Europskiey* (Krakow, 1611), was republished by Fr. Bohomelec as vol. IV of *Zbior dziejopisow polskich* (Warsaw, 1768). I have used the first Latin edition and second Polish edition here. Sobolevskii's comments on the translations are in *Perevodnaia literatura* pp. 76–78.

3. See Sobolevskii, *Perevodnaia literatura*, pp. 88–89, and my remarks in *Kritika* VI:89–91.

4. In Kokhanovs'kyi's chronicle, which exists in two variants—MSS GPB, F.IV.214 and F.IV.215—the sections entitled *O tsarstve astrakhanskom* and *Enealiogiia turetskaia* (fols. 281–291 and 228–231 respectively in F.IV.215) are the indicated accounts from Guagnini (the second a condensed and edited portion of the original). Lyzlov cites Guagnini as a source; so it makes no sense to seek in the separate translations of these passages his source of material on the Turks and Tatars. Cf. E. V. Chistiakova, "'Skif-skaia istoriia' A. I. Lyzlova i voprosy vostokovedeniia," *Ocherki po istorii russkogo vostokovedeniia*, VI (Moscow, 1963):21, 36–37, 54. Textually the evidence for direct reliance on Guagnini is clear, as Chistiakova would have discovered had she checked Lyzlov against his source.

5. See *Poslaniia*, pp. 547–548; the text has been published in *Zapiski Odesskogo obshchestva istorii i drevnostei*, VIII (1872):479–488.

6. In the former, the account is on fols. 4–5 of the final pagination (1578 edition) and in the latter, on pp. 604–611 (1768 edition).

7. For Taranowski's work, see K. Estreicher, *Bibliografia*, vol. XXXI (pt. III, vol. 20), p. 26. The chronicle by Bielski is Joachim Bielski's revision and expansion of the unpublished work by his father Marcin: *Kronika polska Marcina Bielskiego. Nowo przez Joach. Bielskiego syna iego wydana* (Krakow, 1597); republished as *Kronika Marcina Bielskiego*, 3 vols. (Sanok, 1856), where the Astrakhan' campaign is described in vol. II beginning on p. 1176.

8. See above, Chap. 4, n. 64.

9. Cf. comments by Lur'e in *Poslaniia*, pp. 549–551, where he discusses the *Istoriia o prikhode*.

Selected Bibliography

Abramovich, D. I. *K literaturnoi deiatel'nosti mnikha Kamianchanina Isaii.* St. Petersburg, 1913 (*PDP*, CLXXXI).

Akademiia nauk SSSR. Institut russkoi literatury. *Trudy Otdela drevne-russkoi literatury*, 24 vols. to date. Moscow-Leningrad, 1934–.

Akty istoricheskie, sobrannye i izdannye Arkheograficheskoi kommissiei, 5 vols. St. Petersburg, 1841–1842.

Akty, izdavaemye Vilenskoi Kommissiei dlia razbora drevnikh aktov, vol. XXXIV: *Akty otnosiashchiesia ko vremeni voiny za Malorossiiu (1654–1667)*. Vil'no, 1909.

Akty Moskovskogo gosudarstva, izdannye Imperatorskoi Akademiei nauk, 3 vols. St. Petersburg, 1890–1901.

Akty, sobrannye v bibliotekakh i arkhivakh Rossiiskoi imperii Arkheograficheskoi ekspeditsiei Imperatorskoi Akademii nauk, 4 vols. St. Petersburg, 1836.

Al'shits, D. N. "Ivan Groznyi i pripiski k litsevym svodam ego vremeni," *Ist. zap.* XXIII (1947):251–289.

Andreyev, Nikolay, "Interpolations in the Sixteenth-Century Muscovite Chronicles," *SEER* XXXV (1956):95–115.

—— "Kurbsky's Letters to Vas'yan Muromtsev," *SEER* XXXIII (1955):414–436.

Apostol, pub. by Ivan Fedorov. L'viv, 1574. Copy in Houghton Library, Harvard University, Kilgour Collection "A."

Arkhangel'skii, A. S. *Ocherki iz istorii zapadno-russkoi literatury XVI–XVII vv.* Moscow, 1888. Also pub. as *Chteniia*, 1888, bk. i, sec. i.

Avtokratov, V. N. "'Rech' Ivana Groznogo 1550 goda' kak politicheskii pamflet kontsa XVII veka," *TODRL* XI (1955):255–279.

Backus, Oswald P. "A. M. Kurbsky in the Polish-Lithuanian State (1564–1583)," *Acta Baltico-Slavica* (Białystok), VI (1969):29–50.

Beliashevskii, N. F., ed. "Donesenie kniazia Aleksandra Polubenskogo," *Trudy desiatogo arkheologicheskogo s"ezda v Rige 1896*, III (Moscow, 1900):117–138.

[Belokurov, Sergei A.] "Delo o prisylke shakhom Abbasom rizy Gospodnei tsariu Mikhailu Feodorovichu v 1625 godu," *Sbornik Moskovskogo glavnogo arkhiva Ministerstva inostrannykh del*, V (1893):1–48 (also published separately).

—— *O biblioteke moskovskikh gosudarei v XVI stoletii.* Moscow, 1898.

—— *O Posol'skom prikaze.* Moscow, 1906. Also pub. as *Chteniia*, 1906, bk. 3, sec. iv.

—— "O Zapisnom prikaze ('Zapisyvati stepeni i grani tsarstvennye'). 1657–1659 gg.," in his *Iz dukhovnoi zhizni moskovskogo obshchestva XVII v.*, pp. 53–84. Moscow, 1902. Also pub. in *Chteniia*, 1900, bk. 3, sec. ii.

Berry, Lloyd E., and Robert O. Crummey. *Rude and Barbarous Kingdom: Russia in the Accounts of Sixteenth-Century English Voyagers.* Madison, Milwaukee, and London: The University of Wisconsin Press, 1968.

Brailovskii, S. "Novyi variant povesti o rize Gospoda nashego Iisusa Khrista," *Bibliograf: Vestnik literatury, nauki i iskusstva*, 1889, no. 1 (1890), pp. 17–21.

Budovnits, I. U. "Ivan Groznyi v russkoi istoricheskoi literature," *Ist zap.* XXI (1947):271–330.

Buslaev, F. [I.], comp. *Istoricheskaia khristomatiia tserkovno-slavianskogo i drevne-russkogo iazykov.* Moscow, 1861.

Bychkov, A. F. *Opisanie tserkovno-slavianskikh i russkikh rukopisnykh sbornikov Imperatorskoi Publichnoi biblioteki*, pt. I. St. Petersburg, 1882.

Cherepnin, L. V. *Russkaia paleografiia.* Moscow, 1956.

—— "'Smuta' i istoriografiia XVII veka," *Ist. zap.* XIV (1945):81–128.

Chteniia v Imperatorskom Obshchestve istorii i drevnostei rossiiskikh pri Moskovskom universitete. Moscow, 1846–1918.

Churchill, W. A. *Watermarks in Paper in Holland, England, France, etc., in the Seventeenth and Eighteenth Centuries and Their Interconnection.* Amsterdam: Menno Hertzberger, 1935.

Damerau, Norbert. *Russisches und Westrussisches bei Kurbskij.* Veröffentlichungen der Abteilung für Slavische Sprachen und Literaturen des Osteuropa-Instituts (Slavisches Seminar) an der Freien Universität Berlin, XXIX. Wiesbaden: Otto Harrassowitz, 1963.

Danilov, N. N. "V. V. Golicyn bis zum Staatsstreich vom mai 1682," *Jahrbücher für Geschichte Osteuropas*, 1936, no. 1, pp. 1–33.

—— "Vasilij Vasil'evič Golicyn (1682–1714)," *Jahrbücher für Geschichte Osteuropas*, 1937, no. 4, pp. 539–596.

Denissoff, Elie [Il'ia Denisov]. "Une biographie de Maxime le Grec par Kourbski," *Orientalia Christiana Periodica* XX (1954):44–84.

—— "Une biographie de Maxime le Grec par le metropolite Isaie Kopinski," *Orientalia Christiana Periodica* XXII (1956):138–171.

Drevniaia rossiiskaia vivliofika, ed. N. I. Novikov, 2nd ed. 20 pts. Moscow, 1788–1791.

Dubrovskii, S. M. "Protiv idealizatsii deiatel'nosti Ivana IV," *Voprosy istorii*, 1956, no. 8, pp. 121–129.

Duichev, I. "Vizantiia i vizantiiskaia literatura v poslaniiakh Ivana Groznogo," *TODRL* XV (1958):159–176.

Dvortsovye razriady, po vysochaishemu poveleniiu izdannye II-m otdeleniem sobstvennoi Ego Imperatorskogo Velichestva kantseliarii, 3 vols. in 4. St. Petersburg, 1850–1854. *Ukazatel' k Dvortsovym razriadam*, comp. N. N. Golitsyn, St. Petersburg, 1911.

Ekzempliarskii, A., ed. "K rodoslovnoi kn. A. M. Kurbskogo," *Chteniia*, 1895, bk. 3, sec. v, pp. 2–3.

Entsiklopedicheskii slovar', pub. by F. A. Brokgauz and I. A. Efron, 41 vols., 2 vols. addenda. St. Petersburg, 1890–1907.

Fennell, J. L. I., ed. and trans. *The Correspondence between Prince A. M. Kurbsky and Tsar Ivan IV of Russia 1564–1579*. Cambridge: The University Press, 1955.

———— ed. and trans. *Prince A. M. Kurbsky's History of Ivan IV*. Cambridge: The University Press, 1965.

Filaret, Archbishop. *Obzor russkoi dukhovnoi literatury*, vol. I (Khar'kov, 1859), vol. II (Chernigov, 1863).

Geraklitov, A. A. *Filigrani XVII veka na bumage rukopisnykh i pechatnykh dokumentov russkogo proiskhozhdeniia*. Moscow, 1963.

Golubev, I. F. "Dva neizvestnykh stikhotvornykh poslaniia pervoi poloviny XVII v.," *TODRL* XVII (1961): 391–413.

Golubtsov, Aleksandr, ed. "Pamiatniki prenii o vere voznikshikh po delu korolevicha Val'demara i tsarevny Iriny Mikhailovny," *Chteniia*, 1892, bk. 2, sec. ii.

Gorskii, A. V., and K. I. Nevostruev. *Opisanie slavianskikh rukopisei Moskovskoi sinodal'noi (patriarshei) biblioteki*. 6 vols. Moscow, 1855–1917.

Gorskii, S. *Zhizn' i istoricheskoe znachenie kniazia Andreia Mikhailovicha Kurbskogo*. Kazan', 1858.

Gosudarstbennaia ordena Lenina biblioteka SSSR imeni V. I. Lenina. *Zapiski Otdela rukopisei*, 31 vols. to date. Moscow, 1938–.

Gosudarstvennaia ordena trudovogo krasnogo znameni Publichnaia biblioteka im. M. E. Saltykova-Shchedrina. *Kratkii otchet Rukopisnogo otdela za 1914–1938 gg.*, ed. T. K. Ukhmylova and V. G. Geiman. Leningrad, 1940.

Grobovsky, Antony N. *The "Chosen Council" of Ivan IV: A Reinterpretation*. Brooklyn, N.Y.: Theo. Gaus' Sons, 1969.

Gudzii, N. [K.] "Zametki o Povesti kn. Iv. Mikh. Katyreva-Rostovskogo," *Sbornik statei v chest' akademika A. I. Sobolevskogo, izdannyi ko dniu 70-letiia so dnia ego rozhdeniia* . . . , ed. V. N. Peretts. Leningrad, 1928 (*Sbornik ORIaS*, CI, no. 3), pp. 306–309.

Gwagnin (Guagnini), Alexander. *Kronika Sarmacyey Europskiey*. Krakow, 1611. Reprinted in *Zbior dziejopisow polskich*, vol. IV, ed. Fr. Bohomolec. Warsaw, 1768.

Heawood, Edward. *Watermarks Mainly of the Seventeenth and Eighteenth Centuries*. Monumenta Chartae Papyraceae Historiam Illustrantia, I. Hilversum, Holland: The Paper Publications Society, 1950.

Hrushevs'kyi, Mikhailo. *Kul'turno-natsional'nyi rukh na Ukraini v XVI–XVII vitsi*, 2nd ed. N. p., 1919.

Ikonnikov, V. S. *Opyt russkoi istoriografii*, 2 vols. Kiev, 1891–1908.

Istoricheskie zapiski, 84 vols. to date. Moscow, 1937–.

Istoriia o nevinnom zatochenii blizhnego boiarina Artamona Sergievicha Matveeva, ed. N. I. Novikov. St. Petersburg, 1776.

Ivanishev, N. D., ed. and introd. *Zhizn' kniazia Andreia Mikhailovicha Kurbskogo v Litve i na Volyni. Akty, izdannye Vremennoi kommissiei*,

Vysochaishe uchrezhdennoi pri kievskom voennom, podol'skom i volynskom general-gubernatore, 2 vols. Kiev, 1849.

Kagan, M. D. "Legendarnaia perepiska Ivana IV s turetskim sultanom kak literaturnyi pamiatnik pervoi chetverti XVII v.," *TODRL* XIII (1956):247-272.

—— "Legendarnyi tsikl gramot turetskogo sultana k evropeiskim gosudariam—publitsisticheskoe proizvedenie vtoroi poloviny XVII v.," *TODRL* XV (1958):225-250.

—— "'Povest' o dvukh posol'stvakh'—legendarno-politicheskoe proizvedenie nachala XVII veka," *TODRL* XI (1955):218-254.

Keenan, Edward L. "Isaiah of Kamenets-Podol'sk: Learned Exile, Champion of Orthodoxy," forthcoming in *Studies in Eastern Orthodoxy in Honor of Georges Florovsky.*

—— "The *Jarlyk* of Axmed-xan to Ivan III: A New Reading," *International Journal of Slavic Linguistics and Poetics* XII (1969):33-47.

Kharlampovich, K. V. *Malorossiiskoe vliianie na velikorusskuiu tserkovnuiu zhizn'*, vol. I. Kazan', 1914.

—— "Novaia bibliograficheskaia nakhodka," *Kievskaia starina* LXX (1900):211-224.

Klepikov, S. A. "Bumaga s filigran'iu 'golova shuta (foolscap)' (Materialy dlia datirovki rukopisnykh i pechatnykh tekstov)," *ZOR* XXVI (1963): 405-478.

Kliuchevskii, V. [O.] *Drevnerusskie zhitiia sviatykh kak istoricheskii istochnik* Moscow, 1871.

Knigi razriadnye, po offitsial'nym onykh spiskam, izdannye II-m otdeleniem sobstvennoi Ego Imperatorskogo Velichestva kantseliarii, 2 vols. St. Petersburg, 1853.

Kudriavtsev, I. M. "'Izdatel'skaia' deiatel'nost' Posol'skogo prikaza (K istorii russkoi rukopisnoi knigi vo vtoroi polovine XVII veka)," *Kniga. Issledovaniia i materialy*, VIII (1963):179-244.

Kuntsevich, G. Z. "Akt Litovskoi metriki o begstve kniazia A. M. Kurbskogo," *Izvestiia ORIaS*, vol. XIX (1914), bk. 2, pp. 281-285.

—— ed. *Sochineniia kniazia Kurbskogo*, vol. I: *Sochineniia original'nye.* St. Petersburg, 1914. Also pub. as *RIB*, vol. XXXI.

Laucevičius, E. *Popierius Lietuvoje XV–XVIII a.,* 2 pts. Vilnius, 1967.

Leonid, Archimandrite. *Sistematicheskoe opisanie slaviano-rossiiskikh rukopisei sobraniia Grafa A. S. Uvarova*, 4 pts. Moscow, 1893-1894.

—— "Svedenie o slavianskikh rukopisiakh, postupivshikh iz knigokhranilishcha Sviato-Troitskoi Sergievoi Lavry v biblioteku Troitskoi Dukhovnoi Seminarii v 1747 godu. Rukopisi na bumage," *Chteniia*, 1883, bk. 4, sec. ii; 1884, bk. 3, sec. ii; 1884, bk. 4, sec. ii; 1885, bk. 1, sec. ii, with a single pagination throughout.

Letopis' zaniatii Arkheograficheskoi kommissii, 35 vols. St. Petersburg, Petrograd, Leningrad, 1862-1929.

Liewehr, Ferdinand. *Kurbskijs "Novyj Margarit."* Veröffentlichungen der Slavistischen Arbeitsgemeinschaft an der Deutschen Universität in Prag, ser. II, no. 2. Prague, 1928.

Likhachev, D. S. "Izuchenie sostava sbornikov dlia vyiasneniia istorii teksta proizvedenii," *TODRL* XVIII (1962):3-12.

—— *Poetika drevnerusskoi literatury.* Leningrad, 1967.

—— *Tekstologiia na materiale russkoi literatury X–XVII vv.* Moscow-Leningrad, 1962.

Lur'e, Ia. S. "Novye spiski 'Tsareva gosudareva poslaniia vo vse ego Rossiiskoe tsarstvo'," *TODRL* X (1954):305–309.

Lyzlov, Andrei. *Skifskaia istoriia*, 2nd ed. Moscow, 1787.

Maikov, L. "O nachale russkikh virshei," *ZhMNP*, pt. 275 (June 1891), pp. 443–453.

Nikol'skii, A. I. "Sofiia premudrost' Bozhiia," *Vestnik arkheologii i istorii, izdavaemyi Imperatorskim Arkheologicheskim institutom* (St. Petersburg), VII (1906):69–102.

Nørretranders, Bjarne. *The Shaping of Czardom under Ivan Groznyj*. Copenhagen: Munksgaard, 1964.

Novodvorskii, V. *Bor'ba za Livoniiu mezhdu Moskvoiu i Rech'iu Pospolitoiu (1570–1582)*. Zapiski Istoriko-filologicheskogo fakul'teta Imperatorskogo S.-Peterburgskogo Universiteta, LXXII. St. Petersburg, 1904.

Nyenstädt [Nienstädt], Franz. *Livländische Chronik*, ed. G. Tielemann, in *Monumenta Livoniae antiquae*, vol. II. Riga and Leipzig, 1839, second pagination.

Obolenskii, Mikhail. "O perevode kniazia Kurbskogo sochinenii Ioanna Damaskina," *Bibliograficheskie zapiski*, 1858, no. 12, cols. 355–366.

Opisanie Rukopisnogo otdela Biblioteki Akademii nauk SSSR, III, 1, 2nd ed., Moscow-Leningrad, 1959; III, 2, Moscow-Leningrad, 1965; IV, 1, Moscow-Leningrad, 1950.

Pamiatniki drevnei pis'mennosti (later addition to title: *i iskusstva*), published by the Obshchestvo liubitelei drevnei pis'mennosti, St. Petersburg.

Pamiatniki polemicheskoi literatury v Zapadnoi Rusi, 3 vols. St. Petersburg, 1878–1903. Also pub. as *RIB*, vols. IV, VII, XIX.

Petrov, P. N. "Knigokhranilishche Chudova monastyria," *PDP*, 1879, IV (V), pp. 141–199.

Petrovskii, M. P. (M. P——skii). *Kn. A. M. Kurbskii: istoriko-bibliograficheskie zametki po povodu poslednego izdaniia ego "Skazanii"*. Kazan', 1873. Also pub. in *Uchenye zapiski Kazanskogo universiteta*, 1873, pp. 711–760.

Platonov, S. F. *Drevnerusskie skazaniia i povesti o smutnom vremeni XVII veka, kak istoricheskii istochnik*. St. Petersburg, 1888. 2nd rev. ed. pub. as *Sochineniia prof. S. F. Platonova*, vol. II, St. Petersburg, 1913.

——— *Ivan Groznyi (1530–1584)*. Peterburg, 1923.

——— "Ivan Groznyi v russkoi istoriografii," *Russkoe proshloe* (Petrograd-Moscow), 1923, bk. 1, pp. 3–12.

——— "Starye somneniia," *Sbornik v chest' professora M. K. Liubavskogo*, pp. 172–190. Moscow, 1917.

Polnoe sobranie russkikh letopisei, 31 vols. to date. St. Petersburg, Petrograd, Moscow-Leningrad, 1841.

Polosin, I. [I.] "'Igra v tsaria'. (Otgoloski Smuty v moskovskom bytu XVII veka)," *Izvestiia Tverskogo pedagogicheskogo instituta* (Tver' [Kalinin]), vol. I (1926), pp. 59–63.

Popov, A. N., ed. "Perepiska D'iaka Tret'iaka Vasil'eva," *VMOIDR*, bk. IX (1851), *smes'*, pp. 1–29.

[Porfir'ev, I. Ia., et al.] *Opisanie rukopisei Solovetskogo monastyria, nakhodiashchikhsia v biblioteke Kazanskoi dukhovnoi akademii*, 3 pts. Kazan', 1881–1896.

Poslaniia Ivana Groznogo, ed. D. S. Likhachev and Ia. S. Lur'e. Moscow-Leningrad, 1951.

Rozysknye dela o Fedore Shaklovitom i ego soobshchnikakh, pub. by the

Arkheograficheskaia kommissiia, 4 vols. St. Petersburg, 1884–1893.
Russkaia istoricheskaia biblioteka, pub. by the Arkheograficheskaia kommissiia, 39 vols. St. Petersburg, Petrograd, Leningrad, 1872–1927.
Russkii biograficheskii slovar', 25 vols. St. Petersburg, Petrograd, 1896–1918.
Savva, V. I., S. F. Platonov, and V. G. Druzhinin, eds. "Vnov' otkrytye polemicheskie sochineniia XVII veka protiv eretikov," *LZAK za 1905 god* XVIII (1907), third pagination.
Sbornik Russkogo istoricheskogo obshchestva, 148 vols. St. Petersburg, Petrograd, 1867–1916.
[Shakhovskoi, S. I.] "Domashnie zapiski Kniazia Semena Shakhovskogo," *Moskovskii vestnik*, 1830, pt. 5, pp. 61–73.
Shchepot'ev, Lev. *Blizhnii boiarin Artamon Sergeevich Matveev kak kul'turnyi politicheskii deiatel' XVII veka. (Opyt istoricheskoi monografii).* St. Petersburg, 1906.
Shmidt, S. O., ed. *Opisi tsarskogo arkhiva XVI veka i arkhiva Posol'skogo prikaza 1614 goda.* Moscow, 1960.
Skrynnikov, R. G. "Kurbskii i ego pis'ma v Pskovo-Pecherskii monastyr'," *TODRL* XVIII (1962):99–116.
———— *Nachalo oprichniny.* Leningradskii gosudarstvennyi pedagogicheskii institut im. A. I. Gertsena, Uchenye zapiski, vol. 294. Leningrad, 1966.
The Slavonic and East European Review, 47 vols. to date. London, 1922–.
Sobolevskii, A. I. *Perevodnaia literatura Moskovskoi Rusi XIV–XVII vekov. Bibliograficheskie materialy.* St. Petersburg, 1903. Also pub. as *Sbornik ORIaS*, vol LXXIV, no. 1.
Sobranie gosudarstvennykh gramot i dogovorov, khraniashchikhsia v Gosudarstvennoi kollegii inostrannykh del, 5 vols. Moscow, 1813–1894.
Sochineniia I. Peresvetova, ed. A. A. Zimin. Moscow-Leningrad, 1956.
Spasskii, F. G. *Russkoe liturgicheskoe tvorchestvo (po sovremennym mineiam).* Paris: YMCA Press, 1951.
Stählin, Karl, trans. and introd. *Der Briefwechsel Iwans des Schrecklichen mit dem Fürsten Kurbskij (1564–1579).* Quellen und Aufsätze zur russischen Geschichte, III. Leipzig, 1921.
Stroev, Pavel M. *Bibliologicheskii slovar' i chernovye k nemu materialy*, ed. A. F. Bychkov. St. Petersburg, 1882. Also pub. as *Sbornik ORIaS*, vol. XXIX, no. 4.
———— *Rukopisi slavianskie i rossiiskie, prinadlezhashchie pochetnomu grazhdaninu i Arkheograficheskoi kommissii korrespondentu Ivanu Nikitichu Tsarskomu.* Moscow, 1848.
Syrku, P. A. "Iz istorii snoshenii russkikh s rumynami," *Izvestiia ORIaS*, vol. I (1896), bk. 3, pp. 495–542.
Tromonin, K. Ia. *Iz"iasnenie znakov, vidimykh v pischei bumage.* Moscow, 1844. Facsimile edition with translation and supplementary materials, *Tromonin's Watermark Album*, ed. J. S. G. Simmons. Monumenta Chartae Papyraceae Historiam Illustrantia, XI. Hilversum, Holland: The Paper Publications Society, 1965.
[Undol'skii, V. M.] *Slaviano-russkie rukopisi V. M. Undol'skogo, opisannye samim sostavitelem i byvshim vladel'tsem sobraniia, s No. 1-go po 579-i, s prilozheniem ocherka sobraniia rukopisei V. M. Undol'skogo v polnom sostave.* Moscow, 1870.
Ustrialov, N., ed. *Skazaniia kniazia Kurbskogo*, 3 eds. St. Petersburg, 1833, 1842, 1868.
Val'denberg, V. E. "Poniatie o tiranne v drevnerusskoi literature v sravnenii

s zapadnoi," *Izvestiia Akademii nauk SSSR po russkomu iazyku i slovesnosti,* vol. II (1929), bk. 1, pp. 214–236.

Viktorov, A. E. *Opisi rukopisnykh sobranii v knigokhranilishchakh severnoi Rossii.* St. Petersburg, 1890.

Vil'koshevskii, P. V. "K voprosu o redaktsiiakh pervogo poslaniia Ivana Groznogo k kniaziu A. M. Kurbskomu," *LZAK za 1923–1925 gg.* XXXIII (1926):68–76.

Vostokov, Aleksandr. *Opisanie russkikh i slovenskikh rukopisei Rumiantsovskogo muzeuma.* St. Petersburg, 1842.

Vremennik Imperatorskogo Moskovskogo obshchestva istorii i drevnostei rossiiskikh, 25 vols. Moscow, 1849–1857.

Waugh, Daniel C. "Soviet Watermark Studies—Achievements and Prospects," *Kritika: A Review of Current Soviet Books on Russian History* (Cambridge, Mass.), vol. VI, no. 2 (1970), pp. 78–111.

Zaozerskii, A. I. *Tsar' Aleksei Mikhailovich v svoem khoziaistve.* Zapiski Istoriko-filologicheskogo fakul'teta Imperatorskogo Petrogradskogo Universiteta, CXXXV. Petrograd, 1917.

Zhdanov, I. N. "Sochineniia tsaria Ivana Vasil'evicha," *Sochineniia I. N. Zhdanova,* I (St. Petersburg, 1904): 81–170.

Zhurnal Ministerstva narodnogo prosveshcheniia. St. Petersburg, Petrograd, 1834–1917.

List of Manuscripts Cited

(For full description, see reference in bold face)

Index

RUSSIAN RESEARCH CENTER STUDIES

* Out of print.

† Publications of the Harvard Project on the Soviet Social System.

‡ Published jointly with the Center for International Affairs, Harvard University.